"Top-notch. . . . Greenhouse pulls together some key statistics and compelling personal stories to depict the 'broad decline in the status and treatment of American workers.'" —*In These Times*

"Greenhouse has covered the labor beat for *The New York Times* for more than a decade, and his reporting skills serve his book's readers well." —*The Washington Post*

"Important. . . . Reveals how managers extract unpaid work through an array of ingenious tricks, from eliminating bathroom breaks to electronically erasing hours from workers' records." —*The Wall Street Journal*

"An excellent book. . . . Greenhouse exhibits outrage and moral indignation and an idealism one doesn't necessarily expect from a hard-bitten *New York Times* reporter." —*The Washington Monthly*

"As revealing as [the] statistics are, it is the nicely crafted personal experiences of dozens of workers that make the most compelling reading." —*The San Diego Union-Tribune*

"An amazing book. . . . Give[s] us a sense of what is happening to the everyday worker." —Juan Gonzalez, co-host of *Democracy Now*

"An important, ground-breaking book that should be read by everyone." —*Huntington News*

"Puts the meat of specificity on the bones of labor statistics. . . . Well researched and written to be easily read, this book should get people out from in front of their flat-screen HD television sets to try to do something about what has been happening to us and our country." —*Truthdig*

"Gets to the heart of what's stressing U.S. workers." —National Center for Business Journalism

"The best book to be written on the crisis of low-wage work. . . . Superlative. . . . *The Big Squeeze* illuminates the ethical dimensions of decisions made in boardrooms across America." —*Religion Dispatches*

STEVEN GREENHOUSE

THE BIG SQUEEZE

Steven Greenhouse has been the labor and workplace correspondent for *The New York Times* since 1995. He has covered business, economics, and foreign affairs for the *Times* and has been a correspondent based in Paris, Chicago, and Washington, D.C. He lives in Pelham, New York.

www.stevengreenhouse.com

THE
BIG SQUEEZE

Tough Times for the American Worker

STEVEN GREENHOUSE

ANCHOR BOOKS
A DIVISION OF RANDOM HOUSE, INC.
NEW YORK

FIRST ANCHOR BOOKS EDITION, FEBRUARY 2009

The Library of Congress has cataloged the Knopf edition as follows:
Greenhouse, Steven.
The big squeeze : tough times for the American worker / by Steven Greenhouse.
p. cm.
Includes bibliographical references and index.
1. Industrial relations—United States—History—21st century. 2. Working class—United
States—Economic conditions—21st century. 3. Middle class—United States—Economic
conditions—21st century. 4. Industrial policy—United States—21st century. 5. United States—
Economic policy—21st century. 6. Equality—United States. I. Title. II. Title: Tough times for
the American worker. III. Title: American worker.
HD8072.5.G74 2008
331.0973—dc22   2007049054

Anchor ISBN: 978-1-4000-9652-7

Author photograph © James Estrin
Book design by M. Kristin Bearse

www.anchorbooks.com

Printed in the United States of America
10 9 8 7 6 5 4 3 2 1

For my mother and father,
who dreamed of a fairer world,
and
for Miriam,
my favorite American worker

The test of our progress is not whether we add more to the abundance of those who have much; it is whether we provide enough for those who have too little.

I keep a puttin' and a puttin' out
I keep sweatin' like all get out
I work so long that I'm a losin' track
Waitin', waitin' on the big payback.

Contents

Preface to the Anchor Books Edition

When I set out to write this book several years ago, I was frustrated and more than a little annoyed that the nation seemed to be turning a blind eye to the many serious problems plaguing American workers. At the time, the landscape was very rocky for millions of workers—wages were stagnating, health and pension benefits deteriorating, factory jobs disappearing, and countless workers struggling to balance job and family. Perhaps it was presumptuous of me, but I hoped that this book would help make sure that the nation and its leaders saw—and paid attention to—the huge and growing problems faced by many workers and their families.

In the pages that follow, I seek to explain the myriad ways that America's workers have been squeezed, and I'm sorry to say that in the seven months since this book was first published, the big squeeze that I describe has grown considerably more painful for the nation's workers. Day after day, front-page stories tell of thousands of workers laid off, families facing foreclosure, and baby boomers panicking because their 401(k) plans have melted down as they near retirement age. Although many politicians are loath to admit it for fear of making things worse (or making themselves look bad), it looks as if the United States has slid into its worst economic downturn in a quarter century—and perhaps since the Great Depression.

As I write this, the American economy is badly broken. Just look at the fast-rising unemployment rate, the plunging stock market, the failing banks, the colossal trade deficit, and the once-proud automakers struggling to avoid bankruptcy. If there is a central theme to this book, it is that long before the current financial crisis and economic slump hit the United States this year, the economy was already badly broken for millions of workers and their families. Here's one startling statistic about how broken things have been: despite soaring corporate profits, fast-rising employee productivity, and strong GDP growth, median income for working-age households fell by more than $2,100—a nearly 4 percent drop—from 2000 to 2007 (after factoring in inflation).

For many squeezed workers, today's economic downturn has made an already bad situation worse. The evidence is all around us: the spike in foreclosures and personal bankruptcies; the parents who realize they can no longer afford to send their children to college; the families who are so financially stretched that they sometimes go without heating their homes for days at a time during fall and winter.

If there is any silver lining to today's economic slump, it is that the nation, including its leaders and news media, are finally paying attention to just how bad things are for millions of workers. For far too long, the nation seemed to focus on its millionaire investment bankers, its brilliant CEOs, its high-tech geniuses, its visionary entrepreneurs, and its glamorous (and unglamorous) Hollywood celebrities, while all but ignoring the trials and tribulations (and contributions) of its workers, whether factory workers or bank tellers, plumbers or software engineers, supermarket stockers or nursing home aides.

With the economy in such distressing shape, we are at a moment akin to 1932. We have just elected a new president who has promised to do his best to rally the nation and lift the economy out of the mire. But that won't be easy. It wasn't easy for Franklin Roosevelt in 1932, as intelligent and inspiring as he was, and it won't be easy for Barack Obama, as intelligent and inspiring as he is. Let's hope, though, that the nation will finally begin addressing many of the painful problems that I examine in this book: sagging wages, growing income inequality, the loss of manufacturing jobs, the increase in poverty, the widespread wage and hour violations, the huge number of Americans without health insurance, the woefully inadequate system of retirement security, and, last but not least, the increased difficulty in achieving the American dream. This to-do list is dauntingly long, and it is so long largely because we as a nation have failed to face up to these problems.

For the lives of America's workers to improve, the economy will first have to be pulled out of this ugly recession. To do that, the nation will need to undertake serious efforts to jump-start its economy, but those efforts should also aim to strengthen the nation's long-term economic health. Any economic stimulus strategy should include three things: first, major investments in rebuilding the nation's infrastructure, like highways and railroads, to improve the nation's economic efficiency; second, major investments in green industries, like hybrid cars and wind turbines, to increase the nation's energy self-sufficiency; and third, major investments in education, science and research to develop new technologies and industries and increase the nation's competitiveness.

As the financial crisis has raged in recent months, we have seen an unusual amount of creativity and experimentation from Washington's policymakers. The United States could use a similar burst of creativity and experimentation in addressing the squeeze that is hurting so many workers. The nation— government, universities, corporations, and labor unions—should explore how to get companies to share more of their prosperity with their workers and how to make the nation's employers and employees more productive to help assure long-term prosperity and competitiveness. The nation also needs some innovative thinking and policies to fix another worrisome but often over- looked problem: even though we claim to be *the* land of economic opportu- nity, there is too little social and economic mobility. Many children who are born into households with limited resources don't have nearly the opportu- nity of achieving the American dream that children born into wealthier house- holds have.

Sadly, it may take a year or more before we as a nation return to economic growth and prosperity, prosperity that can be translated into improved wages, benefits, and economic mobility. As we await the return of prosperity, we should all take to heart the words of Teddy Roosevelt—words that can be embraced by Republican and Democrat: "Our aim is to promote prosperity, and then to see that prosperity is passed around."

November 5, 2008
Pelham, NY

Introduction

Not long after I began peering inside the nation's workplaces as labor correspondent for the *New York Times*, I was taken aback by what I often found there—squalid treatment, humbling indignities, relentless penny-pinching. The United States may see itself as the City on the Hill, but many of its citizens labor in dismal swamps. Why, I kept asking myself, are there so many unseemly, even shocking things taking place inside the workplaces of the world's richest nation?

I saw great corporations that literally locked employees in their workplace at night, that cheated employees by improperly deleting hours from their time records, that cut employees' pensions in half, that suddenly fired longtime employees and gave them thirty minutes to vacate the premises. One company fired a computer engineer on Take Your Daughters to Work Day as his eight-year-old daughter looked on, and a well-known retailer pink-slipped some workers because they earned fifty-one cents more an hour than the market rate. And then there were the respected multibillion-dollar corporations that hired subcontractors to do their dirty work, with the subcontractors paying many employees half the minimum wage and insisting that they work seven days a week, thirty days a month. One janitor in Houston told me: "They treat us worse than animals."

We all know our own workplaces, but how many of us know what goes on inside a meatpacking plant, a Wal-Mart on the midnight shift, or a corporate office after thousands of layoffs have been announced? In this book, I've aimed to provide a view inside those and other workplaces, and in doing so, I will highlight many unseemly things but also some admirable ones.

This is a decade during which the American economy has thrived by many measures, with corporate profits and CEO salaries soaring, yet wages have languished for most workers, and health and pension coverage has grown worse. Companies are increasingly treating job security as an anachronism, and corporate executives continue to send many good middle-class jobs overseas. Yes, some jobs must move abroad for competitiveness, but it would be foolish not to examine the impact that this has had on American society. Nothing comes without a price.

This book seeks to explain what is happening in the American economy and in the American workplace—in part through the stories of individual, representative workers. I've examined how workers have been squeezed by powerful trends coursing through the economy: the offshoring of white-collar jobs, the Wal-Mart effect, the steeper climb for young workers, the decline of organized labor, the exodus of factories to Mexico and China, the growing power imbalance between management and worker. In an effort to explain these trends, I go beyond the tales of individual workers to weave in analysis—historical, economic, sociological—of such issues as evolving management practices and the weakening of the nation's social safety net. As I complete this book in the winter of 2008, the United States appears on the brink of a recession, possibly a deep one. As a result, many of the problems I write about, such as declining job security and the squeeze on wages, may grow only worse in the coming months.

Many Americans devote more hours to working than to any other activity. It is important therefore that work be a source of fulfillment and dignity. Indeed, both the Old and New Testaments have strong language about the dignity of labor and the moral obligation to treat even the humblest worker fairly and with respect. Proverbs teaches us, "He who oppresses a poor man insults his Maker." And Deuteronomy cautions: "You shall not abuse a needy and destitute laborer, whether a fellow countryman or a stranger in one of the communities of your land."

Over the years I have interviewed thousands of workers—steelworkers and strawberry pickers, Microsoft whizzes and minimum-wage waitresses—and a handful of their faces and tales stick most vividly in my mind. One worker whose story nags at me is Michael Johnson, a father of five who has worked for seventeen years as a security guard in downtown Los Angeles. Johnson is an engaging, earnest man who has come a long way from his days as a drug addict. Now he wants nothing more than to be a good father and to provide his five children with what they need to thrive. He is proud that his three oldest sing in the youth choir at Victory Baptist Church, yet he wishes that he could afford dance lessons and piano lessons for them. When I first met Johnson in the summer of 2006, his big problem was that his security job—he is the post commander in the main lobby of a downtown office tower—paid him just ten dollars an hour. On that salary, about all Johnson can afford is his $975 monthly rent and food for his family. To pay for everything else—utilities, gasoline, car repairs, payments on his 1998 Nissan Quest, clothes for the kids, and furnishings for their gloomy two-bedroom apartment—Johnson took a second full-time job guarding a construction site in L.A.'s northern suburbs. His wife, Denesha, can't work because she hurt her back badly while lifting a 270-pound patient when she was a nursing home aide. One of Johnson's many frustrations is that when he took his second job, the state kicked his family off food stamps. He was told he earns too much.

Each morning Johnson gets up at 5:20 and leaves for work at 6:15, before his children wake up. After putting in eight hours at one job and seven at the other, he returns home just before eleven at night, after his children have gone to sleep. "I'm missing them grow up," he says. "I can't do this forever."[1]

Johnson's story nags at me because it shows that something fundamental is not working. That is exactly why I wrote this book.

THE BIG SQUEEZE

Chapter One

WORKED OVER AND OVERWORKED

In his job at a Wal-Mart in Texas, Mike Michell was responsible for catching shoplifters, and he was good at it, too, catching 180 in one two-year period. But one afternoon things went wildly awry when he chased a thief—a woman using stolen checks—into the parking lot. She jumped into her car, and her accomplice gunned the accelerator, slamming the car into Michell and sending him to the hospital with a broken kneecap, a badly torn shoulder, and two herniated disks. Michell was so devoted to Wal-Mart that he somehow returned to work the next day, but a few weeks later he told his boss that he needed surgery on his knee. He was fired soon afterward, apparently as part of a strategy to dismiss workers whose injuries run up Wal-Mart's workers' comp bills.[1]

∎

Immediately after serving in the army, Dawn Eubanks took a seven-dollar-an-hour job at a call center in Florida. Some days she was told to clock in just two or three hours, and some days she was not allowed to clock in during her whole eight-hour shift. The call center's managers warned the workers that if they went home, even though they weren't allowed to clock in, they would be viewed as having quit.

∎

Twenty-eight-year-old John Arnold works in the same Caterpillar factory in Illinois as his father, but under the plant's two-tier contract, the maximum he can ever earn is $14.90 an hour, far less than the $25 earned by his father. Caterpillar, long a symbol of America's industrial might, insists that it needs a lower wage tier to remain competitive. "A few people I work with are living at home with their parents," Arnold said. "Some are even on food stamps."

∎

At a Koch Foods poultry plant in Tennessee, the managers were so intent on keeping the line running all out that Antonia Lopez Paz and the other workers who carved off chicken tenders were ordered not to go to the bathroom except during their lunch and coffee breaks. When one desperate woman asked permission to go, her supervisor took off his hard hat and said, "You can go to the bathroom in this." Some women ended up soiling themselves.

▪

Don Jensen anticipated a relaxing life of golf after retiring from his human resources post with Lucent Technologies in New Jersey, where he was in charge of recruiting graduates from Stanford, Cornell, MIT, and other top universities. But when Lucent increased its retirees' health insurance premiums to $8,280 a year, up from $180, Jensen was forced to abandon his retirement. He took a job as a ten-dollar-an-hour bank teller.

▪

As part of her software company's last-lap sprint to get new products out the door, Myra Bronstein sometimes had to work twenty-four hours straight testing for bugs. She felt great loyalty to the Seattle-area company because its executives had repeatedly promised, "As long as we're in business, you have a job." But one Friday morning the company suddenly fired Bronstein and seventeen other quality assurance engineers. The engineers were told that if they wanted to receive severance pay, they had to agree to spend the next month training the workers from India who would be replacing them.

ONE OF THE LEAST EXAMINED but most important trends taking place in the United States today is the broad decline in the status and treatment of American workers—white-collar and blue-collar workers, middle-class and low-end workers—that began nearly three decades ago, gradually gathered momentum, and hit with full force soon after the turn of this century. A profound shift has left a broad swath of the American workforce on a lower plane than in decades past, with health coverage, pension benefits, job security, workloads, stress levels, and often wages growing worse for millions of workers.

That the American worker faces this squeeze in the early years of this century is particularly troubling because the squeeze has occurred while the economy, corporate profits, and worker productivity have all been growing robustly. In recent years, a disconcerting disconnect has emerged, with corporate profits soaring while workers' wages stagnated.

The statistical evidence for this squeeze is as compelling as it is disturbing.

In 2005, median income for nonelderly households failed to increase for the fifth year in a row, after factoring in inflation. That is unprecedented in a time of economic growth.[2] In 2006, median income for those households did finally rise, but it still remained lower—$2,375 lower—than six years earlier.[3] That, too, is unprecedented. Even though corporate profits have doubled since recession gave way to economic expansion in November 2001, and even though employee productivity has risen more than 15 percent since then, the average wage for the typical American worker has inched up just 1 percent (after inflation). With the subprime mortgage crisis threatening to pull the economy into recession, some economists say this may be the first time in American history that the typical working household goes through an economic expansion without any increase in income whatsoever.

This, unfortunately, is the continuation of a long-term squeeze. Since 1979, hourly earnings for 80 percent of American workers (those in private-sector, nonsupervisory jobs) have risen by just 1 percent, after inflation.[4] The average hourly wage was $17.71 at the end of 2007. For male workers, the average wage has actually slid by 5 percent since 1979. Worker productivity, meanwhile, has climbed 60 percent.[5] If wages had kept pace with productivity, the average full-time worker would be earning $58,000 a year; $36,000 was the average in 2007.[6] The nation's economic pie is growing, but corporations by and large have not given their workers a bigger piece.[7]

The squeeze on the American worker has meant more poverty, more income inequality, more family tensions, more hours at work, more time away from the kids, more families without health insurance, more retirees with inadequate pensions, and more demands on government and taxpayers to provide housing assistance and health coverage. Twenty percent of families with children under six live below the poverty line, and 22 million full-time workers do not have health insurance.[8] Largely as a result of the squeeze, the number of housing foreclosures and personal bankruptcies more than tripled in the quarter century after 1979.[9] Economic studies show that income inequality in the United States is so great that it more closely resembles the inequality of a third world country than that of an advanced industrial nation.[10]

Many families *are* enjoying higher incomes, enabling them to buy a plasma-screen TV or take a vacation in Orlando, but this is frequently because fathers have taken on second jobs or more overtime hours or because mothers, even with toddlers, have opted for full-time paid employment. Millions of households have not slipped further behind only because Americans are working far harder than before. A husband and wife in the average middle-class household are, taken together, working 540 hours or three months more per year than such couples would have a quarter century ago, mainly because married women are working considerably longer hours than before.[11]

Viewed another way, the American worker's financial squeeze has translated into a time squeeze. In a survey by the Families and Work Institute, two-thirds of employed parents responded that they didn't have enough time with their kids, and just under two-thirds said they didn't have enough time with their spouses.[12] The typical American worker toils 1,804 hours a year, 135 hours more per year than the typical British worker, 240 hours more than the average French worker, and 370 hours (or nine full-time weeks) more than the average German worker.[13] No one in the world's advanced economies works more. Aggravating the time squeeze is a phenomenon known as job creep in which our jobs have spilled increasingly into our leisure time. Americans are finishing work memos on their home computers at eleven p.m., they are reading office e-mails on Saturdays and Sundays, and they are using their cell phones and BlackBerries to answer their bosses' queries while on vacation. The Conference Board, the business research group, found that Americans are less satisfied with their jobs—just 47 percent are satisfied—than at any time since it started tracking the numbers two decades ago. "The breadth of dissatisfaction is unsettling," the Conference Board wrote, its director of research adding, "The demands in the workplace have increased tremendously."[14]

Americans are going deeper into debt than ever before. Millions of households have supersized their credit card balances, and many have taken cash out of their homes by obtaining second mortgages, arguably unhealthy ways to try to maintain a comfortable lifestyle on a less-than-comfortable income.[15] In 2005, for the first time since the Great Depression, the nation's personal savings rate sank below zero, meaning that Americans were actually spending more than they were earning.[16] As a result, among the bottom two-fifths of households, nearly one in four spends at least 40 percent of its monthly income paying down its debts.[17] And foreclosure filings, spurred by the subprime mortgage crisis, are expected to soar to as many as two million by the end of 2008. Two million would represent one in sixty-two households.[18]

Even as wages stagnated in recent years, many government officials triumphantly boasted that consumer spending had continued to rise. But this increase was largely due to soaring incomes at the top. From 1979 to 2005, a period when national output more than doubled, after-tax income inched up just 6 percent for the bottom fifth of American households after accounting for inflation, while it rose 21 percent for the middle fifth. For the top fifth, income jumped 80 percent and for the top 1 percent it more than tripled, soaring by 228 percent.[19] A 2007 report by the Congressional Budget Office found that the top 1 percent of households had pre-tax income in 2005 that was more than two-fifths larger than that of the bottom 40 percent. (After taxes, the top 1 percent's income in 2005 was still nearly 10 percent greater than the bottom 40 percent's.)[20] As Paul Krugman wrote, "It's a great economy if you're a high-level corporate executive or someone who owns a lot of stock. For most other Americans, economic growth is a spectator sport."[21]

The nation appears to be on the threshold of recession, and as a result, America's workers are likely to be squeezed not just by stagnant wages but also by rising unemployment. One of the most worrisome—and puzzling—aspects of the economic expansion that began in November 2001 is that wages have remained stubbornly flat, after factoring in inflation, even though the jobless rate has been low by historical standards. That wages have gone nowhere in a tight labor market underlines the American worker's declining ability to command higher wages, and now with unemployment increasing, workers' leverage to push for higher wages is bound to grow even weaker.

The squeeze is of course worst for those on the lowest rungs, including millions of workers who are part of our everyday lives: fast food workers, cashiers, child care workers, hotel maids, and nurse's aides. Nearly 33 million workers—almost one-fourth of the American workforce—earn less than ten dollars an hour, meaning their wages come to less than the poverty line for a family of four ($20,614 in 2006).[22] Despite strong economic growth, the number of Americans living in poverty jumped by 15 percent from 2000 to 2006—an increase of 5.4 million to 36.5 million.[23] For millions of low-income workers, the promise of America has been broken: the promise that if you work hard, you will be rewarded with a decent living, the promise that if you do an honest day's work, you will earn enough to feed, clothe, and shelter your family.

Not only do workers on the bottom rungs lack money, but they often lack basic benefits. Three out of four low-wage workers in the private sector do not have employer-provided health insurance, while eight out of nine do not participate in a pension plan.[24] Three-fourths of low-wage workers do not receive paid sick days, so if they need to miss two days' work because they are sick or their child is sick, they receive no pay for those days—and often risk getting fired.[25]

A study sponsored by the Ford, Rockefeller, and Annie E. Casey foundations, "Working Hard, Falling Short," concluded, "More than one out of four

American working families now earn wages so low"—defined as income of less than twice the poverty line for a family of four ($41,200 in 2006)—"that they have difficulty surviving financially." The study continued, "While our economy relies on the service jobs these low-paid workers fill . . . our society has not taken adequate steps to ensure that these workers can make ends meet and build a future for their families, no matter how determined they are to be self-sufficient."[26] In her book *Nickel and Dimed*, Barbara Ehrenreich described these workers as "the major philanthropists of our society." Ehrenreich wrote, "They neglect their own children so the children of others will be cared for; they live in substandard housing so that other homes will be shiny and perfect."[27] Across America more than 50 million people live in near poor households, those with incomes between $20,000 and $40,000 a year. Katherine Newman, a Princeton sociologist, has described this large but often overlooked group as "the missing class." The mass of workers who are barely getting by is likely to grow only larger, because the Bureau of Labor Statistics forecasts that low-wage jobs will account for six of the top ten categories in overall job growth between now and 2014: janitors, nursing home aides, waiters, home-health aides, retail sales workers including cashiers, and food-prep and fast food workers.[28]

America's ailing health care system is a big part of the worsening squeeze. From 2000 to 2006, the number of Americans without health insurance climbed by 8.6 million, to 47 million.[29] One study found that more than two-fifths of moderate-income, working-age Americans went without health insurance for at least part of 2005.[30] Not only that, for employees who want coverage, companies are requiring them to pay more for it, and as a result, the cost of family coverage has soared 83 percent in just six years.[31] As health costs consume more and more of the nation's economic output—they account for 16 percent of gross domestic product, or GDP, up from 5 percent in 1960—that necessarily leaves less money for wage increases.

Pensions, the other pillar of employee benefits, are under assault as never before. In May 2005, a bankruptcy judge allowed United Airlines to default on its pension plans and dump them on the federal agency that protects retirement benefits. Because that agency guarantees pensions only up to a certain amount, many United pilots will receive only half what they expected when they retire. United's move was the biggest pension default in American history, releasing it from paying $3.2 billion in obligations over the following five years. One of United's lawyers predicted that more and more companies would use this "strategic tool" to increase their competitiveness.[32] Since then,

US Airways and Delta have followed suit. When Delphi, the auto parts giant, filed for bankruptcy in October 2005, its chief executive, Robert S. Miller, threatened to slash the company's pensions unless the workers agreed to massive wage concessions.

As part of this assault on pensions, Hewlett-Packard, IBM, Verizon, Sears, Motorola, and many other companies have embraced a riskier, far less generous type of retirement plan, 401(k)s, while turning away from the traditional plans that promised workers a specific monthly benefit for life after they retired.[33] When Hewlett-Packard took that step, a company spokesman said, "Pension plans are kind of a thing of the past."[34]

With pensions growing ever scarcer, more and more workers are convinced that they won't have enough money to retire. Ominously, some economists have begun to warn that millions of Americans might have to continue working into their seventies.

Even though this is an era of increased economic volatility, the federal government has decided to let Americans fend increasingly for themselves. Just one-third of laid-off workers receive unemployment benefits, down from 50 percent a generation ago. And even though workers' skills are becoming obsolete faster than ever because of new technologies and globalization, funding for the main federal program for retraining has been reduced by more than $10 billion in the last quarter century.[35] "Americans increasingly find themselves on an economic tightrope, without an adequate safety net if—as is ever more likely—they lose their footing," wrote Jacob S. Hacker, author of *The Great Risk Shift*.[36]

Business executives say they have been forced to tighten their belts on wages and everything else because they face ever-fiercer competition. That is true, but corporate profits have nonetheless soared, climbing 13 percent a year in the six years after the 2001 recession ended, while wages have remained flat. (Employee productivity has also far outpaced wages, rising 15 percent from 2001 through 2007.) Corporate profits have climbed to their highest share of national income in sixty-four years, while the share going to wages has sunk to its lowest level since 1929.[37]

"This is the most pronounced several years of labor's share declining," said Lawrence Katz, an economics professor at Harvard. "For as long as we've had a modern economy, this is the worst we've seen it."[38]

Very simply, corporations, along with their CEOs, are seizing a bigger piece of the nation's economic pie for themselves, leaving the nation's workers and their families diminished.

MANY AMERICANS ARE FEELING the squeeze as part of a growing wave of worker exploitation. Faster line speeds at the nation's meat and poultry plants are causing workers' bodies to break down and leading to more amputations. Workers have died at construction sites when scaffolding or trenches collapsed because supervisors ignored the most elementary precautions.[39] Inside some of the nation's best-known retail stores, immigrant janitors have been forced to work 365 days a year.

Exploitation is of course nothing new, as Upton Sinclair's writings, Lewis Hines's photographs, and the Triangle Shirtwaist fire all made clear. In the decades after the Great Depression, exploitation declined as the United States created the world's most prosperous middle class and as business, labor, and government often worked hand in hand to improve workplace conditions. In recent years, however, worker mistreatment has been on the rise, spurred by a stepped-up corporate focus on minimizing costs and by an influx of easy-to-exploit immigrants. Corporate executives, intent on maximizing profits, often assign rock-bottom labor budgets to the managers who run their stores and restaurants, and those managers in turn often squeeze their workers relentlessly.

A steady decline in workplace regulation has opened the door to greater exploitation. Even though the workforce has grown from 90 million to 145 million over the past three decades, the number of federal wage and hour investigators has fallen. Seven hundred eighty-eight federal wage and hour inspectors are responsible for ensuring compliance at the nation's 8.4 million business establishments.[40] George W. Bush's labor secretary, Elaine Chao, signaled her ambivalent views about enforcement when she said, "Sometimes it's not what you do, but what you refrain from doing that is important."[41] The infamous Sago Mine in West Virginia had been cited 273 times for safety violations in the two years before an explosion there killed twelve miners in 2006. But none of those fines exceeded $460, and many were just $60—a minuscule amount considering that the company that owned Sago had $110 million in annual profits. In the five years before, the Mine Safety and Health Administration, then run by former industry executives appointed by President Bush, failed to collect fines in almost half the cases in which it had levied them.[42]

The rising tide of exploitation has taken countless forms. Target, Safeway, Albertsons, and Wal-Mart have all hired cleaning contractors who required janitors to work the midnight shift thirty days a month. These contractors systematically broke the law by virtually never paying Social Security or unemployment insurance taxes, and they almost never paid janitors time and a half for overtime even though the janitors often worked fifty-five hours or more each week.[43] These contractors sometimes dumped badly injured workers in front of a hospital or at a bus station with a ticket back to Mexico.

At Taco Bell, Wal-Mart, and Family Dollar, many employees complained that managers forced them to work five or more unpaid hours off the clock each week. The workers who were cheated often earned just $12,000 to $18,000 a year. At an A&P in Westchester County, New York, Wilfredo Brewster, a customer service manager, said he worked from six a.m. to six p.m. Monday through Friday, sixty hours, but was paid for only forty. Managers pressured him to donate his Saturdays to the store as well, telling him it would help him earn a promotion. Under federal and state law, he, as an hourly employee, was supposed to be paid overtime for those Saturdays.

Stylists at SmartStyle, the nation's largest hair salon company, said that pressure to minimize payroll costs was so intense that on days when there were few customers, managers often ordered stylists to clock out, then clean up the salon. Several hairdressers said they were occasionally paid for only half the hours they worked, their earnings sometimes slipping to $2.50 an hour, less than half the $5.15 federal minimum wage at the time.[44]

According to many workers and supervisors at Pep Boys, Toys "R" Us, Family Dollar, Wal-Mart, and other companies, some managers illegally tampered with time clock records to erase hours that employees had worked.[45] Dorothy English, a payroll assistant at a Wal-Mart in Louisiana, said that if an employee had clocked forty-three hours in a week, her boss often ordered her to delete three hours from the worker's time records to avoid paying time and a half. "I told them this wasn't right," she said. "But they said, 'This is how we keep people to forty hours.' "[46]

At dozens of upscale supermarkets in Manhattan, including Food Emporium and Gristede's, deliverymen often worked seventy-five hours a week but were paid just two hundred dollars, or less than three dollars an hour. They were told they were independent contractors, a group that is not covered by minimum wage and overtime laws.[47]

Some call centers deduct pay for every minute a worker spends in the bathroom. Workers at Wal-Mart and the Cheesecake Factory complained that managers often refused to give them the lunch breaks and fifteen-minute rest breaks that state law required.[48] Bella Blaubergs, a diabetic who worked at a Wal-Mart in Washington State, said she nearly fainted several times from low blood sugar because managers often would not let her take breaks.[49] At numerous Abercrombie & Fitch stores, African American, Asian, and Hispanic workers complained that they were relegated to back-of-the-store jobs, doing stockroom work and inventory, while white employees were given jobs up front—all to promote Abercrombie's preppy, fraternity, all-American look.[50]

Some cleaning workers at several of the hottest software companies in Silicon Valley earn so little that they live in rented garages in someone else's home. Rosalba Ceballos, a divorced immigrant from Mexico, was one of them; she lived with her three daughters—ages one, three, and seven—in an absurdly cluttered, windowless garage just outside Palo Alto.

Middle-class workers have not been immune. On a day in 2003 that Circuit City workers remember as "Bloody Wednesday," the retailer fired 3,900 senior commissioned salespeople—some earned $50,000 a year—having concluded that their commissions and wages were too high. Circuit City simultaneously hired 2,100 replacement salespeople who were to receive lower wages and far lower commissions.[51] Then in 2007, Circuit City laid off another 3,400 employees because they, in the company's words, earned "well above the market-based salary range for their role." Many of those laid off were earning around $29,000 a year. Circuit City announced that these workers could reapply for their jobs ten weeks later, but if rehired, they would come back at the lower "market rate."

In her ten years at the Circuit City in Hoover, Alabama, Julie Godette was considered a model employee, assigned to train new hires and receiving repeated raises that brought her up to $16.40 an hour. She, too, was suddenly laid off. "To work that long for a company and to be let go because you did a good job really hurts," Godette said.[52]

At JP Morgan Chase, Barbara Parkinson, a customer service representative in the global investment services department in New York City, said managers had repeatedly complained when workers submitted time sheets listing several hours' overtime. To avoid management's continued wrath, she and other workers decided to forgo the overtime pay due them.[53]

At RadioShack's headquarters in Fort Worth, four hundred workers were fired by e-mail. "The workforce reduction notification is currently in progress," the e-mail dryly informed recipients. "Unfortunately your position is one that has been eliminated."[54]

Northwest Airlines gave laid-off workers a booklet entitled "101 Ways to Save Money." But the booklet added insult to financial injury. "Borrow a dress for a big night out" and "Shop at auctions or pawn shops for jewelry" were among the tips it offered. And then it suggested, "Don't be shy about pulling something you like out of the trash."[55]

RARELY HAVE SO MANY economic and social forces been arrayed against the American worker. Downsizing, rightsizing, and reengineering have increasingly made job security an obsolete notion. Many workers fear pink slips so much that they are frightened to ask for raises or protest oppressive workloads. Globalization, including the recent rush to offshore hundreds of thousands of white-collar jobs, has increased such fears. Layoffs have become a fact of life. Nowadays, on nearly a daily basis, some company announces that it is laying off several thousand employees, and except for the workers and their families, virtually everyone who hears about it ignores it.

America has lost one-fifth of its factory jobs since 2000, jobs that have long been a stepping-stone to the middle class. There has been a concomitant decline in the labor movement to its lowest point in decades, undermining the one force that, for all its faults, created some semblance of balance between workers and management during the second half of the twentieth century. The massive influx of immigrants has created a huge pool of easy-to-bully workers that has given managers greater leverage—most visibly in construction and meatpacking—to squeeze wages and worsen conditions for *all* workers. Many companies have embraced the just-in-time workforce—a mass of temps, freelancers, and on-call occasionals whose lower pay and unstable status often undercut the wages, benefits, and job security of the traditional year-round workforce.

The position of the American worker has been further undermined by the economy's evolution from industrial capitalism to financial capitalism. Industrialists were once firmly in control, intent on maximizing production and market share, but now investment bankers, mutual fund managers, hedge fund managers, and, increasingly, managers of private-equity funds wield great power and are forever pressuring the companies that they've invested in to maximize profits and take whatever steps are necessary to keep stock prices at their highest. Companies, in response, often skimp on wages, lay off workers, and close operations.

Wal-Mart, founded in a small Arkansas town in 1962, has spearheaded the rise of a less caring, less generous, and often less law-abiding management style. Wal-Mart employs nearly 1.4 million workers in the United States, far more than any other company. With its phenomenal growth, it has become the world's largest retailer, and its low wages and benefits—it provides health insurance to just half of its workers—have created a downward pull on the way that many companies treat their workers. (For that reason, we will examine Wal-Mart in great detail.) The Wal-Mart effect could be seen most starkly when the three largest supermarket chains in California—Safeway, Albertsons, and Ralphs—grew alarmed about Wal-Mart's plans to open dozens of super-centers in California that would sell groceries in addition to general merchandise. The supermarket chains demanded lower wages and far less generous health benefits for all future hires, and after a bitter four-and-a-half-month strike and lockout in 2003–4, the chains got their way. The California supermarkets said they couldn't compete when their cashiers earned $17.90 an hour on average and Wal-Mart's earned $8.50 an hour.

The squeeze on the American worker has been further exacerbated by corporate America's growing sway over politics and policy, making it harder for beleaguered workers to turn to government for help. When investigators unearthed serious child labor violations at a dozen Wal-Marts, officials in the Bush Labor Department signed a highly unusual secret agreement promising to give Wal-Mart fifteen days' advance notice whenever inspectors planned to visit a Wal-Mart store to look for more such violations. Wal-Mart officials had been major donors to the Republican Party.

As a result of business's strong influence over President George W. Bush and Republicans in Congress, the federal minimum wage remained stuck at $5.15 for nearly a decade. A full-time worker who earns $5.15 an hour grosses $10,712 a year, far below the $16,079 poverty line for a family of three. In 2007, the $5.15 minimum wage, after adjusting for inflation, was 33 percent below its 1979 level.[56] In 2007, the Democratic Congress raised the minimum wage to $7.25 an hour over two years.

Nor have the tax policies emanating from Washington been very friendly to workers. President Bush and Republicans in Congress pushed vigorously to minimize taxes on investors, that is, taxes on dividends and capital gains, while urging elimination of the estate tax. Bush's tax cuts saved the average middle-class taxpayer $744 a year, while saving $44,212 a year for the top 1 percent of taxpayers and $230,136 for the top one-tenth of 1 percent of households.[57]

Even though the government has done little of late to ease the squeeze on American workers, there are plenty of things government can do to alleviate the difficulties that workers face. I will return to this subject later. Now, however, I want to examine in depth a telling instance of the big squeeze.

Chapter Two

WORKPLACE HELL

Eager not to be late for the four-to-midnight shift, Kathy Saumier pushed her storm door shut and clomped down the wooden stairs in front of her house in Syracuse in upstate New York. She slid into the front seat of her Chevy Camaro and began fiddling with its on-again, off-again heater as she edged down the hill. Turning left, she passed the neighborhood factory, HyGrade Metal Processing, and then rumbled past Masello's Auto Repair, Kases and Kegs Liquor, and, perched way up on the hill, St. Vincent de Paul Church. At the stoplight, she sneaked a quick look at herself in the rearview mirror to see whether her mop of dirty-blond hair was under control. She was understandably edgy, because she was heading to a new job.

Kathy, at age thirty-four, was relieved to have left her old job, a tedious position cleaning offices, floors, and bathrooms at Syracuse's largest newspaper. In that job, she was growing more despondent by the day, not because she thought herself too good for toilets and floors, but because she found the work hopelessly lonely—late at night, with no one to talk to.

Many nights after work, Kathy had complained to family and friends about the loneliness of the job as well as the paltry ninety dollars or so she took home each week. She was paid the minimum wage for her twenty hours of work, and her meager paycheck frustrated her because she and her longtime boyfriend, a janitor who earned scarcely more than the minimum wage, were raising a son and a daughter.

Kathy's sister-in-law, Theresa, phoned late one evening to tell her that there were openings at a new plastics factory where she worked. The factory's owner, Landis Plastics, which makes containers for yogurt and cottage cheese, boasted that it represented everything that Rust Belt America did not—it was clean, bright, and forward-looking, it welcomed women workers, and it promised safe and secure jobs.

"My sister-in-law said, 'It's a good place to work. Why don't you come work with me?' " Kathy said. " 'It's a new place. It's more money.' It sounded good." So Kathy applied for a job, and the very next day a manager phoned to hire her.

Heading to work that first day, Kathy pulled on to I-690 and drove through downtown Syracuse, a jumble of decrepit empty lots and stately nineteenth-century bank buildings, of decaying warehouses and soaring steeples. She passed through the city's beaten-down West Side, where she had grown up on welfare. A mile later, Onondaga Lake, the famed lake of Hiawatha, stretched out to her right, a once gleaming beauty carved out by glaciers, now badly scarred and polluted. Just past the lake, Kathy took the exit ramp and entered the Village of Solvay, passing Bridge Street Tavern and then a bowling alley, a pizzeria, and there, right across from Roma's bar, was Landis Plastics.

As Kathy pulled into the Landis parking lot, she felt a tinge of excitement, but some trepidation, too—she had never worked in a factory before. She had worked as a cook, a secretary, a saleswoman, jobs in which she could use her considerable social skills and her gift of gab. Here, she feared, she would be all thumbs with the equipment and would spend her days with forbidding machines rather than with friendly coworkers.

Still, Kathy knew that the factory held out opportunities for advancement, exactly what she hungered for after years of bouncing from job to job. At the factory, she was pleased to hear, workers sometimes climbed from grunt machine tender to trainer or even to supervisor in just four months.

"I wanted to move up the ladder," Kathy acknowledged.

Kathy had grown up in difficult circumstances. The fourth of five children, she was raised on Syracuse's West Side, a neighborhood of corner bars and of Chevies and Buicks rusting from the unforgiving northern winters. Her parents separated when she was just a toddler.

For nearly all of Kathy's childhood, her family—two of her siblings were deaf—was on welfare, and without those monthly checks and without the kindness of the priests and parishioners at St. Lucy's, Kathy's mother might never have been able to hold it all together. Some days all that saved the Saumier children from hunger was an uncle who stopped by to drop off some milk and bread. Every year or two, the Saumier clan bounced back and forth between a muddy-brown row of two-story attached homes that resembled nothing so much as an army barrack and a series of 1920s houses that had similar characteristics: sagging porches, peeling paint, and never enough bedrooms.

"My mother, she could have given us up," Kathy said. "She fought and kept us. She did the best she could."

Kathy's voice swells with pride as she talks about Her Mother, The Battler. At first glance, little, if anything, about Kathy hints that she, too, is a battler. She has a sheepish smile, a pale, almost sallow complexion, and a flat, throaty voice that sometimes turns whiny. She has tried to quit smoking forever. Five foot four and stocky, she has put on a few more pounds than she would like, largely because of a workplace injury that caused two bulging disks in her neck and hampered her mobility.

As soon as Kathy turned sixteen, she dropped out of school, not just because she disliked it, but because she wanted to help support her family. At fourteen, she had taken a job as a receptionist and housekeeper at St. Lucy's rectory. At sixteen, she began working as a cook for Catholic Charities, too. In her years there, she felt the strong tug of the church, and she became more involved by interpreting mass for the deaf, singing in St. Lucy's choir, helping run the Christmas toy drive for the city's poorest children, and helping administer the Eucharist at services. It was at Catholic Charities that Kathy met and fell in love with Michael, who worked there as a janitor. Kathy's two jobs allowed her to achieve her longtime dream of getting off welfare.

After eight years at Catholic Charities, she left to become a cook at Syracuse University. She had needed a change. But after several years of chopping and slicing, Kathy was ready to move on. Confident of her people skills, she decided to pursue a sales job. She went to work as a receptionist at Nationwide Warehouse, a furniture chain, convinced that her sociability and intelligence would earn her a promotion to the sales floor. Within months, she was moved into sales. She did well enough, but it was hard to be a stellar saleswoman when the local economy was so dreary. When Nationwide laid off an African American salesman, it dismissed Kathy as well, to help protect the store, she says, from a potential lawsuit asserting that it was discriminating against blacks.

She soon found a job as a saleswoman at a Caldor's optical department. She loved the job because there was so much socializing with customers, but Caldor's closed that store when it tumbled into bankruptcy. Eager to stay off welfare, Kathy took the first job that came her way, the part-time position cleaning floors and toilets at the newspaper.

"I don't consider any job a lousy job," Kathy said. "I will do whatever I have to do to make money."

Now Kathy was beginning at Landis Plastics in Solvay. She saw the company as a great opportunity, as did all of Solvay, a village of six thousand just west of Syracuse. For the previous decade, Solvay was sullen and sinking because its largest factory, vital to the town's prosperity, had closed. The town and its humble houses had sprouted up around the factory, originally called

Solvay Process, when it opened in 1881. Solvay Process became the nation's largest producer of synthetic soda ash, a chemical used to produce glass, baking soda, and soap. In 1920, the factory became part of Allied Chemical, and for the next six decades it prospered. But demand for soda ash fell so sharply in the early 1980s as glass recycling became popular and plastic bottles increasingly replaced glass that Allied Chemical closed the plant in 1986. It had employed 1,400 workers and paid nearly half of Solvay's taxes. Soon after the plant shut down, neighborhood bars and luncheonettes closed their doors, local trucking companies went bankrupt, and divorces, foreclosures, and car repossessions soared.

When Landis Plastics was surveying the Northeast for a site to build a new factory, Solvay was still aching from the Allied shutdown. Desperate to attract jobs, the town teamed up with the State of New York to offer Landis an extraordinary package of incentives: cut-rate electricity prices as well as $8.5 million in direct aid and tax breaks, amounting to more than $40,000 per worker. In return, Landis promised to create two hundred jobs averaging thirteen dollars an hour. The day that Landis opened on the Allied Chemical site, it was greeted with ribbon cuttings, front-page articles in local newspapers, dignitaries dressed in their Sunday best, and a visit from the governor, Mario Cuomo, who hailed it as a great day for upstate New York.

HOWEVER MUCH TREPIDATION Kathy felt as she pulled into the Landis parking lot that first day, she felt sure that the company represented a step up. The factory was new and well lit, a sprawling one-story building the size of two football fields. Its 180 production workers ran either injection-molding machines that made plastic containers or printing presses that inked bright logos and letters onto containers for products such as Cool Whip, Breyer's yogurt, and Philadelphia cream cheese. Kathy was pleased to be earning considerably more than in her cleaning job and more than some of her waitress friends were making. She was also happy that most of the workers were young women like herself—about half of them were single mothers.

Hired as an inspector-packer, Kathy was supposed to do three demanding tasks at once: inspect the thousands of plastic containers that her injection-molding machine spit out each hour, pack all of them into boxes, and then lug the heavy boxes to a conveyer belt ten feet behind her. Each molding machine was about twenty-five feet long, the front end pumping molten plastic into cup-shaped molds and the back end churning out a constant whirring rush of cups and more cups. Three hours after Kathy began, the trainer who was instructing her and two other new hires suddenly quit. Kathy had been told that she was supposed to receive three full days of training before working on the factory floor, so she was stunned when after just a few hours of training she was sent to the floor. Management immediately ordered her to operate machines that produced a nonstop wave of 10 containers per second, 600 per minute, 36,000 per hour.

On her second day on the job, Kathy felt like Charlie Chaplin playing the hapless, overwhelmed, sprinting-all-the-time factory worker in *Modern Times*.

"I couldn't keep up," Kathy said. "All these cups were coming at me. They're coming out of ten different holes, and you can't slow the machine down. I was ready to cry. They didn't tell you where to put your hands, so sometimes we put them in the wrong place."

Kathy knew how to work hard, and she was intent on making the best of it. But she was shocked when three months after she began, a coworker, Barb Phillips, had part of a finger cut off when it got caught in a printing press. Two months after that, Valerie Yerdon lost the middle finger and index finger on her right hand when she was using a rag to wipe the side of a printing press. The high-speed rollers pulled in the rag and Yerdon's fingers along with it. Not long after, Craig Roberts had most of a finger cut off when he was cleaning the drum of a printing press that unexpectedly started running at full speed even though he thought the power had been turned off. After those three amputations, a sense of fright, even terror, spread through the factory.

Despite a heightened sense of alert, just two months after Roberts's amputation, Wendy Bibbs, an eager, yet anxious twenty-two-year-old, had part of her left pinkie chopped off on her fourth day at Landis. It happened as she was reaching into a printing press to pull out some container lids that were trapped in the rollers; the machine did not have the required guarding apparatus meant to prevent workers from inserting their hands there. For Kathy, who had been promoted to trainer, this accident was especially heart-wrenching because she had gotten to know Bibbs well, having trained her during her first two days of work, teaching her how to operate the injection-molding machines. But on Bibbs's third day at Landis, management had suddenly sent her to run a printing press even though she had received only a few hours of training in printing.

"Wendy said she had heard about the amputations," Kathy said. "She said she did not want to go to printing. She was scared.

"When her finger got caught, it wasn't pretty," Kathy continued. "I lost it. I started crying. I started yelling, 'Are you going to wait till somebody dies until you do something?' "

After Bibbs's amputation—the fourth in thirteen months, almost one hundred times the rate of other plastics factories in the state—several workers complained openly.* Stephen Ellis, the plant manager, issued a statement insisting the factory was safe and its equipment state of the art. "The company," Ellis said, "made every effort possible during the design of its equipment and the development of the guarding equipment to ensure a safe operation. In light of the variety of circumstances under which these four incidents occurred, and the different causal factors, the company does not believe its safety program is sub-par."

Terrible as the amputations were, they were far from the only problem at the factory. Women filled 93 percent of the lowest-rung, lowest-paid, most dangerous jobs, that is to say, the hectic yet monotonous jobs tending the molding machines and printing presses. At the same time, men held all but one of the forty higher-paying, less stressful technicians' jobs, servicing and fixing the machinery. The technician jobs paid $10 to $12 an hour, some 50 percent more than the $6.50 to $8 an hour received by the women. Kathy and several coworkers were stunned when managers told them that the technicians' jobs were for men and the lower-level jobs were for women. The only woman to hold a technician's job was Valerie Yerdon, who was given that position, many workers said, only so management could say it wasn't discriminating against women.

As blatant as the sex discrimination was, many women said the sexual harassment was worse. Male workers often grabbed the breasts and behinds of female workers while the women were tending the molding machines and presses. When women bent over to place the container-filled boxes onto the conveyer belt, they often heard men say, "Nice ass." Sometimes in the middle of a workday, a few technicians enraged the women by asking for oral sex. "They felt they could say anything they wanted and could reach over and grab someone's ass or breast," said Beverly Martin, a longtime Landis worker. "It is common for them to call women bitches or cunts." One male worker greeted new female employees by climbing on top of a machine and performing a crude skit involving a plastic dildo and simulated masturbation. When the women complained to the company about the harassment, the managers shrugged it off as a boys-will-be-boys phenomenon.

*A fifth worker, Kim Stevenson, had the tip of her middle finger cut off when she reached in to clear a jam of containers.

The workers also hated the factory's unforgiving demerit system. It penalized employees whenever they missed a day, arrived late, or left early, no matter if they had pneumonia or had a child who was hurt in a car accident. Missing work for a day was one point, and a five-day sickness meant five points. Workers who received ten points over a twelve-month period were docked fifty cents an hour for three months, while those who accumulated fifteen points over twelve months faced dismissal.[1]

One of Kathy's best friends, Linda Murphy, had racked up points for missing three days because of a kidney infection. Soon after recovering, Murphy had to sprint out of the factory one afternoon because her three-year-old son, Charlie, had badly scalded himself when he knocked a steaming saucepan off the stove, spilling soup on his head and arms. As she rushed out to meet her son in the emergency room, her boss shouted to her that she could face dismissal for leaving early.[2]

KATHY COULDN'T STAND what she was seeing. Her friends, her coworkers, were being maimed, harassed, bullied, threatened, and discriminated against.

"They treat the people who work on the floor like slaves," Kathy said. "I just got tired of hearing all the women complaining that they treat us like dirt, bitching. I just got sick of it."

The workers at Landis were definitely not the type to stick their necks out. Many were high school dropouts, many were single mothers, many had just gotten off welfare, many were barely making ends meet. One day it occurred to Kathy that there were so many single mothers at Landis because the managers knew that these women were so desperate to keep their jobs that they would work hard and hardly make a peep.

Kathy was different. Ever since she was a girl, she had been known for standing up and speaking out, especially on behalf of her two deaf siblings.

Once, when her sister Brenda's school for the deaf was closed for vacation, Kathy took Brenda to school with her. Kathy's teacher ordered Brenda to leave. Just twelve at the time, Kathy insisted that Brenda be allowed to stay, telling her teacher that she was using a double standard because Kathy's classmates were often permitted to bring non-deaf guests to school. The teacher let Brenda stay.

"I've always fought for what I wanted in life," Kathy said. "That's the way it had to be."

Now, with so much amiss at the factory, Kathy felt she had to speak up, even though she feared that doing so would infuriate the factory's managers. So she took three innocent enough steps that the federal government has made available to aggrieved workers.

Her first step was to begin attending a series of meetings at a local motel where an organizer from the United Steelworkers told the factory's employees that only by having a union, only by banding together, could they force management to address their concerns. Like many workers, Kathy was at first hesitant to attend, worried that she might get fired for backing a union. Kathy's second step was to file a complaint with the Occupational Safety and Health Administration (OSHA) about the amputations and the lack of protective equipment on several printing presses. Third, Kathy and a coworker, assisted by a lawyer for the steelworkers, filed a sexual discrimination complaint with the Equal Employment Opportunity Commission (EEOC), accusing Landis of systematically reserving the worst jobs for women and the best jobs for men.

As Kathy feared, the factory's managers treated these moves as acts of insurrection. But she persisted.

"I want dignity. I want respect," Kathy said. "I don't want to be treated like a piece of dirt. I did it for the women in there. They're afraid to speak out. They're afraid of losing their jobs. Someone had to do something."

Because Kathy was so sociable and such a good listener, other workers went to her with their complaints, calling her at home or pulling her aside during smoking breaks. Several women complained to her that managers had pressured them to quit after they became pregnant, telling them they would be rehired a few months after giving birth. (Federal law bars discrimination against pregnant workers.)[3] Many workers complained to Kathy about the point system, noting, for instance, that they often received a point when they cut themselves and left the factory floor to get a Band-Aid. But if they didn't get a Band-Aid and a supervisor saw a drop of blood on their hand, they also received a point. Many workers also complained about the factory's grueling pace and workload.

"You're nothing but a mule," Beverly Martin said. "They feel if you don't like it, if you don't come back, they could always get another warm body."

Some workers complained about being forced to work twelve-hour days or six days a week. (The New York State Department of Labor once fined Landis for violating a law that bars companies from requiring employees to work seven days a week.) The long, wearying days and weeks contributed to the factory's high rate of accidents. Many workers complained of neck sprains, back injuries, herniated disks, and, most of all, repetitive stress injuries. Hundreds of times a day, the inspector-packers had to remove plastic containers from the molding machines, twirl the containers around with their wrists to inspect them, stack them into large cardboard boxes, and lug the twenty-five-to-fifty-pound boxes to a shin-high conveyer belt ten feet away. Many women complained about pains shooting down their backs from repeatedly placing the unwieldy boxes on the conveyer belt. Over a twelve-month period, more than one-fourth of the workers missed at least one day of work because of injuries.

Landis had fired several badly injured workers when they were unable to return to work after being out for a year. One of them was Lorraine Baker. After eighteen months on the injection-molding line, she was laid up with carpal tunnel syndrome. Ten-inch-long braces covered her wrists, which felt numb for days at a time. After she was out for a year, Landis fired her.

THE WORKERS WERE growing angrier by the day, and as a result, the unionization effort was winning converts. So Landis flew in its director of human resources from the company's headquarters in Illinois, and he, in a bullying speech, warned the employees against unionizing. If the factory unionized, he said, customers might sour on the factory, it might lose business, and, he hinted, some workers might lose their jobs. He said unionizing would hurt Landis because it might cause many of the valued male technicians—many of whom were anti-union—to leave. When the human resources director dwelled on how hard it would be to replace the technicians, many women grew enraged, convinced that he favored the men and felt the women were disposable parts.

"He didn't have any respect for women," Kathy said. "He's brutal. He talks down to people. There's no way that I'm going to let anyone talk to me like that. After the meeting, a couple of the men said, 'We don't need a union.' I told them, 'You make the big bucks, and you don't get treated like shit.' "

Kathy was so furious about the manager's speech that immediately after leaving work that day she met with steelworker officials to sign a card declaring her support for a union. Ultimately, officials with the steelworkers say, 60 percent of Landis's production workers signed union support cards.[4] (It might seem odd that the steelworkers union was seeking to organize a plastics factory, but that union claimed Solvay as its turf because it had long represented workers at the Allied Chemical plant.)

"I don't believe our people need to be represented by the union," said Gregory Landis, president of the family-owned company. "We have been in business forty-three years and have done that harmoniously. Why change a good thing? If it isn't broke, don't fix it."[5]

Unfortunately for Landis, the outside world was beginning to take notice of the factory—and of Kathy Saumier. After learning about the amputations, Michael Bragman, the majority leader of the New York State Assembly, arranged for a legislative hearing about Landis in downtown Syracuse. The star witness was Kathy, who in her strong, throaty voice told the legislators, "The way they treat us is not acceptable in this community in this day and age." While testifying, Kathy burst into sobs when she started talking about Wendy Bibbs, the twenty-two-year-old who lost her pinkie on her fourth day at Landis. Kathy described the minimal training that Bibbs had received on the printing presses, adding: "She said she did not want to go to printing. She was scared. She wanted to keep all her fingers."

The next day, Syracuse's main newspaper, the *Post-Standard*, ran a huge front-page color photograph of Kathy wiping away some tears as she testified. When Kathy arrived at work, she discovered that inside the break room where the workers ate lunch and took coffee breaks, someone had pasted up a copy of the photo and scrawled across it, "If you don't like your job, if your job makes you cry, maybe you should find another one."

Kathy's job had now become half crusade and half nightmare. The day after the legislative hearing, a male technician who was friendly with management hovered for nearly two hours in front of Kathy as she ran a printing press. He made whimpering sounds and constantly stuck his face in front of hers, repeatedly wiping his eyes to ridicule her for sobbing at the hearing. He ignored her pleas to go away, even mocking her while a supervisor looked on. When she complained to Linda Russell, the assistant human resources director at the factory, Russell showed little sympathy, telling Kathy, "If you're in the public eye, you're opening yourself to harassment."[6]

Kathy would not be intimidated. Most days at the factory, she wore a button saying, "Woman of Steel." She started chairing the weekly meetings of fifteen to twenty pro-union workers at the Western Ranch motel. She began giving speeches about the amputations and sexual discrimination at churches, union halls, and women's meetings. She even gave a rousing speech to several thousand union members at the New York State Fair's annual labor luncheon. Local newspapers editorialized on behalf of Kathy and the Landis workers, and every Thursday morning, more than a dozen members of the clergy held a vigil outside the factory to pray for fair treatment and an end to the amputations.

At one vigil, Auxiliary Bishop Thomas J. Costello of Syracuse's Roman Catholic diocese said the amputations had special significance to people of the cloth. "In my line of work, the fingers of one's hand are important tools," he said. "I use them to anoint the forehead of a baby at the beginning of her life and that of an elder preparing to meet his God. In my fingers I hold the bread as I speak the words of consecration at the time of Eucharist. I raise these fingers in blessing at the end of every mass I celebrate. Perhaps that explains why we who rely so much on our hands are especially touched and chagrined when we learn that someone has lost a finger, a part of a hand. We know how much more is lost in that severing."[7]

Notwithstanding all the community support the workers received, Kathy felt the heat being turned up. In the break room, she occasionally overheard anti-union workers call her "that blond-haired bitch." In her capacity as a trainer, she sent management a letter saying that many new workers from Vietnam and Latin America might not be able to absorb the safety information they needed because there was nobody to translate the instructions she was giving them. Management's response was hostile, with a Landis lawyer writing Kathy that her letter "smacks of racism."[8]

One morning, the factory's managers suddenly summoned Kathy to a conference room, where a former FBI agent awaited her. The former agent, who was doing work for Landis's law firm, stunned Kathy by interrogating her about whether she had sabotaged an anti-union worker's car whose brakes, he said, had failed. Kathy dismissed that as ridiculous.

"Every time I turned around they were trying to do something to me," Kathy said. "There were days I kept telling myself, 'God, help me get through this day.'

"Friends ask, 'Why don't you just leave?' " Kathy continued. "I don't want the women there to be treated like a piece of dirt. I have a daughter who's growing up. I never want her to have to work in a place like this."

Kathy grew increasingly convinced that Landis's managers were out to get her. She stopped using her locker at the factory, removing the lock and leaving it open, fearing that a conniving manager would plant drugs in it. One day, Beverly Martin, who had joined Kathy in filing the sexual discrimination case, discovered that someone had used bolt cutters to cut through the padlock on her locker. Another outspoken pro-union worker, Linda Murphy, was arrested after another employee accused her of stealing her coat. Management invited the police into the factory, and Murphy was hauled off to jail. The charges were dropped when Murphy's accuser failed to provide any evidence linking her to the coat's disappearance.

Six months after Kathy filed her complaint about safety problems, OSHA announced a $720,700 fine against Landis, one of the largest safety fines ever lodged against a company in New York State.[9]

A dozen OSHA inspectors had found seventy-four violations at the plant, among them repeated failures to install safety guards on the printing presses. OSHA also found that Landis executives had failed to list in the factory's safety log sixty-three separate incidents in which employees had been injured. Federal regulations require companies to record in their safety logs every single injury that results in an employee missing one or more days of work. The agency imposed a $10,000 fine for each of the omitted injuries, including a broken pelvis, concluding that Landis had deliberately failed to list the sixty-three injuries in order to hide the factory's appalling safety record.[10] (The State Workers' Compensation Board had previously fined Landis $48,000 for failing to report twenty-one injuries.)[11] When company officials first listed Valerie Yerdon's amputation in the safety log, they merely reported an injury to the "right hand" even though federal regulations require that the word "amputation" be used whenever a worker suffers an amputation.[12]

Kathy felt vindicated by the OSHA fine, but Landis was livid. Its managers downplayed the penalty. (At the same time, it sought to turn other workers against Kathy by saying that the fine was so big that it might reduce the profit-sharing that went into employees' 401[k] accounts.) Russell, the assistant human resources director, said, "We believe that these violations are the workplace equivalent of old parking tickets."[13] Terri Komuda, administrative assistant to a top manager, all but blamed the victims, saying, "At home you know not to stick your fingers in a running blender."[14]

In an attempt to explain Landis's failure to list the sixty-three injuries, Ellis, the plant manager, said, "Mistakes happen, and we do miss people once in a while. If there's mistakes on it, we correct it. But we do not intentionally leave anybody off of it."[15] His secretary, Patricia Salvagno, later told OSHA that she had been ordered not to list many injuries in the safety log.[16]

The factory's managers soon devised a strategy to neutralize Kathy and perhaps induce her to quit. Many days, Kathy's supervisors assigned her to work by herself in what managers called "hold," an isolated room where she sorted through possibly defective lids and containers to separate the bad ones from the still usable ones. There, Kathy couldn't talk to other workers and spread her pro-union sentiments. "It's like they put you in solitary," Kathy said.

Jim Valenti, the steelworkers' top official in Syracuse and a popular former local football star, said it was clear to everyone that Landis had singled out Kathy. "Landis felt it was not only an insult that anyone would challenge them, but how dare a woman challenge them?" he said. "They had to crush her. The more they went after her, the more courageous she became and the more she stood her ground. They wanted her bad and would resort to anything to get rid of her. They knew if they got rid of her, they'd never have a problem again."

Two weeks after OSHA announced its fine, another worker, Barbara Rotolo, started taunting Kathy in the break room, vehemently arguing that unions did next to nothing to improve safety. Rotolo told Kathy that Crucible Steel, a unionized mill down the road, had recently been fined seven hundred dollars for safety violations. Rotolo screamed so much and so loud that Kathy was convinced she was hoping that Kathy would slug her. That would have gotten Kathy fired.

At work the next morning, Kathy was confronted by a Solvay police officer who had been summoned by Landis. He told her that Rotolo's car wouldn't start earlier that morning. Kathy was questioned about whether she had sabotaged the car, and once again she was convinced that management was setting her up.

"You know if there's any damage, I have to come to get you," the policeman said, according to Kathy.

"I told him, 'Just call me if you have to pick me up. I'll meet you on the street so my kids don't see.' "

After the police interrogation, Kathy had an anxiety attack and started suffering chest pains. As soon as her coffee break arrived, she told a manager that she felt so ill that she needed to leave. She then telephoned the lawyer for the steelworkers, Mairead Connor, who rushed over to meet her. Together they drove to the Solvay police station, where Kathy swore in a statement that she hadn't touched Rotolo's car.

That afternoon, the police informed her that a mechanic at Dave Ball Chevrolet had determined that the problem with Rotolo's car was a faulty sensor light, not sabotage.

The next day, when Kathy went to the factory's front office to pick up her paycheck, she was told that Russell, the assistant human resources director, wanted to see her.

When Kathy arrived, Russell began with a few pleasantries. Then she awkwardly told Kathy that she was sorry to have to tell her this, but Landis had been conducting a six-week investigation into allegations that Kathy had improperly touched two male workers inside the factory.

Kathy was stunned. "I said, 'I know you want to set me up. Everyone else knows that you want to set me up.' "

Russell refused to tell Kathy the names of the two male workers, although she told Kathy that she was accused of pulling down one man's pants and trying to fondle his genitals. Russell told Kathy that she was suspended and had until the next day to respond to the allegations. Kathy said the charges were total fabrications.

"I was sick to my stomach that someone would stoop so low to get me," Kathy said.

Minutes after Russell told Kathy of the sensational allegations against her, Kathy again started feeling chest pains and hyperventilating.

"I was in shock, and I started crying," Kathy recalled. "I told her, 'You can't do this. You made me leave here with chest pains and unable to breathe yesterday, and I'm not going to let you go do it again. I'm so tired of being set up. I came here to do my job. I didn't come here to be harassed. I'm tired of being harassed.' "

Kathy rushed from the factory to St. Joseph's Hospital to be examined for chest pains, but she was soon released.

Immediately after her meeting with Russell, Kathy called Connor for help. Connor is tall and bookish—there's a smartest-girl-in-the-class feel to her—with a bear-trap memory, a bulldog's tenacity, and a visceral resentment to corporate bullying. Later that day, Landis sent Connor a letter with more details, alleging that Kathy had touched a male worker's genitals without his consent, had touched a man's buttocks without his consent, and had attempted to pull down a male employee's pants. The letter further accused Kathy of asking an African American worker whether the size of his penis was related to his race and asking another worker whether the size of his feet had anything to do with the size of his penis.

Kathy and Connor were planning to go to the factory that Monday to respond to the harassment allegations, but early Monday morning, each received a hand-delivered letter saying that Kathy had been fired. Moreover, seeking to humiliate Kathy publicly, Russell told the news media: "This was the most egregious complaint [of sexual harassment] that I have ever investigated. I have terminated individuals for less egregious actions."[17]

Connor said the sexual harassment allegations were especially clever because they appeared designed to drive a wedge between Kathy and a group that was particularly effective in supporting the Landis workers: the clergy. The allegations appeared all the more insidious, Connor said, because they came just days before the clergy were scheduled to issue a report about sexual discrimination and harassment at Landis. Gregory Landis, the company's president, all but called on the priests, ministers, and rabbis to repudiate Kathy, saying, "When it comes to sexual harassment, I'd expect the clergy, of all people, to be the first to rally around the person who was violated, not around the person who perpetrated the harassment."

"We have a harassment policy that is enforced very, very vigorously," he added. "What really isn't plausible is that we wouldn't understand the ramifications if we fired someone like her. Before anything was done to Kathy, it was covered nine ways to Sunday."[18]

Mairead Connor would have none of it. Some two weeks after the investigation of Kathy had supposedly begun, she said, Russell had offered to promote Kathy to supervisor, apparently to buy off management's most effective critic. Kathy turned down the promotion, and then came the damning allegations.

"This shows the extreme and illegal lengths that management will go to, to crucify workers who try to do anything to improve conditions," Connor said. "They must have been calculating, What is the way we can most humiliate her and make her go away with her tail between her legs?"

Within days of being fired, Kathy, joined by Connor and the steelworkers union, filed a complaint with the National Labor Relations Board (NLRB) asserting that the sexual harassment allegations were a ruse to get rid of her. They argued that Kathy was fired because she was the factory's most outspoken champion of unionizing and of ending the safety hazards and sexual discrimination. Federal law prohibits companies from retaliating against workers for supporting a union or for filing complaints with OSHA or the EEOC. (Days after Kathy was fired, the steelworkers union hired her as a full-time organizer, both to ensure that her family did not suffer a financial blow and to continue using her eloquence, energy, and passion.)

According to Landis, two employees, Stanley Washington and Kenneth Mar, had accused her of harassment. Mar, Kathy's main accuser, said she had made lewd comments to him, pulling down his loose-fitting pants, grabbing his buttocks, and seeking to fondle his genitals.[19]

Not long after Landis fired Kathy, Washington, an African American worker with a criminal record and a tenuous hold on his job, told Kathy and Connor that the factory's managers had pressured him to say something bad about Kathy. Washington assured them that he knew Kathy had done nothing improper. By refusing to provide an affidavit against Kathy or to back up Landis's claims, Washington went far to demolish the company's contention that she had harassed him.[20]

Kathy's ordeal became the cause célèbre of blue-collar Syracuse and the focus of the weekly prayer vigils outside the factory. After a concert in Syracuse, Bruce Springsteen met with Kathy to show his solidarity. That was when townspeople and the news media started calling Kathy "the Norma Rae of Syracuse," a reference to the 1979 film in which Sally Field plays a gutsy union activist at a North Carolina textile mill.

The usually conservative *Post-Standard*, never known for carrying Joe Hill's banner, wrote a scathing editorial about Landis's decision to fire Kathy: "Like most central New Yorkers, we cheered when Landis came to Solvay, bringing nearly 200 jobs to a community that had been clobbered by the Allied pullout. But no one expected a seventeenth century attitude toward worker rights to come with the deal. No one expected mangled bodies to be accepted as a cost of doing business.

"Enlightened management," the editorial added, "regards employees as partners, not as the enemy, rabble that must be kept under the boss's heel. Isn't it possible for Landis to treat its workers as human beings and still make money?"[21]

The NLRB's general counsel went to federal district court to seek an emergency injunction that would order Landis to reinstate Kathy, something he almost never did for a fired worker. He did so because her case seemed so egregious and because it was receiving so much attention in the community and the news media. (Workers who are fired for backing a union often must wait two years or more to get reinstated, frequently having to wait for a full trial before a regional labor board judge and then for appeals to the full five-member NLRB in Washington and to a federal circuit court.)

Angry with the NLRB's general counsel, Gregory Landis said, "The message to our employees from this is that if you support the union, the company's rules against sexual harassment don't apply to you."[22]

Linda Russell insisted that no worker had been "set up for dismissal."[23]

THE NORMA RAE OF SYRACUSE was feeling more harried victim than heroine. She felt tense, exhausted, overwhelmed, and at times panicky. At two and three some mornings, not only Kathy but also her mother received obscene phone calls berating Kathy and warning that she had better not return to Landis. Kathy started to fear for her children's safety, asking their school to make sure they were not released to strangers at the end of the day.

The NLRB effort to reinstate Kathy was delayed by months of on-again, off-again settlement talks with Landis, but soon after those talks collapsed came a slam-dunk ruling for Kathy. Federal District Court Judge Rosemary Pooler—now a federal appeals court judge—issued an injunction ordering that Kathy be reinstated. Judge Pooler wrote that Landis had done virtually nothing in response to frequent and flagrant charges of sexual or racial harassment. But in Kathy's case, the judge wrote, the company moved with extraordinary swiftness to fire her without even conducting a thorough investigation. Judge Pooler concluded that the decision to punish Kathy—and virtually no one else, despite myriad sexual and racial harassment allegations at the plant—constituted improper retaliation against Kathy for leading the unionization effort.[24]

"Landis exhibited a pattern of past acquiescence with respect to workplace harassment," Judge Pooler wrote. She noted that when Richard Bentley, a union supporter, complained to management that several workers had called him "Buckwheat" and "Nigger," those workers were not punished.[25]

While Judge Pooler had been weighing whether to issue an injunction to reinstate Kathy, an NLRB administrative law judge was conducting an extraordinarily long trial—forty-seven days—to weigh charges that Landis had unlawfully fired Kathy and engaged in seventy-six other illegal actions to keep out the union and retaliate against union supporters. Local newspapers covered the hearings as attentively as they would a murder case.

Kenneth Mar was the star witness. A six-foot, twenty-two-year-old worker from Puerto Rico, he fancied himself a ladies' man. He testified that Kathy had pulled down his pants and tried to fondle him, saying that he told her, "Don't do that again."

According to his testimony, Kathy responded, "Oops, I hope nobody saw me."[26]

Mar's credibility began to crack during cross-examination. He admitted that Terry McClelland, the factory's human resources manager, had summoned him to his office one day to ask for dirt on Kathy. Mar also acknowledged that in the five weeks after Kathy was fired, he was promoted and given four raises, his pay jumping by more than 25 percent.[27]

At the trial, Connor was merciless toward Mar. In cross-examination, she got him to acknowledge that after nine months in the army he had received a dishonorable discharge for stealing checks and forging signatures on them. She next got Mar to acknowledge that after being discharged, he was convicted on felony theft charges in Georgia for stealing a package that UPS had left in front of a neighbor's home.[28] Mar also admitted that he had lied about having a felony conviction when he applied to the temp agency that had placed him at Landis.[29] Mar was so embarrassed during cross-examination that he repeatedly covered his face with his hands and slumped over in his chair.

The NLRB judge, Steven Davis, ruled that Landis's decision to dismiss Kathy constituted illegal retaliation because it was motivated by the company's anger over her union activities and her long history of speaking out about problems at the factory. Asserting that the sexual harassment allegations were an improper pretext for firing Kathy, Judge Davis wrote that whenever women had previously complained about harassment, management responded with "disbelief, indifference and antagonism."[30] He also wrote, "I do not believe that [Landis] could reasonably have believed that Saumier sexually harassed either Mar or Washington in violation of its policy."[31]

As a result of these rulings, Kathy returned to work thirteen months after Landis had fired her. She felt some trepidation about going back. The day she returned, fifty supporters, including some of Syracuse's leading members of the clergy, rallied outside and cheered her. Some supporters cried. In a raspy voice, Kathy told the small crowd, "Hopefully, it's a safe place to work now, and a place where people can work with dignity."[32]

Inside the factory, union supporters embraced Kathy, while union opponents shunned her. Kathy, who wore a United Steelworkers baseball cap that first day back, was immediately struck by several changes at the factory. The speed of the injection-molding machines had been ratcheted up to seven hundred containers per minute from six hundred. "I couldn't keep up," Kathy said. A far higher percentage of workers were immigrants, from Latin America, Vietnam, Bosnia, and Sudan. Kathy calculated that of the more than one hundred workers who had signed pro-union cards two years earlier, only fifteen remained.

Three weeks after Kathy returned to the factory, her injection-molding machine jammed and the plastic containers began backing up and getting crushed. Kathy lurched suddenly to try to catch dozens of containers before they spilled to the floor. The maneuver was awkward because Kathy was carrying a large plastic tray to help her hold containers—it extended out from her stomach, with a strap around her back—and the weight of the tray threw her off-balance. She tumbled to the floor, tearing the rotator cuff in her left shoulder (that was not the immediate diagnosis) and badly injuring two disks in her neck.

She went to the factory on and off over the next few months, trying to make a go of it, but her neck and shoulder often caused her excruciating pain. After a year, doctors finally realized she had torn a rotator cuff, and only then was it operated on. She missed so many weeks of work because of her pain and injuries that she and Landis mutually decided that she should move on. That decision was made easier because Connor had offered to hire Kathy as her administrative assistant. Now Kathy spends her days setting up appointments with clients, collecting clients' bills, and making sure witnesses get to court on time. Four nights a week, she takes classes to become a paralegal.

Three years after Kathy filed her complaint with the EEOC, Landis agreed to pay $782,000 to dozens of current and former female employees to settle charges that it had improperly discriminated by giving women almost all of the lowest jobs in the factory and men nearly all the best ones. Again, Kathy felt vindicated. "The company always said we were lying about these things," she said.[33]

To Kathy's regret, Landis Plastics is still not unionized. Discouraged by the rapid employee turnover, steelworker officials have abandoned plans to hold a unionization election there. Many of the current workers do not speak much English and know little about unions, and as immigrants, many are terrified about sticking their necks out in an unfamiliar land. Moreover, many have heard of Kathy's travails and know all too well that backing a union can lead to retaliation by management.

Since Kathy left Landis, life has in many ways grown tougher for its employees. A decade after Kathy went to work there, starting pay for most new employees was still around seven dollars an hour, the amount that Kathy first earned there. Employee health insurance premiums have climbed to more than $2,000 a year; with wages of less than $20,000 a year, many workers can't afford the premiums. Almost all the higher-level technical jobs are still held by men. After Landis was acquired by Berry Plastics in 2003, management made the points system even stricter and cut back on matching the workers' 401(k) contributions. The one big improvement is that there are fewer serious injuries, the result of the pressure OSHA brought to bear in response to Kathy's complaint.

Around Syracuse, Kathy is still known as a pillar of strength. Sometimes when she is in a supermarket, strangers approach and say, "Aren't you that brave woman who . . ." The steelworkers union gave Kathy its "Woman of Steel" Award at its annual dinner, and the National Organization for Women named Kathy its "Unsung Heroine of the Year." Kathy testified at a federal hearing on occupational safety, and the AFL-CIO put her on the cover of its monthly magazine. Not bad for a high school dropout.

Looking back at her four-year ordeal with Landis, Kathy said, "I would do it all over again. The fight made me a lot stronger."

———

KATHY'S TALE, indeed the tale of so many of the Landis workers, is an especially egregious example of how companies squeeze their workers. But a squeeze is taking place nationwide, including in a quiet town in the Midwest where a giant corporation encountered far more resistance than it had anticipated.

Chapter Three

THE VISE TIGHTENS

Near the dairy barns and cornfields outside Jefferson, Wisconsin, the signs appeared in one front yard after another. Outside one farmhouse, a sign read GREED IS A SIN. Outside another, it was YOU CAN'T LIVE ON CHICKEN FEED. In town, a two-stoplight affair, the signs continued, voicing the sentiment that no matter what Gordon Gekko told us in *Wall Street*, greed is not good.

For Chuck Moehling, who operates a sausage-stuffing machine in one of Jefferson's largest factories, the Tyson Foods pepperoni plant, the signs were words of encouragement. After twenty-two years, Chuck earned $13.10 an hour, $27,000 a year before bonuses, for doing an arduous job that required him to lift sixty-five-pound racks of pepperoni six hundred times a day. With his wife's income from her public relations job, Chuck's pay was enough to give the Moehlings a solid—or so it seemed—grip on middle-class life. For Chuck, it was no small matter that the plant had paid well enough so that he didn't have to take a second job, giving him time to do what he loved most: coach his twin sons' Little League and basketball teams and his daughter's soccer and basketball teams. His six a.m. to two p.m. shift was ideal, enabling him to coach four, five, sometimes six games or practices a week. Around Jefferson (population 7,338), Chuck was a popular coach. The other parents liked his enthusiasm and dedication, and he certainly looked the part: direct gaze, strong jaw, ruddy athletic glow, and a strapping six-foot-three frame, with Popeye-like forearms. At forty, Chuck was still built like the brawny starting center he once was on Jefferson High's basketball team. He grew up on his parents' pig farm three miles west of town.

But now Chuck found himself in a war, a war he feared would loosen his grip on middle-class life. Tyson had recently acquired the Jefferson plant, which supplied 65 million pounds of pepperoni each year to the nation's leading pizza makers, including Pizza Hut, Domino's, and Tombstone Pizza. Intent on reducing costs at the plant, Tyson wanted to freeze the workers' wages for four years and introduce a two-tier wage scale in which future hires would receive less pay and fewer benefits than current workers. Tyson demanded cuts of almost 20 percent in the plant's starting pay—to $9 an hour from $11.10—and wanted to reduce the maximum base pay that future hires could receive to $11 an hour, down from $13.10 under the old contract with the United Food and Commercial Workers.

Tyson, which calls itself "the world's largest producer and marketer of chicken, beef and pork," also demanded cuts in sick days and vacation days. Additionally, it insisted on instituting a new, less generous health plan—child wellness visits and mammograms would no longer be free—that would require employees to pay far higher premiums, $1,400 a year for basic family coverage, up from $360 under the old contract. Tyson also wanted to freeze the workers' pensions; if that happened, Chuck's anticipated retirement benefits would never grow larger, no matter how much longer he worked there.

Tyson's list of demands—some workers called them Tyson's Ten Commandments—angered not just Chuck but most of Jefferson, a normally quiet town of tidy clapboard houses, humble but handsome churches, and a strong work ethic. Jefferson, like Milwaukee, forty miles to the east, was settled by German immigrants in the nineteenth century, and like many towns in the Midwest, it had begun as a farm community and later developed some ag-related industry. Joseph Stoppenbach, a local entrepreneur, opened the sausage factory in 1876.

When Chuck went to work at the factory right out of high school, Stoppenbach's descendants still owned the plant. They had preserved Stoppenbach's legacy of running a worker-friendly, family-friendly factory, a factory where, decade after decade, loyal workers ground the meat, blended in the spices, stuffed the mixture into casements, and then cooked and smoked the pepperoni. As the meat industry consolidated into a handful of corporate giants, the Stoppenbach family sold the plant to the Doskocil Companies in 1985. Doskocil, which was based in Kansas, was later acquired by IBP, and then Tyson took over IBP and the pepperoni factory along with it.

For Tyson, the newly acquired plant was a symbol of excessive generosity toward workers. Throwing down the gauntlet in Jefferson would show the 115,000 workers at Tyson's three hundred other slaughterhouses and processing plants that it was going to tighten up on pay and benefits.

"Jefferson was in a luxurious position from our perspective," said Ken Kimbro, Tyson's senior vice president for human resources. "We're not pleading poverty. We're not saying the Jefferson facility is losing money. We're saying the cost in Jefferson is out of line and we have to make adjustments."[1]

But the 470 unionized workers at the pepperoni plant feared that if Tyson got its way, their middle-class lifestyle and their hopes of a modestly comfortable retirement would disappear. Chuck and the other workers worried that Tyson was going to transform the factory from an anchor of the community where many Wisconsinites worked twenty-five, even thirty-five years, into a plant that relied on Mexican immigrants who worked there six months or a year and then moved on. At a meeting filled with anger and defiant speeches, the Jefferson workers voted 404 to 9 to strike, rejecting Tyson's argument that far-reaching concessions were needed to assure the plant's competitiveness and future.

When the lunch whistle blew on a surprisingly warm day in February 2003, the workers formed a picket line outside the factory's gates, just one block from Main Street. It was the first walkout since Joseph Stoppenbach opened the plant in 1876.

"The company asked, 'Why should we be sitting on this pedestal in Wisconsin?' " Chuck said. "We're just trying to support a family. We watch our pennies. We cut out our coupons. We're just scraping by. We're making twenty-seven thousand a year. That's not a lot of money. It's just enough to survive in this state. We have high heating bills and some of the highest tax rates in the nation."

Chuck feared that if the workers lost this showdown, it would have a disastrous effect on his family and his finances. "We can't afford to live on the concessions they're demanding," he said. "You hear that the reason kids end up the way they do today is because parents don't spend enough time with them. If Tyson gets what they want, I may be forced to take a second job, and if I have to take a second job, you can forget about the coaching."

"With what they're offering," he added, "it's going to be impossible to put money aside for your retirement or to save for college for your kids."

LIKE CHUCK, millions and millions of Americans have come to feel that their upward climb has stalled. It's no wonder considering the economic squeeze faced by so many workers: downsized white-collar workers, GM, Ford, and Chrysler workers, $7.50-an-hour fast food workers, part-time workers, temporary workers on two-week stints, airline workers and steelworkers battered by bankruptcies, and high-tech and call center workers threatened by offshoring.

Chuck, like these workers, has found himself on the short end of several far-reaching trends in which corporate America is squeezing its workers. These trends include the growing disconnect between profits and wages, the growing inequality between those on top and everyone else, and the growing effort by companies to shift economic costs and risks onto their workers, especially with regard to health coverage and pensions. Fueling all these trends is a profound, overarching shift in the American economy—corporations have been steadily shredding the post–World War II social contract in which they shared their increased prosperity with their workers, helping to create the world's largest and richest middle class. For many workers, a once sturdy structure of solid wages, pensions, health insurance, and job security is being dismantled brick by brick.

The dismantling of the social contract can be seen most starkly in what has happened to wages and family incomes over the past several years. For the first time since World War II, median income for nonelderly households fell five years in a row, sliding from 2000 through 2005, after factoring in inflation.[2] Median income for those households finally rose in 2006, but it still remained 4 percent or nearly $2,400 lower than six years earlier.[3] Since the 2001 recession ended, average hourly wages, after factoring in inflation, have inched up by only 1 percent. It is extremely unusual for wages to languish to such a degree over such a period considering that economic growth, profit growth, and productivity growth were all robust.[4] American corporations have simply kept more of the increased prosperity for themselves.

During the most recent economic recovery that began in 2001, corporate profits have risen 13 percent a year on average, 50 percent faster than profits rose on average during the seven other post–World War II recoveries. But total employee compensation—wages, salaries, and benefits taken together for all workers—rose less than *one-fifth* as fast as profits (and only five-eighths as fast as wages and salaries rose on average in other post–World War II recoveries).[5] In 2006, corporate profits climbed to their highest share of national income in more than six decades, while wages fell to their lowest share since the Great Depression and employee compensation slid to its lowest share since the 1960s (with the exception of 1997).[6]

In recent years, the partnership between pay and productivity seems to have fallen apart—economists use the word "decoupling" to describe this phenomenon. From 2001 to 2007, employee productivity rose by 15 percent, but the average hourly wage barely budged during that period. In late 2006, workers finally saw their wages inch up slightly faster than inflation, principally because of a sharp, temporary drop in energy prices. But in 2007, energy prices soared again, once more causing inflation to eclipse wage growth, a common occurrence in recent years.

Overall employee compensation—wages and benefits, including ever more expensive health benefits—has also trailed far behind productivity increases. Productivity rose nearly 3 percent a year on average from 2001 to 2007, while employee compensation rose by only 1 percent a year.[7] This represents the continuation of an unfortunate trend. From 1947 to 1973, productivity and the average wage rose more or less in tandem with productivity, with each roughly doubling. But from 1973 to 2006, productivity jumped by 83 percent while the average hourly wage essentially remained flat.[8]

Unfortunately for Chuck Moehling, the wage squeeze has been especially harsh for two groups he belongs to: male workers and workers without college degrees. For male nonsupervisory workers, the median hourly wage is 5 percent lower than in 1979, after factoring in inflation. Indeed, wages for the bottom 60 percent of men remain stuck below their 1979 levels. Only among the top 20 percent of male earners has there been anywhere near respectable wage growth.[9] One economist found that for men with just a high school diploma, 87 percent of new jobs paid less than $25,000 a year.[10]

For women since 1979, wages have climbed for all income groups, except the bottom tenth. The median wage for women has risen 24 percent since 1979, after factoring in inflation. Unfortunately, the median wage for women remains 23 percent below the median for men, although that gap has shrunk from 40 percent in 1980.[11]

For workers with just a high school diploma, average hourly earnings slid nearly 2 percent between 1979 and 2005, after adjusting for inflation. The decline was far worse for those without a high school diploma, with their real wage slipping 18 percent. For those with a college degree, real wages climbed 22 percent, and for those with advanced degrees, real wages rose 28 percent.[12]

One explanation for this wage stagnation among the less educated is that since 2000 the United States has lost 3.5 million manufacturing jobs, good-paying jobs that often went to workers without college degrees. The transfer of factories overseas and new technologies, like factory robots, have wiped out many of these jobs. The flood of immigrants has depressed wages for the group they most compete with: American-born workers with limited educations. De-unionization, competition from imports, the decline in the value of the minimum wage, and the rapid expansion of low-wage service sector jobs have also hurt this group of workers. All these factors go far to explain why the earnings gap between college graduates and those with just high school diplomas has climbed to 74 percent from 40 percent in 1979.[13]

As a result of the wage squeeze, in many households both parents have been forced to work. But according to Elizabeth Warren, coauthor of *The Two-Income Trap* and a professor at Harvard Law School, there is often a serious squeeze even in two-income households. The average income in those households was much higher in 2005 than the average for single-earner households in the early 1970s, after factoring in inflation.[14] But today's two-income households actually have less discretionary income than their single-earner predecessors did, Warren found.[15] These households, she concluded, face a financial squeeze because they have to spend so much on the necessities of daily life. "The real increases in family spending," she wrote, "are for the items that make a family middle class and keep them safe (housing, health insurance), and that let them earn a living (transportation, child care and taxes)."[16]

IN RECENT YEARS, the numbers regarding income disparity have been startling. According to a December 2007 report by the Congressional Budget Office, after-tax annual income for the bottom fifth of American households inched up just 6 percent from 1979 to 2005. During those twenty-six years, income for the middle fifth of households grew by a modest 21 percent. But income for the top fifth jumped by an impressive 80 percent, while income for the top 1 percent more than tripled, soaring by 228 percent.[17]

The highest-earning fifth of households received 51.6 percent of the nation's after-tax income in 2005, meaning their income exceeded that of the bottom four-fifths. As for the top 1 percent of households, they received more after-tax income than the bottom 40 percent.[18] A study based on federal tax returns found that this top 1 percent of households, averaging $1.1 million in annual income, received nearly 22 percent of all reported income in 2005, up from 9 percent in 1980, creating the greatest level of inequality since the Roaring Twenties. That study found that the share for the top 10 percent also rose, jumping to 48.5 percent from 33 percent in 1980, leaving a smaller share of the economic pie for the other 90 percent.[19] Were it not for this increased inequality, the bottom 80 percent of Americans would be doing considerably better. According to Lawrence Summers, the former Treasury secretary and former Harvard president, if the distribution of income in the United States today were the same as in 1979, assuming the same level of economic growth since then, income for the bottom 80 percent of Americans would be about $670 billion more or about $8,000 per family a year.[20] For many households in the bottom half, this would mean a 20 to 30 percent increase in income.

An objective outsider who laid fresh eyes on America's economic scene, a twenty-first-century Tocqueville, would probably think that the federal government would be eager to use tax policy to offset these widening disparities. But the tax cuts pushed through by President Bush have in many ways aggravated the disparities, giving $20 on average to the bottom 20 percent of American households, $744 on average to the middle fifth, and $118,477 to those making more than $1 million annually.[21]

At the pinnacle of the inequality pyramid are the nation's CEOs. American corporations may be parsimonious about raises for most workers, but they paid their chief executives $10.5 million on average in 2005, including salary, bonuses, and stock options. That was quadruple their pay a dozen years earlier. This means the typical CEO earns 369 times as much as the average worker, up from 131 times in 1993 and 36 times in 1976.[22]

Warren Buffett, the billionaire investor, had a blunt analysis of these trends: "There's class warfare, all right, but it's my class, the rich class, that's making war, and we're winning."[23] Buffett added that over the past two decades, "the average American went exactly nowhere on the economic scale: he's been on a treadmill while the superrich have been on a spaceship."[24]

The conventional wisdom is that the United States is a land of boundless opportunity and mobility, but some studies show that mobility in America is actually declining and that the United States has less mobility than Canada, Scandinavia, Germany, and France.[25]

Several studies have found that more than half of an American child's long-term income prospects are determined by the income of the child's parents.[26] One study of 6,273 families over two generations found that 66 percent of Americans born into the poorest fifth of earners did not climb above the bottom two-fifths. Only 6 percent of those born into the bottom fifth were able to climb into the top fifth.[27] Another study found that the sons of fathers in the bottom fifth have just a one in five chance of surpassing median income and less than a one in twenty chance of reaching the top fifth.[28] The mobility problem is far worse for blacks than whites. A white born in the bottom fifth by income has a 27 percent chance of remaining in that tier, according to one study, while a black born in the bottom fifth has a 61 percent chance.[29]

A college education is, of course, an important route to economic mobility. Unfortunately, the door to college is much narrower for low-income students, even high-achieving ones, than for high-income students. According to one study, low-income students with high test scores have a 29 percent chance of graduating from college, compared with a 74 percent chance for high-income students with high scores. Indeed, a high-income student with low test scores is more likely to graduate from college than a low-income student with high test scores.[30]

Although there have been some encouraging stirrings of late, most top-tier schools are doing little to educate and elevate those at the bottom. Three-fourths of the students attending the nation's top 146 colleges come from the highest-earning fourth of families, while just 10 percent come from the lowest-earning half and only 3 percent come from the bottom fourth.[31]

Anthony W. Marx, the president of Amherst College—one of the very few elite schools that is aggressively seeking to enroll more low-income students—said in a commencement address at Amherst: "In our society, economic disparities have been growing, not declining. They have grown also in these educational institutions that are supposed to be a source of redress. The assumptions we all once made of steady progress in this country have proven false: Our nation and our colleges are moving toward an inequality not seen since before the Great Depression."[32]

DURING THE NEW DEAL, President Franklin Delano Roosevelt declared war on the economic risks and insecurities that worried millions of Depression-scarred Americans. In a 1938 speech, Roosevelt declared, "There is still today a frontier that remains unconquered—an America unreclaimed. This is the great, the nationwide frontier of insecurity, of human want and fear."[33] Roosevelt saw a forbidding frontier where Americans faced potential financial catastrophe from losing a job, from getting sick, even from living to eighty years of age. Seeking to conquer this frontier, Roosevelt and the New Dealers built a vast protective structure that included Social Security, unemployment insurance, welfare, the minimum wage, housing assistance, disability insurance, even widow's and orphan's insurance. In explaining his decision to weave an expansive safety net, Roosevelt said, "Because it has become increasingly difficult for individuals to build their own security single-handed, Government must now step in and help them lay the foundation stones, just as Government in the past has helped lay the foundation of business and industry."[34] At the same time, the nation's corporations, prodded by organized labor, built a second, parallel safety net that was an essential part of the post-war social contract: health insurance, pensions, job security, and, at many companies, life insurance and disability insurance as well.

In recent years, however, government and business, often working hand in hand, have foisted considerably more risk and insecurity onto America's workers and their families. The effort to dismantle the safety net gathered momentum in the 1980s under President Ronald Reagan. He famously said that "government is not the solution" but rather "the problem." His philosophy, borrowed from the economist Milton Friedman, was that safety nets fostered dependency. Reagan wanted to shrink government and shrink taxes, and to do that, it was necessary to shrink the safety net. The result, as Peter Gosselin wrote in an important series in the *Los Angeles Times,* is that "a broad array of protections that families once depended on to shield them from economic turmoil" has been "scaled back or . . . vanished altogether."[35]

- In 1980, 84 percent of workers in companies with more than 100 workers had traditional pensions. Today just one in three does.[36] Companies are increasingly making their employees rely on far riskier 401(k) plans for their retirement income. In a 401(k) plan, the worker bears the risk of investment losses, not the company.
- Only about one-third of unemployed workers receive unemployment insurance, down from one-half in the 1950s.[37] Less than one in five low-income workers who lose their jobs receive unemployment benefits, largely because government has erected various hurdles—such as requiring applicants to earn a minimum amount each quarter to qualify—that discriminate against low-wage and part-time workers.[38] In the mid-1970s, laid-off workers received fifteen months of unemployment benefits; now they receive six months.
- Three decades ago, employer-provided health insurance protected 70 percent of private-sector workers. Now, it protects 55 percent.[39] Less than one in four workers in the bottom fifth by income have employer-provided health coverage.[40]
- In a fast-changing economy in which millions of Americans need retraining, the federal government's main training program has shrunk to $5 billion annually, down from $17 billion in 1980.[41]
- Federal housing subsidies have nosedived by nearly two-thirds over the past three decades even though rents and housing prices have soared in many cities over the past twenty years, notwithstanding the recent weakness in the real estate market, making housing less affordable for many Americans.[42]
- Pell grants have long made it possible for many poor children to go to college. The value of the maximum Pell grant fell from 84 percent of the average tuition at a four-year public university in the mid-1970s to just 32 percent in 2007.[43]
- The minimum wage, which seeks to ensure that a full-time job keeps work-

ers above a certain floor, slid in mid-2007 (before Congress enacted the first increase in nearly a decade) to its lowest level in more than half a century, after accounting for inflation.

It is an unusual time for government and business to be shifting so much risk onto the backs of American workers because this is an era of greater workplace volatility, faster technological change, and fiercer competition from abroad. Since the 2001 recession ended, unemployed workers have remained out of work for eighteen weeks on average, 50 percent longer than the average in previous post–World War II economic recoveries. As Louis Uchitelle explained in his excellent book on the decline of job security, *The Disposable American*, those who lose their jobs often have a hard time clawing their way back. Two years after being laid off, just two-thirds of the victims say they are working again, and of those, only 40 percent are earning as much as they did in their old job.[44] Underlying this increased volatility, the number of housing foreclosures tripled from 1977 to 2002 while the number of personal bankruptcies soared fivefold.[45] And now, some experts predict that the subprime mortgage crisis will result in two million foreclosures by the end of 2008.[46]

As a result of the unraveling of the safety net, a single bad break—a pink slip, a slipped disk, a rent hike, a broken-down car, a serious illness—increasingly leads to financial disaster and even bankruptcy.

"The modern American family is walking a high wire without a net," Professor Warren said. "Their basic situation is far riskier than that of their parents a generation earlier."[47]

THAT FEBRUARY DAY when the Tyson workers walked off the job, Chuck Moehling felt the quiet, terrifying fear that he might face month after month without a paycheck. But he also felt a stubborn confidence that the strike could bring Tyson to its senses.

Day after day, the Tyson workers stood outside the factory gates, picket signs in hand, often next to big steel barrels filled with burning wood to warm them. From the Tyson plant—a tangle of grinding rooms, kitchens, smokehouses, and warehouses wedged between the railroad tracks and the Rock River—security guards kept a close eye on the goings-on. Many days, the strikers fanned out for miles around, hammering their YOU CAN'T LIVE ON CHICKEN FEED signs into the ground.

"Everyone realizes we're in it for the long haul," Chuck said. "There's no way we can go back with what they're offering."

In an era when labor unions often get much wrong, Chuck's union did an impressive job strategizing during the strike. The UFCW got other unions—the teachers, the auto workers, the steelworkers—to donate hundreds of thousands of dollars, money that helped finance a food bank and the hundred dollars in weekly strike benefits received by each worker. The union deployed small groups of workers to visit state lawmakers, city councils, and newspapers to rebut Tyson's ads and arguments that the Jefferson workers wanted to hold on to unrealistically high wages and benefits. To maintain morale and solidarity, the union organized dinners every two weeks—and once spring arrived, barbecues and picnics—that attracted hundreds of workers and their families. Fifty strike captains—Chuck was one—were appointed, each responsible for keeping up the spirits of the eight to ten workers assigned them.

The support from the Jefferson community was extraordinary. When townspeople walked past the picket line, a block from Main Street and next to the town library, they often gave some strikers five-dollar bills for coffee and doughnuts. Some dropped off freshly baked cookies and brownies. One convenience store donated 328 gallons of milk, while the Towne Inn, the workers' favorite bar, held a beer and pizza benefit that raised more than $1,000 for the strike fund. The Oak Ridge Golf Course agreed not to charge greens fees to the strikers on Tuesdays, while Dave's Piggly Wiggly, Frank's Country Market, and other local supermarkets stopped stocking Tyson products. The supermarkets also donated tens of thousands of dollars in groceries to the union's food bank. "We had to support them," said Dave Lorbecki, a franchise owner of Dave's Piggly Wiggly. "They're our friends. They're our neighbors. Their kids play with our kids. We see they have it tough."

Nearly three hundred strikers went twice a week to the food bank in the union hall, filling two bags of groceries for free—with Chef Boyardee spaghetti, Maypo oatmeal, Mott's applesauce, Kellogg's Frosted Flakes, and lots and lots of potatoes. A union emergency fund gave cash infusions to help the neediest strikers stave off foreclosures, and it paid nearly $10,000 a month to cover the pharmacy bills of the strikers and their families. Outside the factory gates, the union staged boisterous rallies that attracted Senator Russell Feingold, Congresswoman Tammy Baldwin, and John Sweeney, the AFL-CIO president. Not one of the 470 strikers crossed the picket line during the first five months of the walkout.

To prepare for the strike, Chuck had sold the twenty-two-foot powerboat that he kept on a lake up north, getting several thousand dollars to help cushion the financial pain from the strike. Even so, his family had to cut back—there were fewer movies and dinners out, and when the strike dragged into July, the Moehlings sent their three children to summer camp for just one week instead of the normal five, and not to their usual, more expensive "All Star" sports camp at a nearby college.

Two months into the walkout, Tyson upset the workers by hiring permanent replacement workers—permanent if they wanted to stay—to keep the factory running. With this move, Tyson warned the strikers that when their walkout ended, there might not be jobs for them. (The United States is the only major industrial nation that lets replacement workers permanently take the jobs of strikers after a walkout ends.)

At six each morning when the replacement workers arrived at the factory gates, the strikers greeted them with boos, curses, and shouts of "Scabs go home." Sometimes they even spat on them. Many afternoons when Tyson tractor trailers pulled up to the gates to pick up the finished pepperoni, the strikers crowded in front to block them. They often mocked the slogan painted on the Tyson trucks: "This Is What Your Family Deserves." The police fined dozens of workers one hundred dollars for spitting, swearing, and stopping the trucks.

Eager to demonstrate that it was a good citizen, Tyson donated money to the 4-H Club, the town library, and Tomorrow's Hope, a local cancer fund. Tyson also stepped up its public relations efforts and argued that its demands for concessions would be good, in the long term, for Jefferson and the plant's workers.

"We are doing this because . . . we want this facility to continue to operate in Jefferson," said Ken Kimbro of Tyson. "In order for us to stay in business, we have to be able to manufacture at a competitive wage."[48]

But the union insisted that the plant, pre-strike, was both competitive and profitable. Tyson had record earnings the previous year, $338 million on sales of $23.4 billion.

"The plant's profits were increasing, and we felt we should share in those profits," said Mike Rice, a Vietnam veteran who was president of the factory's union. "There's absolutely no need for them to come in and make these kinds of concessionary demands. It's purely out of greed."[49]

The strike stretched into fall. Chuck began to realize that even when a union runs a model strike, it's not easy to defeat a large corporation that can make money from its other plants, all while the strikers suffer week after week without their paychecks. Some of the strikers took seven-dollar-an-hour jobs with retailers and local farms; some took up home repairs and painting. Chuck started a small vending business, placing soda and candy machines in office buildings, the county courthouse, and the police department.

When the new school year approached, the Moehlings swallowed their pride and accepted the kindness of the local Methodist church, which was giving out school supplies to the strikers' children. Chuck's mother-in-law, a cashier at a Citgo station, often dropped by to give them a few bags of groceries. That September, Chuck began working part-time for his brother-in-law, selling fire extinguishers.

In December, ten months in, the union leaders asked to resume negotiations. They were pressured by an important deadline—if the strike passed the one-year mark, the replacement workers would have the right to vote to get rid of the union. That seemed increasingly likely given the venom directed against them. A vote ousting the union would make it much harder for the strikers to win the dispute and get their jobs back.

Back at the bargaining table, Tyson insisted on the same concessions it had sought before the walkout began. This enraged the strikers, but fearing for their jobs and feeling considerable deprivation after months without a Tyson paycheck, they reluctantly voted to approve the company's offer even though it contained nearly all of the concessions they had long opposed. Tyson offered some modest cash bonuses as inducements to ratification.

Chuck grudgingly voted for ratification. "It feels crappy," he said. "A lot of people hated to give in."

Chuck knew that if he lost his Tyson job and had to find work elsewhere, he wouldn't have the twenty-two years' seniority or the four weeks' annual vacation he had accrued at Tyson. Moreover, any decent-paying job he landed was likely to be in Madison or Waukesha, a forty-minute-longer drive.

Chuck still bristles at the contract. He dislikes the wage freeze, the two-tier wage scale, and the new health plan. He now pays $2,340 a year in premiums for the preferred health insurance plan, up from the $360 he paid before the strike. Tyson boasts about a new benefit that it made available to the workers, enabling them to buy its stock at a 15 percent discount. But given the wage and benefit cuts, Chuck and many other workers can't afford to even contemplate that for the foreseeable future.

Nowadays Chuck feels like a struggling member of the working class rather than a farm boy well on his way toward securing his piece of the American dream. In a big setback for him, Tyson eliminated the hourly productivity incentives that had lifted his annual pay by $5,000, even $10,000, some years.

Those bonuses encouraged Chuck and the other sausage stuffers to run their machines faster and to haul more heavy racks of sausage each hour. With those incentives gone, productivity in the plant plunged after the strikers returned to work. With the loss of those bonuses, Chuck now earns just his $27,000 base salary—not the $37,000 he sometimes earned with bonuses.

Chuck now feels little enthusiasm about his job. "When I got out of high school, the factory was considered a great opportunity," he said. "But I think my kids should look for something better." In the years before the strike, Chuck and his wife, Kelly, often squirreled away fifty dollars a week for each child for college. That is a rarity now. They have also had to cut back their contributions to their 401(k)s. They have stopped going out for a family dinner every Friday night, a Moehling tradition, and they no longer take their annual vacation to Florida or out west. They are selling their summer cabin up north.

To help make ends meet, Chuck has expanded his vending business, now devoting ten to twelve hours to it each week. As a result, he only has time to coach two practices a week, half as many as before.

"Tyson says we're on a pedestal," Chuck said. "If that means fair wages, pension, health insurance, and other benefits, darn right, we're on a pedestal, and, in my mind, every American worker should be."

AS MUCH AS TYSON enraged Chuck and his coworkers, it played by the rules— rules that are in many ways skewed in favor of business. Some companies and managers, as we are about to see, are not so scrupulous about following the rules.

Chapter Four

DOWNRIGHT DICKENSIAN

When Farris Cobb gets going about the rats, it's hard to stop him. They were as big as dogs, he says, growing to that size because they feasted all night on the oversize bags of dog food in the back of the Sam's Club in Panama City, Florida, where he worked. He was the night supervisor, and he saw and heard the rats rummaging around much of the time he was there—especially because he was locked in the store each night along with his fellow workers.

"You could see them running across the dog food pallets," Farris said. "You could see the walls soaked in their urine and feces."

As crew leader for the nine p.m. to five a.m. shift, Farris oversaw a dozen workers who unloaded truck trailers and stocked shelves after the customers and day crew had gone home. When the managers left each evening around ten p.m., they locked the doors behind them, leaving the nighttime crew without any keys to get out. And the managers warned the night crew about using the fire door.

"They let us know they'd fire people for going out the fire door, unless there was a fire," said Farris. "They instilled in us that they had done it before and they would do it again."

Generally, no one was allowed to leave the building from ten p.m. until four a.m. when the bakery manager arrived to open the front door.

"They said, 'Don't open the door. Period,'" Farris said. "They said, 'If it wasn't an extreme emergency, like someone losing an arm or leg or someone who's dying, don't open the door.' We tried to call our supervisors when someone was deathly sick, and none of the managers would come and let them out. One guy had a stomach virus and was throwing up pretty bad. I told the manager, 'You need to come to let that person out.' He said, 'Find one of the mattresses. Have him lie down on the floor.'"

For years, these lock-ins were a well-kept secret—and a deliberate business strategy—at Wal-Mart, which owns and operates the Sam's Club chain. Locking in workers prevented employees from sneaking out for a smoke or a snack and, more important, it reduced "shrinkage," a euphemism the company uses for theft by employees or others.

———

THE INDIGNITIES FACED by Farris Cobb are not atypical of those suffered by millions of other workers in the nation's fast-growing service sector, which has come to dominate America's economy. Needing a job, needing to support their families, Farris and two other workers we will soon meet often felt trapped. Their experiences say much about the American way of business, and the often broken bond between employers and their employees.

Farris is in his mid-forties, even-tempered and very patient. He has ramrod straight posture, a strong chin, pronounced cheekbones, a neatly cropped beard, and a thick mane of light brown hair. Raised in Birmingham, Alabama, he speaks with a native accent and has a clear sense of how things are supposed to be—something he says he inherited from his many relatives who were in the military police.

For Farris, being locked in created all sorts of unnerving situations. At one point, he had to deal with a forklift driver who repeatedly showed up late, despite repeated warnings. Farris felt he had to crack down or else the rest of the night crew would begin thinking that they, too, could show up late with impunity. So on yet another night when the forklift driver arrived late, Farris went over to him to lay down the law.

" 'I need to talk with you,' I said.

"He said, 'I'm busy.'

"I said, 'I need to talk to you about your being late. It messes with other people. If they see you come in late all the time, how am I going to teach organization?'

"He said, 'You better be leaving me alone.'

"I said, 'I *am* the nighttime supervisor.'

"He said, 'Leave me alone.' "

Suddenly the forklift driver pulled out a box cutter, wielding it like a knife.

"I jumped way back," Farris said. Scared for his life, he wanted to run out the fire door, but if he did, he might get fired. So he moved carefully to the front of the store, half hiding himself there. He decided he had to telephone the store's top manager at home and tell him that someone had to come to unlock the front door as soon as possible to get the forklift driver out of the store.

"I told him what had happened," said Farris. "He said, 'Just wait till the manager gets there in the morning.' "

Farris realized that the store manager didn't want to be bothered and didn't want the fire door opened because that would set off an alarm that alerted the fire department. Fire engines would then rush over, and the store would be fined for summoning firefighters when there was no fire.

Farris responded to the manager with uncharacteristic sharpness: "I said, 'Dude, I don't feel safe. If you don't come, I'm going to call the police.' "

Normally Farris was reluctant to talk so brusquely to a manager, fearing that it would jeopardize his chances for a promotion. But the store manager didn't want the police called because that could mean embarrassing publicity—perhaps news stories about a knife fight inside the Sam's Club and about workers being locked in. So the store manager called the bakery manager, and three hours later the bakery manager showed up, opened the front door, and ushered the forklift driver out. After three hours of constantly checking whether the forklift driver was sneaking up behind him with the box cutter, Farris finally felt safe.

Farris is not the only Wal-Mart or Sam's worker with a disquieting tale about being locked in. Other overnight workers have said they suffered a heart attack, broke an ankle, or needed stitches after cutting a hand but were unable to seek medical attention—usually because their supervisors feared losing their jobs if anyone opened the fire door. One overnight worker told of not being able to get out after learning that his mother had suffered a stroke, while another said his boss refused to let him leave even though his very alarmed wife had called to say a robber was trying to break into their house. Several longtime Wal-Mart workers remembered that in the 1980s, the fire doors of some Wal-Marts had actually been chained shut. Wal-Mart officials said they halted that practice after an overnight stocker at a store in Savannah, Georgia, collapsed and died in 1988. Paramedics could not get into the store soon enough to save the woman.[1]

When asked about the practice of locking in workers, a Wal-Mart spokeswoman said that workers were locked in at 20 percent of the company's 1,500 U.S. stores that were not open twenty-four hours; the next day she called back to say the practice was used in only 10 percent of those stores. Wal-Mart executives have said the primary reason for the lock-ins was to protect store employees in high-crime neighborhoods.[2] Many workers point out, however, that many of the stores that locked in their employees were located in perfectly safe areas. Wal-Mart executives did not acknowledge that the main reason for lock-ins was to stop shrinkage.

Farris was the type of worker any smart manager would hire in a second. He knows how to take orders and how to give them. He has a way with people, both those above him and those below. He's good-looking and knows how to turn on the charm. He is a self-starter and has a knack for boosting sales, once winning his store's coveted employee-of-the-month award two months in a row. For instance, when sales of paper towels were flagging at his store, he figured out a way to increase sales by redoing the display. He built a massive eight-foot-tall display of paper towels that made customers think, "Wow, if they're selling that many paper towels, it must be a bargain."

"The sales quadrupled," Farris said. "I just had a vision how to do it."

Another time, Farris devised a display that dangled a trampoline from the ceiling, and, presto, trampoline sales soared.

One of the best examples of his initiative and ingenuity involved the rats. To get rid of them, Farris had his crew erect steel racks to hold the hundreds of bags of dog food three feet off the ground, too high for the rats to reach. Not only did this strategy starve out the rats, but, Farris said, the tidier display led to far greater dog food sales.

Farris did not hide his ambition to become the top manager of a Sam's Club. Month after month, year after year, he kept thinking that his excellent work would earn him a promotion to the number two spot at a Sam's, the intermediate step before becoming the top manager. But Farris often felt a tug-of-war between doing what his managers wanted and doing the right thing, as when he wanted to take the deathly sick worker to the hospital.

One summer night Farris and his crew were worried by news reports that a hurricane was about to descend on Panama City. The overnight workers were begging to go home, scared that the hurricane would blow off the store's lightweight roof and jeopardize their lives.

"We were locked inside the Club," Farris said. "Nobody would come let us out of the Club. I actually had the general manager tell me to start stacking copy paper in front of the glass doors, to bring it all out there, stack it up so that if the wind blowed through, it would hit the copy paper first and prevent the glass from hitting anyone. And that if the Club started to fall apart and if the hurricane was to hit, to crawl up under the steel racks, under the merchandise. I told him if you crawl up under there, you know that's tons of merchandise that's gonna come down, crashing down on you. But they didn't really care. He told me, 'Don't leave the Club. If you do, you'll be fired.'

"We were very terrified," Farris said. "We could actually hear the roof lifting. You could hear the wind blowing, and you're thinking the whole building's fixing to lift off now.

"Everybody's wife was calling," Farris continued. "My wife was calling more than anybody else. She was ready to call the police. I said, 'Don't call the police!

That might endanger my job.' " The hurricane passed with only minor damage to the store.

As at other Wal-Mart stores, the employees at Farris's Sam's Club were generally prohibited from working more than forty hours a week on the clock to spare the company from paying time and a half for overtime. The top manager at Farris's store also sought to impose a weekly limit of thirty-seven and a half hours in the hope that employees would somehow do all their required work in the shorter span of time, reducing the store's payroll and increasing the store's profits as well as the manager's bonus. This created a problem for Farris and the rest of the night crew. On Friday nights, they often hit the thirty-seven-and-a-half-hour maximum around two a.m. At that point, they obediently clocked out, but they couldn't leave. When the bakery manager arrived at four a.m., the workers were usually lined up near the front door, eager to go home.

"The manager would come in and say, 'Well, what are y'all doing standing here?' " Farris said. "We'd say, 'Well, we're through working. We're ready to go home.' "

The next day, Farris got an earful from the managers. "They told me, 'Nobody's to be at that front door. You're all supposed to be working.' " At that point, Farris explained that the workers had already reached thirty-seven and a half hours and were not supposed to be working.

"That doesn't matter about the time," said the manager. "You should be working. Period."

"So," Farris explained, "they're pretty much telling you, when they're locking you in the club like that, even though you're outta hours, you have to work off the clock." (Wal-Mart has recently taken some significant but not entirely effective steps to discourage managers from demanding off-the-clock work.) Situations like these so angered Farris that he discreetly told members of his night crew that they would be smart to look for work elsewhere, advising them, "You can go out and get a job ten times better than this and be treated a hundred times better."

As night supervisor, Farris normally showed up for work around seven-thirty p.m.—some ninety minutes before his shift officially began—to talk with the store's managers about what tasks his crew needed to do that night. Farris usually clocked in at nine, took a half-hour meal break around midnight, and clocked out at five a.m. He invariably worked well beyond that, often waiting until the store manager arrived at eight a.m., so he could explain what his crew had accomplished during its shift. Sometimes the store manager ordered Farris to finish something right away, and then Farris would sometimes work until noon, making it a sixteen-hour day. Farris said he often worked sixty, seventy, sometimes seventy-five hours a week, but he was hardly ever paid overtime. His paycheck reflected that he worked far less. (Farris was supposed to be paid by the hour because he was not a salaried manager.)

Tanya, his wife, a real estate manager, kept close track of his hours and figured that he was shorted $200 to $400 most weeks and at least $10,000 a year.

"I got sick of people thinking Wal-Mart is such a good company to work for," Tanya said. She pressed her husband to confront management about all the unpaid hours, but he refused.

"A person has to do things off the clock for the company in order to get a promotion," he explained to his wife. "This was widely known."

Farris never complained to Wal-Mart or to Labor Department officials about working off the clock. "I was afraid that if I did complain about something like that, I'd probably end up fired because then you're getting the company in trouble," he said.

Wal-Mart says its "Open Door" policy is one of corporate America's best programs for employees to air their grievances. If workers are unhappy about how they are treated—about working off the clock or anything else—they can go over their supervisor's head and complain to their store manager, and if they do not receive satisfaction there, they can appeal to the district manager, the regional manager, even to the company's CEO in Bentonville, Arkansas.

Like many employees, Farris says Wal-Mart's Open Door is a joke. "Even though they always call it the Open Door policy, they always shut the door," he said. "They use the Open Door policy to identify troublemakers to get rid of them. I've sat in on many of those meetings, knowing what the people are going to be told. And after that person leaves, the managers look right at you and say, 'Find a way to get rid of him. That's a troublemaker.' "

Farris worked for Sam's Club for eight years. During his last two years, he helped run the export department of a Sam's in North Miami, and it boomed those years, selling millions of dollars in merchandise to Caribbean and Latin American countries. Managers lavished praise on Farris for doing an excellent job, even though he spoke only limited Spanish. Farris was sure this would be his launching pad for a big promotion.

But one day Farris learned that another worker, someone he had trained, had leapfrogged him and been named head of the store's export department. That worker was a buddy of the store manager. Crestfallen and feeling cheated, Farris quit.

Farris is now a plaintiff in a Florida lawsuit accusing Wal-Mart of not paying him for myriad hours of off-the-clock work. He joined the lawsuit a year after quitting, because he had grown so angry with the company. Wal-Mart vigorously denies allegations that it countenanced off-the-clock work, saying that it has repeatedly told its store managers that off-the-clock work is prohibited.*

THE IMMIGRANT'S TALE

While growing up on her parents' coffee and banana plantation in the Dominican Republic, Julia Ortiz dreamed of becoming a doctor. But as the eighth of nine children, she reluctantly gave up that dream when she realized that her parents didn't have the money to send her to both college and medical school.

She instead decided to become an accountant, confident that she could someday work for a cousin's accounting firm in Santo Domingo. But after three months of studying accounting at the University of Santo Domingo, Julia received some bad news. Her father told her he could no longer afford her tuition because the plantation was struggling and because he had already eaten through the family's savings sending five of her brothers and sisters to college. Julia was forced to drop out.

She was devastated. She didn't know what she was going to do with her life. Desperate to cheer her up, her parents sent her on a vacation to the Netherlands to visit an aunt. Julia found Holland exotic and enchanting. She loved its canals, its old-world feel, its quaint architecture, and its nightlife. With few prospects back home, Julia decided to extend her stay and took a job caring for an invalid woman in Rotterdam.

The woman had a son, Domenico, who fell for Julia. She was quite a catch, with her big, liquid brown eyes, glowing dark copper cheeks, finely arched eyebrows, lush brown hair, and disarming smile, not to mention her easygoing manner.

Julia soon warmed to Domenico. He was powerfully built, a construction worker who had grown up on the Dutch island of Aruba. After a six-month romance, Julia and Domenico got married, holding the ceremony in Santo

---

*After I notified Wal-Mart officials in late 2003 that I was working on an investigative story for the *New York Times* about its practice of locking in workers, Wal-Mart announced it was changing its decades-old policy. The company said it would henceforth make sure that in every store that locked in workers, there would always be someone with a key to let workers out in case of emergency. Afterward, workers at several stores told me of improvements, but a few informed me that some nights there was still no one with a key to let them out.

Domingo rather than the Netherlands so that her family could attend the festivities. The newlyweds decided to settle down in Aruba because they preferred its warm weather to Holland's chill. There, Domenico made a solid living from construction and wouldn't let Julia take a job.

She gave birth to a daughter, Raquel, and two years later to a son, Jesse. But soon tensions erupted. Julia thought her husband was far too strict and impatient with the children, and she also grew upset that he was drinking more—and losing his temper more. After eight years together, they divorced, and once again Julia was feeling devastated and lost.

Now a single mother with two children to support, Julia took a job as an order taker at a Taco Bell. It was a struggle, and she sank into a funk. She concluded that she had to start a new life.

"My dream was to go to America," she said. "I had heard so many good things about America. The dream I had was to make enough money in America so I could go back home and someday start my own business in Santo Domingo. I was thinking of maybe opening a restaurant."

Julia bought a plane ticket to New York and left her children with her mother in the Dominican Republic for what she thought would be five, six, maybe nine months at the most.

After landing at JFK, she went straight to her Aunt Jacinto's apartment in Brooklyn, and her first impression was underwhelming. "There was so much poverty," Julia said. But when she visited Manhattan a few days later, she felt far better about coming to America. She loved the excitement, the stores, the crowds, the skyscrapers. After a few weeks, her aunt told her it was time to look for work, so Julia began crisscrossing Manhattan, inquiring about jobs at dozens of stores, delis, and restaurants, including some Taco Bells. She found nothing.

Her aunt then took Julia to Broadway, in Bushwick, a heavily immigrant neighborhood in Brooklyn. Broadway was chockablock with dollar stores, bodegas, check-cashing storefronts, cuchifrito stands, cut-rate furniture shops, and Dunkin' Donuts franchises. A store named Save Smart caught Julia's eye—it sold furniture, kitchen appliances, and clothes—and once they were inside, her aunt asked whether the store was hiring. The manager said yes, and the next day, Julia, having just turned thirty-one, began working on the sales floor.

"I asked, 'How much are you going to pay me?' " Julia recalled. "The manager said, 'You work, and when I have time to pay you, I'll pay you and you'll see how much.' He said, 'If I like the way you work after three months, I'll give you a raise.' "

Julia joined a sales staff that was a mini–United Nations—the workers came from Bangladesh, Colombia, India, the Ivory Coast, Jordan, Nigeria, and Venezuela. Of the store's twenty-five workers, Julia figured, fifteen were illegal immigrants—a status that made them ripe for exploitation. Julia had entered the United States legally, as a tourist, but because she did not have a green card, she, too, was working illegally.

With her beginner's English, Julia greeted customers with her broad smile, directing them to the $4.99 flower-print tablecloths and the $179.99 tubular metal bunk beds. When English-speaking shoppers had questions about the fold-out couches or the rice makers, Julia directed them to workers with better English. The store was an overstocked emporium with armchairs on the sidewalk, strollers hanging from the ceiling, and drapes covering the walls. It boasted of its bargains: sandals for 99 cents, pantyhose for $1.99, pillows for $2.99, three pair of "luxury" socks for $3.99, and kids' hiking boots for $4.99.

Julia worked from eight-thirty a.m. to seven-thirty p.m., with a lunch break from one-thirty to two, but no other breaks. That first week she worked sixty-three hours in six days, so when her supervisor paid her $210 in cash for the week, she was taken aback.

"I at first thought the person who paid me was confused because it was so little," Julia said. "I didn't want to say anything, though, because I was scared."

After discussing the pay situation with her coworkers, Julia learned that the going rate was $35 a day—less than $3.35 an hour, far below the $5.15 federal minimum wage at that time.[3] (Two male workers from Africa were paid just $25 a day.) If Save Smart had complied with minimum wage and overtime laws, Julia should have received, at a minimum, $414 a week. The difference between $414 a week and $210 was the difference between poverty and misery.

"Sometimes I felt like I was working for nothing," Julia said. "Many days I had to walk all the way home because I couldn't even afford the subway."

Her four-mile walk home was by no means the only reason her feet ached. Her boss, Aziz—from a Middle Eastern country, said Julia—required workers to remain on their feet from the moment they arrived until the moment they went home. ("I could hardly stand the pain," Julia said.) Aziz would yell at the workers if they looked idle. When there were no customers to attend to, the workers were supposed to straighten up, fold clothes, and stock shelves. Workers who stayed home sick for a day received no pay for that day; workers who stayed home sick two or three days were often fired. Sometimes when workers arrived twenty minutes late, they were sent home for the day without pay. One day Julia arrived ten minutes late after taking her son to the doctor. Aziz told her he was docking her five dollars. When Julia protested, Aziz sent her home for the day without any pay.

Using an unorthodox strategy to boost sales, Aziz ordered his workers to follow customers around the store to make customers feel pressure to buy something. Once, when Julia was following an African American shopper, the woman began yelling at her and then hit her, asserting that Julia—although she, too, is dark-skinned—was spying on her because she was black.

Julia hated it when she was helping one customer and Aziz would suddenly scream at her to rush over to another customer. "Some of the customers would come into the store and see how bad we were treated," Julia said. "Some customers wrote down addresses on a piece of paper, and said, 'You should apply there for a job.' "

But Julia was afraid to look for another job because she didn't have a green card. Besides, she felt the devil she knew was better than whatever other devils were out there. When Julia suggested to her supervisor, Mercedes, that she was thinking of looking for a higher-paying job elsewhere, Mercedes, who quietly served as Aziz's right hand, told Julia it would be futile and perhaps dangerous to do so.

"Mercedes told me the boss had a lot of connections, and if he found out that I was looking for work anywhere else, he could get them to fire me," Julia said. "Or she'd say, 'If you look for work, the *migras* [immigration officials] are going to get you.' "

"I was a little silly to believe her," Julia admitted.

Julia missed her children terribly, and after six months she told her mother that it was time to bring Raquel and Jesse to New York. "But my mother said, 'I don't think it's a good idea to bring the kids. You're just not earning enough.' "

Two years passed. Julia desperately wanted to improve her financial situation so she could bring her children, but Aziz repeatedly rebuffed her requests for a raise.

"He'd say, 'Later, later, later.' But that time never came," Julia said.

Finally, after three years, Julia decided she just had to have her children in New York. To accomplish that, she persuaded Domenico to increase his support payments by four hundred dollars a month, and she asked her brothers and sisters to chip in to buy airplane tickets for Raquel and Jesse. "I wanted them to come to live with me because no one else could raise them as well as I can," Julia said.

When her children arrived, Julia rejoiced, but her initial exuberance soon disappeared because she had dug herself into a deeper financial hole. Needing more room, Julia and Aunt Jacinto moved with the children from Jacinto's studio apartment into a dank two-room basement apartment that they shared with one of Julia's brothers. Raquel and Jacinto slept in one room, while Julia, her son, and her brother slept in the other. The rent was seven hundred dollars a month, nearly equal to Julia's monthly pay.

Julia usually didn't have enough money to get through the month. After three years at Save Smart, she was still earning thirty-five dollars per day, six days a week. Out of that Julia paid her aunt eighty-five dollars a week to take care of Raquel and Jesse after school, but she also paid twenty dollars a week to a teenage cousin to pick up the children from school. Many weeks she went to the food pantry at St. Barbara's Roman Catholic Church in Bushwick to stock up on beans, rice, canned meat, and other free groceries. She also went to a free health clinic—Save Smart didn't provide health insurance. When she had a bad case of bronchitis, a doctor at the clinic prescribed an antibiotic for her. Shocked to learn that it cost eighty-five dollars, she suffered through her bronchitis without it.

What troubled Julia most was that she could not afford many simple things for her children. Raquel adored Jell-O and begged for it whenever they went to the supermarket together, but Julia often couldn't afford it. When Julia took Raquel and Jesse shopping for a list of required school supplies, Julia decided against buying pencil sharpeners, viewing them as an indulgence she couldn't afford.

"There were times I was so depressed," Julia said. "Sometimes I'd tell Raquel, 'We should move back to Aruba. Life was better there.' But Raquel would say, 'We can't go back, Mommy. I'd have to start school over because I don't speak the language there.' "

Domenico occasionally needled her from afar. "Sometimes when he called to speak with the children, he'd tell me, 'And you thought you were moving to a paradise.' "

Julia's dearth of money was matched by her dearth of time. Many evenings, she returned from work at nine. Jesse would already be asleep, Raquel would be getting ready for bed, and Julia would have to abandon her intense desire to help them with their homework. Julia hardly saw her children on weekends because she had to work Saturdays and Sundays.

"When I was younger, when I first had my kids, I told myself, 'They're not going to be lacking for anything. They're going to have the best mother in the whole world.' " Julia said, tears welling up in her eyes.

A small smile crept back into her face. "At least I can be happy that my children work hard and are doing well in school."

At age eleven, Raquel is a striking girl, self-possessed, with long legs and her mom's dark flowing hair and big brown eyes. She seemed mystified by how hard her mother worked and how little mother and daughter saw each other. "I often told her, 'You're always working. Why don't you get another job?' " Raquel said.

"I don't know why I stayed at Save Smart," Julia answered. "Sometimes you're afraid to leave your job. A lot of us were cowards. We were afraid we would end up without a job. The truth is we hardly had any time to look for other jobs. We had one day off. We had to use that day to clean and shop."

Julia remembers the day she finally became fed up. Raquel called the store three times that day asking for her mother, and each time Aziz told her Julia was busy and couldn't come to the phone. When a sympathetic cashier told Julia what had happened, she marched over to the main counter and asked a supervisor whether she could use the store phone. He said yes, and Julia promptly called Raquel at home. Moments later, Aziz walked over.

"He started screaming at me in front of everyone," Julia said. "He said, 'Hang up that phone right now. You can't call your kids when you're working.' Right then and there, I decided I was going to the Department of Labor. This had gotten ridiculous. At that point, I had lost all fear."

The following week Julia visited the New York State Department of Labor in Manhattan. There, she told the investigators about receiving $210 for working more than sixty hours a week, about never being paid time and a half, about being forced to work twenty-eight straight days during the holiday season. To protect Julia, Labor Department officials assured her that they wouldn't reveal that she was the source of the complaint. (To encourage workers who suffer violations—including undocumented workers—to come forward, the department does not ask workers about their immigration status.)

When two state investigators visited Save Smart several weeks later, the store's managers tricked their fifteen undocumented employees by telling them that the investigators were from immigration. In a panic, the fifteen ran out the back exit. Save Smart's managers then gave the labor investigators a list showing that just ten people worked at the store—the ten with proper papers. A few days later, Julia informed the investigators about the fifteen other workers and their game of hide-and-seek.

A few weeks passed, and Ali, the store's second in command, summoned Julia into his office. He surprised her by telling her that Aziz was angry at her, having somehow learned that she had complained to the Labor Department.

"Ali said, 'I need a favor from you,' " Julia recalled. " 'I want you to go to the Department of Labor and tell them, please, we're actually paying you the right amount and everything conforms with the law. I want you to withdraw the complaint. If you do that, Aziz will take care of you.' "

Julia assured Ali that she would take back her complaint. But when she went to the Labor Department the next day, she instead explained how Save Smart's managers were pressuring her to withdraw it.

Tensions died down at Save Smart, but a month later, Julia received an unexpected phone call at home from a manager.

"He said, 'We don't want you to come back to work. You're too much of a headache.' "

Julia couldn't believe it. Enraged, she hurried to the store to confront Aziz and Ali. But they refused to talk with her.

The next morning, Julia and Consuelo Echeverry, a coworker who was also fired after complaining to the Labor Department, told the investigators that they had been fired in retaliation. (New York State bars companies from firing someone for lodging a wage complaint.) The two women were furious that department officials had apparently broken their promise not to tell management who had filed a complaint.

Julia later said that one state labor official had admitted to her that an investigator disclosed Julia's name to a Save Smart manager when the manager was badgering the investigator to divulge who had complained.

After Julia's initial outrage about being fired, she felt some relief. At least she could spend more time with Raquel and Jesse. Now her hope is to find a part-time job that will give her time with her kids and time to study English. Julia and her children aren't starving thanks in large part to her boyfriend, an immigrant from Niger who works as a Toyota salesman and is studying to be a professional translator.

For more than two years, Julia—represented by lawyers from an immigrants' advocacy group, Make the Road New York—urged the state Labor Department to force Save Smart to pay her tens of thousands of dollars in back wages to cover all the minimum wage and overtime violations. In October 2007, Save Smart agreed to a settlement that called for it to pay Julia $52,000 in back wages and damages.

do Quality of life

LIGHTNING STRIKES AGAIN

Fresh out of the Air Force and newly divorced, Drew Pooters had moved in with his father, a software engineer in Southern California. One afternoon father and son were on a checkout line at a Wal-Mart, and a customer and a manager were screaming holy hell at each other just a few feet away. Drew, a gangly six feet three, with a crisp, booming voice, said to his father, "That's not good. That's not how a manager should handle it."

A woman who overheard Drew's comments suddenly tapped him on the shoulder.

"This lady behind me said, 'What would you do?' " Drew recalled.

"I said, 'Well, ma'am, as a manager you don't engage in yelling matches in front of the customers. You take the person aside and listen to what their problem is.'

"Then she said, 'What are you doing?'

"I said, 'I just got out of the Air Force.'

"She said, 'If you're not working, then I think I have something for you.' She was the store manager, Elaine Braden, a wonderful lady."

After talking further with Drew, Elaine offered him a job in the pet department, where he especially enjoyed helping parents and their delighted children pick out cats and dogs. Drew, who had served in the military police, was also happy that everything seemed to be on the up-and-up at the store. Drew has little patience for anyone who cuts corners.

"None of the rules were broken there," he said. "Elaine made sure everyone was given their breaks. Elaine made sure you worked only when you were clocked in. Elaine was like a mother to everybody."

Drew is a good talker and phrasemaker, with a cutting wit, an eye for detail, and a tendency to talk in ten-minute riffs. His beanpole-thin frame, short light brown hair, narrow face, and glasses make him seem gawky, at times even nerdy. His intelligence is obvious—he has an impressive command of world affairs, military history, computers, science fiction, old movies, and psychology. Many people who meet him are surprised to learn that he has only a high school diploma.

After graduating from high school in Bartlesville, Oklahoma (the home of Phillips Petroleum), he enlisted in the U.S. Air Force. "It was the Reagan years, and everyone was worried about the evil Communists, and most of the guys in my class enlisted," he said. "That's the type of place Bartlesville was. I chose the Air Force because I was always into aerospace—between planes and the space program—and I was hooked on *Star Trek*." With a chuckle, he says he met his second wife, Anna, at "Star Trek: The Experience," a simulated twenty-fourth-century space voyage inside the Las Vegas Hilton. Drew has an unusual hobby, making extraordinarily detailed mini-replicas of *Star Trek* spaceships as well as World War II battleships and bombers. His workmanship is so impressive that several museums have bought his replicas.

In his nearly fourteen years in the Air Force, Drew served as a logistics specialist and military policeman, rising to the rank of staff sergeant. He was stationed at Keflavik Air Base in Iceland, helped build tent cities in Saudi Arabia during the 1991 Gulf War, and served in Somalia in 1993 to supply ammunition, housing, and food to the troops. The stress and travel of Air Force life took a heavy toll on Drew's first marriage, and his wife walked out on him, taking their daughter, Brianna, with her.

After ten months at the Wal-Mart in Southern California, Drew arranged to be transferred to a Wal-Mart in Albuquerque, not far from Cannon Air Force base, where he had last served. He had many friends in the area. In his new job, Drew managed the toy department, earning $9.25 an hour.

Eighteen months after Drew relocated, Phillips Petroleum offered him a job running a company-owned gas station. His father had worked for years as a computer engineer at Phillips and had connections there. Drew weighed his options and, frustrated that he wasn't moving up faster at Wal-Mart, took the $21,000-a-year position with Phillips. It was an opportunity to run a business, and it promised sizable bonuses.

But Drew soon soured on the job. The gas station was chronically short-staffed and as a result, Drew usually put in sixty or more hours a week, often having to work on his days off to fill in when an employee called in sick. Many weeks, his salary translated to less than seven dollars an hour. Nor did he receive the expected bonuses many months, because so many cars drove off without paying for gas. Under Phillips rules, a portion of the losses from those drive-offs was subtracted from the manager's bonus. What upset Drew most of all were the two armed robberies at the gas station.

With four daughters to support—a six-year-old from his first marriage, two stepdaughters, and his own one-year-old from his second marriage—Drew quit the gas station, feeling frazzled, underpaid, and unsafe.

He applied to Toys "R" Us, confident that the company would value his retail experience and his knack with children. Toys "R" Us hired him to run the electronics department at its store at the Winrock Mall, an exclusive shopping center in Albuquerque that includes a Talbots, a Godiva Chocolatier, and a Borders Books.

"I applied to Toys 'R' Us because it's a family-oriented place," Drew said. "Besides, I have girls who go there. It seemed like a nice, relaxed retail environment, and the mall was very nice—it was soccer moms with their 2.2 kids driving a very expensive minivan with a CD player and a DVD player in back."

At the age of thirty-eight, Drew started on September 10, 2001. He was a natural for the job. Children and parents loved his enthusiasm. He knew all about computers and electronics, and he was fond of dispensing advice to parents about which video games were naughty and which were nice.

"I actually felt I was contributing to the community, keeping the wrong videos out of the wrong hands," he said. "I was appalled at some of the violent stuff that passed for entertainment for kids. I felt good keeping Grand Theft Auto out of an eight-year-old's hands. Moms would ask me about video games, and I'd recommend something that was appropriate, rather than a game that is wasted Jell-O."

Things were going swimmingly for Drew until one afternoon when he went into the managers' office to check on some paperwork. Inside the tiny office Drew couldn't help but notice that one of the store's top managers was looking at a computer screen showing the time records of various employees. The manager was changing the times that employees had clocked in and out by moving his mouse around, typing in some numbers and deleting others. It was immediately clear to Drew that the manager was stealthily cheating employees out of wages while also reducing the store's payroll costs. This might help a manager win a promotion, or earn a bigger bonus.

"I saw someone's time change from eight hours and twenty-three minutes to seven hours and fifty-nine minutes," Drew said. "I watched the manager a good long time while waiting to ask him a question. I even saw him editing my name, and I said, 'That's not exactly legal.'

"He said, 'It's none of your business,' and that's when the threats started. He's physically imposing. He's six foot five, a little taller than me, and twice as wide. I weigh one-eighty, he must have been two-sixty. He could have stomped my butt right there.

"He said, 'Mind your own business. You didn't see this. Right? If you say a word about this, I'll kick your damn ass.'

"I backed down and said, 'You're right. I'll do whatever I need to do.'

"He said, 'You damn well better.'

"I left the managers' office and basically had the feeling that I stepped into a hornets' nest."

Drew was seething inside about what he had discovered. "I was military police," he said later. "I have a very strong commitment to doing things right. The rules are there for a reason. If this guy is going to rip me off, he's taking money out of my pocket. One would think that when someone's breaking the law like that he wouldn't do it so brazenly. That would imply he had a blessing from above."

Drew turned to some strategies he had learned in the military police. "I learned that when there's a confrontation, when you discover someone doing something wrong, you should back off from the confrontation and gather evidence," Drew said. He begun sleuthing. He fished through the wastebasket in the managers' office and through the Dumpster outside, often finding the discarded printouts of doctored time records. Those printouts show in black and white that the assistant store manager—the man Drew had observed—had manipulated employee time records and had used his computer to override the times that workers had clocked in and the times they had clocked out. With the manager's name printed wherever he made changes, the printouts show where he added time-clock punches, deleted punches, and altered punches dozens and dozens of times.

A few days after the confrontation in the managers' office, Drew was demoted from running the electronics department to a grunt job, unloading trucks and stocking shelves. He was sure the move was designed to get him to quit, but he hung on.

On three different occasions, Drew said, the assistant manager he had tangled with ordered him to do a specific set of tasks but then a few hours later would start screaming at Drew, "Don't you remember, I told you to do something else." He questioned Drew's competence; he accused Drew of insubordination.

"But he had never told me to do those other things," Drew said. "I think he wanted a confrontation as a reason to fire me."

Drew, who was earning $10.50 an hour, became increasingly unhappy. Not only did he fear that the assistant manager would beat him up, but he felt it would be futile to go over that manager's head because he had a sister in the corporate hierarchy.

"I thought, I'm not going to take this anymore," Drew said. "I'm not going to let one bad apple ruin my life." So he quit.

Drew immediately posted his résumé on Monster.com, and within days he received a promising reply. Family Dollar, a nationwide discount chain that was expanding rapidly in New Mexico, said it wanted to interview him about joining its management team. Drew came away encouraged from his interview with the chain's district manager for Albuquerque.

"He said they wanted to make sure that their people had lives," Drew said.

That assurance, the good vibes from the district manager, and an offer of $26,000 a year persuaded Drew to sign on. Family Dollar hired him to be a manager-in-training at a store in Albuquerque. Three days after Drew began work, he was promoted to store manager—another manager had suddenly quit.

In no time, Drew saw that it was a vastly different job—and world—from Toys "R" Us.

"It's basically like a dollar store: low-cost food, low-cost everything, soda, chips, beanie-weenies—they're baked beans with franks—all the junk food that anyone could ever want," Drew said. "The clothes would sell anywhere between five and ten dollars—dresses, children's clothing, work clothes. The quality wasn't high, but you couldn't argue with the price."

The Toys "R" Us job had been fun for Drew, but there was little fun at Family Dollar, which has more than 6,300 stores nationwide. He was unloading trucks and stocking, unloading and stocking, punctuated by sprints to the cash register to ring up customers. And his store was on the wrong side of town.

"Not a day would go by when we didn't have rolling lights in front of the store—the cops would pull someone over for doing this or that wrong," Drew said. "And there were a lot of snatch-and-grabs. People would run into the store and grab some underwear, some glue for sniffing, or something and run back out."

Much of Drew's work was dictated by Family Dollar's vaunted Matrix, essentially a computer-generated plan that told him how many employees he would have in his store and what hours they should work. Matrix told Drew he could have two full-time employees, including himself, and three part-timers. Drew said the payroll came to around 5 percent of the $50,000 in sales the store was supposed to generate each week. Matrix required that his store unload delivery trucks at the rate of more than 4,000 items per hour—garbage cans, laundry detergent, soda bottles, girls' jumpers, bags of Doritos. Matrix also declared that within twenty-four hours of a delivery truck's arrival, all its items had to be on the shelves.

Drew soon told the newly appointed district manager that Matrix was demanding the impossible. "It was crazy. I figured we had twenty-two seconds to unload each box off the truck and put it on the shelves. When I complained to her about unloading the trucks, she said, 'You're just going to have to suck it up.'

"Now there's leadership," Drew said.

After a few weeks as store manager, he concluded that Matrix did not assign his store nearly enough workers. It usually called for having just two employees work at a time—to run the cash register, stock shelves, price items, do inventory, show customers where to find things, watch for shoplifters, and clean up.

"The store would close at nine, and the cleanup was supposed to last an hour or two, but often you'd get out of there at one or two a.m., and then you'd have to get back at seven a.m.," Drew said.

For his wife, Anna, a medical assistant for an HMO, a big worry was that Drew would fall asleep one night while driving home at two a.m. Sometimes he was so overwhelmed with work that he spent the whole night at the store by himself, unloading trucks and stocking shelves and then sneaking a few hours' sleep in the back room. He often worked fourteen-, sixteen-, even eighteen-hour days, sometimes more than one hundred hours a week. But his pay was limited to five hundred dollars a week, meaning that some weeks his pay amounted to just five dollars an hour.

"There was no quality of life. There was none," said Anna. "Some days when he spent the night there, I'd have to take a change of clothes and shaving supplies to him. Some weeks he'd work ninety hours and he'd see the girls for maybe thirty minutes. The girls would wake up and say, 'Daddy, where's Daddy?' and the only way they could see him was to take them to the store."

There were days that Anna missed her husband so much that she resorted to a not-terribly-romantic way to see him—she spent a few hours working alongside him, unpaid, straightening up the apparel, sweeping the floors, mopping the bathroom. That way she was able to talk more with her husband and help him get home a few hours earlier.

One week when Drew felt particularly snowed under, he assigned the store's four other employees more hours to help with all the unloading, stocking, and straightening up. Drew was soon told he had committed a major sin: assigning more paid hours than the Matrix allowed.

Then, Drew said, "Right after a huge managers' meeting where we had gone over our budgets and headquarters was reducing our available hours [the number of payroll hours his store could use], my district manager made clear that you had to reduce your hours one way or the other."

Drew thought that her demand to reduce hours meant that she wanted only one employee working at times when there used to be two.

"I said, 'But you can't have a store so undermanned.'

"She said, 'Just delete the hours.'

"I said, 'You can't do that. That's a violation of company policy.' "

When Drew balked, the district manager said she'd do it herself. She sat down at a computer in the back of the store, Drew said, and started tinkering with the time records of his employees.

"She started rejiggering the hours right in front of me," Drew said. "I was looking over her shoulder when she did it. I said, 'But that worker didn't take a lunch that day,' and she said, 'Now she did.'

"I told her, 'I'm not going to get involved in this stuff. I'm not going to be a part of this.' " (Drew made many of these points in a deposition in a lawsuit accusing Family Dollar of off-the-clock violations.)

Drew told his four employees to keep their daily time slips and to check them against their paychecks to make sure they were paid for every hour worked. (At Family Dollar, employees clocked in and out by punching a numerical code into the cash register, which was connected to a company computer, and at the end of each day, they could have the cash register print out a slip showing their hours worked.)

"I told them, 'If you show me there's a difference, I'll put the hours back and make sure you're paid,' " Drew said.

He figured the district manager was shaving workers' hours—and paychecks—because she was eager to show corporate higher-ups that the stores in her district were not exceeding their assigned payrolls. Toys "R" Us redux.

Drew felt that Family Dollar's managers might someday be prosecuted for fraud and nonpayment of wages, and he was intent on staying on the side of the angels. He did not bow to his managers' illegal demands, lest he become an accomplice.

"I asked myself, Are you going to go to jail so someone else could get a promotion?" he said. "The pressure has come from on top for someone to look good at the expense of other people, but if something hits the fan, I am not going to be the one held responsible. These people work for me. I'm supposed to watch out for them. In the military, they teach you that you're responsible for what happens to your people. If we had a system like that on the civilian side, there would be more personal responsibility taken. The buzzword is more accountability, but there isn't any."

"When you don't have enforcement of the law, you breed disrespect for the law," Drew added. "If there's no respect for the law, society falls apart."

Drew's refusal to erase workers' hours caused huge friction between him and his district manager. Then Drew requested a week off around New Year's so he could drive back and forth to Missouri to pick up Brianna, his daughter from his first marriage; under the divorce settlement, he was supposed to take Brianna that week. But the district manager told Drew that Family Dollar couldn't possibly give him those days off.

Drew was furious. "I was working seven days in a row, working more than one hundred hours some weeks, and they were refusing to give me time off to see my daughter," he said. "It was crazy."

So he quit, recalling the words of the Family Dollar district manager who had first interviewed him—they wanted to make sure that their people had lives.

DREW AND ANNA NOW DECIDED to move to the Midwest because they wanted to be nearer Anna's parents and grandmother, who live in the Detroit area. Drew and Anna moved 140 miles away, to Middlebury, Indiana, just south of the Michigan border, lured by Middlebury's highly regarded school system and by Indiana's lower taxes.

Once again Drew posted his résumé on Monster.com, and once again a well-known national retailer came knocking. Rentway, a chain of 750 stores that rent—or sell on installment—furniture, computers, heavy appliances, and consumer electronics, invited Drew for an interview at its store in South Bend.

"They asked me, 'Do you like to work with people?'

"Yeah," Drew said.

" 'Do you like to work with computers?'

"Yeah. I could show people different systems for families and for improving their education.

" 'Okay, you're hired.' "

He was assigned to a Rentway store in Sturgis, Michigan, just north of the Indiana border. Part of the new job was trying to persuade consumers to rent or buy television sets, fold-out couches, and computers. And part of the job was making deliveries throughout northern Indiana and southern Michigan. In addition, Drew became the chief computer troubleshooter for Rentway customers for miles around.

He began working for Rentway in September 2003, and his early weeks there were often frenetic. Many days Drew and his partner, Bill Coombs, were assigned fifteen deliveries for which they had to drive 200 to 300 miles, often forcing them to work through lunch to keep on schedule. Drew and his partner often wolfed down a sandwich and soda as they drove from one delivery to another.

When the store manager gave Drew his paycheck on the first payday in November, the accompanying time sheet said that Drew had taken a half-hour lunch break every day the previous week.

"I said, 'I'm not going to sign this because it's incorrect. I didn't have a chance to take lunches at all.' "

"He said, 'If you don't sign, you don't get paid. If you don't sign, you'll be looking for work somewhere else.' "

Once again Drew felt a mixture of shock and revulsion at seeing a manager brazenly cut corners. He also felt personally offended that the manager was insisting that he had taken lunch breaks those days. "The delivery log shows when we were supposed to be having lunch, and it shows we were at this person's house making a delivery during lunch," Drew said. "Isn't it a violation of the law of physics to be in two places at once?"

Drew realized that by standing up to his boss so soon after being hired, he had put a target on his own head. When Drew was sick for five days around Christmas—at one point, Anna rushed him to the hospital—the store manager sought to fire him, accusing him of missing too many days. Drew clung to his job thanks to a doctor's note that said Drew had had fever of 105 and pleurisy in his lungs.

Then, two months later, the store manager fired Drew, saying he had violated Rentway's rules by lending three dollars out of his own pocket to help a low-income customer make her monthly installment payments to buy a foldout couch. Drew was attempting to save the woman from having her couch repossessed and her son sleep on the floor. Drew said Rentway employees often lend customers a few dollars to make their installment payments. He was fired all the same.

"I'm so disappointed with the retail world—they've broken every covenant with the American worker," Drew said. "I long for the days when you worked for a company, and the company was loyal to you and you were loyal to the company."[4]

The days that Drew longed for began not long after the most devastating war the world had ever seen, a war in which Americans pulled together as never before. Looking back at those days is particularly instructive as regards the evolution of the American workplace. It is also a bit nostalgic.

Chapter Five

THE RISE AND FALL OF THE SOCIAL CONTRACT

Nineteen forty-five was a year of great celebration, but it was also a year of great uneasiness. The United States and its allies had vanquished Germany and Japan, and America could justly boast about its fighting men overseas and its industrial prowess at home. With Europe's and Japan's factories decimated, American industry reigned supreme and unchallenged. Nonetheless, America's industrialists and workers were uneasy about the uncharted route that lay ahead in converting World War II swords into postwar plowshares, a painful process that would involve shutting scores of defense plants and laying off hundreds of thousands of workers.

Before the war, the United States had suffered through by far the worst slump in the nation's history, a time of bread lines, bitter despair, and mass unemployment, with one in four Americans out of work. The Great Depression lasted from 1929 through the late 1930s, and it was not until industrial output soared to meet the military's needs during World War II that the nation finally pulled itself out of its economic malaise. At war's end, there was some fear that the nation could slip back into a depression as it shifted to a civilian economy. Nineteen forty-five thus became a pivotal year when America had to chart a new economic course that would carry it forward. As a result, debates raged about many economic questions: Should the federal government continue to run the economy with the same forceful, interventionist hand as it did during the war? Should post–New Deal America become a social democracy like Britain and France, in which government provided workers with cradle-to-grave benefits? To what extent should American corporations share their prosperity and profits with their workers and the public (during the war, the government had imposed a special tax on excess profits)?

Considering that Detroit was the nation's industrial hub, it seems fitting that two men from there—Charles E. Wilson, the president of General Motors, and Walter Reuther, the president of the General Motors division of the United Auto Workers—did more than anyone else to set the nation's new economic course. At the end of World War II, GM was the brightest jewel in America's industrial crown. During the war, it manufactured one-eighth of all the metal goods used by the American armed forces: 13,000 bombers and fighter planes, 206,000 aircraft engines, 97,000 aircraft propellers, 854,000 trucks, 198,000 diesel engines, 190,000 cannons, 1.9 million machine guns, and 14 million shells.[1] Though Wilson ran what was by far the nation's largest company— GM's legendary chairman Alfred P. Sloan, Jr., had largely entrusted him with the keys to the kingdom—he felt horribly hemmed in. Wilson detested the price controls that the federal government had placed on automobiles and many other products because it feared that pent-up consumer demand would cause prices to explode. Reuther felt just as hemmed in, even though he ran the largest division of the nation's most dynamic labor union in an era when organized labor was feared and mighty. During the war, the federal government had imposed strict wage controls, and Reuther, knowing that his rank and file were behind him, was spoiling to do whatever it took to secure hefty raises, not just to boost GM's workers but to use GM's prominence to set a generous pattern for all of the nation's workers.

In November 1945, the can-do industrialist and the can-do unionist clashed in a titanic showdown—175,000 GM workers walked off the job at eighty assembly plants and warehouses, shutting down GM's assembly lines for nearly four months. It was a showdown between two extraordinary men, described in impressive detail in Nelson Lichtenstein's biography, *Walter Reuther: The Most Dangerous Man in Detroit*.[2] Wilson, an electrical engineer by training, had sprinted up the corporate ladder at the world's leading corporation thanks to his uncanny mastery of the most intricate details as well as his extraordinary ability to plan ahead. Reuther, trained as a tool-and-die maker, was a man of perhaps even greater vision, a fiery, charismatic speaker who knew how to rally the troops, a man revered in some quarters after he had been severely beaten by Ford Motor Company goons a decade earlier.

In the days leading up to the strike, Reuther made demands that were ambitious, to say the least. He sought not only a 30 percent raise, but a pledge from GM to keep its prices frozen. He recognized that if car prices and other prices bounded upward, those increases could wipe out the value of any raises won by workers at GM and elsewhere. Reuther hoped that a decisive victory in this showdown would catapult him into the UAW's presidency. Borrowing a page from John Maynard Keynes, he also desperately wanted to put more money into workers' pockets as a way to boost purchasing power and help prevent the postwar economy from slipping into recession. In pamphlets, the UAW asserted, "Mass purchasing power is our new frontier," while Reuther peppered his speeches with catchy slogans such as "Purchasing power for prosperity."[3]

"We make this fight," Reuther told a convention of the Congress of Industrial Organizations, "not only because Joe Smith needs more money to buy his kids food and get them adequate clothing and provide decent shelter, but in the aggregate, millions of Jones[es] and Smiths throughout America need this greater purchasing power because the nation needs this greater purchasing power."[4]

Even though Reuther and the 175,000 GM strikers kept their picket lines solid for 113 days, Reuther fell badly short of his goals, in large part because several other unions and the Truman administration had undercut him. During the GM strike, the United Steelworkers and the United Electrical Workers agreed to an eighteen-cent hourly raise in negotiating their contracts, making it nearly impossible for Reuther to continue insisting on a 30 percent raise, which was equivalent to thirty-three cents an hour. And the Truman administration had, to Reuther's dismay, eased price controls and given General Motors the green light to raise its sticker prices. Despite having to back down on several key demands, Reuther still claimed victory, boasting that he had gotten GM's workers a nineteen-and-a-half-cent (17.5 percent) raise, slightly more than other unions had received.

After the strike ended, Reuther kept maneuvering to get GM's workers what he thought they deserved. Wilson, meanwhile, had his own grand plans. Sensing the pent-up consumer demand from years of war and depression and noting the construction boom in the nation's suburbs, Wilson realized that demand for cars was going to explode. He therefore announced an ambitious strategy to invest $3.5 billion—equal to $30 billion in today's dollars—to expand GM's car production by 50 percent. This served to give Reuther considerable leverage because Wilson recognized that the UAW's crippling work stoppages could undermine GM's expansion plans.

In late 1947, Reuther, having narrowly won the UAW's presidency, was once again clamoring for large raises for GM's workers. The government's decision to remove price controls on GM and other companies had, as Reuther feared, turned out to be hard on GM's workers, causing inflation to soar by 18 percent in 1946, largely negating the raises that the workers had received after their 113-day strike. This time Reuther was demanding a 26 percent increase. But he had another ambitious goal as well. Reuther was disappointed, although not surprised, that Congress had voted down proposals to create a national health insurance program like that embraced by Britain's ruling Labor Party. He was also dismayed that Congress had rejected proposals to transform Social Security into a far more generous pension system. Seeing that Congress would not embrace his social democratic vision, in large part because the Republicans had won control of Congress, Reuther opted for an ambitious back-up plan—to have General Motors provide what the government would not.

In 1948, Reuther was wounded and nearly assassinated by a shotgun blast. During months of convalescing—no one was ever charged with the crime—Reuther refocused his energies on pressuring GM to create a private welfare state. That was when Wilson surprised Reuther by offering a grand bargain: labor peace for labor prosperity. Wilson had grown tired of industrial warfare, tired of annual labor negotiations and annual strike threats, not just because they drained his and GM's time and energy but because they dangerously threatened production. To realize his ambitious expansion plans, he needed GM's factories to run without interruption. Wilson asked Reuther to sign a contract that would ensure two years without work stoppages. In return, Wilson made a far-reaching economic offer with three unusually generous components: an 11 percent raise over two years, an annual cost-of-living adjustment to help workers keep up with inflation, and a newfangled notion—an additional 2 percent-per-year raise, called the annual improvement factor, which was designed to let GM's workers profit from the company's steadily improving productivity.

Wilson's offer did not contain the ambitious package of health and pension benefits that Reuther was seeking, but it was an offer hard to refuse. GM could certainly afford such generosity; it controlled 45 percent of the domestic auto market and had productivity growth of more than 3 percent a year, as well as a startling 28 percent return on investment. GM was also in a strong position because competition from abroad remained decades away, and competition from Ford and Chrysler was gentlemanly, part of a cozy oligopoly that ensured plentiful profits. Detroit's Big Three did not sully their hands by competing on wages or prices; rather, they competed through advertising, product innovation, and car design, such as who had the fanciest tail fin.

Not only did GM's generous 1948 contract with Reuther generate a cascade of large me-too raises at companies across the land, but it worked so well for the automaker and the autoworkers that they signed a similar, even sweeter deal in 1950—a five-year contract. The deal was a breakthrough because it promised a then remarkable five years of labor peace. Not only did the contract contain a better formula on cost-of-living increases and on the annual improvement factor than the 1948 deal had, but it gave GM workers much of the private welfare state that Reuther had been seeking. GM agreed to pay half of its workers' health insurance and, following Ford's example, to fatten its retirement plan to provide pensions of $125 a month—the highest employee pensions in the country.[5]

By any measure, "the Treaty of Detroit," as it was often called, was startlingly generous—the autoworkers were all but guaranteed a 20 percent increase in living standards over five years. The contract caused huge ripples across America, and by the early 1960s, more than half the union contracts in the nation had copycat provisions calling for annual improvement factors and cost-of-living adjustments, putting the nation's workers on a steadily rising escalator.[6] With labor unions representing one in three workers and threatening to unionize millions more, many nonunion companies adopted a me-too approach, providing cost-of-living adjustments and annual improvement factors, both to keep their workers happy and to keep them from unionizing.

The contract that Wilson and Reuther negotiated was pivotal in creating the world's largest middle class, although generous contracts signed by two other giants, the Ford Motor Company and United States Steel, also gave it important impetus. That era established a social contract in which workers were to share in a company's growing profits and productivity. (This did not mean the end of strikes; workers always want a little more while companies want to give them a little less.)

These developments ushered in an era of mass economic progress unprecedented in modern times, although blacks, migrant workers, and residents of Appalachia were largely left behind, as Michael Harrington pointed out so powerfully in his book *The Other America.* Worker productivity overall more than doubled from 1947 to 1973, soaring by 104 percent, while median family income rose by an identical 104 percent, after accounting for inflation.[7] *Fortune,* that tribune for the managerial class, lavished unusual praise on Reuther, saying that his union had "made the worker to an amazing degree a middle-class member of a middle-class society."[8]

Charles Wilson is often remembered—and derided—for something that he never actually said: "What's good for General Motors is good for the country." But considering how GM served as a model that helped persuade corporate America to share its prosperity, there was considerable truth to what Wilson actually did say. After President Dwight D. Eisenhower nominated Wilson to be secretary of defense in 1953, a senator at a committee hearing asked Wilson whether he could make a decision contrary to GM's interests. Wilson responded, "I cannot conceive of one because for years I thought that what was good for our country was good for General Motors, and vice versa."[9]

With the cold war raging, the great strides that Reuther and other union leaders made in getting American corporations to share their fast-rising profits and productivity gave much-needed ammunition to American leaders in their ideological confrontation with the Soviet Union, helping them boast how well blue-collar Americans—with their Hotpoint refrigerators, Philco televisions, and tail-finned Oldsmobiles—were doing compared with Russia's proletariat.

President Eisenhower, speaking at the National Automobile Show's dinner in Detroit, said, "An American working man can own his own comfortable home and a car and send his children to well-equipped elementary and high schools and to colleges as well. They [the Soviets] fail to realize that he is not the downtrodden, impoverished vassal of whom Karl Marx wrote. He is a self-sustaining, thriving individual, living in dignity and in freedom."[10]

In 1959, in his famed kitchen debate with Soviet premier Nikita Khrushchev, Vice President Richard Nixon boasted that three-fourths of America's 44 million families owned homes, and that those families owned 50 million televisions, 56 million cars, and 143 million radios. In a jab at Marxist idealism, Nixon added, "The United States comes closest to the ideal of prosperity for all in a classless society."[11] America may not have been close to a classless society, but Nixon spoke during an era of extraordinary shared prosperity, when the divide between the rich and the rest of America was the smallest it was at any time in the twentieth century.[12]

TO WHITE-COLLAR AND blue-collar workers alike, job security was just as important a part of the social contract as good pay and benefits. To white-collar workers, corporations all but promised lifetime job security, and in return companies expected hard work, loyalty, and a willingness to upgrade one's skills. White-collar workers were hardly ever laid off, except when their company plunged into bankruptcy or when there was glaring misconduct or incompetence. Blue-collar workers could expect layoffs by order of seniority during downturns, but they could fully expect to be rehired once the economy picked up. IBM served as the standard that the rest of corporate America strived to emulate—Big Blue was famous for having a no-layoffs policy for more than five decades.

It was an age of extraordinary job security and stability, when one-third of corporate executives had worked at just one company their whole career, while another quarter had worked for just two employers.[13] William H. Whyte's book *The Organization Man* caught the essence of the times, describing the millions of corporate men who took "the vows of organization life" and were "the mind and soul of our great self-perpetuating institutions."[14] In return, these organization men received job security, a comfortable income, periodic raises, and, as often as not, periodic promotions, too. As one economist put it, the United States had "an overall system for wages and careers that placed a heavy emphasis on continuity and fairness."[15]

For American corporations, the formula for success involved several none-too-secret ingredients: bigness, economies of scale, employee loyalty, and patiently grooming and training executives so they developed the know-how to coordinate the many branches of a company's vast empire. One of the leading industrialists of the day, Eugene Holman, president of Standard Oil of New Jersey—John D. Rockefeller's old company—said corporations must find ways of "protecting the individual against the more damaging effects of inevitable change." He added, "So far as the management of my own company is concerned, we have formed the habit of thinking in terms of . . . lifetime employment. That is our goal."[16]

Richard Deupree, president of the nation's leading consumer products company, Procter & Gamble, sounded just as committed to his workers, wanting to regularize employment for blue-collar workers who were often laid off for weeks at a time when orders dipped. In a 1948 speech, Deupree said, "Steady, year-round employment is so right from the standpoint of the employer, so right from the standpoint of the workers and so right for the country as a whole . . . that it is hard to see why we manufacturers have not made more progress in its application."[17]

In the nineteenth century, in the United States as in Dickensian Britain, corporations were rarely known as benevolent employers, but the executives who ran America's companies after World War II deliberately adopted a kinder, gentler philosophy. They followed the advice of Elton Mayo and other sociologists and industrial experts who propounded "the human relations perspective," which in everyday jargon was sometimes called "the happy worker model." Its philosophy, based on extensive studies at Western Electric and other corporations, was simple: the surest way to get the most productivity out of your employees (and to discourage unionization) was to keep them happy. The human resources model superseded the so-called scientific management model propounded by the renowned industrial engineer Frederick Winslow Taylor, who essentially called for treating production workers as hapless machines who were expected to perform X number of functions in Y minutes. In stark contrast, the human relations school emphasized employee morale, job security, increased communication, and treating a corporation's workers as a big family.

Two decades before Jack Welch took over at General Electric, that company took the human relations perspective to heart. "Maximizing employment security is a prime company goal," GE's manager of employee benefits, Earl S. Willis, wrote in 1962. "The employee who can plan his economic future with reasonable certainty is an employer's most productive asset."[18]

The era of hothouse capitalism that corporate America enjoyed in the postwar years made it unquestionably easier for companies to provide workers with such an enviable social contract. American industry flourished because it faced little competition from overseas, because there was huge pent-up consumer demand after war and depression, and because astute government officials fueled economic growth with such programs as the Interstate Highway System and the GI Bill of Rights, which provided subsidized, low-interest mortgages that encouraged a housing boom. In addition, corporate America—like Henry Ford of old, paying his mass-assembly workers the then generous sum of five dollars a day—paid its workers so well that their collective purchasing power was able to sustain economic growth.

At times, America's postwar economy seemed like the City on the Hill in which prosperity and fairness reigned. When corporations did their workers wrong, it was a shock, and Republican and Democrat alike often denounced such behavior as a betrayal of the system. When the Studebaker Corporation collapsed in 1963, leaving 4,100 of its workers with just 15 percent of their promised pensions, the move was widely seen as treason to its loyal workforce. Senator Jacob Javits, a Republican from New York, then pushed for legislation to protect workers' pensions from future defaults, and his worker-friendly bill, the Employee Retirement Income Security Act, became law in 1974. It was an era when Republicans were so attentive to the interests of workers that President Nixon signed what is widely considered the most pro-worker piece of legislation enacted since the 1930s, the Occupational Safety and Health Act.

This golden age was badly shaken by the Arab oil embargo of 1973. In its wake came the deep recession of 1974–75, double-digit inflation, rising unemployment, and a mysterious slowdown in productivity growth—all of which did serious damage. Then came a second serious oil shock in 1979. During the seventies, wages for many workers failed to keep up with inflation. Adding to the troubles, American industry started to feel the first serious pressures from imports, which began as a trickle, first with apparel, shoes, and radios, and then became a torrent, with higher-value products such as steel and cars.

Even though the decade was a roller-coaster ride of economic shocks and jitters, there remained an enduring belief in the social contract. It was stated no more clearly than in the era's best-selling business book, *In Search of Excellence*. In seeking to explain the secrets of success for the nation's best-run companies, the book noted that most of those companies had an unswerving commitment to their employees. "You must treat your workers as your most important asset," wrote the authors, Thomas J. Peters and Robert H. Waterman, Jr., noting that many of the best companies didn't even lay off workers during downturns. "When we look at excellent companies," they wrote, "we see . . . full employment policies in time of recession . . . Caring runs in the veins of the managers of these institutions."[19]

THE 1980s brought major new cracks in worker prosperity. To this day, there is a vigorous debate about which forces were most responsible for undermining the lofty postwar position of the American worker. Some say it was the surge in imports, especially in two pivotal industries, steel and automobiles, while others say it was the recession of 1981–82, the worst downturn since the Great Depression. Others point to the wave of deregulation—first in trucking, then in airlines and telecommunications—which, by opening the door to aggressive, low-cost start-ups, gave a cold, hard slap to sheltered industries and to long-established unionized companies. Still others say worker prosperity suffered a lasting blow when President Ronald Reagan fired 11,500 air traffic controllers after they went on strike in 1981, a move that emboldened American corporations to take a tougher line with their workers.

Imports, recession, deregulation, the offensive against unions—all of these made the early 1980s a witching hour for American workers, especially blue-collar workers. Since then, the position of the American worker has steadily eroded. The early 1990s brought the downsizing craze, which hit white-collar workers hardest, and the early years of the twenty-first century brought a sharp decline in factory jobs as well as the offshoring boom, which has hurt high-tech workers most. But it was the developments of the early 1980s that irreversibly changed the mind-set of corporate America. In the golden age of the 1950s and 1960s, America's corporate executives worried little about controlling costs, knowing they could always tack a few more cents or dollars onto the price tag and pass it on to the consumer. But because of imports and deregulation, blue-chip companies that had long been above the fray no longer felt unassailable. U.S. Steel had to contend with low-cost steel coming from Belgium, Romania, and Brazil. Pan Am and TWA had to worry about the twenty-nine-dollar airfares of People Express. GM, Ford, and Chrysler were staggered when Japanese auto imports surged from 20 percent of the American market in 1981 to 30 percent a decade later.

Corporations rather than unions were now taking the offensive at the bargaining table, and labor negotiations began focusing on freezing wages rather than raising them, on eliminating cost-of-living adjustments rather than adopting them. The word *concessions* seemed to dominate the management lexicon. As one example of the about-face at the bargaining table, the International Brotherhood of Teamsters—a mighty union that many feared could cripple the nation's economy with a coast-to-coast truckers' strike—was so shaken by deregulation and by competition from new low-wage, nonunion trucking companies that it agreed, in 1982, to a three-year freeze in base wages for more than 300,000 long-haul drivers, although the cost-of-living adjustment remained in force.

While deregulation and imports were hell to millions of American workers, they were of course a boon to American consumers, bringing them lower airfares, dependable Sony televisions, and fuel-efficient Toyotas.

At many companies, deregulation and imports caused managers and workers to unite against a common enemy—lower-cost competitors. In this new spirit of cooperation, unions would often agree to end archaic work rules that undercut efficiency. But deregulation and imports more naturally caused companies and workers to clash, especially when management insisted on freezing wages or closing plants. With competitive pressures growing, many corporate executives seethed at lackadaisical worker attitudes that undermined not just productivity and product reliability but also the workers' own jobs, as when employees went to work high on drugs, took sick days to go hunting, or didn't bother to do their jobs right, leading to shoddy products that were often less reliable—think cars—than Japanese products.

In the early eighties, corporate America focused as never before on another unhappy phenomenon: overcapacity. Imports were, Pacman-like, gobbling up a growing percentage of the market for autos, steel, and tires, while the 1981–82 recession (caused largely by the Federal Reserve's efforts to reduce double-digit inflation) meant there was insufficient purchasing power to support all of the nation's factories. Plant closings turned into an epidemic in the 1980s. In 1983, just two days after Christmas, U.S. Steel, a symbol of industrial might since the days of Andrew Carnegie, stunned the nation by announcing it was shutting down nearly 20 percent of its steelmaking capacity and laying off

15,000 workers. That was part of a devastating decline in which the company, hobbled by imports and outmoded technologies, cut its steelmaking workforce from 106,000 in 1979 to 30,000 a decade later and reduced its production capacity from 30 million tons to less than 15 million.[20]

Given all that was going wrong, it was no surprise that corporations often presented their workers with the choice of accepting a wage freeze or watching their factories close. The workers usually opted for the pay freeze.[21]

Until President Reagan's aggressive response to the air traffic controllers, no president had ever fired thousands of striking workers. Neither had a president ever dissolved a union before, as President Reagan did with PATCO, the Professional Air Traffic Controllers Organization. The air controllers had brazenly defied a law that bars federal employees from striking. As one of the few unions to endorse Reagan in the 1980 election, the air traffic controllers had expected him to repay them by backing their demands. After the election, the Reagan administration was feeling somewhat generous toward the controllers, at first offering the union an 11.4 percent one-year pay increase, more than double the 4.8 percent received by other federal workers. PATCO's leaders accepted that offer, but then the rank-and-file controllers, who viewed themselves as highly valuable and hugely overworked, overwhelmingly voted it down. They wanted to hold out for the 30 percent pay hike and thirty-two-hour workweek—down from forty hours—that the union had initially demanded.[22]

The union then badly overplayed its hand, infuriating the White House and much of organized labor by calling a strike, without even seeking last-minute negotiations. The air traffic controllers were confident their walkout would paralyze the nation's airports, but their confidence was badly misplaced. The administration, relying on 2,500 supervisors, 5,000 non-strikers, and 1,000 military air traffic controllers, got the nation's airports running at 75 percent of their normal flight load soon after the controllers walked out.[23]

With the union routed, many companies now felt they could borrow from the president's playbook. Traditionally, companies that were hit by strikes hired temporary replacement workers, and the strikers knew that once their walkout ended, their employer would bring them back and say good-bye to the replacements. But now companies began hiring permanent replacement workers to cope with strikes, a hard-nosed tactic that had rarely been used before, even though the Supreme Court had declared it legal in 1938. Companies now warned workers that if they went on strike they might permanently lose their jobs. "Managers," *Fortune* wrote, "are discovering that strikes can be broken, that the cost of breaking them is often lower than the cost of taking them, and that strikebreaking (assuming it to be legal and nonviolent) doesn't have to be a dirty word. In the long run, this new perception by business could turn out to be big news."[24]

In June 1983, Louisiana-Pacific, then the nation's second-largest timber company, parted ways with seven other large wood products companies and shunned the industry-wide contract, which called for a ten-dollar-an-hour starting wage. Louisiana-Pacific instead insisted on seven dollars, a move that enraged its two unions and sparked a strike by 1,700 of its workers. Louisiana-Pacific hired 600 permanent replacement workers to keep its mills operating. A month later, when 2,900 miners went on strike against Phelps Dodge, the nation's second-largest copper company, management followed Louisiana-Pacific's example and hired 1,345 workers to keep its mines running. Hurt by a flood of low-cost copper imports, Phelps Dodge had proposed eliminating the miners' cost-of-living adjustment, but the miners' union rejected that demand. The Louisiana-Pacific and Phelps Dodge strikes lasted more than a year, but both companies continued running more or less successfully thanks to their replacement workers. In a crushing setback for organized labor, the replacement workers at the two companies, along with union members who had crossed the picket line, voted to get rid of the labor unions in 1984, spelling doom for the two strikes.[25]

Bill Keller, then the labor reporter for the *New York Times*, wrote, "Union members and leaders are approaching Labor Day 1984 with a growing feeling that the balance of power in the workplace has shifted dramatically in favor of employers."[26]

Boise Cascade, Greyhound, Eastern Airlines, International Paper—all embraced replacement workers. In strike after strike, the union was voted out or it surrendered, forced to cede concessions on pay and benefits. Seeing the disastrous results of these walkouts, unions and their members increasingly hesitated to use their most powerful weapon: the strike. "Labor's trump card in a dispute, the strike, is no longer trump," said Mark A. de Bernardo, director of the Labor Law Action Center at the United States Chamber of Commerce.[27]

These developments hastened the decline of America's labor unions. The percentage of truck drivers who belonged to unions plunged from 60 percent in 1975 to 25 percent in 2000. During that period, drivers' pay fell 30 percent after factoring in inflation.[28] The percentage of telecommunications workers in unions fell from 55 percent in 1983 to 29 percent a quarter century later, with nonunion telecom workers typically earning 25 percent less than unionized ones.[29] During the 1980s, the number of steel jobs nationwide plunged to 170,000 from 450,000. As a result of the industry's crisis and a weakened union, steelworkers' wages fell by 17 percent, after inflation, in the decade after 1981. Wages for meatpackers plunged from $13.98 an hour in 1981 to $9.15 an hour a decade later—a trend, as we've seen, that later spread to the Tyson workers in Jefferson, Wisconsin.[30]

The 1980s represented the humbling of the blue-collar worker. During that decade, the nation's white-collar workers were, by and large, still confident that the social contract would protect them. But then came the 1990s.

THE NICKNAMES SAY A LOT: "Chainsaw" Al Dunlap, "Neutron" Jack Welch. More than any other executives of their day, these two men exemplified a new, rougher and tougher way to manage workers. Dunlap and Welch became the kings of downsizing, the lords of the layoff, and in those roles they became the darlings of Wall Street and models for corporate executives across the land.

In early 1994, Scott Paper, the world's largest producer of tissue products, was languishing. With the industry suffering from overcapacity and its worst price slump in decades, Scott was losing money and market share, and its longtime head, Philip E. Lippincott, was slowly, perhaps too slowly, carrying out a plan to cut costs and restore profitability. Growing impatient, Scott's board of directors pressured Lippincott into resigning. To replace him, it hired Dunlap, a West Point graduate and former paratrooper who decorated his desk with circling sharks made of brass and his conference table with a pouncing brass lion. "I like predators," Dunlap said. "I like them because they live by their wits."[31]

Within weeks of his arrival, Dunlap announced plans to lay off nearly 11,000 of Scott's employees, more than one-third of its workforce. He slashed the headquarters staff from 1,600 to less than 300, and he cut Scott's respected research and development staff by 60 percent.

"You must get rid of the people who represent the old culture, or they will fight you," Dunlap said.[32]

Fashioning himself as part of a swashbuckling, new corporate vanguard, Dunlap accused Lippincott and other Scott executives of ignoring, even abusing, shareholders because Scott had lost $300 million the previous year.

"There was a high cost structure; there was no vision and no leadership," Dunlap said. "If you ask me about the shareholders, they would have been abused less if they had been captured by terrorists."[33]

Dunlap had a bulldozer voice that was matched by his bulldozer personality, and he recognized that his bold moves and biting words would win him respect and media attention—although the layoffs he ordered generated far more hostility than he had anticipated. Sometimes he seemed to go out of his way to be mean, pounding his fist at meetings and dressing down subordinates. He called a best-selling book he wrote *Mean Business*. He prohibited Scott's managers from participating in community activities, saying it would distract them from their corporate responsibilities. He even reneged on the last $50,000 of Scott Paper's $250,000 pledge to the Philadelphia Museum of Art. He also closed headquarters in Philadelphia, where Scott had long been a beloved corporate citizen, and moved the headquarters to Boca Raton, Florida, where he had purchased a home not long before.

Dunlap asserted that the principal obstacle to turning around a company was that people dislike change and will criticize you. "That's where managers fail," he said. "They succumb to criticism. I don't have that problem. If you want to be liked, get a dog. In business, get respect."

He owned two dogs, prompting his former boss, Sir James Goldsmith, to quip, "I see you're hedging your bets."[34]

One day while touring a Scott factory, Dunlap asked a worker how long he had been with the company. The employee proudly responded, "Thirty years." Dunlap's response stunned the employee: "Why would you stay with a company for thirty years?"[35]

Wall Street loved how Dunlap had transformed Scott Paper. He boasted of pushing though cuts that would save Scott $420 million a year and restore its profitability. In Dunlap's fifteen months as CEO, he became a corporate superstar because the company's stock price more than tripled, increasing shareholder value by $6.3 billion. By the time he sold the company to Kimberly-Clark, another major paper manufacturer, he had earned an impressive $100 million in salary, bonus, stock gains, and a $20 million non-compete payment for promising not to work for a competitor for five years.

As proud and defiant as Dunlap was, he resented the criticism leveled at him for being heartless toward his workers. He said he was merely trying to save Scott from collapse. "People say I've made a lot of money off the backs of people by cutting all these jobs," he said. "I find that personally offensive. I come from a working-class family, a father who was a union steward at the shipyards and a mother who worked in the five-and-dime. If I have to get rid of 35 percent of the people to save 65 percent, that's what I am going to do."[36] And that is exactly what he did.

The day Scott Paper was acquired, Kimberly-Clark's chairman, Wayne R. Sanders, said Dunlap "has been a wake-up call to a lot of CEOs, and he has been good for American business."[37]*

WHEN REGINALD JONES, Jack Welch's predecessor at GE, turned over the reins in 1981, Jones was considered the nation's most respected CEO. But there was one major blemish to Jones's legacy: in 1981, GE's stock price was less than half the level of a decade earlier, after factoring in inflation. Welch saw his primary mission as getting the stock price up, and to that end, he cut costs with abandon, especially by hacking away at a workforce that he considered bloated and complacent.

In his first year as chief executive, Welch laid off 35,000 workers; the next year, 37,000. All told, he eliminated 130,000 jobs (25 percent of the workforce) in his first six years as chief executive, saving GE $6.5 billion a year.

To be sure, Welch's exalted status stems not from these cuts, but from the magic he wrought with GE's stock price—the value of the company increased from $13 billion when he became chief executive in 1981 to $500 billion when he retired in 2001. From his position atop America's leading business conglomerate, Welch changed the calculus of corporate decision-making so that the shareholder was king and employees were disposable pawns. He made large-scale layoffs not only acceptable but, to the corporate mind, desirable.

Under Welch, Schenectady, New York, GE's original headquarters, lost 22,000 jobs. Louisville, the home of appliances, lost 13,000. Evendale, Ohio, which made lighting, lost 12,000; Pittsfield, Massachusetts, home to GE's plastics division, 8,000; Erie, Pennsylvania, which made locomotives, 6,000.[38] "What made Welch's reductions notable," wrote Thomas F. O'Boyle, a Welch biographer, "was that his actions had been taken not to curtail losses but to enhance profitability, and in that regard, they presaged a change in philosophy that would become the prevailing attitude in the 1990s."[39]

Welch gave GE the highest stock valuation of any company in the world.

---

*Years later the Securities and Exchange Commission accused Dunlap of artificially inflating Scott's profits by misrepresenting its liabilities. After leaving Scott, Dunlap went to Sunbeam, the appliance maker, and, true to form, he turned that company upside down as well. But the board fired him in 1998 for accounting irregularities, and the SEC later charged him with fraudulent accounting practices that inflated Sunbeam's earnings. Although Dunlap denied any wrongdoing, he settled the charges by paying $500,000 and agreeing never to serve again as an officer or director of a publicly traded corporation.

He jettisoned layers of management and ordered that GE should be number one or number two in every business it was in. He sold off several bread-and-butter businesses, including small appliances and consumer electronics, and he acquired NBC and Kidder Peabody. He endlessly emphasized staying ahead of the competition and being nimble enough to adapt to the times. Among his mottos were "Change before you have to" and "Control your destiny, or someone else will."

He adopted a much-praised policy of worker involvement called "Work-Out" in which various levels of employees, from lowly machine tenders to division presidents, met at a retreat to thrash out how to improve operations and cut costs. But Welch also brought a brutal approach to human resources. "According to former employees," *Fortune* wrote, "Welch conducts meetings so aggressively that people tremble. He attacks almost physically with his intellect—criticizing, demeaning, ridiculing, humiliating."[40]

Welch thought his nickname cruel. He told *Fortune*, "Let me tell you why the name Neutron Jack is wrong. Competitiveness means taking action. Nuking somebody means you kill him. We start a renewal process."[41]

Welch argued that the waves of layoffs were justified, insisting that he had to fortify GE against ever-fiercer low-wage competition from abroad. Welch said he might have sacrificed some jobs, but he was saving whole operations. "I believe that people coming into these insecure, weak businesses are worse off," he said.[42] He spoke of empowering workers, of improving the lives of those who survived, even as he laid off thousands. His goal, he said, was to leave behind "people whose real income is secure because they're winning and whose psychic income is rising because every person is participating."[43]

Welch added to his repudiation of the postwar social contract by showing contempt for the notion of loyalty. "Loyalty to a company, it's nonsense," he once said.[44] To his mind, loyalty bred complacency. Loyalty had been a bedrock notion for Reginald Jones.[45]

Under Welch, employees were explicitly warned not to expect loyalty. The handbook for new employees warned, "If loyalty means that this company will ignore poor performance, then loyalty is off the table." New hires were also told, "The only job security is a successful business."[46]

In his never-ending push to improve performance, Welch had all GE employees ranked into three groups—the top 20 percent of hotshots, the middle 70 percent of solid, if not spectacular performers, and the lowest 10 percent, who were treated as untouchables to be cast off. (Some employees called the system "rank and yank.") "Some think it's cruel or brutal to remove the bottom 10 percent of our people," Welch wrote. "It's just the opposite. What I think is brutal and 'false kindness' is keeping people around who aren't going to grow and prosper."[47] As for the prized top 20 percent, he had no intention of cosseting them with promises of job security. "No one is assured of staying in the top group forever," he wrote. "They have to constantly demonstrate that they deserve to be there."[48]

So influential was Welch that *BusinessWeek* called him "the gold standard against which other CEOs are measured,"[49] while *Fortune* called him "the manager of the century." "Welch," *Fortune* wrote, "wins the title because in addition to his transformation of GE, he has made himself far and away the most influential manager of his generation."[50]

Jim Daughtry, an official with the International Union of Electrical Workers, had a different take on Welch's far-reaching influence. When GE gave workers at its electric motor plant in Fort Wayne, Indiana, the choice of swallowing wage concessions or seeing their plant closed, Daughtry said: "It used to be that companies had an allegiance to the worker and the country. Today, companies have an allegiance to the shareholder. Period."[51]

AL DUNLAP AND JACK WELCH signified, along with other things, the end of the era of job security. Workers were suddenly being viewed as costs, not assets. Downsizing became all the rage, and so did its first cousins: rightsizing, delayering, and reengineering. Corporate executives feared being seen as weak-kneed if they failed to send at least a few thousand workers packing, no matter the health of the company. The 1990s represented the humbling of the white-collar worker, especially the middle manager, who was suddenly no longer exempt from job cuts. In 1997, two-thirds of large companies questioned in one survey said they had ended their policies of job security.[52]

The hugely greater importance of the shareholder over the worker represented a sea change in American capitalism. In the fifties and sixties, corporate executives had plenty of latitude in running their companies as they wished, and if profits languished, shareholders might grumble, but they did not become apoplectic. Many CEOs were gentle and generous toward employees, especially white-collar ones, because they knew it could be tense and unpleasant to preside over a grumpy workforce that felt underpaid and underappreciated. In the late eighties and early nineties, the executive mind-set changed profoundly as the American business world metamorphosed from "managerial capitalism" to "investor capitalism."[53] Now all the talk was of shareholder rights and maximizing shareholder value, of underperforming companies and lagging price-earnings multiples. If the stock price languished, top executives faced either the Scylla of institutional investors who might seek to oust them in proxy fights or the Charybdis of corporate raiders eager to snatch up underperforming companies and "unlock" their shareholder value—a process that often involved jettisoning the CEO, shutting down operations, and laying off thousands of workers.

It was the age of corporate buccaneers, financial engineers, and takeover artists. Michael Milken, Ivan Boesky, T. Boone Pickens, and Carl Icahn all became household names, appearing on business magazine covers as often as celebrities on glamour magazine covers. CEOs knew that to protect themselves from takeover attempts they had better push up their stock price, and fast; slashing their workforce was often a good way to accomplish that.

The rise of institutional investors was equally threatening. When companies were predominantly owned by individual shareholders, there was little chance they would band together and challenge the executives of an underperforming company. But the rise of institutional investors, such as pension funds and mutual funds, meant that tremendous pressure could be brought to bear. In 1965, institutional investors owned 16 percent of corporate stock; in 1990, they owned 46 percent.[54] Fund managers were determined to meet their quarterly and annual goals, and they expected the CEOs of the companies in which they invested to make their quarterly goals, too. This pressure led to more layoffs. (Ironically, managers of workers' pension funds often served as a catalyst for laying off workers.)

The 1990s were a time when Wall Street investors came to love layoffs. The day that Sears surprised the retailing world by announcing a layoff of 50,000 workers—one-seventh of its workforce—its shares climbed 4 percent.[55] When Xerox announced plans to shed 10,000 workers, more than 10 percent of its workforce, the company's stock jumped 7 percent.[56] But when Wall Street thought a company too timid about job cuts, as happened when Kodak announced it was laying off 10,000 workers, the stock would continue its slide. When that happened, Kodak announced layoffs of 6,600 more workers a month later and its stock rose. "You cannot ignore important constituencies like shareholders," said Charles Smith, a Kodak spokesman.[57]

The surge in mergers during the 1990s also spurred wave after wave of layoffs. When corporate giants merged, they often did so in the expectation that they could do the same amount of business or more while laying off thousands of now redundant workers. After Chemical Bank and Chase Manhattan merged in 1995, 12,000 workers—one-sixth of the total—were laid off and 100 of the two banks' 480 branches were closed. When Lockheed merged with Martin Marietta, 12,000 workers were laid off. The merger of Travelers Insurance and Citicorp resulted in 10,000 layoffs, and the Exxon-Mobil merger, 9,000.

Soon after Chase and Chemical banks merged, workers circulated a mock memo, "Frequently Asked Questions," supposedly signed by Thomas G. Labrecque, Chase's chief executive.

Q. Why am I facing layoffs, why is my career in ruins, why can't I sleep at night?

A. Your largely insignificant life is being sacrificed to bring into existence the best banking and financial services company in the world, bar none . . .

Q. When will I know if I'm being laid off?

A. You, you, you, is that all you care about, you? Please understand that we need to think about "us," which probably doesn't include you. It's about time you started to think about the greater whole, buddy . . . It should be an honor to be laid off.[58]

In 1994, three years after the 1990–91 recession ended, the nation's corporations laid off 516,069 workers, 63 percent more than in recession year 1990, according to Challenger, Gray and Christmas, a leading outplacement firm.[59]

For many workers who still clung to their faith in the social contract, it was shocking to see massive layoffs even when their companies were thriving. On July 15, 1993, Procter & Gamble's chairman, Edwin L. Artzt, predicted that his company would have record operating earnings that year, and on the same day, he announced that P&G planned to close thirty factories and lay off 13,000 employees, 12 percent of its workforce. In a message designed to reassure investors, Artzt said, "The public has come to think of corporate restructuring as a sign of trouble, but this is definitely not our situation . . . However, we must slim down to stay competitive."[60]

Xerox, a company long known as a benevolent employer, posted net income of $794 million in 1994, a happy reversal from the loss it suffered the previous year. Notwithstanding this rebound, the company laid off 10,000 workers. Judd Everhart, a Xerox spokesman, said, "I know it can sound very heartless when you're making these decisions when individuals' careers are affected, especially when the company's making money. But I think it is a new reality."[61]

JUST AS THE "investor revolution" changed how companies operated, so did the "high-tech revolution." Networked computers and new software vastly improved efficiency. Computers could handle tasks that once required scores of accountants, bookkeepers, and order takers. A new technology like voice mail made thousands of secretaries redundant. General Motors laid off 5,000 design engineers after new CAD (computer-aided design) software made it possible to use far fewer engineers to design products and to link new designs to the manufacturing process.[62]

The high-tech revolution gave birth to a practice known as "reengineering," a process in which companies used sophisticated software to increase efficiency and streamline their workplaces by combining and redefining jobs and making many positions unnecessary. To be sure, it meant lots of layoffs. One of the leading business books of the nineties was *Reengineering the Corporation: A Manifesto for Business Revolution.* The book's authors, Michael Hammer and James Champy, wrote about IBM's Credit Corporation, a subsidiary that provided credit to customers who wanted to buy products from IBM. In one department, workers logged in each credit application, while specialists in another department typed in data involving special conditions for particular customers. A third department set the interest rate for a proposed deal, and a fourth department assembled all that information and prepared a formal offer that an IBM salesman then presented to the customer. Reengineering specialists eliminated all four departments and replaced them with a single employee, who, aided by new software, accomplished the same thing.[63] As a result of reengineering, software was used to replace thousands of insurance adjusters, credit specialists, and mortgage application processors. A 1995 survey found that nearly 80 percent of the nation's largest companies had embraced reengineering and "would be increasing their commitment to it over the next few years."[64]

The layoffs came in waves. In the 1990s, AT&T laid off 123,000 workers, Sears laid off 50,000, and Delta Airlines, 18,800. In a series about downsizing, the *New York Times* wrote that one-third of all U.S. households had a family member who had lost a job between 1980 and 1996, and that one in ten adults, 19 million people, acknowledged that layoffs had precipitated a major crisis in their lives. The series described Americans such as Rene Brown, who, though still in her forties, had been downsized three times, out of an $8.50-an-hour meatpacking job, a $7.25-an-hour job in a bank mailroom, and a $4.75-an-hour job loading newspapers. When the *Times* series appeared in 1996, she was earning $4.25 an hour, then the minimum wage, cleaning office buildings in Baltimore.[65] The Labor Department found that three-fourths of Americans who had lost jobs between 1993 and 1995 had found new ones by February 1996, but only one-third of those workers were earning as much as they did in their old jobs.[66]

Further eating away at job security was a flood of new management fads and concepts. Many companies divided each of their operations into "profit centers," and when any profit center missed its goal, the answer often was lay-offs. When companies embraced "benchmarking" to compare the efficiency of their operations with those of their competitors, if theirs fell short, workers would often be let go. Thousands of companies embraced the strategy of focusing on their "core competencies," and that made many non-core workers expendable. As a result, many companies "unbundled," usually meaning that they sold off or closed their non-core operations. Inspired by Jack Welch, many corporations embraced "delayering," helped by sophisticated software that eliminated the need for several layers of managers who monitored and coordinated managers below them. The software often enabled one or two layers of managers to do what four or five layers once did.

Throughout corporate America, the leitmotif was maximizing flexibility and minimizing fixed costs to make it easier to adapt to fast-changing business conditions. The title of Bill Gates's book was telling: *Business @ the Speed of Thought*. Wall Street seemed ready to pillory any executive who was perceived as showing undue loyalty toward longtime employees—just more fixed costs that got in the way of needed flexibility.

Paul Osterman of MIT, one of the nation's most astute analysts of labor markets, noted the effects of these trends. "The institutional structure has been blown apart," he wrote, "and with it has gone the sense of order that undergirded people's notion of the economy. The loss of order is what explains the unease that persists even in the face of good economic news."[67]

In that era of downsizing and reengineering, not only was more work heaped upon those who survived the initial round or two of layoffs as they took over tasks once done by departed colleagues (those that couldn't be done by computers or other machines), but those survivors often went far beyond the call of duty, hoping to prove that they were Stakhanovite superworkers who should be spared in the next wave of downsizing. After Westinghouse ordered several rounds of layoffs in the early nineties to cope with financial losses, Pam Cromer, a marketing coordinator there, began putting in eighty-hour weeks to demonstrate her commitment and her ability to work wonders. When Westinghouse was solidly back in the black in 1994, Cromer received a pink slip. She was stunned.

"I thought they wanted people like me, who would give up their lives and do anything to keep their jobs," she said. "I felt like a rat running on one of those little wheels."[68]

Seeing the wonders wrought by anxious yet dedicated workers like Cromer, corporate executives realized that high anxiety often translated into high productivity. In this way, companies moved beyond the "human relations" paradigm and its "happy worker" corollary. The new paradigm seemed to be that worried workers could be productive workers.

And there was anxiety aplenty. A poll done in 1996 found that 46 percent of workers at four hundred large corporations answered yes to the question, "Are you frequently concerned about being laid off?" During the 1980s, no more than 24 percent of those surveyed ever answered yes to that question.[69] In a 1994 survey, the American Management Association found that 86 percent of companies that had downsized reported a drop in worker morale. But 70 percent of those companies reported that productivity had risen or held constant, while 80 percent reported that profits had risen or held constant.[70]

As Peter Cappelli of the Wharton School wrote in *The New Deal at Work*, "While it is difficult for many of us to admit, [the happy worker] model more or less went out the window in the 1980s and was replaced by what might be called the 'frightened worker' model."[71]

THE RISE OF HIGH TECH, some experts predicted, was to be the salvation for America's economic ills and its beleaguered workers. And in the late 1990s, the high-tech boom did in fact do wonders for the economy, helping to reduce the jobless rate to its lowest level in decades and to lift real wages at their fastest clip in recent memory. But the high-tech bubble burst in 2000, and now it seems that if high tech is going to be a salvation for anyone, it will be for workers in Bangalore and Beijing.

"Profits, Not Jobs, on the Rebound in Silicon Valley" said a headline on a *New York Times* story in the summer of 2005. Profits at Silicon Valley's seven largest companies had more than quintupled the previous three years, while employment in the valley had declined by nearly 20,000 during the same period. In contrast, during the high-tech boom from 1995 and 1997, Silicon Valley added more than 82,000 jobs. The *Times* story focused on Wyse Technology, a respected producer of computer terminals, whose sales and profits were soaring and whose job growth was taking place overseas. In 2005, Wyse added 100 workers in India and 35 in China, increasing its worldwide workforce to 380, but Wyse's employment in California remained flat. Just 15 percent of Wyse's engineering talent remained in America.[72]

Another *Times* story that summer was headlined "Cutting Here, but Hiring over There." The story began, "Even as it proceeds with layoffs of up to 13,000 workers in Europe and the United States, IBM plans to increase its payroll in India this year by more than 14,000 workers." Defending these moves, an IBM senior vice president said the decision to increase the company's workforce in India had nothing to do with the cheaper labor costs there. Rather, he said, IBM was expanding in India because of "the surging demand for technology services in the thriving Indian economy and the opportunity to tap the many skilled Indian software engineers to work on projects around the world."[73]

These news stories point to a growing disconnect between what's good for American corporations and what's good for American workers. These stories also demonstrate that high tech will not be a salvation for many American job seekers in the future unless the United States develops some revolutionary new technologies that spawn large new industries.

When factory jobs were heading overseas in the 1980s, young Americans were told there would be plenty of high-paying high-tech jobs to replace the jobs that disappeared. Then in the early nineties, many companies moved their computer chip production overseas, and we were told the good software jobs would remain in America. Now many of those software jobs are moving overseas, fueled by some stark numbers. American software engineers start at $75,000 a year, while many in India start at $15,000.[74]

One respected consulting firm, Forrester Research, estimates that 3.4 million American white-collar jobs will be sent offshore between 2003 and 2015. Tax returns once prepared by accountants in New York or Los Angeles are now being prepared in the Philippines. Radiologists in India are reviewing X-rays e-mailed from the United States. Paralegals in India are helping budget-minded law firms in Chicago and Seattle prepare wills and contracts. Forrester Research estimates that from 2003 to 2015, the offshoring exodus will include 542,000 computer jobs, 259,000 management jobs, 191,000 architecture jobs, 79,000 legal jobs, and 1.6 million back-office jobs.[75]

Offshoring may produce other perils as well. Joseph Stiglitz, a Nobel Prize–winning economist and a professor at Columbia University, said, "What worries me is that it [offshoring] could have an enormous effect on wages, and that could have a wrenching impact on society."[76] Offshoring has already held down the wages of software workers up and down the West Coast. At a Sprint call center in North Carolina, 180 customer service representatives, scared that their jobs would be shipped abroad, accepted a pay freeze for 2004 and no definite increase in 2005. A limited group of the "best performers" were promised 2 percent merit raises, raises that lagged behind inflation. "Sprint said they had to restrain wages because the company's performance wasn't so good, but we think a lot of it has to do with offshoring," said Rocky Barnes, president of the union local.[77]

Paul Samuelson, the famed MIT economist, textbook writer, and Nobel Prize winner, has warned that if American companies shift too many high-tech jobs and too much high-tech expertise to India, China, and other developing nations, that could ultimately undercut American industry and reduce the nation's per capita income. Samuelson also warned of a downward effect on worker pay, saying, "If you don't believe that [offshoring] changes the average wages in America, then you believe in the tooth fairy."[78]

Indeed, more and more economists are voicing fears that if American technology companies continue to send so much of their work and expertise overseas, that might someday enable India's and China's high-tech industries to outinvent, outthink, and outstrip America's high-tech industry in some key areas, leaving the United States at a costly disadvantage in a field of critical importance.

GLOBALIZATION IS PROVING to be a great leveling force, throwing America's workers, white collar and blue, into direct competition with hundreds of millions of workers in China, India, and other countries with wages just a fraction of American wages. From Portland, Maine, to Portland, Oregon, managers often tell workers not to expect sizable raises not only because their companies face intense foreign competition but because their companies are weighing whether to transfer jobs to lower-wage locales overseas. Indeed, some companies repeatedly use globalization as a sword to keep workers on the defensive, often warning that globalization portends cuts and catastrophe.

Globalization's powerful hand can be seen in the enormous loss of manufacturing jobs in recent years—from 17.3 million in 2000 to 13.7 million in early 2008, a loss of one in five factory jobs. (To be sure, globalization is not the only factor destroying factory jobs—automation has also played a part.) Factory jobs were often a direct ticket to the middle class, even for millions of workers without a college degree, because those jobs might pay $40,000 a year and provide excellent health and pension benefits. But now American companies are rushing to build refrigerators and televisions in Mexican *maquiladoras* that pay workers less than $5,000 a year.

Globalization also means that people are flowing more freely between countries. For the United States, this has of course meant a huge influx of immigrant workers, legal and illegal. Over the past dozen years, roughly 700,000 illegal immigrants—equal to the population of Maine—entered the United States each year, with the number of undocumented immigrants climbing to 12 million. Immigrants pick our oranges and tomatoes, process our chickens, and clean our hotel rooms, and they hold down the cost of any number of services, from restaurant meals to landscaping. But their huge numbers have unarguably squeezed down wages in some jobs, especially those requiring few skills. For example, many immigrants are willing to take grueling jobs in meat- and poultry-processing plants for eight dollars an hour while few Americans would take those jobs for thirteen dollars an hour.

There is another important aspect of globalization. On any given day, trillions of dollars are sloshing around the globe as investors maneuver to maximize the return on their money. In this age of global capital, mutual funds, hedge funds, and private-equity funds have more power than ever before, and they use that power to pressure the companies they've invested in to maximize the return on their assets and operations—wherever they are located. In this respect, many CEOs show little loyalty to having operations in the United States as opposed to, say, Sri Lanka. For American workers, this means their job security grows ever more tenuous.

The full brunt of globalization can be seen very clearly at the company where Walter Reuther and Charles Wilson once sparred: General Motors—as well as at Delphi, the nation's largest auto parts producer, which GM spun off in 1999. GM's North American operations lost $8.2 billion in 2006, and Delphi filed for bankruptcy in September 2005 after losing $741 million in the first half of that year. (Delphi also faced up to $11 billion in unfunded pension liabilities.) After declaring bankruptcy, Delphi called for slashing the wages of its 33,000 unionized workers to $9.50 an hour from $27 an hour, which is far more than what Delphi pays workers at many of its overseas plants.

"Today we are paying double, triple or more for hourly labor compared to what prevails in the marketplace," said Robert S. Miller, Delphi's CEO. "No business can survive doing that."[79]

The UAW's president, Ron Gettelfinger, angrily responded that "Delphi's proposal is designed to hasten the dismantling of America's middle class by importing third world wages to the United States."[80]

GM's problems are so great that its domestic market share has fallen from 44 percent in 1980 to 24 percent and Toyota seems poised to replace it as the world's number one automaker. GM has been hurt badly by foreign competitors such as Toyota and Honda and by misguided strategies, like focusing far too much on SUV fuel hogs and far too little on fast-selling fuel-efficient cars. But GM has also suffered competitively because of its astronomical health costs, which totaled $5.2 billion in 2007 (about $1,900 per car). In 2007, General Motors employed just 74,000 UAW workers, down from 400,000 in 1970, and had the burden of financing first-class health benefits for 340,000 retirees and surviving spouses. In one of his columns, George Will decried GM's "function as a welfare state." "The $4 billion that goes annually [for health care] to retirees does not go into developing products people want to buy," Will wrote.[81]

Fearing that its high costs, especially health costs, would lead to further large losses and possibly bankruptcy, General Motors has taken some potent and painful steps. In November 2005, it announced that it would close twelve plants and offer buyouts to one-third of its blue-collar workforce. Ultimately GM bought out 35,000 workers (while Delphi did likewise for 12,600). GM took an unusually tough stance in its 2007 contract talks, demanding that its obligation to pay for retiree health care—an obligation estimated at $51 billion over several decades—be transferred to an independent trust, known as a voluntary employees' beneficiary association, with GM pledging money toward that trust. After a two-day strike in September 2007, the UAW, fearing further job losses and an eventual GM bankruptcy, agreed to creating such a trust, with GM promising to contribute about $30 billion to it over several years. Even so, many GM retirees worried that the new trust would be underfunded and that they would ultimately have to pay more toward their health care. In other major concessions, the UAW agreed to a freeze in base wages and a two-tier contract with far lower wages for new hires who do not do assembly work. All those concessions are expected to save GM around $12.50 an hour and to cut Toyota's hourly labor cost advantage nearly in half. GM officials hailed the contract as going far to make the company competitive, but many Wall Street analysts said it did not cut costs enough.

But many workers complained that the concessions went too far. Defending the two-day strike and the UAW's resistance to further cuts, Maurice Faust, a fifty-one-year-old repairman at the GM assembly plant in Hamtramck, Michigan, said, "We fight not just for ourselves, but we fight for the young coming behind us. This is middle-class employment, and we want to keep it that way."[82]

With Chrysler and Ford also in crisis, the UAW soon agreed to similar cost-cutting contracts with them. As for Delphi, the union, worried that a bankruptcy judge would approve even deeper cuts in wages, reluctantly agreed to a deal that reduced the company's $27-an-hour base wage to around $16 an hour. The one sweetener was that Delphi offered buyouts of more than $100,000 to some longtime workers.

The great irony is that in many ways the crisis at GM stems from the fabulous job that the UAW has done over the years for its members. Now GM has become a pivotal test of whether American manufacturing and the American middle class can survive in a globalized world.

FOR MANY WORKERS, the pressures brought to bear on a daily basis have become as difficult to bear as job insecurity. The often fierce winds of globalization have intensified those pressures, as we shall soon see, and have produced a generation of more demanding, more unforgiving and, too often, more cold-hearted managers.

Chapter Six

LEANER AND MEANER

At age thirty-one, Melissa Jerkins became the top manager of a Wal-Mart store in Decatur, Indiana, that had 120 employees and $24 million in annual sales. One day, her boss, a district manager, was touring her store, and while she was showing him the stockroom in back, he saw something that made his blood boil—three pallets piled with boxes were sitting on the floor, unloaded from the night before.

He ordered Melissa to go to his car, where he launched into a tirade. "What kind of fucking store are you running?" he screamed. "I thought you were better than that."

After he had finished, he dropped her at the store's entrance, asking, "Are you going to cry now?"

The next day, Melissa's office phone rang. "I didn't know if you'd still be there," Melissa recalled the district manager saying. "I thought you might jump in front of a train."

"They really managed by fear," she said. "They wanted you to be intimidated."

Melissa is a sweet, engaging woman who grew up in a Bible Belt farm town in southern Indiana. She has long chestnut hair, an animated smile, a strong, jutting chin, and the smooth skin of a sixteen-year-old. She is just five feet one, but she projects authority. Her voice is powerful and her penchant for efficiency unmistakable, but those are leavened by her direct, friendly manner. Propelled by those qualities, Melissa zoomed up Wal-Mart's ladder, praised for running a tight ship, keeping her stores neat, maintaining good employee morale, and not exceeding her assigned payroll.

In climbing from six-dollar-an-hour salesclerk to store manager for the world's largest retailer, Melissa got a crash course in how tough and even bullying many of today's managers can be. In her decade at Wal-Mart, she saw managers break the law, act sadistically, spew profanity at workers, endanger workers' health, and treat employees as disposable parts. In an era in which corporate America aspires to be lean and mean, Melissa saw how today's management style often seems to be mean and meaner. All too often Wal-Mart exemplifies this harsher style—setting ever-tougher goals for its managers, using sophisticated computer systems to monitor their every move, ousting those who fall short of expectations, allowing managers to use foul language and savage criticism to bully subordinates.

"They never say anything without cursing or threatening you," Melissa said. "I think some of them thought that's how to get results. They thought, 'If I'm nice to that person, they're going to run all over me. But if I am Number One Asshole, I'll get results.' "

One Wednesday, Melissa received orders to drive the very next day to Wal-Mart's headquarters in Arkansas along with her district manager and the eight other store managers from her district. The company's top brass was angry that the stores in her district had too much shrinkage.

Melissa and the others left Indiana at daybreak Thursday, arriving in Bentonville late that night. The next day, they endured one brutal meeting after another with their regional vice president, their divisional vice president, and several loss-prevention executives.

"Everything was derogatory," Melissa said. "Everything was 'damn' and 'suck.' It was across the board how we were costing Wal-Mart all this money, and we should be ashamed of ourselves. They said we're worthless.

"When we left, I told the others, 'I never knew how many levels you can suck. When they say, "You suck," then you're okay. When they say, "You really, really suck," that's clearly not good for you. And then when they say, "You really, really, really suck," then you know you're in real trouble.' "

That same day, Melissa's district manager was demoted because of all the shrinkage. In addition, Wal-Mart executives ordered Melissa and the eight other store managers from her district to attend the company's Saturday morning meeting, a gathering packed with more than 1,000 headquarters personnel and store managers that helps spread the gospel of Wal-Mart as well as spread the word about hot new products.

"They announced that folks from the district in Indiana that cost them a million dollars were there, and everyone had to stand up and look at us," Melissa said. "We were laughed at and called the 'million-dollar losers.' "

Two months before that trek to Bentonville, Melissa had been promoted from managing the Decatur store to running a new, much larger 450-employee Wal-Mart in Bluffton, Indiana. Melissa had to endure the boy-do-you-suck ordeal even though top management had not found worrisome shrinkage problems at her new store or her previous store. In Bentonville, several executives pulled her aside and told her not to worry about all the nasty words, that they didn't apply to her, that management, as evidenced by her recent promotion, was indeed happy with her. Melissa, understandably, was confused.

Melissa says her years at Wal-Mart changed her for the worse. "I screwed plenty of people in my career there," she said. "Honestly, you have to. It's either you do it, or there's the door. They told us in meetings, 'I can go hire anyone off the street and pay them fifty thousand dollars to run a store.' "

At two Wal-Marts where she was a manager—Watseka, Illinois, and Decatur, Indiana—Melissa, like managers we met earlier, locked in the twelve-person night crew, usually from ten p.m. to seven a.m. "I think it's wrong, and I was part of it," she said. "All the smaller stores did it. They just said, 'It was payroll,' and they couldn't afford another manager to work at night with a key."

For store managers like Melissa, the most important metric was to keep the amount her store spent on wages below the bare-bones weekly payroll that headquarters assigned her. One year her store's weekly payroll was not to exceed 5.9 percent of its weekly sales. And if her store's sales fell from one week to the next, perhaps because of a snowstorm or road construction, she was expected to cut payroll to stay under 5.9 percent. To do that, Melissa followed orders and often fired or pushed out more experienced, higher-paid workers. Sometimes she would assign them to unload trucks from ten p.m. to six a.m., knowing that the hours and work would be so grueling that they would quit.

"They said, 'Just make this person mad and they'll quit,' " Melissa said. "Then they'd bring in people at six dollars an hour replacing nine-fifty-an-hour workers."

To meet her payroll targets, Melissa often reduced forty-hour-a-week workers to thirty-five hours, and sometimes to as few as twenty-eight. Some workers pleaded with her not to cut their hours because they were just scraping by. "They couldn't afford their bills, they couldn't afford food for their family, they couldn't afford diapers for their children, but we were told to cut them back," Melissa said. "You hated to do it, but by the same token, you can't have a heart. I fired hundreds and hundreds of people during my time there."

Melissa said that when she was a store manager, Wal-Mart required new employees to work full-time six weeks in a row before they qualified for some benefits. So Melissa often did what many Wal-Mart managers did—after new employees worked full-time five straight weeks, she assigned them to part-time work the sixth week. By preventing these workers from qualifying for benefits, she reduced her store's costs.

"When I was there, I knew what I had to do," Melissa said. "I had to meet the bottom line or my ass was in trouble. They didn't care how I got to that bottom line . . . so long as I got there."

Melissa dutifully followed a Wal-Mart practice of challenging—with rare exception—every discharged employee who filed for unemployment insurance even when that employee rightly deserved such compensation. Even if someone was laid off as a straightforward cost-cutting measure, Melissa, like many Wal-Mart managers, would try to persuade state officials that the worker was fired for serious misconduct and therefore shouldn't qualify for jobless benefits.

Day after day, computers at Wal-Mart's headquarters tracked the sales and payroll at Melissa's store, and day after day her district manager zealously acted on those numbers. On Thursdays he would warn her if her payroll numbers were trending too high for the week. If she needed to do some last-minute payroll trimming, she often sent a dozen stockers, cashiers, and department managers home after lunch on Friday, the last day of the weekly payroll. As a result, on Friday afternoons at her store, as at many Wal-Marts, there were few sales assistants to answer shoppers' questions and so few cashiers that the checkout lines snaked into the aisles.

Every Saturday morning, the store managers in Melissa's district participated in a conference call. The district manager—and sometimes the regional vice president—would chastise whichever managers had overshot their assigned payroll for the previous week. "They're hollering and screaming, 'You need to control your store. That's what we pay you for. I can't babysit you. I'll write your ass up,' " Melissa said. "If you were on the good side, they didn't say anything."

"If payroll was 6.1 percent of sales one year, and I was able to run my store at 6.1 percent of sales, then the next year I had to run at 5.9 percent," she said. "Every year you were constantly cutting. It was a never-ending battle."

At Wal-Mart, many managers faced an additional quandary—their stores were habitually short-staffed because the payroll assigned them didn't give them enough employee hours to get everything done that needed to get done. Managers like Melissa confronted three painful choices with regard to getting everything done: (1) work fifteen or more extra hours a week; (2) pressure subordinates to do more of the work needed, often by getting them to work off the clock; or (3) risk getting demoted or fired.

Melissa usually chose to work the extra hours. She sometimes cleaned the bathrooms herself, put up new merchandise displays, or helped round up shopping carts in the parking lot.

"Wal-Mart says store managers are supposed to work fifty-four hours a week," she said. "I usually worked seventy, seventy-five hours."

Ruefully, she admits that for many years her daughter, Mikaela, spent far more time with her babysitter than with her mom.

Many managers took the option of pressuring employees to work off the clock.

"The Wal-Mart system is hurting the assistant manager who wants to have a family, wants to be an honest person, wants to get the job done," said Robert Eckert, who was an assistant store manager at several Wal-Marts in California. "The assistant manager is put in a position of 'If I want to go home to my wife and family, I have to put pressure on someone to work off the clock.' They tell you that working off the clock is against the law, is not allowed by Wal-Mart, and then they tell you to get the job done. But they didn't give you the budget to get the job done."

In her first eight years at the company, Melissa was a Wal-Mart true believer. She had bought in to such a degree, she was so eager to climb the ladder, that she was willing to put up with the abuse. But soon after she was promoted to head the larger store in Bluffton, she started to see things differently. Her salary there was $50,000, while her top two subordinates, both men, were earning $65,000 and $60,000. When she complained to her district manager, he reassured her that even though her salary was lower, she, as the store manager, stood to receive a much larger annual bonus, perhaps $50,000 or more, if her store thrived. Melissa reminded him that her bonus could also be zero.

That was not the only sexual discrimination Melissa felt. (She has become a plaintiff in the giant sexual discrimination lawsuit against Wal-Mart.) Once a month the nine store managers from her district gathered at the district manager's office in Fort Wayne for a meeting before going out to a business lunch together. Twice, the group—she was the only woman among them—headed to Hooters.

"I don't like the atmosphere, the girls in tight shirts and tight skirts," Melissa said. "The guys would flirt. When the girls bent over, the guys would make comments about their breasts and what they'd like to do with this girl when she was bending over. Sometimes I'd say, 'Shut up,' and they'd laugh at me. They'd say, 'Oh, Melissa, you're no fun.' "

When the managers from Indiana were driving to Bentonville after being summoned there, her district manager—the man who had screamed at Melissa in his car—had them stop, en route, at an anonymous concrete building that Melissa thought was an innocent enough bar. Once inside, she was shocked to see pole dancers.

"I had never been to a strip club," she said. "I wanted to leave, but I was scared to. I didn't want to sit outside by myself. One of the dancers leans over and was talking to my district manager, and he turns to me and says, 'Melissa, we could go out back. She said that for fifty bucks we can have a threesome.'

"I said, 'Hell no.'

"He said, 'If you're scared, I'll just watch.' "

During that trip to Bentonville, Wal-Mart replaced that district manager with someone who had long carried a grudge against Melissa. She thinks the new district manager disliked her because she was a woman who had risen so fast. Years before, the new district manager, while overseeing a Wal-Mart district in Illinois, had yelled and cursed at Melissa while visiting a store where she was the second in charge. He had raged at her because her store had run out of some plastic cutlery, leaving an embarrassing empty space on a shelf.

The new district manager pumped the assistant managers who worked for Melissa—all male—for dirt on her. He didn't hide his intentions to get rid of her.

"He said my job was home raising my daughter and not running a Wal-Mart store," Melissa said. "Then it got to 'You know if you don't step down now, I will make your life hell. You'll be gone in six weeks one way or the other.' " (In sworn testimony in the sexual discrimination lawsuit against Wal-Mart, the district manager denied saying that.)

So Melissa quit.

Looking back at her years at Wal-Mart, Melissa feels anger and guilt. "I feel bad that part of me wasn't a very nice person when I was at Wal-Mart," she said. "To think I would compromise my morals and values for them. But when you're wrapped up in that type of corporate culture, you got to do what you got to do. Your brain wants to believe that what you're doing really isn't wrong."

EVERYTHING STARTS at the top in business, but as it works its way down it reveals its human face. As we have seen, managers fire people to make budgets, pressure employees to work without pay, cheat workers by manipulating data on computers, and punish people for taking fully justified days off. These are not isolated incidents but a way of life for millions of American workers. The pressure for maximum profit leaves a wide range of abuse in its wake.

There is no denying that America's corporations have grown tougher in recent decades. Books with titles like *Mean Business, Lean and Mean, The New Ruthless Economy, White-Collar Sweatshop, The Disposable American,* and

War on the Middle Class attest to that. If there is competitive upheaval, "who knows if your job will even exist," Andy Grove, Intel's chairman, wrote in his book *Only the Paranoid Survive.* "And, frankly," he continued, "who will care besides you?"[1]

Far too often today's high-pressure management style has swept away inhibitions about doing what was once considered callous or onerous. Radio-Shack, as we saw, used a mass e-mail to inform four hundred employees at headquarters that they were being dismissed. At a BankOne call center in Florida, managers often pressured, sometimes even prohibited, workers from going to the bathroom while working. At one company where workers were left shell-shocked by yet another round of downsizing, a manager told a female employee to "smile more often so that people would know just how grateful she was to still have a job."[2] A Tyson poultry plant in Virginia lowered the temperature from the high sixties to an uncomfortable fifty degrees in order to save money by reducing bacterial growth and thus the need for an extra washdown of the plant's equipment.

In an anonymous posting circulated on the Internet, the wife of a programmer for Electronic Arts, the video games giant, bemoaned today's push-it-to-the-max management style. She complained that she rarely saw her husband because his work hours were so insane. And when she did see him, he was usually dog-tired and plagued by headaches.

"The current mandatory hours are 9 a.m. to 10 p.m.—seven days a week—with the occasional Saturday evening off for good behavior (at 6:30 p.m.)," she wrote. "This averages out to an eighty-five-hour work week . . . The stress is taking its toll. After a certain number of hours spent working the eyes start to lose focus; after a certain number of weeks with only one day off fatigue starts to accrue and accumulate exponentially. There is a reason why there are two days in a weekend—bad things happen to one's physical, emotional, and mental health if these days are cut short."[3]

This unhappy wife, who called herself "ea_spouse," raged against the company's decision to stop giving comp time to offset the hundreds of hours that programmers had worked above and beyond a forty-hour week. Ea_spouse was also furious that Electronic Arts seemed to treat all fifty-two weeks of the year as crunch time, as a perpetual last-minute sprint to get the hottest, newest project out the door.

She described the company's human resources policy as "Put up—or shut up and leave." She said the message to workers was "If they don't want to sacrifice their lives and their health and their talent so that a multibillion dollar corporation can continue its Godzilla-stomp through the game industry, they can work someplace else."[4]

Some business executives argue that today's managers are no tougher than those of yesteryear. In the late 1800s and early 1900s, Carnegie Steel, Republic Steel, and many coal companies certainly used Pinkertons and state militias to brutally intimidate strikers, with workers dying in confrontations. And of course the working conditions were often Dickensian.

A century ago many companies squeezed out more production by using the harsh "drive system" in which foremen motivated their workers through stress and intimidation. In 1912, a steel industry expert testified before a congressional committee about these hard-driving foremen, who were known as "pushers."

"Who does he push?"

"He pushes the gang."

"Explain how he does this."

"It is done in various ways, through motions and profanity"—in other words yelling at, cursing, threatening, and sometimes hitting workers.[5]

The great Harvard University labor economist Sumner Slichter wrote in 1919, "The reason why coercive 'drive' methods have prevailed in the past has been that the central management has been indifferent to the methods pursued by foremen in handling men but insisted rigidly upon a constantly increasing output and constantly decreasing costs."[6]

Fear fueled the drive system. The historian Sanford Jacoby described one episode in which the assistant superintendent of a plant asked, "Has anyone been fired from this shop today?" When told no, he replied, "Well, then, fire a couple of 'em. It'll put the fear of God in their hearts."[7]

The drive system declined during the Roaring Twenties, and then the New Deal brought a strong national sense that workers, battered by the Depression, should be treated better. American companies, by and large, treated their workers far better from the 1940s through the 1970s. Then came the late-twentieth-century tightening, spurred by numerous forces, including foreign competition and pressures from Wall Street.

"The people at the top are pressuring their workers more because there's more pressure on them," said Carl M. Van Horn, executive director of the Heldrich Center for Workforce Development at Rutgers University. "They're feeling pressures day to day, week to week, quarter to quarter, and they're in turn pushing those pressures down the line."[8]

In this fiercer business climate, high performance has become a central concept. It is expected of CEOs, and they expect it from those below, and those who fall short do not last. "Management," says Eric Greenberg, director of surveys at the American Management Association, "is more thick-skinned about letting people go, and workers are more thick-skinned about accepting layoffs as a condition of employment."[9]

In *The New Deal at Work,* Peter Cappelli of the Wharton School describes how downsizing devastated employee morale in the 1990s and how management hardly seemed to care. Cappelli noted that a survey by the Conference Board, a respected business-backed research group, found that "employee morale ranked eighth out of a possible nine management priorities."[10] He quoted one executive whose comments highlighted the huge change in managers' attitudes. Not long ago, said T. Quinn Spitzer, chief executive of Kepner-Tregoe, a management consulting and training firm, "your reputation was on the line if your hire didn't work out. So you did everything you could to make them better. Now, your reputation is on the line if you don't get rid of them fast enough."[11]

One of the main trends in compensation, for managers and employees alike, is performance-based pay. More and more of each manager's pay takes the form of bonuses and/or stock options, creating sizable incentives for managers to do their utmost to cut costs and maximize profits. These incentives have caused "executive and lower-level managers to take risks, to work harder and to engage in the unpleasant personnel tasks associated with reorganization and staff reductions," wrote Martin Feldstein, the Harvard University economist and adviser to President Reagan.[12]

"We're asking managers to do a lot more with less," said Richard S. Wellins, a senior vice president at Development Dimensions International, a human resources consulting firm. "Expectations have changed. Things have gotten far more demanding. The stress of the job, along with the economics and expectations, is causing nastier behavior."[13]

In the fast-growing service sector, many managers are being asked to squeeze out more production while having very limited money for bonuses or merit raises to reward greater productivity. Jerry Newman, a management professor at the State University of New York at Buffalo, gained some perspective on how this played out when he spent a year working as a cook, counter man, and floor cleaner at seven fast food restaurants.[14]

"One way to get people to work hard is to reward them," said Professor Newman, coauthor of a textbook on employee compensation. "Another way is to punish them. If you don't have money to reward them because you have to control costs, then you have to go with the punishment model. That means you put more pressure on people. You set higher expectations and you try to achieve that by intimidating people. I call that the bullying model.

"Corporate officials never say they want bullies," he continued. "They would say they want people who were performance-oriented. I don't even think they're looking for bullies. They're looking for people who get results, and those people just happen to be bullies."[15]

THEY CALL IT THE SCRIPT. But it's actually an arcane list of things you're supposed to say and things you had better not say. At the TeleTech call center in Niagara Falls, New York, the script sometimes seems only slightly less sacred than the Bible.

If any of the 550 customer service representatives (CSRs) stray too much from the script on one call, they risk a tongue-lashing. If they are caught straying on three or four calls, they risk their job.

You must always say, "Thank you for calling Verizon Wireless"—that's the call center's main client. You should never call a customer sir or madam—it's always Mr. or Ms. with the last name. And you had better not mispronounce the last name, even if it's Krzyzewski. If you don't slip in the customer's name at least three times during a call, that will mean some demerits. And you'd better mention Verizon's Worry-Free Guarantee at least once each call. You need to sound chipper and energetic, and you shouldn't spend more than four minutes on a call. You also need to slip in at least two "proactives," such as "Do you know that if you punch star-two-twenty-two on your phone, it will tell you how many minutes you have left this month?" And when a call is about to end, you had better not forget to ask, "Have I resolved all of your concerns today?"

These are a small fraction of the rules at the TeleTech call center, where pod after pod of customer service reps are spread throughout a cavernous hall a half mile from the thundering falls. TeleTech has set up shop in a defunct nightclub, the Pleasure Dome, in Niagara Falls's shabby downtown, just yards from the convention center. When New York's former governor, George E. Pataki, did the obligatory ribbon-cutting when TeleTech opened in 1997, he hailed the call center's arrival, saying, "This is the single largest increase in jobs we've had in downtown Niagara Falls in the twentieth century."[16]

The TeleTech center may be in a languishing city, but it is part of a flourishing industry—there are more than 60,000 call centers in the United States and an estimated 4 million call center workers.[17] It's an industry at the heart of the

American economy. Call centers are the connective tissue of modern commerce, handling airline reservations and stock sales, selling HBO subscriptions and cell phones, taking orders for L.L.Bean and Dell computers, troubleshooting problems with your hard drive or credit card.

Call centers are sometimes viewed as factories that supply an invaluable product: customer service. One academic study found that "call centers introduce principles of mechanization and industrial engineering into a much wider array of service transactions than was hitherto possible"—thanks to specialized software, networked computers, sophisticated equipment that distributes calls, and recording devices that keep tabs on a CSR's every word.[18] While call centers rely on modern technologies to maximize productivity, their techniques often seem borrowed from the "drive" principles of old.

"You had a script—they were incredibly complex scripts," said James Hufnagel, a TeleTech employee who fielded calls from Verizon customers who were having DSL problems. "If you didn't follow the script and if you left a single thing out or if you misspoke or spoke with a mistake in grammar, you got a QA [quality assurance] report, and they were murder."

Every call was recorded, he said, and each month a quality assurance supervisor reviewed four or five of each worker's calls, meticulously going down a checklist.

"You got scolded for anything and everything," Hufnagel said. "I've worked in factories and on assembly lines, but this job was the most dehumanizing of all. It was so inflexible. The whole underpinning of the job was, day in and day out, 'You are lucky to work here because you suck.' They were always threatening you with termination. You were always doing something wrong."

The TeleTech center was not always so oppressive. When Greta Kargatis began working there in 1997, it was genteel and fairly low-key. The men usually wore dress shirts and ties, the women, stockings and heels. Many of the managers and employees had worked at a nearby Fleet Bank office that had closed not long before.

"When I first started, they treated us very well," said Greta, who joined TeleTech after working for seven years as a legal secretary, losing that job when her firm downsized. Greta is thin with stylish glasses and neatly coiffed straight dark hair, a bit prim and conservative. She began at TeleTech at age forty-four, when GTE was the center's main customer. GTE's primary goal was getting the phone reps to persuade customers to upgrade their cell phone service with such lucrative add-ons as paging and cellular Internet. Back then, management had a far different approach toward boosting productivity. For doing a stellar job selling GTE upgrades, Greta got to choose from a gift cata-log, and her gifts included a washing machine, a vacuum cleaner, and an eigh-teen-carat gold watch.

But the work environment turned sharply worse after Verizon Wireless took over GTE's cell phone business and negotiated a new, lower-cost contract with TeleTech. In 2001, TeleTech announced it was laying off 511 of the center's 875 workers. Soon afterward, it contacted many of the 511 and told them that they could stay on the condition they agree to a three-dollar-an-hour pay cut. Greta's pay fell from $14.50 an hour to $11.50; many less experienced or less stellar performers fell from $12 an hour to $9.

"There were no other jobs to leave to," Greta said, "and certainly not jobs that provided health insurance."

The call center's focus—and metabolism—soon changed. There was now an unrelenting push to handle calls quickly, to hew to the script, and to be on the phone every single minute. Greta was a strong performer—she was even-tually promoted to quality assurance supervisor—but she said the pace of work was often brutal.

"There were unbelievable amounts of work you were supposed to do," she said. While on a call, perhaps answering a customer's questions about a monthly bill, the CSRs not only were supposed to slip in all the elements from the script, but were supposed to verify names and addresses and type them into the computer. And if customers changed their cell phone plan during a call, the CSRs had to type in a great deal of additional information and do a credit check, all while navigating among various computer screens. The phone reps were also supposed to discreetly ask customers what time of day they made long-distance calls, in theory to determine whether there might be a more profitable plan for Verizon to offer them. "If there was ever an opportu-nity to offer the customer something better and you didn't, you could get in trouble," Greta said.

If while juggling all these tasks a call center rep concentrated so much on her typing or her computer screen that she didn't listen to the customer for a second or dropped a beat in the conversation, there would be consequences. "If you ever asked a caller to repeat something, the supervisors had a fit," Greta said. "And you couldn't have dead air."

In the call center business, the customer is king, the CSRs servants. TeleTech Holdings—a Colorado-based company with 62 centers, 41,000 employees, and $1 billion in revenues—calls its CSRs "customer loyalty specialists."

As soon as Greta and the other CSRs finished one call, they were supposed to grab another—for hours on end. Their phones showed how many calls were in the center's queue—usually twenty or more—and if they ever waited more than four seconds before answering a call, the all-knowing computer that monitored them piled on the demerits. The pressure to handle the call flow was so great that when Greta stayed on a call for more than four minutes, a supervisor patrolling the floor often gave her a cut sign, like a movie director cutting short a scene that has gone awry. Greta hated that sign. "You shouldn't rush people off a call," she said. "I wanted the account taken care of properly."

For Greta, the hardest part was satisfying TeleTech's requirement to complete all the paperwork for a screwed-up monthly bill or an upgraded cell phone plan during a three-to-four-minute conversation. On days when calls were backed up, meaning most days, it was forbidden to finish up that work after a call ended.

"If you put yourself in ACW [after-call work]," notifying the computer that you were doing after-call work and were not picking up new calls, according to Greta, "the supervisor would yell, 'There are calls in the queue. Take the next call.' When you're working and getting calls back to back, it's hard to concentrate on what you didn't finish up three or four calls ago. You try to do that and do your call flow and do your order 100 percent accurate, and that's where the stress came in. It would be different if once you got that order, they would give you the lousy five minutes to finish writing up the order."

Hufnagel, the CSR who fielded calls about DSL problems, echoed her complaint about trying to keep up. "It's like holding down a lid on a kettle that's boiling," he said. Hufnagel wasn't a typical customer service rep. He majored in biology at Cornell University and then obtained an MBA from Baruch College in Manhattan. He returned to his native Buffalo to work for a stock brokerage, but when the brokerage collapsed, he became a computer consultant. His timing was bad and when high tech sputtered, he settled for a twelve-dollar-an-hour job at TeleTech. It paid the bills while he studied to pursue a less stressful career: massage therapy.

To attract workers, TeleTech's Web site advertised, "Cool jobs, fun people, big paychecks." The Web site also asked, "Do you like to work hard and have fun?"[19] But TeleTech's management made such stringent demands, workers said, that once or twice a month ambulances were called to the Niagara Falls center because employees were having stress attacks.

Rosemary Batt, a professor of industrial relations at Cornell and the nation's leading academic expert on call centers, said the nation's CSRs average one hundred calls a day. That means they typically handle a new call every 4.8 minutes for eight hours.

Professor Batt divides the call center world into two halves. One half emphasizes excellent service—think of your calls to your mutual fund company or to Land's End. These "professional service" centers are usually run in-house. The other half emphasizes high volume and low cost. These call centers are often called "mass service centers," and they are often run by outside contractors. Wages in the high-volume centers are often far lower and the stress levels far higher.[20]

Some industrial experts have called these centers "electronic sweatshops." At the worst ones, employee turnover exceeds 200 percent a year.

Many companies, Professor Batt said, "have tried to routinize these jobs, making them as similar as possible to the old assembly line work where you left your mind at home and tightened bolts all day."[21] The industry trend, she said, is to push for ever-greater standardization and automation to get the biggest bang—the highest volume of calls—for the buck.

As one academic study put it, the job may be lowly and low paid, but it is highly demanding: "CSRs must handle elevated customer expectations, understand complex products and services, explain creative pricing strategies, navigate sophisticated technology, operate within regulatory limitations, and meet or exceed challenging individual performance expectations for variables such as talk time and sales quotas."[22]

And all that for often under eleven dollars an hour.

The "mass service" centers, several studies found, are inherently problematic for their workers. "The aims of employee well-being, cost minimization and operational efficiency appear incompatible in such call centers," one study in the *Human Resource Management Journal* concluded, adding that these centers' practices are "likely to reduce employee well-being."[23]

TeleTech's managers often seemed to go out of their way to undermine employee well-being, many workers said. The company gave workers five sick days a year, but there were strings attached. "You got penalized for using your sick time," said Ella Moore, a CSR. "They frowned on you taking it. You got written up."

The CSRs were supposed to receive a break every two hours—either a fifteen-minute coffee break or a half-hour lunch break. "If you took an unauthorized bathroom break, you'd hear about it," Hufnagel said. TeleTech's managers told their CSRs that they wanted them on the phone every single minute they were clocked in because Verizon Wireless paid TeleTech only for the minutes workers were on the phone.

In a lawsuit that accuses TeleTech of requiring off-the-clock work, more than a dozen employees and managers said CSRs were ordered to arrive at work at least fifteen minutes before they were scheduled to clock in. During that time, they had to read up on any newly announced changes in the subjects they were handling, such as cell phone promotions and pricing. They were also required to boot up their computers and get all their programs running so they could answer their first call the moment their shift officially began.

Off-the-clock work at TeleTech took many other forms. CSRs said they were often required to work through breaks without being paid for those fifteen minutes. One top call center manager said workers sometimes received no pay for staying an extra fifteen or thirty minutes after their shifts ended to catch up on all the paperwork and computer work they couldn't complete during phone calls.

"TeleTech had the ability to capture all of a CSR's working time accurately, but chose not to," said Michael Gregory, who was the second in command at TeleTech's call center in Topeka. "Working off the clock was a condition of a CSR's employment. Hourly workers who complained were weeded out and terminated." In an affidavit in the off-the-clock lawsuit, Gregory added, "TeleTech management, including managers in TeleTech's corporate headquarters in Colorado, were aware that the CSRs were working off the clock, but did nothing to stop it."[24]

A TeleTech spokeswoman denied that off-the-clock work occurred at TeleTech's centers. (This phenomenon was by no means limited to TeleTech. Cingular and T-Mobile each agreed to settlements of $5 million after the Labor Department accused them of not paying thousands of CSRs for pre-shift work that the companies required them to do.)

The workers at the Niagara Falls center felt that their every move was being watched. Some sociologists refer to call centers as "electronic panopticons"— likening them to prisons where the guards can see all the inmates at once. The CSRs were prohibited from talking to workers in other pods except during breaks. Hufnagel remembers an incident in which a boyfriend and girlfriend who worked in different pods were suspended for three days after the boyfriend telephoned his girlfriend one morning to make lunch plans. Rose Russell, a CSR, was threatened with dismissal when she missed work for two days to take care of her daughter because her child care worker needed to leave town to attend her mother's funeral.

Many workers dreaded the dressing-downs at their monthly quality assurance reviews, which were held after supervisors listened to recordings of their calls and graded them. Getting less than sixty-five out of one hundred on three or four calls could result in termination. CSRs lost twenty points for failing to mention Verizon's Worry-Free Guarantee, and another twenty points if they missed a word in the scripted opening or closing. One's grades had a heavy bearing on one's raises; some CSRs with mediocre scores received no pay increases for two or three years.

To many workers, the ratings system took things to the point of absurdity. "It was unbelievable the stuff you had to do to get a perfect rating," Greta said. "If the customer hung up on you, you got in trouble because you weren't able to say everything you were supposed to say." Even when enraged customers screamed and cursed, the CSRs were to stick to their script and maintain their chipper tone. "Someone is on the phone 'mother——ing' you," Greta said, "and you still had to give your proactives."

One call sticks in Hufnagel's mind. "It was a two-minute call, and we never got off the ground," he said. "The person was confused. It was a wrong number. And they QA'd me on it. I got a score of twenty out of one hundred. You can get fired for that.

"I think they've probably done behavioral studies that there are people who respond more to an intimidating atmosphere," Hufnagel added. "Another factor is you have a shrinking middle class, and in this part of the world, a twelve-dollar-an-hour job isn't so bad, and there's a lot of competition for these jobs."

COMPUTERS HAVE CLEARLY BECOME the Big Brother of today's workplace. Not only are computers used for the kinds of reprehensible acts we have already seen, like erasing employees' hours, but at innumerable work sites, management uses them to exact more labor from workers. Computers can keep track of how many e-mails employees send each day, how many keystrokes they type each minute, how long it takes a worker to process an insurance claim, register a hotel guest, take a Burger King order—or handle a call from a Verizon Wireless customer. Computers are often tied to monitoring systems at workplace entrances, allowing managers to know that a particular worker left for lunch at twelve-thirty and returned at three. In some workplaces, like the TeleTech call center, computers know when employees take eighteen minutes for their fifteen-minute coffee break, how often they go to the bathroom during regular work hours, and how many minutes they spend there. The computer at TeleTech will know that in a particular week a CSR handled 401 calls that averaged five minutes, thirty seconds, far more than the desired four minutes. As the chief operations officer of one call center put it, "We can reach down from the executive level to see that Billie Sue isn't cutting it. A poor performer can be more easily trapped and dealt with."[25]

Computers keep a watchful eye on not just shirkers but also the hardworking CSR who needs to take twelve minutes away from the phone call queue because her babysitter's car broke down. At call centers, computers enable managers to monitor every second of an employee's work time, something that even the most vigilant bosses could not do before the computer age. If your supervisor wants to get rid of you, an all-seeing, all-knowing computer can usually be relied on to provide the ammunition. It can easily show that a worker took too many two-hour lunches, left early on too many Fridays, or spent too much time writing e-mails to his girlfriend.

In a *Los Angeles Times* profile of a call center, one worker said, "Weren't computers supposed to allow us to work less? Instead, they're being used to make us work harder."[26]

Workers recognized early on that computers would not be a balm for workplace stress. In 1991, at one of the first congressional hearings on computer monitoring, Harriet Ternipsede, a TWA reservations agent, said, "During my thirty years as a reservations agent, I have personally witnessed how my workplace has been turned into an electronic sweatshop by monitoring . . . Today, through computer programs and communications systems, employers can electronically observe and review employees' every move—every word."[27]

If anything, such monitoring has gotten only shrewder and more sophisticated since Ternipsede testified. One major academic study said, "The continuous monitoring and emphasis on results takes all control away from the employee and places it with an unseen manager, potentially creating a work environment filled with such pressure that workers experience increased stress, greater dissatisfaction, a loss of valued privacy, and lower morale."[28]

Computers have also been used to restrict workers' ability to think for themselves. Companies often use computers together with sophisticated recording equipment to make sure that a call center rep or the counter server at a fast food restaurant sticks to the script. In his book *The New Ruthless Economy*, Simon Head wrote, "Today's scientific managers are trying . . . to control the minds of their white-collar employees. That is what the whole superstructure of control, scripting, and surveillance along the digital assembly lines is designed to achieve."[29]

Julian Barling, a professor of organizational behavior at Queen's University in Toronto, suggested that computers give managers more information than they need and that managers then use all that information to pressure employees too much. "In the good old days, if you wanted the data on how a particular unit was doing, it took quite a while to get that data," said Professor Barling, who is editor of the *Journal of Applied Psychology*. "But now you can get that virtually immediately. You can get data on employee behavior and performance any time of day. That enables managers to say, 'You may not spend more than forty seconds on a call and, remember, your goal is to provide superior customer service.' Where does that leave us?"[30]

Before computers came along, senior managers often had a difficult time trying to assess the effectiveness and efficiency of lower-level managers. But computers have changed all that. Just as a manager knows whether a call center rep is averaging a minute too long handling calls, a call center's top executive will now know whether a middle manager's team of forty CSRs is averaging forty-five seconds too long on their calls. And that might mean thunder from above. Not surprisingly, that thunder is often passed down the line.

The science of computer-controlled payroll management has become so sophisticated that Taco Bell installed a system in which if sales at one of its restaurants dipped from two to three p.m., the computers could immediately determine whether a manager had complied with corporate rules by reducing the number of employees working during that time slot. To control costs, Taco Bell adopted rules to ensure that every one of its restaurants did not exceed a specific hour-by-hour staffing-to-sales ratio. Lower-level managers know that if they violate such rules or exceed their payroll numbers, their bonuses might disappear, and perhaps their jobs as well.

In 2003, Taco Bell agreed to a $1.5-million settlement after a jury in Oregon found its managers guilty of requiring off-the-clock work and using their computers to erase employees' hours. Some business experts say computers have made it easier for individual managers to cheat workers on payroll because they can now, for example, erase hours on their own, whereas in decades past they would have probably had to conspire with bookkeepers or accountants to do such cheating. And that becomes all the easier in an era when unions are weaker and there are fewer government investigators pursuing wage fraud.

So not only does computer monitoring from above increase pressures on low-level managers to make budget, but computers often make it easier—with just a few mouse clicks—for those managers to cut corners in order to make budget.

William Rutzick, a lawyer who represented the one thousand workers in the off-the-clock case against Taco Bell, said many low-level managers know that unless they cheat to make budget, they may be fired. "The store managers have a toehold in the lower middle class," he said. "They're being paid twenty thousand, thirty thousand dollars. They're in management. They get medical. They have no job security at all, and they want to keep their toehold in the lower middle class, and they'll often do whatever is necessary."

NO GROUP KNOWS BETTER that the American workplace is no longer the stable, secure place it once was than the millions of Americans who work as temps, freelancers, independent contractors, and on-call workers. The next chapter examines this vast sea of disposable workers.

Chapter Seven

HERE TODAY, GONE TOMORROW

In the 1980s, many American manufacturers embraced a practice known as "just-in-time inventory." The idea was simple—to keep only enough parts in inventory for immediate needs. This practice saved corporations considerable sums by reducing the need for huge warehouses containing mountains of components that might sit around for months.

American corporations have embraced a similar strategy for 18 million people, more than one-eighth of the nation's workforce—a just-in-time workforce. Economists have dubbed them "contingent workers," and for corporate America they're essentially a disposable workforce, discarded as soon as they're not needed anymore. If a customer places a big new order, just-in-timers are brought in, and when demand subsides, they are sent packing, with the companies not needing to worry about unemployment insurance and severance packages. The just-in-time workforce includes agency temps, freelancers, on-call workers, day laborers, direct-hire temps, contract employees, and independent contractors. For these workers, there is no job security, and employer-provided benefits such as health insurance and pensions are a rarity. These workers are cheap labor for corporate executives who are loath to hire new full-time employees lest it undermine their companies' preoccupation with maximizing flexibility and minimizing fixed costs.[1]

A whole vocabulary has developed to describe just-in-time workers, ranging from the perfunctory (*consultants* and *contingent staffers*) to the euphemistic (*special assignment representatives* and *flexible staffers*), to the colorful (*hired guns, floaters, temp slaves, 1099ers, lone rangers, permalancers,* and, in the high-tech world, *E-lancers* and *information backpackers*). Paul Osterman, an economist at MIT, described them as "America's new migrant laborers, moving from job to job without security and without benefits."[2] They have also been called the "vanguard of insecurity" in today's increasingly globalized economy.[3]

"Employers broke the old deal because they didn't want long-term commitments," said Peter Cappelli of the Wharton School. "But increasingly they don't want employees at all."[4]

The just-in-time concept has been used, shall we say, innovatively by many companies. Pacific Bell, the West Coast phone company, hired more than one thousand temps and independent contractors who had previously worked for it as regular employees—that is, until they were downsized out of their jobs.[5] Companies with human resource policies that make employees "permanent" with access to benefits after their ninetieth day often lay off temps on their eighty-ninth day. Microsoft once fired ninety receptionists while telling them they could reapply for their jobs on a just-in-time basis through an outside contractor that Microsoft planned to use.[6] A small auto-parts manufacturer in Chicago, the A&E Service Company, announced one day that it would "no longer hold general labor employees on the payroll." The notice added that anyone who wanted to continue working for the company had to "be employed by Elite Staffing effective immediately." On the notice, the workers were to check a box accepting or declining their new temporary status.[7]

The just-in-time workforce began to expand dramatically about the same time that massive downsizing began. These trends represent two sides of the same phenomenon—reduced employer commitment to workers.

The number of agency temps has soared from 980,000 in 1982 to nearly 3 million today, according to the American Staffing Association.[8] Indeed, in the first four years after the 2001 recession ended, temp jobs accounted for one out of every seven new jobs added. Temps have grown so prevalent that one business research group found that they make up more than 10 percent of the workers at nearly one in five American corporations.[9] Even at prestigious giants like Microsoft, temps have represented more than 20 percent of the workers.

Temping has become a booming $72 billion-a-year business, up from $1 billion in 1975.[10] Temp agencies have aggressively maneuvered to upgrade their image, calling themselves staffing agencies and describing their métier as helping corporate America with "flexible staffing arrangements." Nowadays, just 20 percent of agency temps do office/clerical work, while 35 percent do industrial jobs, 21 percent do professional/managerial jobs, and 16 percent do information technology work.[11] The legendary Kelly Girl has spawned such offspring as the Kelly Law Registry, which provides paralegals, and Kelly Scientific Resources, which grosses more than $100 million a year providing chemists and other scientists by the day to clinics and laboratories. Temp agencies also provide nurses, substitute teachers, accountants, and even acting CEOs for companies whose leaders suddenly left or were ousted. Including temps hired directly by companies, day laborers, and on-call workers such as substitute teachers, the United States, by some estimates, now has 8 million temporary workers.[12]

The just-in-time workforce also includes 10.3 million independent contractors.[13] They are the elite of the contingent workforce even though some of them struggle every bit as much as lowly temps. Independent contractors earn 14 percent more per hour on average than standard workers who do the same work.[14] Many of them—accountants, management consultants, movie editors, Web designers—earn more than $100,000 a year and are secure in their niches, having developed stable, dependable relationships with their customers and clients. But many independent contractors—such as freelance writers—have a much harder time.

The rise of the just-in-time workforce has helped companies by reducing their costs and increasing their flexibility. Wall Street, of course, loves when CEOs cut costs by reducing *permanent* headcount.

All too often temps are treated as second-class citizens. At a computer consulting firm outside Washington, the temps had to wear a large badge around their necks with the word "Temporary."[15] At Microsoft, temps are prohibited from using the company basketball court and are often not invited to parties celebrating the completion of projects they worked on. "As a temp, you mainly feel like an appendage," said David Larsen, who has worked several temp stints at Microsoft. "It's like Vietnam syndrome. Toward the end of Vietnam, the new guy would come on the line and no one wanted to get to know him because they figured he will be dead soon anyway."

Jeff Kelly, editor of the magazine *Temp Slave*, described temping as a "never-ending treadmill of low pay, no benefits, no security and no respect."[16] Richard Pauli, a temp at Microsoft, said that many managers deliberately pushed temps to their limit. "When you know these are temp positions, there's this attitude of really burning people out," he said.

It is no surprise that the Bureau of Labor Statistics found that 59 percent of temps said they would prefer a traditional job.[17] Still, there are many Americans who prefer working as temps, including college students who take a summer job or retirees who work during the holiday season to earn a few extra dollars for gifts. And some workers like to start as temps because it gives them an inside look at a company or an industry, helping them decide whether that is where they would like a permanent job. Similarly, many companies use "temp-to-perm" or "try-buy" strategies because it gives them a close look at a person's skills and work ethic before they decide whether they want to hire that person as a regular employee.

Not only do temps face less stability and status than regular workers, but they are paid 10 percent less on average than their counterparts in standard jobs.[18] In one study of temping agencies, economists at the Federal Reserve Bank of Chicago found that temps "receive much lower wages than permanent workers, although they frequently perform the same tasks as permanent staff members."[19]

Whether temps or independent contractors, America's just-in-time workers face a far worse situation regarding benefits than other workers. While 64 percent of full-time workers have employer-provided health insurance, just 9 percent of agency temps do. Similarly, just 7 percent of agency temps participate in their employer's pension plans while 58 percent of standard workers do.[20] Independent contractors and freelancers must fend for themselves on health and pension coverage. Proponents of the just-in-time phenomenon argue that it's not so bad that these workers rarely receive employer-provided health and pension benefits, under the assumption that they get those benefits through their spouses. But a study done by the Upjohn Institute found that more than half of the nation's agency temps have no health insurance from any source. Moreover, four out of five temps do not have pension coverage, while three-fifths of independent contractors do not.[21]

Corporations increasingly treat workers as independent contractors to save money, but they often skirt the law in doing so. Although independent contractors typically receive higher wages than regular workers, companies can often save 25 percent or more by using them because companies pay no employee benefits for them and don't pay the employer's share of Social Security and Medicare taxes, normally 7.65 percent of an employee's wages. Nor do companies have to pay unemployment insurance taxes or workers' compensation premiums. Another advantage for companies is that independent contractors are not protected by federal minimum wage and overtime laws or laws that bar discrimination by race, religion, sex, or disability.[22] Nor do independent contractors have a right to unionize.

In light of all these advantages, it is little wonder that the IRS once found that one in six American employers wrongly classify workers as independent contractors. The IRS found that employers had misclassified 3.4 million workers.[23]

WHEN JEAN CAPOBIANCO was diagnosed once again with breast cancer, her doctors ordered a mastectomy. She had first contracted the disease three years earlier and had suffered through seven months of chemotherapy. After her cancer came back, her husband walked out on her. "He told me he wasn't sexually attracted to me anymore," Jean said. "He got a girlfriend and left."

For more than a decade, Jean and her husband had been working together as a truck-driving team, doing long hauls in their eighteen-wheeler, driving hazardous waste from Massachusetts—Jean lives in Brockton, just south of Boston—to Alabama and other distant destinations. Now, with husband and truck gone, her career as a long-haul driver was gone as well.

After recovering from her second bout with breast cancer, Jean started looking for work. She spotted a Help Wanted ad from Roadway Packaging Systems, which said it was looking for independent contractors to deliver packages, entrepreneurial types who wanted to be in business for themselves.

"I needed a job," said Jean, who was forty-three when she went to work for Roadway in 1993. "I was too stupid to know what I was doing. They made it look so beautiful. They tell you you'll make all this money working for yourself. There'll be no one breathing down your back."

With her broad face, wavy brown hair, big eyes, and warm but awkward smile, Jean bears an uncanny resemblance to *All in the Family*'s Jean Stapleton. She is five feet one and stocky. She is down-to-earth, without airs and with a thick Boston accent, having grown up in a working-class section of Cambridge, Massachusetts.

Jean's work as a package driver soon became a maddening mixture of rush and routine. At six each morning, she arrived at the Roadway terminal in Brockton. She spent the next ninety minutes loading and arranging 100 to 140 packages in her boxy white truck, although some days, wholly unpredictably, she was given more than 200 packages to deliver. In the cavernous terminal, a series of conveyer belts ferried the packages to the forty-five trucks, which were parked in several rows, one alongside the other. Jean usually left the terminal around seven-thirty a.m. For the next ten to eleven hours she crisscrossed the crowded suburbs south of Boston, making deliveries to stationery stores, auto parts shops, factories, office buildings, even a few schools. Despite her small stature, she was strong, somehow managing to deliver 150-pound packages, relying at times on the assistance—and kindness—of strangers who were walking past her truck. She often picked up dozens of packages, too, typically returning to the terminal between six and seven at night. The managers often relied on Jean to make unexpected last-minute pickups, sometimes forcing her to work until eight or later.

She virtually never stopped for lunch. "I used to eat lunch and drive at the same time," she said. "I got real expert at eating a salad while it sat on top of my steering wheel."

In the late 1990s, Jean was forced to leave her delivery job for two years when she suffered a severe back injury while lifting an unwieldy package. Before she was able to return to work in 2000, FedEx, which had acquired Roadway and renamed it FedEx Ground, required her to purchase a truck from a FedEx-designated dealer, a truck that had to have FedEx-approved shelving and FedEx's logo painted on the outside. The truck's list price was $37,800, with the purchase contract calling for Jean to make sixty monthly installments of $781.12 and then a final one-time payment of $8,000.

In Jean's view, it was ludicrous for Roadway and then FedEx to call the drivers independent contractors.

"You're under their one hundred percent control," Jean said. "We're told what to do, when to do it, how to do it, and how much to do, when to take time off and when you can't take time off. You have to wear their uniform. You have to wear black sneakers. You can't wear your hair certain ways. You have to drive their truck. You have to deliver every single thing they put on the truck. You have to answer to them for everything that goes wrong. You have to do the pickups when they tell you to do them."

She talked of a driver who wanted to put an American flag decal on his truck after the terrorist attacks of September 11. FedEx wouldn't let him.

Jean realized that it's shrewd business for FedEx Ground to treat its 15,000 drivers as independent contractors. "It's a great deal for FedEx," she said. "They don't have to pay for trucks, for the insurance, for fuel, for maintenance, for tires. We have to pay for all those things. And they don't have to pay into the government with our Social Security."

By some estimates, this arrangement saves FedEx's Ground division up to $400 million a year, giving it a significant cost advantage over UPS, its main rival, which treats its drivers as regular employees. FedEx Ground argues that the drivers at its 500 terminals have no right to unionize, under the theory that they are independent contractors and not employees.[24] (FedEx Ground is separate from FedEx's air-freight operation, which employs its drivers as direct employees.)[25]

FedEx Ground insists that its drivers are independent contractors because they make major investments in their "businesses," specifically the purchase of their trucks, and because they can hire helpers and operate multiple routes. "These drivers are more like businesspeople," said Perry Colosimo, a spokesman for FedEx Ground. "They can set their own hours. They can buy routes.

They can develop their business. There are three hundred drivers who gross more than a quarter million a year."

But Jean says, "It's not true that we can set our own hours. Sometimes they didn't let us leave the terminal until eight. They blocked the doors so you can't get out. They wouldn't let you out until every single package was sorted."

In more than thirty lawsuits, FedEx Ground drivers have argued that they are employees, not independent contractors, and that the company should, as a result, pay for their trucks, insurance, repairs, gas, and tires. Many drivers mock FedEx Ground's claim that they are independent entrepreneurs who can "grow" their business, considering that their business is delivering packages that FedEx assigns them. Similarly, many drivers ridicule the company's assertions that they can show their business acumen and increase their profits through such supposedly enterprising steps as finding cheaper ways to repair their trucks.

In a lawsuit that FedEx Ground drivers filed in California, a state judge ruled that the company was essentially engaged in a ruse in maintaining that its drivers were independent contractors. The judge wrote that FedEx Ground "has close to absolute control" over the drivers, adding that the operating agreement that the drivers sign "is a brilliantly drafted contract creating the constraints of an employment relationship . . . in the guise of an independent contractor model."[26] An appeals court upheld that decision in August 2007, writing that FedEx has "control over every exquisite detail of the drivers' performance, including the color of their socks and the style of their hair."[27]

In December 2007, FedEx acknowledged another setback: the Internal Revenue Service had ordered it to pay more than $319 million in taxes and penalties for just the year 2002 because it has misclassified employees as independent contractors. FedEx could face similar IRS penalties for subsequent years. Asserting that it had "strong defenses," FedEx said it would appeal.

To attract drivers, FedEx Ground often runs ads claiming that its drivers can earn $60,000 to $80,000 a year. Many drivers say those ads are deceiving. Gross income can exceed $60,000, but for many, their net income is $25,000 to $35,000 a year, compared with $60,000 a year for a UPS driver, before overtime. Jean, echoing many drivers, said she had to pay nearly $800 a month for her truck, $125 a week for gas, and $55 a week for business equipment that FedEx all but requires, including an electronic scanner to track the packages. She also paid $4,000 a year for various company-required insurance policies and made additional outlays for tires, maintenance, repairs, and renting a FedEx uniform.

Some years, Jean said, her net pay was just $32,000. Jean usually worked sixty hours a week, and if one calculates straight time, her pay came to $10.25 an hour, and if one factors in time-and-a-half pay for when she worked more than forty hours, her base pay came to $8.80 an hour. (Because of an industry-inspired quirk in federal wage laws, most truck drivers are not entitled to time-and-a-half pay for overtime work.)

In order to get a two-week vacation, the drivers generally had to pay FedEx $17.50 a week, or around $900 a year. That helped pay for replacement drivers while they were on vacation. On days that Jean called in sick, she often had to lay out around $450: $125 in wages to each of two drivers because her route was too large to be handled by a single substitute unfamiliar with her route, $80 to rent a truck for each driver, and another $25 in gas for each truck. On those days, FedEx would usually pay her $250 for the deliveries that the replacement drivers made. That left her with a net loss of around $200 for each sick day.

Jean and many other FedEx Ground drivers found it hard to walk away, as much as they might like, because they had invested so much in their trucks. If they left, they might still be stuck with two or three years of payments of $800 a month as well as a final one-time payment of $8,000. Besides, Jean liked her customers.

One morning in August 2004, Jean doubled over in pain while making deliveries at her first stop of the day. When she visited her doctor several days later, he discovered a large bulge in her lower abdomen. The doctor ordered a CT scan, and a day later, while Jean was doing her route, her doctor called to tell her she had a massive tumor and ovarian cancer.

"The doctor told me to stop working immediately, but I didn't have that option," Jean said. She not only finished working that day, a Friday, but worked the following Monday and Tuesday as she struggled to find a replacement driver. She was mindful of FedEx's requirement: "Your route had to be covered." Jean approached her terminal's two on-call replacement drivers—one wanted $900 a week to do her route, the other $750. "They knew they had me over a barrel," Jean said. Since she grossed $1,250 a week on average, she figured that if she paid a replacement driver $750 a week while also paying $125 a week for gas and the equivalent of $200 a week in truck payments, it would have left her about $175 a week to live on, which was "not feasible."

Tuesday became Jean's last day on the job because she started bleeding badly. The next nine days—the days leading up to her surgery—were a blur of CT scans, MRIs, blood tests, and meetings with doctors. For those nine days, the terminal manager assigned an emergency replacement driver to do Jean's route.

On August 21, 2004, surgeons removed a large malignant tumor from Jean's abdomen. They also did a hysterectomy. The next week the doctors told her that she had stage-4 cancer; it had spread to her lungs. They also told her that she would need chemotherapy through the end of December.

Jean had twice beaten breast cancer, and she was intent on beating this, too. "I prayed every day," she said. Ever the optimist, Jean expected to return to her FedEx job in January. She called FedEx Ground's headquarters in Pittsburgh to ask for a leave of absence, and someone there said they would get back to her. Weeks later, a letter arrived from Pittsburgh. It said she was terminated.

"I said, 'Oh, my God,' " Jean said. "I got in my car immediately and went right down to the terminal. I said to the terminal manager, 'I'm not accepting this. You cannot fire me.' I was crazy with anger. I said, 'I can't deal with this right now. I have bigger stuff on my plate. I have stage-4 cancer.' I sat in his office and cried my eyes out because I didn't know what I was going to do. He said there was nothing they could do about it."

Fired and with no income, Jean saw no option but to stop paying the monthly installments on her truck. She had already paid more than $40,000 on it, but now she was powerless to prevent the truck from being repossessed.

"I was devastated," Jean said. "Ten years of beating my brains out for them, and they throw me away like I was a piece of garbage. I'm devastated to think that any human would do that to somebody who doesn't know whether she's going to live or die."

FedEx Ground officials said they had sympathy for Jean's plight, but said they had to terminate her under the company's rules—she was no longer covering her route and she hadn't found a replacement driver.

"I had tried finding a replacement, and then I was on the damn operating table," Jean said. "My hands were tied. How was I supposed to find a replacement?"

Company officials said they were free to terminate Jean because in FedEx's view she was an independent contractor and therefore not protected by the Americans with Disabilities Act. That federal law requires companies to make reasonable accommodations to keep employees who have cancer or other disabilities. Jean has sued FedEx Ground under federal law, asserting that it violated the disabilities act on the grounds that she was an employee, not an independent contractor. Her lawsuit also accuses FedEx Ground of violating a

Massachusetts law that bars companies from discriminating against both employees *and* independent contractors.

"To this day, I still can't understand how they can get away with it," Jean said. "If I was a schlub who didn't do my job, I can understand. But someone who did a real good job and had to fight for my life, who had one year left on my truck after making four years of payments, I just don't understand.

"I held my own to any man. I was equal to the best guy. When someone was interested in working at FedEx, they always had that person ride with me for a day to see what it's all about. They'd say, 'You're going to go with Jean because she'll show you how to do the job right.'

"You work for a company for ten years and you give a hundred and fifty percent," Jean continued. "Customers call in and say how much they like you. I used to go above and beyond. And then I get sick, something totally out of my control. And then to get fired."

Her voice dropped off, then tears streamed down her cheeks.

WHILE SOME COMPANIES try to twist logic and the law to have workers considered as independent contractors, many workers become independent contractors by choice. For many Americans who were downsized or laid off, or saw they were about to be, independent contracting was a lifeboat. Downsized Web designers and accountants wooed away clients they had served while still with their old employers. Laid-off television producers contracted with cable networks to make documentaries. Many of these workers loved their more flexible hours and loved not having to suck up to the boss in vying for raises and promotions. They could take more vacations and have time off with their children when they wanted to. After surveying some of these newly independent workers, the Freelancers Union, a Brooklyn-based group that provides benefits to thousands of freelancers, wrote, "Many of New York's freelancers have happily traded the stress of corporate life for the possibilities—and the insecurities—of working independently."[28] Unlike temps, independent contractors overwhelmingly say they prefer their contingent status to holding a standard job—84 percent say they prefer their alternative arrangement, while just 9 percent say they would prefer a traditional job.[29]

In his book *Free Agent Nation*, Daniel Pink hailed the rise of independent contractors and freelancers, describing free agency as a liberating new form of work that would replace the regimented Taylorism of old with what he called a new "Tailorism"—free agents tailoring their careers to meet their individual needs.[30] Pink points out that it is far easier than in decades past for Americans to make a go of it as free agents because owning the means of production merely requires buying a home computer, a phone, and whatever software is needed. Even though the conventional wisdom is that independent contractors and other free agents have less job security than workers in standard jobs, Pink writes, "As many free agents fashion a diversified portfolio of multiple clients, customers, and projects, they often find themselves more secure than traditional employees."[31]

In surveying 2,836 freelancers and independent contractors, the Freelancers Union found that 87 percent said their flexible schedules were an advantage, 71 percent saw the diversity of projects as a good thing, and 63 percent praised the freedom from office politics.[32] The study found disadvantages, too. Sixty-one percent complained of always having to look for work, while 28 percent said they spent part of the previous year without health insurance. The same portion, 28 percent, said they had no retirement savings whatsoever, while 53 percent said they did not put away anything each month for retirement.[33]

There was an unusual uprising of freelancers in December 2007. One hundred such workers at one of the nation's hippest workplaces, MTV Networks, staged a walkout to protest the company's pre-Christmas announcement that it was cutting health and dental benefits and ending 401(k)s for many long-term freelancers. In some departments, 75 percent of MTV's workers are freelancers. Carrying a protest sign that read SICK-ELODEON, Matthew Yonda, who works at Nickelodeon, one of MTV's networks, said, "They call us freelancers in order to bar us from getting the same benefits as employees." Embarrassed by the walkout, MTV scaled back some of the announced cuts.[34]

In *Free Agent Nation,* Pink does plenty of cheerleading for independent contractors and freelancers, seeing a wonderful new style of work in which they peddle their valuable talents for a flexible, low-stress work life. But for many free agents, the reality isn't quite so rosy. Many have of course thrived, but many have stumbled and struggled. Sara Horowitz, founder and president of the Freelancers Union, has developed a slogan for these well-educated but woefully undercompensated free agents: "Welcome to middle-class poverty." Thanks to their solid educations, she said, many freelancers feel middle-class, but their economic life is one of scraping by. Horowitz, whose paternal grandfather was a vice president of the International Ladies' Garment Workers Union, came up with the ingenious idea of creating a union for freelancers. The Freelancers Union is not a typical union that bargains with employers and threatens strikes. Rather, it pools the freelancers' buying power to obtain more affordable health, dental, and disability insurance, and it pools their political power to push for policies such as unemployment insurance for freelancers.

"We're saying that in this century the world has changed, and people are not going to get their benefits from an employer," Horowitz said. "We're creating a new model for how workers get their benefits."

While independent contractors and temps are the quintessential contingent workers, some economists include part-time workers in the category as well. Many companies use part-time workers the same way they use independent contractors and temps, hiring them when business swells and shedding them when it slackens, treating them as a shock absorber to complement their "permanent" full-time employees. For this reason, some economists say, the nation's 18.4 million part-time workers should be viewed as part of the just-in-time workforce.

Whereas temps are more or less balanced between the sexes, more than two-thirds of part-time workers are women. Like temps, part-timers tend to receive worse wages and benefits than standard workers, with one study finding that female part-timers are paid 15 percent less per hour and male part-timers 25 percent less than comparable full-time workers.[35] Only 19 percent of part-timers receive health insurance through their employers and just 23 percent participate in their employer's retirement plan.[36] As for why companies are fond of using part-time workers, Wal-Mart's executive vice president in charge of employee benefits, Susan Chambers, gave a surprisingly explicit explanation in a confidential memo to the company's board. "The shift to more part-time associates will lower Wal-Mart's health-care enrollment," she wrote.[37]

Not long ago some critics of the just-in-time phenomenon were predicting that it would mushroom in size, leaving far more workers insecure and impermanent. But the contingent workforce has not grown nearly as much as some had feared. The number of just-in-time workers climbed from 15.5 million in 1995 to 18.1 million in 2005, but because the workforce grew over that decade, just-in-timers remained more or less unchanged as a percentage of all workers (12.8 percent in 2005).[38] Even when part-time workers are included, the percentage of contingent workers has remained relatively flat over the past decade.

The impermanent workforce has not grown faster for several reasons. Whenever there is a downturn, temps are usually the first workers to be laid off, often causing a sharp drop in temp employment. And in strong economic times, like the second half of the 1990s, the percentage of part-time workers often tumbles because many part-timers who want full-time jobs are finally able to land them. Although corporate executives love just-in-time workers for their lower cost and greater flexibility, they frequently point to three major problems that keep them from hiring more of them: these workers are not committed enough to the firm's success, their turnover rate is too high to enable them to develop the requisite skills and experience, and companies feel they don't have enough control over them. Still, as Paul Osterman of MIT has observed, the just-in-time workforce "has an impact beyond the absolute numbers because regular employees are well aware of contingent employment within their organization and the implicit threat it entails."[39]

Catherine Clarke, a client services officer at JP Morgan Chase, said the threats weren't just implicit. She said several managers had explicitly warned workers that if they continued filing for a lot of overtime—many worked fifty or fifty-five hours a week—they might be replaced with "consultants." Clarke said she and her coworkers took these warnings seriously because they had already seen the company jettison longtime colleagues in favor of so-called consultants. These consultants were often independent contractors who did not receive benefits or time-and-a-half overtime pay when they worked more than forty hours a week.

Clarke said her coworkers continued to come in early and stay late to meet all of their responsibilities, working well over forty hours a week but recording considerably less overtime on their time sheets than before.

In effect, the bank's managers deployed their contingent workers as unconventional weapons to squeeze their conventional employees.

JENNIFER MILLER STILL BRISTLES at the memory of those Christmas Eves. Many Hewlett-Packard workers were away on two-week end-of-year vacations, but there was Jennifer toiling until nine at night, straining to help HP meet its deadline to release its newest laser-jet printer. If Jennifer had a choice, she would not have been there but instead with her twelve-year-old son, preparing for the holiday. But HP's managers knew they could lean on Jennifer to work late on Christmas Eve because she led the precarious, need-to-please life of a temp.

"Basically you're expected to contribute more than a regular employee," she said. "But you shouldn't expect any recognition for it. They can always say, 'You're just a temp. You're out the door tomorrow. Good-bye.' "

But Jennifer wasn't just any temp. Back in 1995, a manager at a temp agency offered Jennifer, then twenty-nine, a three-week assignment at Hewlett-Packard's laser-jet factory in Boise, Idaho. Ten years later, amazing as it might sound, she was still a "temp" at HP, receiving lesser pay, benefits, and status than regular workers. She had become that rara avis among contingent workers—a permatemp, a walking and talking oxymoron in the same long-term limbo as thousands of other long-term temps, not just at Hewlett-Packard but at other blue-chip giants including Microsoft, Verizon, and Intel.

Jennifer is five feet four and unusually open, friendly, and talkative. She has a warm, uninhibited smile, lively brown eyes, and long dark brown hair with bangs that cover her thick eyebrows. In her years as a temp at HP, she held a surprising number of jobs. She did "competitive analysis," comparing the performance of other companies' laser-jet printers with HP's. She worked as a customer service rep at HP's call center, ever so patiently helping consumers who had technical problems with their printers. She coordinated the final tests on various generations of printers, including a $50,000 digital laser-jet printer, before they were released to the outside world. She had actually served as a manager for several long stretches; at one point she managed thirty-six call center workers, and at another she supervised a dozen techs who conducted a range of tests on printers about to be released. Although Jennifer's highest degree is a high school diploma, she has an impressive knack not just for learning high-tech processes and procedures but for explaining them to others.

Jennifer's ambivalence about HP is palpable. One minute she hails the company for the opportunities it gave her, and the next she damns it for taking advantage of her. "They have a certain culture and it's really great," she said. "I wouldn't have gotten the opportunities that I did if I wasn't a temp at HP. But it's still kind of a sweatshop mentality. Many nights I worked until ten or eleven. I often had to work sixty, seventy hours a week.

"In everything I did," she continued, "I contributed to a group of people who were all working as a team, working to make profits for the company. When you're working with a team, you feel respected, you feel like part of the team, you're making equal contributions or in a lot of cases a higher contribution. But then they can say, 'You're out of here tomorrow.' That doesn't feel so good. They expect you to invest everything in them, but they don't expect to invest anything in you."

Jennifer had the notion that because she did the same work as HP's regular employees and worked in teams with HP's regular employees, HP should make her a regular employee and give her the same benefits. HP employees often paid $1,800 a year in premiums for family health insurance; Jennifer had to pay $8,400 a year to her temp agency for coverage. "That was so prohibitively expensive," she said. HP's regular employees were enrolled in a comparatively generous retirement plan, but Jennifer said her temp agency contributed nothing to her 401(k). HP provides sizable tuition subsidies to regular employees when they take courses; temps like Jennifer were not eligible.

"The benefits were outrageously better for regular employees," Jennifer said. "And their pay was slightly higher, but that was before you count the profit sharing." Each year HP's regular employees received profit sharing that at times equaled 8 percent of their salaries. There was no profit sharing for the temps.

It is far harder for temps to buy a home than for regular workers, chiefly because mortgage lenders are concerned that the temps could be laid off at any time. As one of Jennifer's coworkers put it: "Here I am working side by side with people who have far more disposable income and far more days off than I do, while I essentially do the same job. They can buy a house, and I pretty much can't. It just doesn't feel right."

The Boise complex where Jennifer worked was immense, resembling a college campus, with its handsome buildings, tidy landscaping, and impressive athletic facilities, which included a jogging track, a basketball court, soccer and baseball fields, and an elaborate fitness center with dozens of exercise machines. At its peak in the mid-1990s, HP's Boise campus had 5,000 employees, and by some estimates more than one in four were temps. But temps couldn't use the athletic facilities.

Temps faced other daily indignities. For more than a year, Jennifer was put in charge of coordinating tests for various laser jets to make sure that the printers and their accompanying software worked properly before a new model was released commercially. "If I didn't say it was ready to go out the door, it wasn't released," Jennifer said. At times, it was Jennifer who made the announcement that a new printer was ready to be shipped to stores and consumers, prompting various underlings to prepare special T-shirts and a party to celebrate the launch. But to Jennifer's dismay, she and the other temps were not invited to those parties.

"You had an HP manager sitting at a meeting saying, 'This project is going to contribute to HP's welfare overall and you're all a valuable part of it, and now we're going to give out gifts,' and then he'd say, 'The temps have to leave,' " Jennifer said. "And then they'd have a cake or give out gifts, maybe a T-shirt, or maybe they'd take all the workers skiing. You know you contributed. You know you did a good job. It's like when someone gives kids cookies, and you're the kid who doesn't get a cookie."

At HP, regular employees were given holidays off, but the company often pushed its staffing agencies to pressure temps to work Memorial Day, July Fourth, and Labor Day to help make sure the company met its deadlines. "If you refused to work those days, you looked bad," Jennifer said. "Besides, the temps didn't get any paid holidays. If we didn't work Memorial Day, we weren't paid anything for that day."

Denying temps the normal perquisites was part of a deliberate HP strategy to ensure that neither the IRS nor a judge would ever conclude that the temps were regular employees. Such a decision might entitle them to many of the benefits provided to regular employees.

Since Jennifer was hired as a temp, she probably wouldn't have considered it unfair if Hewlett-Packard and her first temp agency, Veritest, had given her a pink slip after three months. But when HP kept her on year after year, Jennifer felt that someone was pulling a fast one. At the same time she acknowledged that HP could get away with it because there were so many unemployed and underemployed techies desperate for work. A coworker described HP's reliance on temps this way: "Why buy the cow if you get the milk free? If there is no reason for them to hire you, why bother?"

HP, of course, is by no means alone. Companies across the nation are increasingly using permatemps. The share of agency temps who remained on a job for more than a year climbed from 24 percent in 1995 to 34 percent in 2005.[40]

Jennifer first went to work for HP in 1989 as a full-time permanent worker; her job was installing components into circuit boards at HP's printer factory in Boise. Before that she had been a manager at McDonald's. In 1994, HP was so eager to reduce its headcount as it moved its circuit board production overseas that it persuaded Jennifer and hundreds of others to take a generous buyout.

Just four months after the buyout, a manager that Jennifer knew and liked offered her a three-week "temp" stint at HP—and Jennifer thought, why not try temping? She started at eleven dollars an hour. By 2002, seven years after she began temping, her pay had jumped to twenty-nine dollars an hour, some $60,000 a year, and that was before overtime. Jennifer said that when Manpower—the world's largest temp agency and the one that "employed" her for most of her ten years at HP—was paying her twenty-nine dollars an hour, HP was paying Manpower more than forty-six dollars an hour for her services.

As frustrated as Jennifer was with permatemp-dom, she never considered quitting, partly because she was a single mother with a son to support. (She was divorced in 2000.) "Do you know how many places I can make that type of money with as little education as I have?" she said. "Here in Boise, there's nowhere else to make that kind of money or use those kinds of skills."

In March 2005, Jennifer was laid off because HP was offshoring her job coordinating tests for new printers. (That was the fourth HP position that Jennifer held that was sent overseas.) She is certain she could have gotten HP and Manpower to offer her yet another temp job, but that wasn't going to happen after she joined a lawsuit that asserted that some 3,000 HP temps should be classified as regular employees and be given the same benefits as regular employees. The lawsuit sought class action status and asked for more than $300 million in damages for benefits it said were improperly denied.

HP asserted that the lawsuit had no merit and that Jennifer and the other temps worked for outside contractors, such as Manpower, and not for HP. Manpower did indeed pay her and wrote her performance evaluation, but Jennifer maintains that HP managers oversaw virtually every step she took.

"We were totally managed by them," she said. "Ninety-nine percent of the management came from HP people. It is all a game to make it seem that you're not a permanent employee."

For now HP has prevailed: Jennifer's lawyer withdrew the lawsuit, fearing that the workers would lose because upon being hired Jennifer and the other permatemps were required to sign statements saying they were not HP "employees"—even though they later grew convinced they were employees in everything but name.

HP's top executives certainly have been aware of what happened when permatemps brought a class action lawsuit against Microsoft in the 1990s. They accused Microsoft of improperly excluding them from the discount stock purchase plan available to its regular workforce. (Thousands of regular Microsoft employees had become rich when the shares they purchased skyrocketed in value.) In the late 1990s, Microsoft had 5,000 temps working next to its 17,000 regular U.S. employees, with nearly one-third of those temps working there for more than a year, some for more than five years.

Under federal rules governing discount stock purchase plans, companies must make their plans available to all common-law employees. Microsoft's permatemps said they fit that description because Microsoft supervisors had full control over them, telling them what to do day to day, when to do it, and how to do it. Microsoft asserted that the temp agencies were the real employers. "Many of these agencies are just parasites," said Mike Blain, an organizer with the Washington Alliance of Technology Workers, an affiliate of the Communications Workers of America that has sought to unionize high-tech work-ers. "They hire whomever Microsoft tells them to put on their payroll. Then they process their paychecks, and that's it."[41]

During the litigation, Microsoft said it had the right to choose whom to hire as a permanent employee and whom to hire as a temp. Microsoft's chief exec-utive officer, Steven A. Ballmer, said the permatemps were trying to get some-thing beyond what they had a right to expect. "A temp is a temp," Ballmer said. "People know when they sign up. It's not like we fool anybody."[42]

Microsoft took a public relations beating during the permatemps battle, fueled by workers like Rebecca Hughes, who temped for Microsoft for three years. "If Microsoft cannot afford to treat all its employees well, then no com-pany in the history of the world could," Hughes said. Amy Dean, who headed the AFL-CIO's office in Silicon Valley, said permatemps were "one more strat-egy in which companies are seeking to avoid their responsibilities to their workers."[43]

The United States Court of Appeals in San Francisco ruled against Microsoft, finding that its permatemps were common-law employees and thus should have been included in the discount stock purchase plan. The liti-gation dragged on for thirteen years and ended in 2005 when Microsoft ulti-mately agreed to a $97 million settlement that covered 8,500 workers.[44]

Microsoft overhauled its policies as a result of the dispute. But even when Microsoft ordered its temp agencies to improve their health and vacation benefits and 401(k) offerings, the benefits they offered remained far worse than what Microsoft offered its regular employees. To ensure that its temps would never again be considered common-law employees, Microsoft decreed that as soon as temps reach their 365th day with Microsoft, they have to take a 100-day break before working at the company again.

Despite Microsoft's loss in the courts, HP continues to ape Microsoft's failed practices. The courts may someday rule on the wisdom of that decision.

IF ANY COMPANY HAS COME to symbolize tough-minded management and the squeeze on American workers, it is Wal-Mart, the nation's largest corpora-tion. The giant retailer maintains that its low prices make it the best friend of America's working families. But Wal-Mart's many critics assert that for its workers, its business practices demonstrate that Wal-Mart is leading a race to the bottom. It's time to take a close look at the colossus from Arkansas.

Chapter Eight

WAL-MART, THE LOW-WAGE COLOSSUS

Lee Scott is the head of Wal-Mart, the biggest retailer on the planet, with sales greater than the combined sales of the nation's five next largest retailers and with more employees—1.9 million in 2008—than the combined populations of Vermont, Wyoming, and North Dakota. "The world's most powerful CEO," according to *Fortune* magazine, he earned $29.7 million in salary, bonus, stock awards, and stock options in 2006.[1] Yet Wall Street has essentially given him a "D" in the subject that CEOs care about most—the company's share price. During Scott's first eight years as chief executive, Wal-Mart's stock price fell by 27 percent, representing a $77 billion loss in value—this at a company that posts its share price in the lobby of its headquarters and even outside some employee restrooms. For Scott, the stock's poor performance is frustrating because under him, Wal-Mart's sales and profits have more than doubled; its sales were $345 billion in 2006, its profits were $11.3 billion.[2]

Scott, a down-to-earth guy whose father ran a gas station in Kansas, has other troubles. Not a day goes by that his company isn't pilloried by groups with names like Wal-Mart Watch and Wake Up Wal-Mart, upset that he pays his workers only 59 percent of what his discount rival, Costco, pays, or that tens of thousands of his employees must turn to taxpayer-financed Medicaid because they earn too little to afford the premiums and deductibles for Wal-Mart's health plan. When Alice Walton, a Wal-Mart heiress, paid $35 million for *Kindred Spirits,* an 1849 painting that is a defining work of the Hudson River School, to install it in a museum near Wal-Mart's headquarters in Arkansas, one anti-Wal-Mart group issued a news release pointing out that the $35 million could have bought health insurance for 8,572 uninsured Wal-Mart workers.

Scott has also been criticized by journalists who have written about Wal-Mart's illegal and unethical activities, such as forcing employees to work off the clock and locking its workers in at night, activities we've already discussed, as well as violating child labor laws in Arkansas, Connecticut, Maine, and New Hampshire; having illegal immigrants work seven days a week cleaning its stores; and buying goods from Chinese sweatshops where managers beat workers and hold them in virtual slavery.[3] Blaming the messenger, Scott and other Wal-Mart executives often complain that the company's stock price and image have been hurt mostly because of these *stories* and not the practices themselves.

But in fact Wal-Mart's sales and its share price have been held down partly because of some major marketing mistakes, including apparel designs that didn't catch on, but far more so because the bulk of its customer base, 42 percent of whom have household incomes under $35,000, are hurting due to stagnating wages and soaring fuel prices.[4] Even though Scott and Wal-Mart's corporate PAC donates lavishly to Republicans, Scott has quietly complained that President George W. Bush's tax cuts went disproportionately to the rich, helping lift sales at Neiman Marcus and Saks Fifth Avenue but doing little for Wal-Mart's customers and revenues.[5]

More than forty lawsuits have been brought against Wal-Mart over off-the-clock work, and the company is the defendant in the biggest class action employment discrimination lawsuit in American history. That lawsuit is seeking billions of dollars in damages and accuses Wal-Mart of discriminating in pay and promotions against 1.6 million current and former women workers.

Wal-Mart deserves to be examined in detail because it is immense—it is not just the world's largest retailer but the world's largest company—and because it has a huge influence on retailers and business practices across the United States. Business executives and MBA students alike are assiduously studying how to mimic its low-cost ways. Its sales represent an astonishing 2.6 percent of the nation's gross domestic product. It is three times as large as the world's second-largest retailer, Carrefour of France. Its sales are greater than the combined sales of Target, Sears, Kmart, JCPenney, Kohl's, Safeway, Albertsons, and Kroger. Some retail consultants predict that it will become the world's first $1 trillion company in a dozen years.[6] Each week 130 million shoppers visit its 4,100 U.S. stores, and each year 82 percent of American households shop at Wal-Mart. It is the nation's largest grocer, and will have 35 percent of the nation's food market and 25 percent of the pharmacy market by the end of this decade, according to Retail Forward, a consulting firm.[7] Wal-Mart already sells one-third of the nation's disposable diapers, toothpaste, shampoo, laundry detergent, paper towels, and nonprescription drugs, and some say it could soon capture a 50 percent share for those products. It is the biggest customer of Walt Disney and Procter & Gamble and accounts for 28 percent of Dial's sales, 24 percent of Del Monte's, and 23 percent of Revlon's.[8] Wal-Mart also accounts for 15 percent of the nation's single-copy magazine sales and nearly 20 percent of all sales of CDs, videos, and DVDs.[9]

Over the past decade Wal-Mart has opened more than 250 new stores each year in the United States. Its expansion efforts employ 30,000 construction workers, and its plans call for adding 60,000 employees a year. Wal-Mart has more than 4,000 stores in the United States, including 2,300 supercenters—giant stores that sell groceries in addition to general merchandise—and top company officials say they hope Wal-Mart will one day have thousands of additional supercenters.[10] "In the United States, we have between 8 and 10 percent of the retail sales, non-automotive, non-restaurant, so we can be a much larger company," says Scott.[11]

Ironically, while it is easy for critics to find grounds for demonizing Wal-Mart, it is hard to imagine Scott as some Mephistophelian force. He is a charming man who speaks with Andy Griffith–like folksiness. Under Scott, Wal-Mart has become a national leader in promoting energy conservation and in making low-cost generic drugs available to consumers. When Hurricane Katrina struck, Scott put FEMA to shame by immediately dispatching a giant fleet of trucks to carry bottled water and other necessities to the stricken Gulf Coast.

When Scott became CEO in 2000, his mission was to spread Wal-Mart from rural America into the nation's cities, to expand overseas, and to turn Wal-Mart into a snazzier merchandiser to compete more effectively with its archrival, Target. Scott was responsible for overseeing the efficient shipment of 5 billion cartons of goods each year to more than 5,000 stores worldwide. Scott's mission was also to safeguard Wal-Mart's credo: "Always low prices."

Scott sees himself as a champion of the value-seeking consumer. He is constantly talking up Wal-Mart's role in saving American consumers billions of dollars each year.[12] He often portrays Wal-Mart as the best friend of "working families" (borrowing the vocabulary of the AFL-CIO), saying its jobs and prices have helped millions of struggling families "achieve a higher standard of living." Its low prices give them "a raise" every time they shop at Wal-Mart, he says.[13] Wal-Mart, he adds, is a boon to low-income Americans, its low prices a blessing to the poor, partly because its prices have forced other retailers to cut theirs. But the low wages and modest benefits that Wal-Mart offers have induced other companies to cut their wages and benefits, too, thus squeezing the living standards of the "working families" that Wal-Mart has embraced.

EARLY ON, SAM WALTON, Wal-Mart's founder, recognized Scott as a man to watch. Scott was a quick study, a good talker, an attentive listener, and an astute strategist. He was a wizard at logistics, and he knew how to analyze a difficult situation and then get the job done. He was also hypercompetitive in a company that thrives on competitiveness. (In the years before Wal-Mart helped push Kmart into bankruptcy, Wal-Mart's offices were filled with pictures of Wal-Mart's yellow smiley-faced mascot strangling a red K with a devil's face.)

Scott grew up in Baxter Springs, Kansas, a town of 4,600 best known for a robbery staged there by Jesse James. His mother was a music teacher, and his father owned a Phillips 66 filling station. To pay his way through college—he majored in business at Pittsburg State in Kansas—Scott worked nights at a tire-molding factory. He married before his junior year, and the young couple started humbly, moving into a trailer court. After graduation, Scott went to work for Yellow Freight, the giant trucking company. One day in 1979 he confronted a Wal-Mart transportation executive, David Glass (who later rose to become CEO), complaining that Wal-Mart had failed to pay a $7,000 bill to Yellow Freight. Glass was so impressed by Scott's mix of tenacity and charm that he offered him a job as Wal-Mart's assistant director of trucking. At the time, Wal-Mart had 276 stores, 21,000 employees, and $1.2 billion in sales. An investor who bought $10,000 worth of Wal-Mart stock that year would now be sitting on shares worth more than $4 million.

Scott was perhaps an overly zealous manager. Whenever a Wal-Mart truck driver was caught drinking or arrived late, Scott dashed off notes to every driver, warning of potential discipline. He got under the drivers' skin so badly that one day nine of them went to see Sam Walton to demand that Scott be fired. Walton told Scott to apologize and made him tell the drivers that he appreciated that they had used Wal-Mart's Open Door policy to go over his head to complain.

Chastened, Scott became a kinder and gentler manager. Indeed, he has developed a reputation as a people person with some of Sam Walton's common touch. He inhabits the same modest ground-floor office, laminated wood desk and all, that Walton once used—facing the company parking lot. Like Walton, Scott is a genial, get-along guy. He seems genuinely surprised by all the broadsides that Wal-Mart faces. Regrettably, he says, his job has increasingly evolved into giving speeches and television interviews to try to beat back wave upon wave of criticism. "It has been a hard transition for us going from being the darling to being under attack," he said.[14]

Scott tells everyone who will listen that Wal-Mart's detractors are often unfair and even dishonest. But it seems clear that the critics only want the company to start providing better wages and health benefits. According to

Wal-Mart, its average hourly wage for full-time workers was $10.51 in 2007. One study found that Wal-Mart's average wage was 25.6 percent below the average at large general merchandise stores and 17.5 percent below that at large grocery stores.[15] The annual pay for Wal-Mart's full-time hourly workers averaged $19,100 in 2007—some $1,500 below the poverty line for a family of four.

Wal-Mart provides health insurance to just 50 percent of its employees, compared with 53 percent for large retailers in general and 83 percent for Costco, one of its main competitors.[16] According to an internal Wal-Mart study from 2005, 19 percent of Wal-Mart workers had no health insurance, while 5 percent of its employees turned to Medicaid for coverage. To Wal-Mart's embarrassment, that internal study found that 46 percent of the children of Wal-Mart workers were either uninsured or had Medicaid coverage.[17] This means that taxpayers are paying for health coverage for many of Wal-Mart's workers and their families. In 2005, Wal-Mart paid just $2,660 for health coverage for each of its 560,000 insured U.S. employees, while the nation's major corporations paid an average of $5,600 per insured worker.[18]

Scott often boasts that several studies have found that Wal-Mart's grocery prices are 5 percent to 17 percent lower than those of other grocery stores.[19] But Scott hardly ever mentions that his company's rock-bottom costs make its rock-bottom prices possible.

WAL-MART'S EXTRAORDINARY EXPANSION has of course been fueled by those "everyday low prices." It has made its famously low costs—and prices—possible by pressuring suppliers to hold down prices, building the most efficient transportation system in retailing, creating an extraordinary computer and inventory system, and maintaining rock-bottom labor costs. It creates a ripple effect.

"Wal-Mart comes up in every single labor negotiation we have, whether it's Safeway or Schnucks in St. Louis or the IGA in any number of communities," said Joseph Hansen, president of the United Food and Commercial Workers (UFCW), the main union representing supermarket workers. "They all say, 'We need to reduce our wages and benefits to maintain our profit margins and stay competitive with Wal-Mart.' "

Craig Cole, the chief executive of Brown & Cole Stores, a supermarket chain in the Pacific Northwest, has been vocal about "Wal-Martization" as the retail colossus has expanded in his region.

"Wal-Mart has developed a business model based on being an employer of the working poor," said Cole, whose company provides health insurance to 95 percent of its workers, twice the level at Wal-Mart. "Wal-Mart's business model is undermining communities by pushing out locally owned retailers while driving employee wages down.[20]

"Socially, we're engaged in a race to the bottom," says Cole.[21]

A study led by David Neumark, an economics professor at the University of California at Irvine, concluded that Wal-Mart's arrival in a community depresses wages. The study found that eight years after Wal-Mart enters a county, earnings per worker in that county, retail and nonretail, fall between 2.5 and 4.8 percent.[22] The drop happens because Wal-Mart often drives out retailers that pay higher wages or pressures those that survive to cut their wages.

Wal-Mart's downward pull manifested itself most clearly in Southern California when the state's three largest grocery chains—Safeway, Albertsons, and Kroger, which owns Ralphs—demanded deep wage and benefit concessions because they feared Wal-Mart's plans to open forty supercenters in the state. The grocery chains repeatedly pointed out that their cashiers earned $17.90 an hour on average while Wal-Mart's earned $8.50. The UFCW balked at the huge concessions these chains demanded, but after a four-and-a-half-month strike and lockout in 2003–4 involving 59,000 workers, the union agreed to drastic concessions, including vastly inferior health and pension plans for newly hired workers. (The union's fight was badly undercut by its own poor planning and by embarrassing revelations about the exorbitant salaries paid to its top officials in California.) Under the resulting contract, the three supermarket chains contributed less than $2,000 a year for health coverage for each new full-time employee, enough only for bare-bones health coverage. That was far lower than the $6,900 a year the companies contributed for each full-time worker before the contract showdown. The contract cut starting pay by 90 cents an hour and reduced the maximum that newly hired workers could earn from $17.90 an hour to $15.10.[23] The UFCW was forced to agree to somewhat lesser concessions in its contracts in San Francisco, Sacramento, and Seattle.

"We have been in business for sixty-eight years, and in that period of time we have seen dozens of competitors come and go," said Jack Brown, president of Stater Brothers, a unionized California grocer. "However, Southern California has never seen as big a competitive threat as the Wal-Mart supercenter."[24]

Wal-Mart is known for placing unusually intense pressure on its 61,000 suppliers, often forcing them to squeeze their domestic workers on wages or move their operations overseas or both. Bill Nichol, CEO at Kentucky Derby Hosiery, said Wal-Mart pressed him to move production overseas: "Their message to us, surprisingly, is, 'There's a broad market out there. If you want to focus on the lowest part of the market, it's obvious that you can't do that [by manufacturing] in the United States.' "[25]

Lakewood Engineering and Manufacturing, a Chicago-based company whose plight was analyzed in a Pulitzer Prize–winning series by the *Los Angeles Times*, makes a twenty-inch box fan that sold for twenty dollars in the early 1990s. But the company, facing pressures from Wal-Mart, cut its costs and prices to such a degree that Wal-Mart now sells those fans for ten dollars. Lakewood's owner, Carl Krauss, said he could satisfy Wal-Mart's demands only by increasing automation and by importing the electrical guts of each fan from Shenzhen, China, where Lakewood now makes heaters and desktop fans. As a result, it takes seven workers in Chicago to produce a fan, down from twenty-two a decade ago. In Chicago, Lakewood's workers earn thirteen dollars an hour; in Shenzhen, the going rate is forty cents an hour. Eager to please Wal-Mart, Lakewood now produces 40 percent of its volume in China.

"My father was dead set against it," Krauss said about opening a plant in China. "I have the same respect for American workers, but I'm going to do what I have to do to survive."[26]

WAL-MART'S PHENOMENAL SUCCESS stems from Sam Walton's idea to make money by selling more goods instead of selling goods for more, and from his determination to cut costs to the bone and then cut them some more.[27] Walton founded his empire in 1962 with a single store in Rogers, Arkansas, and he practiced what he preached. When he and other Wal-Mart executives took business trips, he would insist that everybody double up in hotel rooms. When he summoned store managers from miles around to join in the weeklong sprint to prepare a new store for opening, instead of putting them up in hotels, he had them camp out in the soon-to-be-opened store. When Wal-Mart's buyers traveled to Manhattan, they were told to stay at cheap hotels near Madison Square Garden and to walk everywhere, forgoing taxis. In his first few stores he paid many of his workers less than the federal minimum wage, asserting that each store was an individual company that should enjoy a wage exemption available to very small businesses. The Labor Department disagreed.[28]

"In the beginning . . . we really didn't do much for the clerks except pay them an hourly wage, and I guess that wage was as little as we could get by with at the time," Walton wrote in his autobiography.[29]

At the urging of his wife, Helen, he eventually became somewhat more generous, offering his employees modest bonuses, a bare-bones health insurance plan, and discount stock purchases. (Thanks to those stock purchases, some workers who joined Wal-Mart early on have become millionaires.)

Sam Walton's cost-cutting legacy has been passed down to Wal-Mart's current management. Following Walton's example, the company's senior executives have generally viewed overtime—paying time and a half when employees work more than forty hours a week—as an outlandish luxury. In many stores, signs next to the time clock proclaim "Absolutely No Overtime," while managers at some stores use the PA system to tell employees, "No overtime this week."

Wal-Mart tells its store managers that their annual bonus, which can exceed their base salary, will hinge largely on the profitability of their stores. Base salary for store managers generally ranges from $50,000 to $80,000, with annual bonuses for strong performers running from $70,000 to $150,000. In seeking to increase store profits, managers have little control over sales, so they focus on what they can control—costs, especially labor costs.

As discussed earlier, Wal-Mart also orders store managers not to exceed the payroll assigned to their stores. Headquarters tells many store managers to keep weekly payroll between 5.5 and 8 percent of weekly store sales, far lower than the 8 to 12 percent level at most retailers. To squeeze out more profits, headquarters usually requires store managers to reduce that percentage from one year to the next. If store managers exceed that ceiling several weeks in a row, they can be fired or demoted to assistant manager or even to hourly employee, their pay perhaps falling from $150,000 a year to less than $50,000.

These rules, as we've seen, made life miserable for Wal-Mart managers like Melissa Jerkins and Wal-Mart supervisors like Farris Cobb. But Wal-Mart's rules and cost-cutting culture can also play havoc with the lives of its regular employees.

TWO, THREE, EVEN FOUR TIMES A WEEK, Verette Richardson, her husband, and their four children piled into their car and headed south on I-435 to the Wal-Mart supercenter in Kansas City. They viewed the store as the next best thing to Six Flags. The kids loved the toy department, the vast expanses of children's clothes, and the pint-sized jet fighter ride out front that bobbed them up and down for a minute or two.

"I shopped there so much that I thought it would be fun to work there," Verette said. "That was my mistake."

Verette, a large African American woman with a commanding voice and booming laugh, began there as a cashier, but in her eight years at Wal-Mart, she also worked as a front-door greeter, overnight stocker, forklift driver, truck unloader, shopping cart fetcher, guard for the changing rooms, sales assistant in apparel, sales assistant in sporting goods, manager of the layaway department, and manager of customer service.

At first Verette adored working at Wal-Mart—she liked the camaraderie, the atmosphere, talking to the cashiers and customers. But she slowly soured on it. Sometimes, she said, she was forced to work ten straight hours without a break. The store was so understaffed, she said, that some days managers did not let her take her thirty-minute lunch break or the two fifteen-minute rest breaks that Wal-Mart rules promised. One holiday season, the employees were so overstretched and the breaks so rare that the only way Verette could eat lunch was to sneak into a changing room to wolf down a sandwich and chips.

She said the managers were especially stingy about giving bathroom breaks. "They'd say, 'What do you mean, you need me to watch the register for you to go to the bathroom?' They'd say, 'Why don't you hold it in?'" Verette said. "There was one woman—she kept saying, 'I have to go to the bathroom, I have to go.' The woman menstruated on herself. Afterward we had to wrap bags around her so she could get to the bathroom to clean herself up."

Worried that her colleague would get in trouble, Verette shut down her own cash register and rushed over to run her coworker's register. To provide further help, Verette asked another employee to run to get some sanitary napkins and a washcloth, which Verette paid for herself. She was punished for this act of kindness.

"They said I was going to get written up because I left my register without permission. Then I also got written up because I bought some things while I was on the clock."

Fearing that she might someday face a similar emergency, Verette started keeping spare underpants and a washcloth in her pocketbook. Several weeks later, a manager demanded that Verette show him a Wal-Mart receipt to prove that she had not stolen the underpants that were stuffed into her pocketbook.

"I told them, 'Who's going to want this raggedy underwear from home?'" Verette said.

There was one inspiring moment, however, that caused Verette to keep some faith in Wal-Mart. Soon after she was hired, Sam Walton visited the store, and he shooed away the managers to talk with Verette and several other employees.

"You could see the sincerity in his face," Verette said, as if describing an audience with the pope. "When he said, 'People came first' and 'This was family,' you believed him."

Verette said she was willing to put up with a lot because she believed in those preachings. But she grew disillusioned because of an accumulation of things, large and small. Some days, minutes after she punched out to begin her thirty-minute lunch break, the PA system called for Verette by name. The manager then ordered her to run to apparel to answer a customer's questions or rush to sporting goods to help a customer fill out forms to buy a rifle. She was told not to clock back in until after she had finished serving the customers, and as a result, she would work those ten or fifteen minutes unpaid.

At times, the moment she entered the store, even before she walked past the two dozen cash registers up front, a manager ordered her to rush over to a register because the lines were so long and the store so short-staffed. And there was no time, she was told, to go to the back of the store to clock in. Once, she recalled, she worked for two hours at the registers before she had a chance to clock in, but she was never paid for those two hours.

"They wanted us to do a lot of work for no pay," Verette said. "They treated us like little slaves. A company that makes billions of dollars doesn't have to act like that."

Sometimes as soon as Verette clocked out for the day—Wal-Mart workers clock in and out by swiping their identification badges in front of the time clock's electric eye—a manager ordered her to collect shopping carts in the parking lot or to straighten up the apparel and linen departments. That meant working thirty minutes off the clock. Once she worked four extra hours because she was ordered not to leave until she had finished putting together an elaborate floor display of infant cribs. She said she was never paid for those hours; she was too scared to put in for them because that would have pushed her over forty hours for the week. Management had repeatedly warned that if employees did that, they would face the managers' wrath and a write-up.

"They'd say, 'No overtime is permitted, it's not in the budget,'" Verette said. "But they would wait till we got off the clock, and say, 'Can you finish that up? Please wait to take care of these customers here. Can you keep an eye on the front door while I return this item to the shelf? Can you return some items? Can you help finish that project? Because the district manager is doing a surprise visit tomorrow and I want it to look good.' They'd do it every night. The managers sat at the clock, and if they weren't sitting at the clock, they were sitting by the front door. They'd look like parrots just sitting there. One time I'm going home, and they said, 'Did you finish the soft lines?' I told them, 'No, my time is up.' And they said, 'If you don't finish it, I will write you up.' "

Verette said Wal-Mart's managers have ways of getting rid of workers who complain or protest. She is convinced that was why, in her final year at Wal-Mart, management put her on the worst shift and most arduous job—the midnight shift, unloading trucks.

"They worked off intimidation," she said. "They'd get people frustrated, not paying them correctly, not giving them enough hours, giving them too many tasks, giving them mediocre jobs, putting them on the overnight shift, not allowing them to advance. And then they would quit." She said managers often schemed to get African American employees to quit instead of firing them, because if they quit they would have a hard time suing for discrimination.

Verette remembers several times when managers ordered her to spend an additional hour straightening up off the clock even though her husband and kids were waiting outside the front door to pick her up. "Once it got to the point that my husband came in, and he was angry, and he was going off at the manager, and the manager said, 'If your wife can't handle the work we do in the time allotted her, maybe she should look for employment elsewhere.'"

At one point Verette took two months off under the Family and Medical Leave Act to take care of her husband, who was seriously ill. When she returned to work, the store manager told her she was being switched to part-time work. Verette protested because that would slash her weekly pay and jeopardize her health coverage.

"The manager said, 'You have to choose between your family and your job,'" Verette said.

She grew so fed up that she quit.

Verette said she stayed as long as she did only because of her allegiance to Sam Walton and his vision. (He died in 1992.)

"When he said, 'People come first' and 'We're all family,' that was in my head," Verette said. "I felt obligated to this dead man. I promised him I was going to remain a family member. But the new people running Wal-Mart don't treat you like family."

MORE OFTEN THAN HE CARES to remember, Mike Michell stripped thieves of their knives—and sometimes their guns—when he stopped them as they sought to slip out the front door. Surprising as it may seem, Mike loved his job, loved the adrenaline rush of apprehending shoplifters, and he was good at it, catching 180 over a two-year period at the Wal-Mart stores he patrolled in East Texas.

Mike, a member of Wal-Mart's loss-prevention team, was also responsible for cracking down on internal theft. He spied on cashiers to make sure they weren't pilfering money, and he installed hidden cameras not just to watch customers but to keep an eye on the employees who unloaded trucks. Twenty eight years old and built like a linebacker, he was so loyal and trusted that when the retailer's Texas operations needed someone to carry out the delicate—and illegal—task of installing secret cameras to spy on some meat department employees who supported a union, Mike got the assignment. (Federal law prohibits companies from spying on workers because they support a union.) Mike slipped into the stores after they had closed and installed the cameras, including one in a store's walk-in freezer.[30]

Mike loved being part of "Wal-Mart's praetorian guard." "I'd do anything for Wal-Mart," he said. "I couldn't believe they were paying me to do it. Most people said they were going to work. I said I was going to fun."

In the five stores that Mike policed, he had one last, highly unusual responsibility. He was ordered to spy on Wal-Mart workers who had filed workers' compensation claims. Specifically, Mike said he was told to find a pretext to fire those employees once they returned to work after being out for weeks or months with injuries.

"I didn't look at associates as employees," Mike said (*associates* is the word that Wal-Mart uses for employees). "I looked at them as potential thieves. Anytime anyone was injured and filled out a workers' comp claim form, we were told they were trying to get something for nothing, so let's get rid of them. If anyone filed a workers' comp claim that cost Wal-Mart a lot of money, we tried to terminate them. The rationale was, they're faking it."

Mike's love for Wal-Mart began to crack one April afternoon when he was doing what he had done dozens of times before—apprehending a thief. That afternoon, a store manager told Mike that a female shopper was using stolen checks, and Mike chased the woman into the parking lot. She jumped into a bright green Cadillac—he vividly remembers the car—and when Mike approached to write down its license plate number, the woman's companion gunned the accelerator and the car lunged at him. Mike jumped onto the Cadillac's hood and tried clinging to the windshield wipers for dear life. The driver started swerving wildly, hoping to throw Mike off, and it quickly dawned on Mike that to maximize his chances of survival, he had better get off the car before it accelerated to sixty miles an hour and then tossed him off. So Mike let go of the windshield wipers.

"After I hit the ground, the car's front tire came so close to my head I could see pebbles in the tread," he said. "I wound up with a torn rotator cuff and two ruptured disks in my spinal cord. I also wound up with part of my kneecap broken on my left knee. They removed a section of my kneecap."

Eager to show that he was an exemplary employee, Mike went back to work the next day even though he was all bandaged up. "I caught a shoplifter that day," Mike said. "My doctor told me I should do just light duty, but I was so loyal to Wal-Mart that I did everything I could to fulfill all my duties."

Mike tried to work forty-hour weeks, but he soon realized that he couldn't; the pain was too great.

"Just driving to work killed me. Just standing for a few minutes began to hurt. I went to my supervisor. I told him, 'I'm hurt. I need help doing my job.' "

Mike told his bosses that he would need knee surgery and then some disability leave. But Mike said his managers warned him that if he took disability leave, they would demote him to door greeter when he returned. That position paid six dollars an hour and was often reserved for seventy-year-olds supplementing their Social Security. It was far less prestigious than Mike's loss-prevention job, which paid more than twice as much.

Notwithstanding the managers' warnings, Mike opted for surgery and disability leave because the pain was so overwhelming. He told Wal-Mart's managers of his plans to have surgery in a month's time.

A few days later at work, Mike saw the manager of the Wal-Mart where he was based, in Canton, Texas, forty miles east of Dallas, spying on him, keeping tabs on when he arrived and how he spent his time. Mike was sure the manager was looking to find a pretext to fire him.

One afternoon the following week, the store's number two manager got on his walkie-talkie and ordered Mike to rush to the front door to help catch an unruly shoplifter. It was a strapping, overweight seventeen-year-old, and as Mike approached, he saw that the youth was wielding a knife. Mike, his adrenaline pumping, lunged at the shoplifter's hand, tugged the knife out, and jerked the youth's arms behind his back. He then walked him toward the holding area in the back of the store.

"As I tried to search the guy, he kept pulling away," Mike said. "I said, 'If you don't stop, I'm going to put you on the floor.' I believed he was trying to go for another weapon so I pulled his leg out from under him. I didn't slam him down. I just took him to the ground. I had not done anything that had not been done before."

When the police arrived minutes later, they found that the shoplifter was hiding another knife. Mission accomplished, Mike thought he was going to win high praise from management.

But the next day Mike was called into the store manager's office. "They said

I took the guy in back and beat the snot out of him for no reason," Mike said. "I spent an hour and a half in the office arguing with them. I was saying, 'This isn't right. This isn't true.' "

Mike was ordered to step out of the manager's office. "They called me back twenty minutes later and said, 'You're fired for excessive use of force and for assaulting a customer.' "

Mike is convinced he was set up to be fired, just as he used to set up other injured employees. "I know they fired me because I was having a costly workers' comp case," Mike said.

Nowadays Mike hobbles around, unable to run, unable to play baseball or basketball. For three years after the incident in the parking lot, he took Oxycontin to keep the pain at bearable levels. He is in too much pain to hold a job, and, financially depleted, he had to move back into his parents' house. Mike's doctor says he needs fusion surgery on the ruptured disks to relieve the pain, but Wal-Mart insists that its workers' comp subsidiary should not have to pay for the $20,000 operation on his back; it maintains that Mike's disks were deteriorating even before the car crashed into him.

Mike said Wal-Mart was refusing to pay for the operation simply because it wanted to skimp on medical expenses. During his years at Wal-Mart, Mike learned that the costs of a worker's injury—the doctor's visits, the surgery, the paid weeks off—were deducted from the profits of the store where the injured employee worked, hurting not just the store's profits but the store manager's bonus.

After two years of litigation to try to get Wal-Mart's workers' compensation subsidiary to pay for his back operation, Mike and his lawyer surrendered. Injured, unemployed, and with his resources dwindling, Mike turned to the State of Texas for help. Now the taxpayers of Texas, rather than Wal-Mart, will pay for his operation.

ASK LEE SCOTT ABOUT documented abuses of Wal-Mart employees, and he often lays the blame on "knuckleheads," a term that suggests the abuses are unintentional slipups by careless managers. But scores of interviews, affidavits, depositions, and personal statements as well as court testimony make clear that these are not random occurrences.

David Glass, Scott's predecessor as CEO and currently chairman of the board's executive committee, said at the 2005 shareholders meeting, "The original philosophy [of Wal-Mart was] not an employer-employee relationship, but let's make everyone a partner."[31] But at stores across the nation, Wal-Mart managers have systematically used improper and often illegal strategies:

THE END-OF-SHIFT LOCK-IN: When the evening shift ended, some managers locked workers in their stores until they had spent thirty to sixty minutes, sometimes off the clock, straightening up the merchandise.

INTERNAL BANISHMENT: Two union supporters—Katherine McDonald at a Wal-Mart in Aiken, South Carolina, and Angie Griego at a Sam's Club in Las Vegas—said their store managers ordered them not to talk to coworkers during their workday out of fear that they might spread their pro-union views. (Federal labor law prohibits such intimidation and retaliation against union supporters.)

CHILD LABOR: In 2000, the State of Maine fined Wal-Mart $205,650 for 1,400 child labor violations—violations at every one of its twenty stores in the state. The violations included making children work past ten p.m. on school nights and making them work seven hours on school days when the law set a four-hour limit.[32] In 2005, Wal-Mart paid $135,540 in fines after the United States Labor Department found eighty-five child labor violations at stores in Arkansas, Connecticut, and New Hampshire. The department's investigators had found underage workers using dangerous machinery, including cardboard balers and a chain saw.[33]

SLASHING SCHEDULES: In store after store, Wal-Mart managers often drastically slash many employees' work schedules to make their budgets.[34] Sally Wright, an $11-an-hour greeter who worked twenty years at a Wal-Mart in Ponca City, Oklahoma, said that one day management inexplicably cut her back from thirty-two hours a week to just eight. She was convinced the store manager wanted to push her out because the store could hire lower-wage newcomers to take her place. Belva Whitt, a $7.40-an-hour cashier at a Wal-Mart in Tampa, complained that her store reduced her from full-time to part-time many weeks—and some weeks assigned her no hours at all. "I'm a single mother trying to raise my son, so not having that money makes it hard," she said. "Sometimes I have to decide, Am I paying the rent or will I have food on the table?"[35]

OVERNIGHT LOCK-INS: Despite a death in 1988 because of this policy, this practice was still going on in 2004.[36]

MISSED BREAKS: Wal-Mart managers often strong-armed employees not just to work off the clock but to work through their required breaks. A jury awarded $172 million to 116,000 current and former Wal-Mart employees in California over the company's systematic failure to give those workers their thirty-minute lunch breaks over a four-and-a-half-year period even though state law expressly required it. "From the top down to the store manager, it seemed that there was disregard for the laws," said one of the jurors, Jeff Pector, a fifty-two-year-old software developer.[37]

SHAVING TIME: Dorothy English, a payroll assistant at a Wal-Mart outside New Orleans, said one of the store's managers often told her that when employees worked more than forty hours during a given week, she was to log on to the computer and erase several hours from their time records. Jon Lehman, who was the top manager of several Wal-Marts in Kentucky, said shaving time was so prevalent and accepted that a Wal-Mart district manager instructed store managers gathered at a district meeting about a handy trick to keep them from exceeding their assigned payrolls—go into the computer and delete employee hours. Victor Mitchell said that when he became a store manager in Alabama, an aggressive district manager ordered him to start shaving hours. "I was told to get rid of our overtime," Mitchell said.

HIRING ILLEGAL IMMIGRANTS: For years, Wal-Mart had more than five hundred illegal immigrants washing and waxing floors at its stores. Many of these immigrants worked seven nights a week but never received overtime. They were paid off the books and were almost always kept out of the Social Security and workers' comp systems. Wal-Mart's top executives asserted that they knew absolutely nothing about these undocumented workers, saying that they had turned their floor-cleaning operations over to outside contractors. Between 1998 to 2001, federal immigration officials arrested 100 illegal immigrant janitors at Wal-Mart stores in Missouri, New York, Ohio, and Pennsylvania, and in October 2003 they arrested 245 more at sixty Wal-Marts in twenty-one states.

SEX DISCRIMINATION: Evidence in the sex discrimination lawsuit shows that 65 percent of Wal-Mart's hourly employees were female, but just 33 percent of its managers were. In contrast, among a group of large retailers that compete with Wal-Mart, 57 percent of the managers were women, according to a study commissioned by the plaintiffs' experts. Those experts found that full-time female hourly employees at Wal-Mart earned $1,150 less per year than men, while women store managers at Wal-Mart earned $16,400 less than male store managers.[38] Diane Durfey, an assistant store manager at a Wal-Mart in Utah, said that when she told her superiors she wanted to become a store manager, one top manager let her know that "it was maybe not something for women because it means you have to be away from home a long time each day." While working as an assistant manager of a Sam's Club in Riverside, California,

Stephanie Odle learned that a male assistant manager at the store was making $23,000 more than she was earning. "When I went to the district manager, he first goes, 'Stephanie, that assistant manager has a family and two children to support,'" Odle said. "I told him, 'I'm a single mother and I have a six-month-old child to support.'"[39] Wal-Mart denies any system-wide discrimination, saying the problem was limited to a few of its stores.

Other dubious practices have marred Wal-Mart's reputation. David Glass did not distinguish himself for candor when NBC's Brian Ross once asked him about a factory in Bangladesh that made private-label shirts for Wal-Mart. At that factory, child workers, some as young as ten, were often locked in past midnight. Glass insisted that all the workers were over fourteen, even though Wal-Mart's own inspectors had found otherwise. (In Bangladesh, it is often considered appropriate for fourteen-year-olds to work, but not ten-year-olds.)[40]

When *BusinessWeek* found that Wal-Mart was importing goods from a handbag factory in China where managers hit workers and prohibited them from leaving the factory compound for more than one hour a day, a senior Wal-Mart executive denied that his company used the factory, calling the allegations lies. He later admitted that he was not telling the truth and that Wal-Mart had long used the factory.[41]

Embarrassed by news reports about the large number of Wal-Mart workers on Medicaid and food stamps, Wal-Mart officials have denied that their stores ever gave forms to newly hired workers that explained how they could apply for food stamps and Medicaid. But many workers said Wal-Mart managers had distributed those forms during orientation.

In 2006, Wal-Mart workers in many states complained that their managers had pressured them to agree to open availability, that is, to agree to make themselves available for work any time of the day or night, making it difficult to arrange child care or to take college courses. Those who refused open availability often had their hours of employment cut severely. A Wal-Mart spokeswoman in Bentonville insisted that Wal-Mart did not have such a policy.[42]

In the fall of 2005, Susan Chambers, then Wal-Mart's executive vice president for employee benefits, sent the company's board a memo recommending that Wal-Mart cut its health costs by seeking to attract a healthier workforce. To that end, her memo recommended that Wal-Mart "design all jobs to include some physical activity (e.g., all cashiers do some cart gathering)." Her memo added that such moves would "dissuade unhealthy people from coming to work at Wal-Mart." Chambers nonetheless told the news media in interviews that the memo in no way called for discouraging unhealthy people from applying.[43]

Lee Scott said in a CNBC documentary that Wal-Mart had not accelerated the process in which American companies were moving production to China, notwithstanding companies such as Lakewood, the Chicago-based fan manufacturer. In fact, Wal-Mart doubled its imports from China between 2000 and 2005 to $18 billion a year.[44]

"We will always be committed to the highest standards of integrity, even when it hurts," Scott told the 2005 shareholders meeting. "It's just like Dr. Martin Luther King said, 'The time is always right to do the right thing.' "[45]

LEE SCOTT CLEARLY BELIEVES that the good that Wal-Mart does hugely outweighs any misdeeds. He repeatedly boasts that Wal-Mart not only has created more than 120,000 jobs in the last two years but saves American consumers tens of billions of dollars a year. He deserves considerable credit because he has moved to end many of the most glaring illegalities that victimized Wal-Mart workers, illegalities that, when exposed, shocked Wal-Mart's customers, unnerved its investors, and undercut its stock price.

At times, Scott made clear that a major reason for the cleanup was to avoid embarrassment. On an internal Wal-Mart Web site, he warned managers against taking shortcuts such as cheating on payroll. "It's not unlikely in today's environment that your shortcut is going to end up on the front page of the newspaper. It's not fair to the rest of us when you do that," Scott wrote. "Your value to Wal-Mart is outweighed by the damage you could do to our company when you do the wrong thing."[46]

It remains to be seen whether Scott's cleanup campaign will persuade Wal-Mart's managers to comply fully with the law.[47] Many managers will still be tempted, for example, to demand off-the-clock work because of the continuing pressures to minimize costs. It's not easy to change corporate culture overnight.[48]

Scott's campaign to put Wal-Mart on a more law-abiding path has included numerous praiseworthy steps. Orientation for new employees and managers makes clear that off-the-clock work is illegal and will not be tolerated. The company has reprogrammed its cash registers and the handheld electronic gadgets that post prices for merchandise so that workers cannot operate either piece of equipment when they are off the clock. Wal-Mart's computerized time-clock system now signals cashiers when they are due to take their breaks, and both cashier and manager can get in trouble if breaks are not taken. To prevent child labor violations, Wal-Mart has begun using sophisticated software to ensure that teenage workers are not scheduled to work too late or too many hours. To halt the practice of shaving hours, managers are now supposed to obtain an employee's signature every time they use the store computer to adjust that employee's hours. (Some time adjustments are perfectly valid, as when a manager notices that a worker left for the day without clocking out.) Employees can still be locked in, but now a supervisor with a key is always supposed to be on hand to let them out in case of emergency, as I mentioned earlier. To stop sex discrimination, Scott has sought to end the old-boy network, in which Wal-Mart did not post openings and store managers tended to tap their male favorites to become management trainees. Scott has ordered that managerial openings be posted and has called for cutting the bonuses of senior executives who fall short on diversity goals.

In a variation of the Web site message cited earlier, Scott told the 2005 shareholders meeting, "We are stepping up in a way that not only are we going to be subject to less criticism, but we actually will be a better company."

Critics who never have a kind word for Wal-Mart should be applauding these steps. Alas, illegalities continue. Long after Scott began his crackdown on off-the-clock work, Aaron Payne, an army veteran who served in Iraq and then worked at a Wal-Mart in Camden, South Carolina, said an assistant store manager had repeatedly forced him to work unpaid hours after his shift ended. "It happened almost every night," said Payne, who earned $6.25 an hour working in the sporting goods department. "I'd usually have to stay one and a half or two extra hours."[49] Houston Turcott, an overnight manager at a Wal-Mart in Yakima, Washington, said, "They gave big speeches saying they'd fire people for working off the clock, and then they'd take you around the corner and say, 'You have to do what has to be done even if it means working off the clock.' "

Abi Morales, a pet department employee at a Wal-Mart in Orlando, said that even though he regularly worked forty hours a week, some weeks his paycheck mysteriously compensated him for only thirty hours. Morales said that no manager ever asked for his approval before tinkering with his time records. After Morales threatened to hire a lawyer, the store's manager agreed to give him seven hundred dollars in back wages, equivalent to eighty hours of pay that had disappeared through some unexplained legerdemain.[50] Catherine Kandis, a cashier, said that at her Wal-Mart in Kissimmee, Florida, more than a dozen workers complained in late 2004 that their paychecks cheated them out of more than ten hours' pay. The store manager, she said, had told the workers that he needed to cut costs because a series of hurricanes had hurt sales. The manager all but admitted shaving their hours, Kandis said, when he gave the complaining workers an unprecedented "bonus" check.[51]

Jon Lehman, the former manager of several Wal-Marts in Kentucky, warns that managers will continue to feel huge and often irresistible pressures to take shortcuts that harm workers. "Wal-Mart might tell store managers to stop doing this and stop doing that, but they won't show they're serious about ending abuses until they give store managers a more realistic payroll to operate with," Lehman said.

Even though Scott has taken many positive steps, Wal-Mart's critics continue to fire salvos at him day after day for paying wages below the retail industry average and for providing health benefits far worse than what most large companies provide.

The nation's two largest teachers unions, the National Education Association and the American Federation of Teachers, with more than four million members combined, have urged families not to buy school supplies at Wal-Mart because, they say, it treats its workers so shabbily. An anti–Wal-Mart film, Robert Greenwald's *The High Cost of Low Price*, generated a storm of unwanted attention for Wal-Mart, and so did the vote by the Chicago City Council to require Wal-Marts there to pay all employees at least ten dollars an hour and provide three dollars an hour worth of benefits. (Chicago's mayor vetoed the bill.) The large number of Wal-Mart employees who have turned to Medicaid to obtain health coverage has attracted much press attention. In Florida, newspapers wrote that the state's Medicaid program covered 12,300 Wal-Mart workers and dependents when the company had 91,000 employees in the state.[52] At a meeting of the National Governors Association, Christine Gregoire, the governor of Washington State, complained that 20 percent of the Wal-Mart workers in her state receive public health care assistance.[53] Prominent Democrats, including John Edwards and Barack Obama, have taken Wal-Mart to task. "Wal-Mart is making enormous profits and yet it has chosen to go with low wages and diminished benefits," Obama said on a union-sponsored conference call with workers and reporters. "You've got to pay your workers enough that they can actually not only shop at Wal-Mart but also send their kids to college and hopefully save for retirement." All the criticism and bad publicity have taken a toll; a Wal-Mart-commissioned study found that between 2 and 8 percent of consumers have stopped shopping at Wal-Mart because of all the negative press about the company.[54]

For its part, Wal-Mart boasts that it has a generous health plan. Its executives cite occasions when Wal-Mart's health plan spent more than a million dollars on procedures to save a baby born prematurely. Despite such laudable examples, Wal-Mart's main family health insurance plan has long been prohibitively expensive for many workers. The company's standard plan for family coverage called for employees to pay $2,300 a year in premiums as well as an additional $3,000 in deductibles. That's a daunting amount for Wal-Mart's full-time hourly workers, who earn $19,100 a year on average. Susan Chambers, Wal-Mart's top employee benefits official, said in a memo to the company's board that nearly 40 percent of the retailer's employees spend at least one-sixth of their Wal-Mart income on health care.

Wal-Mart says that while its plan is certainly not as generous as a General Motors plan, it is typical for retailers. But one study found that Wal-Mart spends 27 percent less per worker on health insurance than the typical large retailer and that a smaller percentage of its workers are insured.[55]

Distressed by all the bad publicity, Wal-Mart introduced a new health plan in 2005, in large part to increase the embarrassingly small percentage of Wal-Mart workers who sign up for its health insurance. Wal-Mart hailed the new plan as a huge step forward, boasting that its new "value" option had premiums of "as low as $11 a month" with the first three doctor visits free. Despite the huge fanfare, the new plan barely increased the percentage of workers in Wal-Mart's health plan—it remained below 50 percent. Many workers shunned the plan because after the three free doctor visits, the plan's high deductibles kicked in: $1,000 for an individual and $3,000 for a family. Moreover, the "value" plan required workers to pay 20 percent of their medical bills even after they paid their deductibles. These provisions are prohibitive for a group of workers who earn less than $20,000 a year on average.

That much-ballyhooed plan did little to silence Wal-Mart's critics. So in late 2007, again with great fanfare, Wal-Mart introduced another "improved" health plan. In the latest version, premiums remain enticingly low, and employees can get hundreds of prescription drugs for four dollars. But the deductibles, while somewhat lower—now $2,000 for families—remain prohibitive for many Wal-Mart workers. Wal-Mart announced with great pride in early 2008 that employee participation in its health plan had inched up by two percentage points, enabling it to proclaim that it had reached the 50 percent mark.[56]

Scott often responds to critics by saying that Wal-Mart offers competitive wages and benefits. Why else, he asks, would 11,000 people from the San Francisco Bay area apply for 400 openings at a supercenter planned for Oakland?

Why, he asks, should Wal-Mart offer higher wages and benefits if it can obtain the employees it needs at its current pay levels? "It is clear to me that people want Wal-Mart jobs," he said.[57]

Scott recognizes that Wal-Mart has replaced GM and Microsoft as the archetypal American corporation, but he argues that critics are wrong to think that Wal-Mart can provide the pay and benefits that those corporations do. He wrote in a 2005 advertisement that while "Wal-Mart earned roughly $6,000 in profit per associate, Microsoft, by contrast, earned $143,000 per associate." Scott added: "If we kept our low prices and raised our average wages and benefits above today's market levels by a few dollars an hour or so, we would sacrifice a hefty chunk of our profits, hurting shareholders . . . If on the other hand we raised prices substantially to fund above-market wages, as some critics urge, we'd betray our commitment to tens of millions of customers, many of whom struggle to make ends meet."[58]

In response, many argue that Wal-Mart, as the nation's largest corporation, has basic societal responsibilities, and those include paying its workers enough so that they don't have to turn to taxpayers for medical coverage, food stamps, and housing subsidies. Others, such as the retailing analyst Burt Flickinger, argue that Wal-Mart's customer service and efficiency would improve markedly if it raised its wages and benefits enough so that employee turnover dropped sharply. Some say Wal-Mart's internal theft would fall substantially as well. (This strategy has worked wonders at Costco, as we shall soon see.)

Scott's strategy aims to maximize Wal-Mart's profits, but it has not lifted Wal-Mart's share price. Critics argue that if Scott improved wages and benefits, that would help increase the share price by reducing ill will and negative publicity, and just might do so without doing much harm to profits. Such a strategy might defuse the opposition that Wal-Mart faces in New York, Chicago, Los Angeles, and other cities where its expansion efforts have been frustrated. Such a strategy might also win back some of the millions of shoppers who have shunned Wal-Mart in response to all the negative publicity.

If Wal-Mart raised its wages to the very modest average for other general merchandise retailers—other retailers pay about $1.70 more an hour than Wal-Mart on average—that would increase Wal-Mart's costs by roughly $3.5 billion a year.[59] Such an increase would represent 1.3 percent of Wal-Mart's annual U.S. sales ($270 billion). This could be offset by raising its prices by 1 percent, yielding $2.7 billion in extra sales and paring its operating profits by $800 million, still leaving it $10.5 billion in net profit.

Even if there were to be a wage increase, many critics assert that they will not stop battling Wal-Mart until it provides a respectable health care plan. That might mean spending three dollars per hour per worker, the same figure embraced by several big box ordinances. Wal-Mart now spends less than one dollar per hour per worker.[60] The proposed increase in wages and health costs would amount to an $8.1 billion increase in annual spending. To offset that, Wal-Mart might have to increase prices by 2 percent, yielding $5.4 billion, and cut its profits by $2.7 billion. That would still leave $8.6 billion in profits.

Scott would no doubt argue that this would do grievous damage to Wal-Mart's shoppers and shareholders. Scott objects strenuously to the idea of raising prices, even by 1 or 2 percent, to help pay for higher wages and benefits, even though he has often boasted that Wal-Mart's prices are at least 15 percent lower than its competitors' prices. This certainly indicates that Scott's company should face little injury from such a modest price increase. Nonetheless, Scott might well argue that Wall Street would take him to task for such things. But by taking such decisive action, Scott might placate Wal-Mart's critics, eliminate much of the negative publicity, and lift Wal-Mart's stock price.

There's another alternative to improve health coverage for Wal-Mart's workers. With their combined worth of more than $80 billion, Sam Walton's heirs—the world's richest family—could easily donate, say, $3 billion a year to help create a good health plan for Wal-Mart's employees. Just as Bill Gates has donated billions to improve health care for the world's poor, the Walton heirs could donate billions to improve health care for Wal-Mart's poor.

ALAS, IT'S ALL TOO EASY to catalog the ways that myriad companies mistreat their workers, whether leviathans such as Wal-Mart or a small discount store in Brooklyn. Fortunately, there are companies that treat their workers in an exemplary manner, offering far better wages and benefits than their competitors do and showing employees respect and considerateness. These businesses are far too few, but as we shall now see, they have a lot to teach us.

Chapter Nine

TAKING THE HIGH ROAD

James Sinegal is often called the greatest retailing genius since Sam Walton. The gruff, plainspoken Sinegal founded Costco in 1983, and since then he has built the discount warehouse chain into the nation's fourth-largest retailer and the world's eighth-largest.

Costco makes a compelling case that its prices are actually lower than Wal-Mart's vaunted "everyday low prices." As part of its fierce rivalry with Sam's Club, a division of Wal-Mart, Costco also boasts that its discount warehouses, with $130 million in annual sales on average, ring up nearly twice the sales of the average Sam's Club. Costco also bests Sam's with higher sales per square foot, higher sales per employee, and a higher market share. Sam's executives, however, often boast that their prices are lower than Costco's.

"They're full of shit," says Sinegal. "The customers vote on that. They vote at the checkout lines. And why would we do almost twice as much volume as Sam's if their prices are so great?"

Costco and Wal-Mart endlessly debate who has lower prices, but there is no debating which company treats its workers better. Costco is recognized as having the best wages and benefits of any general retailer in the land. Costco workers earn $17.92 an hour on average, 70 percent more than the average full-time Wal-Mart worker and 40 percent more than the average Sam's Club worker.[1] A cashier with five years' experience at Costco can earn as much as a Wal-Mart assistant store manager.

To some hard-nosed observers, it is mystifying why Sinegal would be so generous to his workers. Some suggest that it must be because of his Roman Catholic upbringing. But Sinegal, who grew up in Pittsburgh, the son of a Jones & Laughlin steelworker, said religious teachings have nothing to do with it.

"We are not the Little Sisters of the Poor," he said. "This is not altruistic. This is good business."

When Sinegal founded Costco, he worried that consumers would suspect that the only way Costco could charge such low prices was by paying sweat-shop wages. So, in developing Costco's business model, Sinegal decided that

Costco's workers would receive the best wages and benefits of any general retail workers in the nation. That, he believed, not only would prevent shoppers from thinking that Costco exploited its workers, but would also ensure that his company had a dedicated and productive workforce.

Costco of course is not the only company to do well by its workers. Wegmans, a supermarket chain based in Rochester, New York, has given away $54 million for employee scholarships over the past twenty years. Timberland, the boot company, gives its workers forty hours of paid leave each year to do community service and two weeks of paid leave to take care of an ailing family member. As we shall see, there are other similarly minded employers who do not have extraordinary profits and have more or less typical workforces.

As a result of the business model Sinegal adopted in the 1980s, Costco's wages remain the envy of retail workers everywhere. Costco workers, whether full-time or part-time, start at $11.50 an hour (one dollar above the average wage for all Wal-Mart full-time workers). After four and a half years, Costco workers reach $19.50 an hour, the top of the scale. For full-time employees, that translates to more than $46,000 a year when one includes the $4,200 annual bonus and the company's automatic 4 percent contribution to each employee's 401(k). The annual bonuses rise to $5,400 a year after ten years with the company and to $8,200 after twenty years, while the 401(k) contributions rise to 6 percent of annual pay after ten years and to an unusually high 9 percent after twenty-five years.

"That's good money," said Mark Sjoboen, who was the top manager of a Costco in Missoula, Montana. "These are great jobs in these small towns. Nobody ever leaves." In comparison, a Wal-Mart worker might average $23,000 after four years, a McDonald's shift manager, $27,000, and a Montana teacher with four years' experience, $34,000.

As evidence of how happy his workers are, Sinegal cited the results of a survey that Costco did of its 85,000 U.S. employees. Their main complaint was surprisingly minor—that Costco didn't allow them to wear shorts year-round. (Costco has since changed that rule.)

Wall Street analysts frequently badger Sinegal to be more tightfisted with Costco's workers so that the company can boost its profits. (Its profits were $1.1 billion in 2007 on revenues of $64 billion.) Some of these critics also urge Sinegal to nudge Costco's low prices upward—its low prices have inspired 25 million households and 5 million small businesses to become members. (Membership costs fifty dollars for households and one hundred dollars for businesses.) Costco's five hundred warehouse stores also pull in shoppers because of their unusual mix of merchandise, including bulk groceries, such as giant jars of mayonnaise and huge slabs of cheddar cheese, but also status items such as Coach bags and Waterford crystal, which often cost less than half what they cost in department stores.

One Wall Street analyst took a poke at Sinegal by saying, "At Costco, it's better to be an employee or a customer than a shareholder."[2] But in Sinegal's worldview, the employee and customer come before the shareholder. The first page of Costco's employee handbook states: "In order to achieve our mission we will conduct our business with the following Code of Ethics in mind: 1: Obey the law. 2: Take care of our members. 3: Take care of our employees. 4: Respect our suppliers. If we do these four things throughout our organization, then we will achieve our ultimate goal, which is to 5: Reward our shareholders."

Sinegal has borrowed Sam Walton's idea of seeking to sell more goods instead of selling goods for more, but he has taken that idea a step further than Wal-Mart. Sinegal rarely lets Costco's markups exceed 15 percent. Most supermarkets mark up products by 25 percent, while department stores usually mark up by 50 percent or more. Wal-Mart marks up many products by less than 15 percent, but it marks up some merchandise, especially imports from China, by 100 percent.

I interviewed Sinegal in his astonishingly informal office in Issaquah, a suburb of Seattle. During that visit, he gave me a personal tour of the Costco store 150 yards from corporate headquarters. In the grocery department, he grabbed a package of granola snack mix, ripped it open, and started gobbling it down. "You got to try this," he said. "It's delicious. And just nine ninety-nine for thirty-eight ounces."

Some twenty-five yards away, Sinegal crowed about a private label pinpoint dress shirt. There were boxes and boxes of them—solid white, solid blue, and blue pinstripe—stacked on pallets.

"Look, these are just twelve ninety-nine," Sinegal said while fingering a crisp blue 100-percent-cotton button-down. "At Nordstrom or Macy's, this is a forty-five-, fifty-dollar shirt." Two years earlier, Costco charged $17.99 for these shirts when it was ordering 200,000 of them a year. But they have become such a hit that Costco now orders more than a million a year, enabling it to buy them at a far steeper discount. Sinegal has dutifully passed the savings along to customers.

Sinegal says that if he kowtowed to Wall Street and raised prices, that could spell Costco's doom. "If you follow the evolution of retail, you know that over the years there have been a lot of people who have had very great values who then started raising their prices and raising their prices," he said. "When I started, Sears, Roebuck was the Costco of the country, but they allowed someone else to come in under them [in terms of price]. We don't want to be one of the casualties. We don't want to turn around and say, 'We got so fancy, we've raised our prices,' and all of a sudden a new competitor comes in and beats our prices.

"The traditional retailer will say, 'I'm selling this for ten dollars. I wonder whether I can get ten-fifty or eleven?' " he continued. "We say, 'We're selling it for nine dollars. How do we get it down to eight? We understand that our members don't come and shop with us because of the fancy window displays or the Santa Claus or the piano player. They come and shop with us because we offer great values."

James Sinegal got into the retailing business by accident. After growing up in Pittsburgh, he moved to sunnier California to live with an uncle. In 1954, he was attending San Diego Community College and holding a part-time job—picking up dirty laundry from the sailors on navy ships in port and taking it to a laundry—when a friend told him about a one-day gig unloading mattresses for $1.25 an hour for a new, bare-bones warehouse store called FedMart. Sinegal was invited back the following day, and soon he had a permanent job there. At age twenty-six, he was running FedMart's largest store. Several years later, he was the company's executive vice president for merchandising.

At FedMart, Sinegal learned at the feet of Sol Price, the man who invented high-volume, members-only discount warehouses. Price, whose father was a union organizer in New York's garment district, was also a maverick in the retailing world because he firmly believed in paying his workers handsomely. (Price tells a startling tale about advertising for workers when FedMart opened a store in San Antonio in the 1950s. He placed a Help Wanted ad that offered wages double those of the city's other retailers. Angry at this high-wage upstart, the city's retailers pressured the newspaper to stop running FedMart's ad because it could force them to raise their wages.) After selling FedMart to a German company, Price founded Price Club, and Price Club merged into Costco in 1993.

Costco is able to offer great values while paying its workers handsomely because Sinegal is such a shrewd merchandiser. He knows what customers want and how to drive a hard bargain with suppliers. He keeps costs down by operating no-frills stores (the floors are cement) and by not advertising. For most retailers, advertising represents 2 percent of sales. Sinegal passes that savings on to consumers.

Sinegal says his strategy of paying workers well actually saves money. Sixty percent of American retail workers quit their jobs each year. That means the average worker lasts slightly more than a year and a half. At Costco, turnover is 20 percent, and the average employee stays for five years. Among employees who work at Costco for at least a year, the turnover drops to 6 percent. Those workers stay nearly seventeen years on average. As a result, Costco does not have to train a steady stream of new workers about where to stock the Huggies and how to drive a forklift. Since it costs an estimated $2,500 to hire and train each new employee, that leads to significant savings, helping Costco hold down its prices. At Wal-Mart, annual employee turnover is around 50 percent, in large part because of its lesser wages and benefits. As a result it needs to hire and train more than 600,000 workers a year for its U.S. stores, which costs Wal-Mart more than a billion dollars a year.

Sinegal believes that good pay and benefits translate into a hardworking, loyal workforce that provides superior customer service. That loyalty, he says, helps explain why Costco has one of the retailing world's lowest rates of theft by employees. At Costco, shrinkage is just over one-tenth of 1 percent of sales; the industrywide average is fifteen times that.

With its high wages, Costco has a flood of job applicants, and it usually hires one out of every fifteen who apply. "It's a hard company to get into and it's a hard company to leave," said Joel Benoliel, Costco's director of administration. "You work really hard for your money at Costco. There's a tough work ethic. We tell people, 'You have to work long and hard and smart, and you don't have a choice of two out of three.'"

Karen Jackson, a cashier in Clearwater, Florida, feels huge gratitude toward Costco because in her fifteen years with the company it accommodated her so many times. It transferred her from her first Costco in Fresno, California, to a Costco in Montana and then to one in Orlando, Florida, as her husband transferred between colleges, then tried out for a professional football team, and then began a career in business. "This job helped pay my husband's way through college," said Jackson. She was so eager to remain with Costco that at one point she commuted 107 miles each way to work.

Her latest reason to celebrate Costco is its dental plan—she paid less than $2,000 for braces for each of her two teenage daughters. Without Costco's insurance, she would have had to pay between $10,000 and $20,000 for each daughter. She loves Costco's pay rate of $19.50 an hour for experienced cashiers, nearly triple what cashiers earn at many stores in Florida. "You can't beat that anywhere," she said.

Jackson says she wants to be good to Costco because it has been good to her. "If we're running around when we do our jobs, it's not because someone is cracking a whip," she said. "This may sound corny, but when I go home every day, I want to make sure I've earned my money."

Wal-Mart executives say Costco's wages are so much higher than Sam's mainly because Costco's stores are concentrated on the coasts, with their higher wages and cost of living, while Sam's, like Wal-Mart, is concentrated in rural America. Sinegal says that when Costco's stores are in lower-cost locales, such as Missoula or Florida, they still pay far more than nearby Wal-Mart and Sam's stores. Wal-Mart claims that when a Sam's store is in the same city as Costco, Sam's wages are fully competitive. Sinegal responded to that assertion with a barnyard epithet.

Sam's employees often start at $1.50 an hour less than Costco's $11.50 starting level, but they soon fall far behind. Costco workers receive raises averaging $1.75 (12 to 18 percent a year) for each of their first four and a half years, while Sam's workers receive raises averaging 50 cents a year. After four and a half years, Costco workers jump from $11.50 to $19.50 and receive the equivalent of $3 an hour more in bonus and 401(k) contributions. At Sam's, workers will typically go from $10 an hour to $12.50 after four and a half years, with the company's profit-sharing and 401(k) contribution adding the equivalent of 50 cents more an hour. This means that a full-time Costco worker with four and a half years' experience earns $46,550 a year, 72 percent more than the $27,000 average for a full-time Sam's worker.

Costco's benefits package may be even more generous than its wages. When *Money* magazine ran an article hailing the fifty companies offering the best benefits, Costco was the only retailer on the list, standing alongside investment banks, high-tech companies, and Detroit's automakers. Costco workers generally pay 10 percent of their annual health costs, far lower than the 25 percent average for companies nationwide and the nearly 40 percent paid by Wal-Mart workers. Eighty-three percent of Costco's workers are in their company's health plan, compared with 50 percent at Wal-Mart.

Costco's dental plan, which costs five dollars a week for family coverage, provides free annual checkups and pays for more than 50 percent of most dental bills. Its optical plan provides for free eyeglasses each year and one hundred dollars toward new contact lenses.

"When Jim [Sinegal] talks to us about setting wages and benefits," says John Matthews, Costco's senior vice president for human resources, "he doesn't want us to be better than everyone else; he wants us to be demonstrably better."

Costco has other benevolent oddities. If a store manager wants to fire someone with two or more years on the job, the decision must first be approved by a senior vice president at regional headquarters, perhaps saving a worker from being fired because a manager was having a bad day and lost his temper. To help employees with their family life, Costco tries hard not to schedule work between ten p.m. and five a.m., although employees occasionally must report at four a.m. when trucks are backed up for unloading. Unlike most discount retailers, Costco has thousands of unionized workers and a good relationship with its union, the Teamsters, which represents 14,000 Costco employees.

Costco, of course, is not perfect. An assistant Costco store manager filed a national class action lawsuit against Costco in 2005 accusing it of discriminating against some 650 women in promotions. The lawsuit noted that 17 percent of Costco's top managers were women, while 50 percent of its workers were. Costco denies any discrimination.[3]

Sinegal has made clear that a huge retailer can pay its workers well and still thrive. For that reason, Costco is often called the anti-Wal-Mart. Even though Costco's profits ($8,600 per worker in 2006) were about $2,300 more per worker than Wal-Mart's, Costco's compensation per full-time worker was roughly $20,000 more than Wal-Mart's. Of course, Wal-Mart could choose to pay its workers more if it settled for somewhat lower earnings per share, just as Sinegal has done.

Sinegal's emphasis on treating workers right has, perhaps counterintuitively, made Costco the darling of a sizable group of investors. Many see Costco as a highly ethical company that they want to be part of. Bill Dreher, a retailing analyst, described Costco as a "cult stock."[4] That is one reason its price-to-earnings ratio substantially exceeds Wal-Mart's.

Despite Costco's spectacular record under Sinegal, his salary is just $350,000 a year, with Costco's board giving him an $80,000 bonus and an annual award of some Costco stock.[5] His compensation comes to just one-tenth that of many other CEOs, even though Costco ranks thirty-second in revenue among all American companies.

"I've been very well rewarded," said Sinegal, whose wealth exceeds $150 million thanks to his Costco stock holdings. "I just think that if you're going to try to run an organization that's very cost-conscious, then you can't have those disparities. Having an individual who is making one hundred or two hundred or three hundred times more than the average person working on the floor is wrong."

MANY EMPLOYERS OFFER a few catchy perks, like on-site haircuts, massages at one's workstation, or a valet to take one's clothes to the dry cleaner. But only a handful of employers do an excellent job across the board in how they treat their workers. These companies usually act as they do for one of three reasons: they are carrying out their founder's vision, they are bowing to union pressures, or they want to do their utmost to attract and keep workers who are highly sought after.

Nathan Swartz, Timberland's founder, had a vision of creating an unusually worker-friendly company and then made that vision a reality, even though it often meant accepting slimmer profit margins. "Our company is organized around values," said Jeff Swartz, Timberland's CEO and a grandson of the founder.[6] He carried on his grandfather's employee-friendly legacy by introducing programs like lactation rooms on site and a lifestyle leave program in which workers can accrue up to 144 hours for personal time off, whether to attend their kids' soccer games or to go kayaking or climbing.

"My grandfather taught me how to cut leather," Swartz said. "He also taught me to be courageous and stand up for what you believed in."[7]

As I said, some companies are pressured to take the high road by a powerful labor union and often conclude afterward that it was good business. Kaiser Permanente, the California-based health care provider, after years of friction with the twenty-six unions representing 82,000 Kaiser workers, agreed to a far-reaching partnership with labor that has sharply reduced employee injuries, cut patient waiting times, and yielded $150 million in annual productivity savings for Kaiser. As part of that partnership, Kaiser has promised to retrain every worker it lays off and then place that worker in another Kaiser job with equal or better wages.

High-end employers that depend on a highly skilled workforce, such as accounting firms, law firms, investment banks, and Silicon Valley giants, often provide everything from creature comforts to the ne plus ultra in work-family balance, having concluded that running a model workplace is a smart way to recruit and retain the highly sought-after skilled workers they need. SAS Institute, a software company in Cary, North Carolina, with 5,000 employees, has on site two Montessori child care centers, a health clinic, auto detailing facilities, masseuses, a basketball court, a ten-lane swimming pool, and three cafeterias, one with a lunchtime piano player. The company also maintains a referral system to help employees choose the right college for their teenagers or the right nursing home for their parents. Its corporate culture encourages employees to criticize their bosses, albeit constructively. SAS's chief executive, Jim Goodnight, explained his company's unusual approach this way: "SAS recognizes that 95 percent of its assets drive out the front gate every evening. Leaders consider it their job to bring them back the next morning."[8]

In its 2006 list of the one hundred best companies to work for, *Fortune* wrote that even this pantheon of companies is not immune from the pressures of global competition. It noted that in 2001, thirty-three of the "best 100" paid 100 percent of their employee health care premiums. By 2005 that had dropped to fourteen. The number that offered traditional pensions to new employees had fallen to twenty-seven from forty in 2001. "Sorry, the expectations of even a great employer have to be recalibrated," *Fortune* wrote.

When *Fortune* first published its best 100 list in 1998, seventy-one of the companies were publicly traded; in 2006, just fifty were. Clearly executives at publicly traded corporations feel they need to bow to Wall Street pressures to minimize costs, and that often means less generosity toward their employees. Still, in assessing the best 100, *Fortune* concluded that it is unwise to be ungenerous. "These firms are highly successful," it wrote. "Being a great place to work pays."[9]

"HERE, IT'S MORE LIKE FAMILY"

Wilfredo Graulau wakes up at six-thirty each morning in a dark, quiet apartment in the South Bronx. Thirty-six years after a gunshot wound left his legs paralyzed, Wilfredo remains frustrated, even bitter, that he cannot do more for himself. Though confined to a wheelchair, he used to get around remarkably well, driving himself to work for two decades as a computer instructor at the Fashion Institute of Technology in Manhattan. But because of a hip infection that nearly killed him, he can no longer drive. He cannot even leave his apartment by himself.

Many mornings, Wilfredo says, he feels trapped, wondering how he will ever get through the day. At eleven each morning, his deep funk begins to dissipate with the arrival of Margarita Pillot, a home-health aide who has been caring for him for a year. She puts some Busto coffee up to brew. She lifts the blinds. She starts chatting with him about the Yankees, about politics, about the flowers blooming outside, about her son at Cornell. She asks whether he wants an omelet or a *pollo asado* for lunch. She has gotten to know exactly what buttons need to be pushed to lift him out of his morning melancholy.

The two have been drawn closer by their Puerto Rican roots. Day by day, as she checks his blood pressure and breathing, as she tidies up his apartment full of files and floppy discs, Margarita has grown more attuned to what subjects he loves to talk about and what conversational booby traps she should avoid. Margarita was assigned to Wilfredo after a placement counselor at the agency where she works, Cooperative Home Care Associates, interviewed him at length to determine which home-health aide would be the best one for him.

"I still wake up at six-thirty even though I'm not going anywhere," Wilfredo says. "By ten-thirty, eleven, I'm feeling depressed, thinking that I should be out somewhere, and that's when she starts talking to me, and I start feeling better. She animates me. She gets me to do something."

He thanks Cooperative Home Care for blessing him with Margarita, who is fifty-six, five years older than he is. She is a sturdily built five feet three, with short, reddish-brown hair and old-fashioned steel-rimmed glasses. She has a purposeful air and a cautious smile, as if she carries more than her fair share of worries. For more than a dozen years, Margarita had hopped from one home-care agency to another, finding the same problems at each: low pay, paltry benefits, and callous managers who treated the aides as if they were anonymous, interchangeable parts. But a friend told Margarita about Cooperative Home Care, and she applied, not knowing just how unusual an agency it is.

Tucked into three floors of a pedestrian brick building on 149th Street in the South Bronx, Cooperative is employee-owned, a rarity in the field. Many workplace experts and health care professionals are studying it as a model for low-wage workers across the nation. Cooperative has 1,100 home-care aides—99 percent of them female, nearly all of them Hispanic or African American. Seventy percent of them have spent some time on welfare. Cooperative is also unusual because workers control two-thirds of its twelve-person board of directors, giving the workers the ultimate voice in determining their own wages, benefits, and bonuses (actually dividends). These worker-owners have learned that if they are too generous to themselves financially, that could jeopardize Cooperative's future, as well as their jobs and their ties with their patients.

"The economic literature says workers are inherently stupid and selfish, but that has not played out here," said Rick Surpin, Cooperative's chairman. "They've consistently made decisions that show they care about the longevity of the company and its long-term ability to pay better wages and benefits."

Right away, Margarita could tell that Cooperative Home Care was different. It didn't require that she pay three hundred dollars for a training course, as other agencies do. Nor did it demand fifty dollars for a physical. Even though Margarita had received previous home-care training, Cooperative required her to enroll, at no charge, in its elaborate four-week training program, twice as long as the training offered by most agencies. At other agencies, much of their two-week training is understandably devoted to practical necessities, such as how to do housekeeping and how to arrange for a van to take clients to a doctor appointment. The two extra weeks of training at Cooperative allow far more time to focus on health—how to recognize symptoms of a heart attack, what to do if a patient has a seizure, how to get through to depressed patients.

"Cooperative is better," Margarita said. "They focus more on what's good for the patient."

Cooperative also focuses more on what's good for the worker. At the other agencies where Margarita worked, there was neither health coverage nor paid sick days. The other agencies sometimes threatened to fire Margarita when she called in to say she had to miss work because her son was having an asthma attack. Many weeks the other agencies assigned her just fifteen or twenty hours of work, leaving her unable to make ends meet. (She has three children to support.) At Cooperative, workers with at least three years' tenure are guaranteed a minimum of thirty hours of pay a week, even if they are assigned fewer hours.[10]

In Margarita's previous jobs, she said, "There were no benefits, no nothing. They didn't care about you. At Cooperative, you know everybody, and if you have a family problem, they have a counselor who tries to help you."

Cooperative's average pay is 10 to 15 percent higher than at other home-care agencies in New York, although its average wage—$8.80 an hour—is certainly modest, held down by the reimbursement rate that the State of New York pays home-care agencies.

Because its workers receive better wages, benefits, and treatment, Cooperative has a turnover rate of around 20 percent a year, meaning its workers stay for five years on average. At other New York agencies, the typical worker leaves after eighteen months. For long-term clients, care will necessarily be better—more knowledgeable and more dedicated—if the home-health aides remain the same. Cooperative's low turnover is one reason that health care experts are looking to it as a model.

Marilyn McDowell, a longtime nurse who suffered a stroke that left her right side paralyzed, can attest to the benefits of low turnover. She said that a Cooperative aide had once saved her life because the aide had gotten to know her distinctive needs. Once, McDowell had a seizure, leaving her unable to talk, but thankfully, Celeste Garcia, the aide who had cared for her for three years, knew how to stop her from choking.

"If I have a seizure, she knows exactly what to do," McDowell said. "She knows exactly what to say to the doctor if I can't speak for myself. She's a god-send."

Michael Elsas, Cooperative's president, put the agency's philosophy this way: "The worker is at the center of everything we do. Everything else revolves around that."

At many workplaces, such words are hollow rhetoric. Most home-health agencies do little or nothing to help their employees train for better jobs, for fear of losing them. But Cooperative, with a worker-controlled board that wants to do what's best for the workers, provides low-interest loans and partial scholarships so aides can train to become, for example, nurses or respiratory therapists. If Cooperative's workers arrive late to a client's apartment because of child care problems, the agency doesn't summarily fire them the way many agencies do. Instead, its counselors help employees track down child care to prevent such problems from recurring. Cooperative also gets many of the little things right that make workers feel valued—it has Christmas parties, not just for the workers, but for the workers and their children. To build camaraderie and make Cooperative more than just a place to work, it holds annual boat rides as well as "Fun Fridays"—evenings when dozens of aides gather to watch movies, play bingo, dance, or do arts and crafts.

"I worked at other agencies where you didn't feel any sense of unity, where you felt like just an employee, where you got your paycheck and just went to your cases," said Sabrina Horry, a Cooperative employee for four years. "Here it's more like family. They have things that make you feel good about yourself. You always have someone to talk to if there's a problem."

At Cooperative, one of management's responsibilities is to listen to what the workers have to say. "Here you don't have to be afraid of speaking up," said Vivian Carrion, a Cooperative employee for thirteen years. "If you say something that many people don't agree on, they won't hold it against you. That's what having a voice means. There's respect. I have worked in so many places where the managers are in one place and the workers are on the other side. So many times there is a partition that goes up. Here there is no off-limits. There is no partition."

Surpin, Cooperative's chairman, founded the agency in 1985 after writing his thesis about alternatives to nursing homes. His thesis was a reaction to the 1970s revelations about the horrific conditions in many New York City nursing homes. Inspired by the success of worker-owned cooperatives in the Basque region of Spain, Surpin came up with the idea of creating a worker-owned home-care cooperative instead of a traditional for-profit or nonprofit home-care agency.

"I realized that nonprofits and for-profits treated their workers equally badly," Surpin said. "For-profits did it because it was the way to make money, while nonprofits did it because for them their workers didn't count and their patients and professional staff counted a lot more."

Cooperative's managers say they are able to pay higher wages than for-profit agencies because at those agencies 5 to 8 percent of total revenue typically goes to the owners as profits. At Cooperative, most of that is pumped into wages. Cooperative's far lower turnover rate helps it keep its training budget down. In addition, because so many of the people Cooperative hires are coming off welfare, it receives many government grants to help finance its training efforts, again freeing up more money for wages.

Margarita Pillot will be the first to say that all is not perfect at Cooperative. Many workers complain that the board members they elect are too tightfisted about raises and end-of-year bonuses.

"We'd definitely like a better salary," said Margarita, who earns $8.25 an hour. "It's really hard when you have to pay seven hundred dollars in rent for your apartment."

Over one especially arduous five-year stretch, when government reimbursement rates remained flat, Cooperative's board voted no raises. That pay freeze infuriated many workers, but what helped assuage their anger was knowing that the worker-owners on the board of directors were not receiving raises either.

"When you're a worker-owner, you have to understand what it means to be a worker and owner," said Joann Poue, a longtime board member. "You share in the good, and you share in the not so good."

A MOUNTAIN CLIMBER TAKES A WORKPLACE TO NEW HEIGHTS

The second-floor men's room had a surprisingly pungent smell. Just inside the door was a rack that held a mix of dirty socks, sweaty biking shirts, damp bathing suits, and clammy running shoes. Six wet towels hung near the shower stall, several hinting at mildew. Not just the aroma but the scene itself seemed to belong more to a high school locker room than to a corporate headquarters. But this was the house of Patagonia, the outdoors apparel company that prides itself on letting its employees take their play every bit as seriously as they take their work.

At lunchtime many days, Patagonia designers, marketers, info tech specialists, even the receptionist, go surfing for two hours, while a half dozen employees take a one-hundred-minute twenty-seven-mile bike loop in the hills overlooking the Pacific. Many other workers jog four or five miles, while a handful go kayaking.

One of the sweaty biking shirts belonged to Andy Welling, a sales manager at Patagonia's headquarters in Ventura, California, nearly sixty miles northwest of downtown Los Angeles. Welling had just returned from a lunchtime bike ride, freshly showered and with a ruddy glow. At forty-one, he is a fiend about staying in shape—he bikes several days a week at lunchtime, and joins Patagonia's weekly pick-up soccer game. When Welling takes a two-hour lunch to go cycling, he often makes up for it by working a few hours at home in the evening. Patagonia is mellow about flextime, so much so that the receptionist at its headquarters, an eleven-time world Frisbee champion, is allowed to take three months off each summer to run a surfing school. "I could make quite a bit more money working somewhere else," Welling said. "But to have the quality of life and to remain physically fit, by cycling or going surfing, you can't put a dollar amount on it."

Welling has taken full advantage of another unusual Patagonia offering: the child care center at corporate headquarters. His two boys, five and three, have thrived there, dropped off at nine each morning and picked up at five, with Dad sometimes dropping in to have lunch with them or just to say hi and give a hug. "Being able to have my kids a few feet away from me all the time is fantastic," Welling said. "It is a bonding relationship I never would have had if I were working somewhere else."

Patagonia is not like anywhere else. With 1,200 workers and $250 million a year in sales, it donates 1 percent of its annual sales to environmental groups—over the past two decades, those grants have totaled $20 million. The lunchroom at headquarters is an organic café, with tofu salads, chai tea, and eight types of whole grain bread, with "Save the Condor" posters on its walls. Four days a week at lunchtime, the company offers yoga and Pilates sessions; there are also occasional classes on fly-fishing and knife sharpening. Each year Patagonia lets forty employees take paid two-month internships with the environmental group of their choice—some have worked to protect buffalo in Yellowstone Park or to preserve tropical forests in Guatemala. Patagonia gives a $2,500 subsidy to employees who buy a hybrid car or convert their vehicles to run on recycled cooking oil, for example, the grease left over from making McDonald's french fries. The best spots in the parking lot at headquarters are reserved for the most fuel-efficient cars, and above dozens of parking spots are solar panels, supported by ten-foot stilts, that supply all the power for one of Patagonia's administration buildings.

Patagonia has nine hundred job applicants for every opening. With starter houses in Ventura costing $500,000, it is thinking of building company-owned garden apartments to house newly hired employees who are unable to afford a home in the area. The company sponsors civil disobedience training for employees who want to participate in environmental protests, and it pledges to post bail for workers arrested in such peaceful protests. The company's mission statement calls for making the best outdoor products while doing the least damage to the environment. Its Synchilla fleece vests are made from recycled plastic bottles, and it is one of the few apparel makers that use only organic cotton, which is made without pesticides and thus does less damage to the environment. A half dozen times a year Patagonia brings in well-known speakers to hold forth on environmental issues or on their sporting achievements, such as scaling mountains or surfing Hawaii's famed Pipeline. At headquarters, twenty surfboards are tucked under the stairs to the second floor, and employees are welcome to work barefoot. "When you walk through the front door, we don't want you to stop being the person you are," said Lu Setnicka, a former ski patrol worker who is Patagonia's director of training.

This unusual blend of work, play, family, and environmentalism grows out of the philosophy of Patagonia's extraordinary founder and principal owner, Yvon Chouinard. Born in Maine and raised in Burbank, California, Chouinard was an indifferent student who felt passionate about just one activity during high school: the Southern California Falconry Club. As part of the club's activities, he learned how to rappel down cliffs to visit falcon nests, and out of that grew a lifelong passion for mountain climbing.

Dissatisfied with the soft-iron pitons that were then used for climbing—pitons are small spikes that climbers drive into rock and attach ropes to—Chouinard set out to fashion stronger pitons for himself. He taught himself blacksmithing, but only after going to a junkyard to buy a coal-fired forge, a 138-pound anvil, and some hammers and tongs. He made his first pitons out of an old harvester blade of chrome-molybdenum steel, and soon he was selling friends his high-quality pitons for $1.50 apiece. Many summer days, Chouinard went surfing for three or four hours, then dragged the anvil from his car and started cutting pitons with a cold hammer and chisel right on the beach. For months at a time, he lived on less than a dollar a day, selling his pitons out of his car and pursuing his passions by climbing in Wyoming, Canada, Yosemite, and the Alps.

As demand for his pitons grew, Chouinard decided to be a little less Henry Thoreau and a little more Henry Ford. He rented a corrugated metal shed in Ventura and hired a few smith's assistants, a sales manager, and a bookkeeper. By 1970, his company had become the nation's largest producer of climbing equipment. That year, during a winter excursion to Scotland, he purchased a rugby shirt, and he concluded that the thick, sturdy shirt was ideal for rock climbing. Its collar kept the metal climbing slings from cutting into his neck. When he returned to California, his climbing friends asked for a shirt just like it, and soon Chouinard expanded into the apparel business, importing rugby shirts first from England and then from New Zealand. As the company, then called Chouinard Equipment, grew, it had one unbending rule: the business closed whenever the waves in the Pacific, a quarter mile from the black-smithing shed, were running six feet, hot, and glassy.

"Since none of us wanted to be in business, we wanted to blur the distinctions between work and play," Chouinard said. "We didn't want to go to work slouching every day. We wanted to skip up the stairs two steps at a time. That meant we had to break a lot of rules of business. And that meant we had to have flextime."

To describe his human resources philosophy, Chouinard often cites a quotation from François-Auguste-René de Chateaubriand, the nineteenth-century French writer: "A master in the art of living draws no sharp distinction between his work and his play; his labor and his leisure; his mind and his body; his education and his recreation. He hardly knows which is which. He simply pursues his vision of excellence through whatever he is doing, and leaves others to determine whether he is working or playing."[11]

Back then, Chouinard often joked about his "MBA" philosophy: management by absence. Many years he disappeared from his company for six months at a time—to go ice climbing in the Alps, bonefishing in the South Pacific, or surfing, skiing, and climbing in South America. His was the ultimate flextime, and he trusted his employees to get the job done when he was gone, while of course taking time themselves to go surfing. In his autobiography, *Let My People Go Surfing*, Chouinard makes clear that if he was going to be a businessman, he was going to be an iconoclastic one. "I also knew that I would never be happy playing by the normal rules of business," he wrote. "I wanted to distance myself as far as possible from those pasty-faced corpses in suits I saw in airline magazine ads. If I had to be a businessman, I was going to do it on my own terms."[12]

Chouinard has a simple philosophy that he says ensures that Patagonia's employees do their jobs and don't abuse the extraordinary flextime given them. "Hire the people you trust, people who are passionate about their job, passionate about what they're doing. Just leave them alone, and they'll get the job done," he says.

Shannon Ellis, Patagonia's vice president for human resources, says she is convinced that the company's unusual flextime policies do not hurt productivity. "It gives people an opportunity to clear their minds," she said. "A lot of people recognize that what they have here is unique, and I don't think they want to jeopardize that. They realize, 'Hey, I get to go surfing at lunch. If I screw up, I'm not going to have that opportunity to do that anywhere else.' This is a carrot that you need to manage on your own. What happens if you don't respect that is you go back to work in the rest of corporate America. They've been there, they've done that, and they realize, I don't want to go back."

As Chouinard's business grew in the late 1970s, he and several of his employees began having families. His wife, Malinda, also a climbing enthusiast, proposed setting up a child care center in the administrative building after several workers began bringing their babies to work in cardboard boxes. After months of debate about costs and rules, the Great Pacific Child Development Center came into being. The center, which now cares for seventy-two children, is housed in three of Patagonia's headquarters buildings. The two sections for children under two are in large, brightly colored rooms overflowing with toys, blocks, cribs, and pictures of fish. In the two preschool sections, the children take Spanish lessons and celebrate Peace Week by making flags and talking about the importance of getting along without fighting. There is plenty of playground space, including a slide, monkey bars, swings, and—to make sure the apples don't fall far from the trees—a climbing wall and a space trolley, a ride in which the children, held by a harness attached to ropes, glide several feet above the ground.

Soon after the child development center opened, mothers just days out of the delivery room were dropping off their infants. The center's employees complained that they were in no way equipped to care for days-old infants. Chouinard then decreed that babies had to be at least eight weeks old before they could be left at the center. His decree sparked protests by several Patagonia employees who said they would be forced to stay home for eight weeks without pay to feed their families or make their mortgage payments. Several threatened to quit. At the urging of his wife, Chouinard agreed to give eight weeks' paid maternity leave, quite an unusual policy in the early 1980s.[13] Not long after, he agreed to eight weeks' paid paternity leave as well as eight weeks' paid leave to any employee who adopts a child.

"The paternity benefit is amazingly powerful when you have a career," said Rich Hill, Patagonia's vice president for sales, who took a one-month leave when his son, Zane, was born. "It's one of the most special times in my life. Being away for a month, it's nice to have the support of everybody here. In many other companies, if you're gone for a month, you're gone. Reentry is almost impossible."

To explain his worker-friendly policies, Chouinard said: "All of these things I'm doing are not to have a socialist birth-till-death utopia here. Every one of these things is good business."

If Patagonia didn't have paid maternity leave and on-site child care, Chouinard said, many employees—71 percent are female—might quit after giving birth. With workforce experts estimating that it costs $55,000 to lose a skilled white-collar worker and hire and train a new one, Chouinard figures that the $600,000 annual subsidy that Patagonia gives to the child development center is a smart investment. Thanks to the subsidy, Patagonia's workers pay 23 percent less than the market rate for child care.

Patagonia pays 100 percent of the health insurance premiums for not just full-time workers but also part-time workers. This makes business sense, too, Chouinard says, because it helps attract the gung-ho outdoors types that Patagonia wants—workers who love to climb and surf, who test the company's products as they pursue their passions, who can then convey their expertise and enthusiasm to customers.

Chouinard describes his company in a way that would make most CEOs blanch. "It's an experiment," he says. Patagonia's main goal, he says, is not to make profits but to generate resources and money to promote environmental activism.

Alyssa Firmin, an editor of Patagonia's catalog, benefited from Patagonia's environmental largess, spending a paid two-month internship with Rare, a group that seeks to preserve wildlands in developing nations. She traveled to Guatemala and Mexico to teach classes to local people on how to improve marketing for the ecological tours they give to Americans and Europeans. "I think it is phenomenal that Patagonia would support my interest in making a difference in the world with their money," Firmin said.

Yvon and Malinda Chouinard acknowledge that the company they own could not be nearly so generous toward its workers or the environment if it had gone public. "I went through the process of what it means to go public," Chouinard said. "It would have been the death of my company. You lose all power. You can't take risks. The accountants would say, 'When you do this or that, there is no benefit to the company. What are you doing with other people's [the shareholders'] money?' "

Lisa Pike, who oversees Patagonia's environmental grants and programs, said Chouinard's iconoclastic ways were paying off: "He's proving Wall Street wrong. You can do the right thing and still have an extremely profitable company."

HITTING THE JACKPOT IN LAS VEGAS

Walk down Las Vegas's famed strip and you'll see all these only-in-Vegas wonders: an ersatz Eiffel Tower, a miniature Brooklyn Bridge, a pseudo Venetian palace, and an Egyptian-like pyramid that sends a towering shaft of light into the black desert sky. Another wonder is Graciela Diaz, a petite woman with a jet-black ponytail, driving in her white Dodge Ram pickup to her waitressing job inside the pyramid.

Graciela, a native of Jalisco, Mexico, represents a large and growing number of unskilled newcomers, many of them immigrants, for whom Las Vegas has become a Shangri-la, thanks to a booming economy and an extraordinary collaboration between industry and labor. In Las Vegas, dishwashers, busboys, hotel maids, and hotel janitors can easily gain a foothold in the middle class as well as the opportunity to climb ever higher. In most other cities, those workers would be consigned to poverty.

In 1991, helped by some money sent by a brother in Los Angeles, Graciela flew from Jalisco to Tijuana with her sister to cross into the land of her dreams. Before dawn the next morning, the two women met a coyote, who was to bring them across the border. As he lifted the barbed wire so they could crawl into the United States, a Border Patrol helicopter suddenly appeared, its blades cutting through the still morning air. Graciela nearly panicked.

"We try to hide," she said. "We waited one hour under some bushes."

The helicopter finally flew away, and Graciela and her sister quickly walked a half mile into America to meet a car that took them to San Diego. From there, they were driven to her brother's house in Los Angeles.

Graciela soon landed a job ironing clothes at a cramped apparel factory, a classic sweatshop. The work was dreary, the monotony broken only when the managers screamed and cursed at some unlucky worker. Even after Graciela was promoted to seamstress, she still earned just thirty dollars for her ten-hour days. The sweatshop offered one important dividend, however. It was there that Graciela met Manuel, a burly six-foot immigrant from Mexico who worked as a bundler. Manuel was drawn in by Graciela's broad smile, lustrous dark hair, and easygoing affability, and Graciela was flattered by his attentions.

Obeying Mexican tradition, Manuel asked Graciela's father—he also had moved to Los Angeles—for permission to date her. But Graciela's father refused it, upset that Manuel had once lived with another woman and convinced that he would not be a good provider, for he, too, was earning only thirty dollars a day, just $7,500 a year.

Resolute as always, Graciela let her love trump parental objections. Within a year, she and Manuel were living together in his tiny apartment and Graciela was pregnant. But their rejoicing soon gave way to worry.

"There was no money," Graciela said. "The rent was too high. Some days if we eat, we don't pay the rent. We say, okay, we have to do something because it is not only you and me, it is the baby. We got to go. We have to find something else."

Manuel's sister, a hotel housekeeper in Las Vegas, told them there were good jobs in the city's hotel casinos. Soon they were Las Vegas bound, moving in with Manuel's sister and her husband. Graciela found a job making beds and cleaning bathrooms at a Best Western—monotonous, low-paid work that didn't provide benefits—while Manuel took a job washing eighteen-wheelers at a truck stop. The pay was lousy and the work unpleasant, leaving him filthy at the end of each day. When Manuel heard of a better-paying job removing asbestos, he took that, but after a week he quit, swayed by friends who warned him of the dangers of asbestos.

Soon Manuel's brother-in-law told him that workers were needed to build a giant new hotel casino, the Bellagio, that the entrepreneur Steve Wynn envisioned as the zenith of Las Vegas opulence. Manuel landed a construction job there, became a member of the laborers union, and was delighted with the wages and benefits.

In her imperfect English, Graciela said, "In California, we never thought of buying a house. We couldn't buy many things. Here it's more easy."

In her first three years in Las Vegas, Graciela jumped from one dispiriting job to another. After the Best Western, it was back to seamstress work, sewing costumes for nightclub performers; then back to hotel housekeeping at the Horseshoe Casino and then at the Venetian.

"It's really hard when you come, and you don't know the language," Graciela said. "You want to be somebody, but it's very hard."

When the wife of Manuel's foreman told Graciela of some restaurant openings at the Luxor, the hotel with the pyramid and towering shaft of light, she jumped at the opportunity. She applied for an entry-level unionized job bussing tables, and La Salsa, the Mexican restaurant inside the Luxor, offered her a job. That good news came on her thirtieth birthday.

Her humble job putting out tortilla chips and salsa and clearing enchilada-encrusted dishes paid $10.14 an hour, and that did not include the $5 an hour she averaged in tips. (The waiters share tips with the bussers.) Her $10.14-an-hour wage was the base pay for bussers and waiters in Las Vegas, the highest in the nation. (It's $4.60 an hour before tips in New York City.) Working a seven-hour day, Graciela was on pace to earn $27,000 a year, nearly twice what she made as a hotel housekeeper and three and a half times what she made at the sweatshop. Graciela obtained a green card and became an American citizen through her father, who worked at a car wash in Los Angeles. He had obtained legal status because he had moved to California before the 1986 federal law that granted amnesty to many illegal immigrants.

When the Luxor hired her, Graciela gained access to an extraordinary career ladder. She could take whatever courses she wanted for free at the nation's best training center for hotel and restaurant workers, the Las Vegas Culinary Training Academy. With three thousand workers attending each year, the academy offers a series of courses that enable $27,000-a-year bussers to become $50,000-a-year waiters and, if they continue their studies, $75,000-a-year bartenders and sommeliers. Some even take courses to become sous-chefs and master sommeliers, positions that sometimes top $100,000 a year.

The academy is the offspring of the city's two most powerful institutions: Las Vegas's fast-growing casino and hotel industry, which has a ravenous appetite for trained workers, and Culinary Workers Local 226, an unusually farsighted union. By many measures, the Culinary, as it is called, is the nation's most successful union local. Its membership has more than tripled to 60,000 from 18,000 in the late 1980s, even as the rest of the labor movement has shrunk. The Culinary is such a force that one in ten Las Vegas residents is covered by its health plan. More than 90 percent of the hotel workers on the Strip, where the Bellagio, the MGM Grand, the Paris, and other giant hotel casinos are situated, belong to the union. The Culinary is a rainbow coalition: 65 percent nonwhite, 58 percent female, and 55 percent immigrant, including peasants from Central America, refugees from the former Yugoslavia, and African Americans from the Deep South.

By unionizing such a high percentage of the Strip's workers, the Culinary has made itself a force that the hotel casinos must reckon with. In a remarkable example of the Culinary's strength and willpower, the 550 workers at the Frontier Hotel and Casino went on strike for six years, four months, and ten days, and not a single one crossed the picket line before the Frontier capitulated in 1997. Thanks to its ability to inflict serious economic damage on the hotel casinos, the Culinary has succeeded in pressuring these employers to pay its members well.

"These workers are marvelously better off than elsewhere, and it's largely because of the Culinary union," said Hal Rothman, a longtime history professor at the University of Nevada, Las Vegas. "I call Las Vegas the last Detroit. It's the last place where unskilled workers can still make a middle-class wage."[14]

To be sure, the Culinary's success cannot be separated from the industry's wealth and generosity. But the hotel casinos decided to be generous toward their workers only after the Culinary fought back against several that had sought to break the union. In 1984, the hotel casinos decided to go on the offensive in wage negotiations, all but forcing the union to go on strike. The striking workers stuck together, swarming the streets in massive demonstrations and picket lines. Ultimately nine hundred were arrested. With television cameras whirring, the disturbances and arrests undermined Las Vegas's expensive campaign to present itself as a wholesome (or at least pretty wholesome) resort that had left its tainted past behind. Moreover, the city's hospitality industry realized it was wiser to have a satisfied workforce than a surly one.

"In the service business, the first contact our guests have is with the guest room attendants or the food and beverage servers, and if that person's unhappy, that comes across to the guests very quickly," said J. Terrence Lanni, chairman of MGM Mirage, which owns the MGM Grand, the world's largest hotel, with 5,035 rooms and 8,200 employees.

The Culinary pressured most hotel casinos into signing a good contract, but the union was badly shaken by the 1984 dispute, especially because six hotels that refused to sign a contract had managed to get rid of their unions. To gird itself for future battles, the Culinary brought in veteran organizers who set up vigorous rank-and-file committees in every hotel. To lessen the industry's appetite for confrontation, the union also hired a team of young college graduates to do negative research on the industry. They unnerved several gambling companies by issuing elaborate reports warning Wall Street that certain casinos had dangerously high debt levels and might not be able to withstand a strike.

Seeing that the union had become such a formidable force, the casinos made a strategic shift toward peace and partnership. In 1989, Steve Wynn, who transformed Las Vegas with his grandiose theme hotels, signed a ground-breaking agreement with the Culinary when he opened his first hotel casino, the Mirage, famed for its white tigers and erupting volcano. Wynn said he would recognize the Culinary as soon as a majority of the Mirage's workers signed cards saying they favored a union. In return, the Culinary gave Wynn two big things he wanted. It rewrote archaic contractual language to whittle 134 job classifications down to 30, going far to increase flexibility and efficiency. And the Culinary's parent union, the Hotel Employees and Restaurant Employees Union, used organized labor's lobbying clout to help block legislation in Congress that would have required that taxes be withheld whenever foreign gamblers racked up large winnings. The industry feared that such legislation would drive foreign gamblers away. Inspired by Wynn's example, Caesars Palace, Bally's, Circus Circus, and other hotel casinos soon signed similar labor agreements.

"The last thing you want is for people who are coming to enjoy themselves to see pickets and unhappy workers blocking driveways," MGM's Lanni said. "I swore then that we would never have such problems again."

The casino industry has certainly given the Culinary's workers lots to make them happy. The Culinary's health coverage requires no premium payments whatsoever by union members. Workers pay only a few hundred dollars a year in copayments for prescriptions, doctor appointments, and hospital visits. The Culinary's members usually pay nothing for a basic dental checkup or a filling and ten to forty dollars for a more complicated dental procedure, while workers at nonunion hotels often pay upwards of two hundred dollars.

The Culinary's contract guarantees housekeepers a forty-hour week, while in many cities housekeepers are assigned just twenty-five or thirty hours a week. (Many hotels prefer to keep them part-time to deny them benefits and to leave slack in their schedules so that if occupancy rises, the hotels can increase their hours without pushing them over forty and having to pay time and a half for overtime.)[15] Unionized Las Vegas housekeepers typically earn $548 a week, $29,000 a year. Nonunion housekeepers earn less than three-fifths that in most other cities, averaging $16,000 a year, far below the poverty line.

For members of the Culinary union, all courses at the training academy are free, because the academy's $3 million budget is financed by two dozen unionized hotel casinos that contribute 3.5 cents for every hour that the Culinary's members work. With the help of state and federal training grants, many unemployed workers also take the academy's courses for free.

"Our union's goal and the training center's goal is you can come in as a non-English-speaking worker, come in as a low-level kitchen worker, and if you have the desire, you can leave as a gourmet food server, sous chef, or master sommelier," said D. Taylor, the Culinary's secretary-treasurer. "We want to have a situation where the only limits are your own ambition."

To pursue her own ambitions, Graciela started the academy's course to become a waitress three years after she began working as a busser at La Salsa. On Wednesdays and Thursdays, her days off, she took the academy's six-hour-a-day course to become a waitress.

"I want to jump another step," Graciela said. "I want things to be better for my family. I don't want my family to miss anything."

For five months, she studied the fine points of the food server's trade, such as how many pancakes are in a short stack and the difference between fettuccine and farfalle. One Wednesday afternoon, Graciela and eight other students—a mix of dishwashers, hotel maids, bussers, and the unemployed—were sitting at the Culinary Academy's seven-table diner-cum-classroom. The students came from Russia, Bosnia, Thailand, the Philippines, Mexico—and Montana. The teacher, Natalie Rodriguez, was simulating taking customers' orders in a high-pressure environment. Speaking at machine-gun speed, she rattled off what the daily specials and side dishes were and which salad dressings were available. The teacher then turned to each student and placed an imaginary order, asking each student a few minutes later exactly what she had ordered. One student with scant English fumbled badly, butchering the term "french fries."

Suddenly, the teacher wheeled around and asked Graciela to recite the three daily specials. Graciela, wearing a black apron and black pants, hesitated for a second but then recovered, answering in a low voice, "Chicken Vesuvio, barbecue chicken, and seafood salad."

The teacher was pleased, but said, "Graciela, you have to speak up more."

As soon as Graciela finished the course, La Salsa promoted her to waitress. Now she is responsible for a half dozen tables in the ocher-colored restaurant, where songs from a Mexican crooner are piped in. She greets customers with her big smile and tentative English, often recommending her favorite dish, the fajita salad. La Salsa's signs boast that it sells margaritas by the yard, and Graciela knows to push the restaurant's trademark drink.

Graciela is doing so well that Manuel jokingly tells friends: "She'll be earning so much that I'm going to be able to quit my job and take care of the house. So when she arrives home, there will be steaming food on the table."

In 2002, Graciela and Manuel paid $125,000 for their house on Gold Sluice

Avenue. Their gated community, called Sutter Creek, was built in the desert ten miles north of downtown and is so new that not a single one of its trees is taller than twelve feet. Manuel said they wanted a gated community because they were unhappy with their previous neighborhood. "People from Mexico—I call them paisanos—were burning tires," Manuel said. "They played radios real loud. I was afraid of Cecilia [their daughter] playing outside, that someone would run her over. Here it's quiet and safe for her."

With a sheepish grin, Graciela said her parents could hardly believe how she lives. She and her husband have a forty-eight-inch television set, a satellite dish, a gleaming kitchen with track lighting, and his and hers pickup trucks.

After landing his construction job at the Bellagio, Manuel did grunt work at first, lugging heavy building materials. His large biceps and chest attest to his hard work. He later worked on Steve Wynn's dream project, Wynn Las Vegas, a hotel casino intended to surpass the Bellagio in opulence. There, Manuel worked more with his head than his hands, helping grade the land so that plumbers and electricians could lay pipe and wire. He earns $23.66 an hour, and, with overtime, he grosses more than $60,000 some years.

"I get like twenty times more money than I made in Mexico," Manuel said. He sounded a little guilty about his immigrant success.

"We don't want to take nobody's place," he said. "A lot of people born over here, they don't work so hard because they don't appreciate the opportunities they got. They didn't suffer crossing the border and all that stuff we put up with."

The Diazes have big ambitions for eight-year-old Cecilia: college and then maybe law school. Relaxing after a dinner of rice and chorizo, Graciela and Manuel beamed as they read some comments that their daughter's teacher made on her report card: "With her creative imagination and flair for details, Cecilia has become one of the class's favorite story writers."

One of Graciela's major worries is that she has unwittingly become an inappropriate role model for her eight-year-old. "My daughter says, 'Mommy, let me have your apron,' " Graciela said. " 'I'm going to play. I want to be a waitress. I want to be a waitress because you always have money.'

"I say, 'No, don't be like me,' " Graciela continued. "My husband says to her, 'You have to learn and do everything the teacher says, because one day you're going to be somebody.' "

———

AS WE HAVE JUST SEEN, many corporations believe a happy worker will be a productive worker. Other employers, as we've also seen, are indifferent to this notion. In this age of business at Internet speed, the callousness often manifests itself in a desire for employees to pick up the pace. We will now examine this speed-up and why so many workers feel like the overwhelmed Charlie Chaplin figure in *Modern Times*.

Chapter Ten

OVERSTRESSED AND OVERSTRETCHED

A photograph first published in 1953 shows a throng of men in fedoras streaming onto the train platform in Park Forest, Illinois, with an accompanying caption that reads "5:57, back from the Loop." At the time, the photograph of similarly attired businessmen on a similar schedule returning from work pointed to a worrisome conformity. The picture ran in *Fortune* to accompany an unusually astute article by William H. Whyte, which he expanded into his landmark book about corporate conformity, *The Organization Man.*[1]

Stand on the platform at Park Forest at 5:57 today, and not only are the fedoras gone, but so is the crush of workers streaming home. Many men—and now there are women, too—are pulling into Park Forest two or three hours later. And those who arrive at 5:57 are just as likely to have begun work at 7 a.m. as at 9 a.m. For many of Park Forest's residents, a ten-hour day seems as much the norm nowadays as an eight-hour day did in the 1950s. The 1953 photograph highlighted a haunting conformity, but at least those organization men were home in time to have dinner with the family or catch the last three innings of Johnny's Little League game.

For too many Americans, the conventional, comfortable forty-hour week has given way to the overloaded, overstressed sixty-hour week. If any aspect of the economic squeeze is hitting American workers across the board—white-collar and blue-collar, high-income and low-income, chief executives and janitors—it is the phenomenon of increased stress on the job, a combination of longer workweeks and having to toil harder and faster during one's hours at work.

In most households, not only are both parents working but they, together, are working far more hours than parents did a generation ago, making it harder to juggle work with raising a family and managing a home. Further intensifying the stress, even when Americans are officially done with work, they're increasingly tethered to their jobs, connected by their BlackBerries and cell phones, by the e-mails they receive on their home computers, by the laptops that many feel compelled to take with them on vacation.

"With technology, we're supposed to be available 24/7," said Carl M. Van Horn, executive director of the Heldrich Center for Workforce Development at Rutgers University. "Technology is a stress increaser, not a stress releaser. There used to be an excuse that we couldn't get it out in the mail. But now there is no excuse. The boss might ask, 'Why didn't you respond on your Black-Berry? You mean, you didn't have your BlackBerry with you? What the hell is wrong with you?' This is the new reality. You're supposed to be connected to your business all day long."[2]

One out of six managerial employees worked more than sixty hours a week in 2004, according to the Bureau of Labor Statistics.[3] A sixty-hour week means, for instance, working from eight a.m. to eight p.m., five days a week—and that does not include commuting time. And some CEOs seem eager to let their workers know that sixty or seventy hours might not be enough. Jeffrey Immelt, Jack Welch's successor as GE's chief executive, has boasted that he has worked one hundred hours a week for more than two decades. Little wonder that 67 percent of employed parents say they don't have enough time with their kids and 63 percent of married employees say they don't have enough time with their spouse, up from 50 percent in 1992.[4]

Not just young lawyers seeking to make partner but even many law firm partners in their forties and fifties are toiling seventy hours a week, staying in the office until two a.m. to finish drafting a contract or writing a brief. Middle managers, investment bankers, and many accountants and attorneys com-plain of being called on their cell phones while on vacation, having to jump to attention to answer the boss's demands. One engineer at Electronic Arts, the video game manufacturer, protested about having to work 179 out of 180 days, eighty-five to ninety hours a week, as company officials constantly insisted that there was an all-out sprint to get the next game out the door.[5] Gregg Slager, a senior accountant in Ernst & Young's mergers and acquisitions prac-tice, used to work so many eighty-hour weeks that his wife sometimes took their two boys to the firm's Times Square headquarters in their pajamas so they could have some time with Dad.[6]

At the other end of the economic ladder, low-end workers face a different version of on-the-job stress. Some hotels have ordered housekeepers to clean sixteen rooms each eight-hour shift, up from fourteen rooms, pressuring many to work through their lunch breaks and coffee breaks. Wackenhut, the nation's largest security company, routinely required its guards to work more than sixty hours a week at a nuclear weapons storage facility in Oak Ridge, Tennessee, making federal inspectors worry that Wackenhut's workers were too exhausted to guard the weapons properly.[7] And other security guards, as we've seen, earn so little per hour that they need to work two full-time jobs to support their families.

With many companies shedding one group of workers after another, the employees who survive often have more and more responsibilities heaped on them. Many workers feel internal pressures to perform above expectations, fearing that if they don't, they might be next to lose their jobs to downsizing or offshoring. With organized labor on the decline, fewer workers can turn to unions to check management's demands for them to step up their pace and output. In countless offices, workers feel additional stress from having to do more multitasking than ever before—juggling desk phone and cell phone, plowing through e-mails, poring over spreadsheets, having to put presentations together themselves by using PowerPoint instead of farming those presentations out to the graphics department. Not only that, many companies are using internal instant-messaging systems, so when one's boss IMs a question, an immediate response is expected.

"You're supposed to suck it up," said Professor Van Horn. "The business world is still a very macho world. It usually doesn't accept soft values, notwithstanding a lot of the B.S."

One study found that 40 percent of workers report that their jobs are "very or extremely stressful," while in another study, 26 percent said they were "often or very often burned out or stressed" by their work.[8] In a survey done by the Families and Work Institute, 54 percent of those who responded said they felt "overwhelmed" by how much work they had "at least sometimes" during the previous month, and 27 percent said they felt overwhelmed by their workload "often or very often" during the previous month.[9] In one survey, 29 percent of workers acknowledged that they had yelled at coworkers because of workplace stress, while 23 percent said they had been driven to tears. Fourteen percent said they had worked someplace where machinery or equipment had been damaged because of workplace rage, and 12 percent said they had called in sick at least once because of job stress.[10]

Just a few decades ago, the average number of hours Americans toiled each year put them in the middle ranks among industrial countries, far behind Japan, which many Americans derided as a nation of workaholic drones. But in recent years the United States has surged into the lead. From a certain perspective, this reflects that the U.S. economy has grown far faster than Europe's and Japan's, creating a greater need for workers and hours worked. But the downside is that the average American worker clocked 1,804 hours of work in

2006—three full-time weeks more per year than the average British worker, six weeks more than the average French worker, and nine weeks more than the average German worker.[11]

One surprising result of this spurt in hours is that American workers are no longer the most productive in the world per hour, although because of the huge number of hours they toil each year, Americans can still boast the highest annual productivity per worker.[12]

In many countries there is, in essence, a legal brake that limits overwork. In the twenty-seven countries of the European Union, employers are required to give workers at least four weeks' vacation each year. In Norway and Sweden, workers are guaranteed five weeks' vacation, while workers in France and Spain generally receive six weeks. The United States is the only advanced industrial nation that does not legislate a minimum number of vacation days each year.[13] American workers average just twelve days of vacation annually, and 36 percent of Americans say they do not take all the vacation days due them.[14]

Today's overstressed workplace has spawned the phrase "extreme jobs"— jobs of sixty, seventy, eighty hours a week that often destroy weekends. A group named the Hidden Brain Drain Task Force estimates that 20 percent of the nation's high-income workers hold extreme jobs—jobs in which people are "working harder than any human can sustain for very long." In a survey, 69 percent of these workers said their job undermined their health, 46 percent said their job hurt their relationship with their spouse, and 58 percent said it got in the way of strong relationships with their children.[15]

"Over the past two decades, workaholism has become a creed among Americans of all classes," said an article in the magazine of the Conference Board. "Business magazines and even mainstream media glorify sixty-hour workweeks and Palm Pilot–centered working weekends and vacations." That article further noted that the trend among companies to run around the clock "has begun to reverse the two-century-old industrial paradigm of equating progress with increased leisure."[16]

"ALMOST EVERY DAY I take Motrin 800," said Jackie Branson, a guest room attendant in the elite Towers section of the Chicago Hilton. "It's for my back and my shoulders, mostly."

By the time Jackie finishes cleaning fourteen rooms a day on the "executive" floor of the glamorous Hilton, once the world's largest hotel, her body feels beaten and bone-weary—from pushing her 200-pound supply cart around the hotel's halls, from lifting super-thick 115-pound mattresses to tuck in sheets, from kneeling on bathroom floors to scrub toilets and tubs.

Fifty years old, Jackie looks more like sixty. For the last three years she has taken medication for her blood pressure. Her doctor told her that her blood pressure has climbed in tandem with the pressure of her job.

"The work is harder than when I started," said Jackie, a hotel housekeeper for twelve years. "The mattresses are different—they're heavier. There are more pillows on the bed, and there are heavier mattress pads—they're as thick as sponges."

Jackie is a big-boned African American woman, powerful but not heavy, with strong cheekbones, chestnut-brown eyes, a shock of straight dark hair, and a stern demeanor that occasionally gives way to a sly smile. She wears stylish glasses with sharply curving black frames.

"When I started, we didn't have the coffeemaker, we didn't have the ironing board, we didn't have an iron in the room," she explained. "We didn't have an extra two pillows and a blanket in every room. When I started, it was more focusing on cleaning the room."

The Chicago Hilton, built in 1927 on South Michigan Avenue, boasts that it has 1,544 "richly appointed guest rooms" that combine "historic luxury and contemporary amenities." The double beds used to have two pillows; now they have four. The king beds had three pillows; now they overflow with five. Now each bed takes three sheets instead of two—there is a new, plusher mattress pad, then the bottom sheet, then the traditional top sheet, then a new, fluffier duvet, then a third sheet on top of the duvet. To add a regal touch, there's also a three-foot-long gold-colored roll pillow for every bed.

As hotels make their rooms ever more luxurious to pamper—and attract— business travelers and affluent tourists, Jackie is experiencing the ways that America's widening income disparities can play out in the workplace. The affluent get ever more indulged while many of those who serve them work ever harder.

At times Jackie, one of the nation's 350,000 hotel housekeepers, feels like a foot soldier caught in a competitive war—the Battle of the Beds—in which hotel chains have deployed ever-fancier beds and bedding. The Westin chain fired the first shot with its Heavenly Bed, which includes a nine-hundred-coil mattress, three sheets, a down blanket, a crisp white duvet, and five goose down or goose feather pillows. Then Hilton volleyed back with its Suite Dreams Bedding Program, offering a twelve-and-a-half-inch-deep mattress, a billowy duvet, and a plethora of pillows. Marriott later weighed in with its Revive program, with duvets, softer sheets, a feathered pillowtop, and a stylish bed scarf.

"Every time you turn around there's something new that has been added," Jackie said. "We have to do more and more in each room, but they still have us do the same number of rooms.

"The mattresses we have now—they are so heavy. You can't make the bed without lifting the mattresses. After three or four beds, you feel it in both shoulders. You used to just be able to slide the bedding under—that's when there were two sheets and just a regular blanket. But now you have to lift and hold the mattress. You have to take your knee to help you hold it."

Jackie said her doctor keeps telling her to quit because of all the pressure. "But I can't afford to," she said. "I just think management should do this job for a week. They would see it needs some changes."

Jackie said she doesn't dislike her job. She likes her coworkers and loves the clientele. Her wearied tone turned enthusiastic as soon as she told about some of the celebrities who have stayed on the executive floor: Whitney Houston, Gladys Knight, and Les Brown of the famed "Band of Renown." Her biggest thrill was meeting Muhammad Ali. "You get to talk to them when they're coming out of their room, but you just can't ask for their autograph," Jackie said.

"The only part I'm not happy with the job is how you're treated. The bosses ask you nothing. They tell you everything. They demand this. They demand that," she said.

Jackie grew up on Chicago's South Side. Her mother died when she was five, and she never knew her father. An aunt and a grandmother raised her, and they were painfully strict, insisting that Jackie go to church and not go out with boys. Not surprisingly, Jackie rebelled. Lured by the excitement of gang life, she was drawn to the Disciples, the rivals of the notorious Blackstone Rangers. Before long, she grew terrified of the knife fights and shootings. She joined the federal Job Corps and moved to Oklahoma City, where she received job training and obtained her high school diploma. After returning to Chicago as a far more mature young woman, she worked as a barmaid, grocery store stocker, and office clerk. Hoping to move up, she returned to school to learn more word processing and computer programs. After a semester in school, she saw a want ad for hotel housekeepers and, with her savings account nearly depleted, she applied. "I really needed a job," she said.

Now Jackie arrives at the Hilton around seven-fifteen each morning even though her shift doesn't officially begin until eight. Upon arriving, she fetches a linen cart and hauls it to the stockroom on the twenty-fourth floor, loading it with king-size sheets, double sheets, pillowcases, bath towels, hand towels, floor mats, tissue boxes, toilet paper, and a panoply of Crabtree & Evelyn products, including shampoos, conditioners, and body lotions.

To Jackie, it makes sense to arrive forty-five minutes before clocking in. "We look at it as a way that is helping us, to get our carts ready to help us finish in time," she said.

After loading her cart, Jackie slowly pushes it to her assigned rooms, the linens literally piled up to her eyes. From behind, she resembles a nineteenth-century peddler shoving a pushcart overflowing with household goods.

The moment Jackie enters a guest room, she becomes a model of Taylorist efficiency. First, she does the bathroom, cleaning the tub, checking the drain for hairs, removing the wet towels, scrubbing the sink and toilet, mopping the floor, emptying the wastebasket, wiping the mirror. Then she gets on her tiptoes to clean the bathroom vent. She replenishes the towels, shampoo, soap, and other amenities, and she had better not forget to check inside the hair dryer for dust and stray hairs. "I always say, 'First you take out the dirty, and then you do the fresh,' " she said.

After seven minutes working the bathroom, she's doing the closet. She arranges the hangers, replaces the plastic laundry bags, and straightens up the spare pillows and blanket. Next she's moving through the main part of the room, washing the four water glasses and two coffee cups, taking apart the coffeemaker and removing the grounds, checking if there is any water to be emptied from the iron. It's all continuous movement, not fast, but never slowing. She is dusting the telephone, then the Philips flat-screen television, then the window ledges, then vacuuming the rug, emptying the trash basket, straightening papers on the desk, dusting the nightstand and dresser.

If she finishes a room and there is a stray hair on a duvet or a smudge on a mirror, a supervisor might slap her with demerits. Too many demerits can mean a suspension or firing. Management says it should take fifteen to twenty minutes to clean a regular room and thirty minutes to clean a "departure" room, but Jackie insists that it takes twenty-five minutes to clean a regular room properly and forty-five to clean a room after a guest departs. As a result, she says, many housekeepers are forced to take shortcuts, some days not vacuuming, other days not dusting the television, telephones, and window ledges.

"If you have four or five departure rooms, it's hard to finish everything on time," Jackie said. "Sometimes they'll order you to stay late to finish. But I tell them I can't. I have to pick up my granddaughter, Jasmine, at daycare. And when I say I can't work overtime, they sometimes give me a write-up."

When doing rooms, Jackie saves the hardest task for last—making the bed. After pulling four pillowcases off and pulling four pillowcases on, Jackie strips the bed and then puts on a bottom sheet, a top sheet, the duvet, and then another top sheet. She bends over, strains to lift one edge of the mattress, wedges her knee in, and pushes the sheets and duvet under. She winces.

One man's luxury is one woman's shoulder pain. Some hotel maids complain of having to make twenty-five beds some days, which can mean at least three hours of just doing beds, changing one hundred pillowcases and lifting mattress corners dozens of times. One academic study of 971 hotel housekeepers found that 75 percent experience "very severe" pain and that 84 percent often take painkillers to deal with that pain.[17]

Jackie once sprained her right wrist when a heavy laundry bag filled with dirty sheets got snagged on a stairway landing as she was dragging it to a supply room. "If you injure yourself, they write you up—they say it's your fault," Jackie said. That discourages many workers from reporting injuries. Many workers do not report injuries immediately, hoping they will simply go away. But if an injury nags for several weeks and a worker then reports it, that worker can get written up for not reporting the injury promptly.

The new plusher rooms are a recipe for injuries, say experts such as Phyllis King, professor of occupational therapy at the University of Wisconsin at Milwaukee and the author of an ergonomics guide for hotel housekeepers. "The Heavenly Bed and all that, it's an added strain," she said. "There are bigger things to move, requiring more force. It creates an overexertion problem. Injuries result when there are heavy objects and awkward positions and people start taking shortcuts because they're in such a hurry all day long."[18]

At the Hilton, Jackie says, the housekeepers have so much work during their eight-hour shifts that many skip their lunch breaks or coffee breaks. "The managers say, 'I can't understand why you aren't having lunch,' " Jackie said. "But they know some ladies can't finish their rooms in time unless they don't take lunch."

"I feel wupped, beat, especially at the end of a bad day," Jackie added. "There are ladies that start at eight and don't leave the hotel till eight. They're not happy. Your body shuts down after eight hours. You're just dragging, trying to get finished."[19]

———

IN 2003, the *New York Times Magazine* ran a cover story, "The Opt-Out Revolution," about highly successful women, some with law degrees or MBAs, who had stepped off the career ladder in order to raise families. The story, which focused on several Princeton graduates, was at first applauded for identifying a trend in which women, struggling to balance family and work, had "opted out" in order to focus on family because they thought that would be more meaningful and satisfying than remaining in the careerist rat race. One of the women, a graduate of Columbia Law School, quit her job at a prestigious law firm after she grew frustrated about having to work week after week of thirteen-hour days on a major case, leaving her little time with her six-month-old daughter.[20]

Several feminists attacked the story, saying it improperly suggested that many women were opting out of the workforce. These critics said that only an elite group of women with highly paid husbands or trust funds had the luxury of opting out.[21] "Most mothers do not opt out," said a leading critic, Joan C. Williams, a professor at the University of California's Hastings College of Law in San Francisco. "They are pushed out by workplace inflexibility [and] the lack of supports."[22]

Some feminist critics said that these Princeton graduates didn't have any choice but to quit. The *Times* article described one Princeton graduate, a local television news celebrity in Atlanta, who complained that her fifty-hour weeks were becoming sixty-hour weeks when she was telling her bosses she wanted her schedule scaled back so she could have more time with her son. "The station would not give me a part-time contract," she said. "They said it was all or nothing." So she walked away from her job and her six-figure income.

Professor Williams would call that a push-out, not an opt-out. Williams says too many workers, women and men, feel huge stress because too many employers make it hard to balance work and family. In the days of *Ozzie and Harriet,* this balance was hardly a problem for women, because just 13 percent of mothers with children under seventeen had paying jobs in 1950; today, 70 percent do.[23] In two-thirds of married couples with children, both the husband and wife work, and in half of married couples with children, the wife works full-time.[24] In her book on the work-family balance, *The Time Bind,* Arlie Russell Hochschild noted that 59 percent of mothers with children under six do paid work, and so do 55 percent with children under one, about half of them full-time.[25] One reason for today's increased time bind, as we've seen, is that in the modern middle-class American household, both parents taken together work 540 more hours per year—13.5 more weeks per year—than parents did a generation ago.[26] In two out of three American families with small children in which both parents work, the couples work more than 80 total hours per week.[27] It's hardly surprising that two-thirds of employed parents said in a survey that they didn't have enough time with their children.[28]

Many employers do surprisingly little to help workers juggle work and family. Some retailers post their workers' weekly schedules only a few days in advance, making it hard to plan child care. Many businesses require employees to work overtime at a moment's notice, leaving many workers in a bind when their babysitter is scheduled to leave. Nearly half of American workers are not entitled to paid sick days, and as we have seen, many workers risk getting fired when they stay home to care for their sick children.[29] In a disquieting article called "One Sick Child Away from Being Fired," Williams writes of a bus driver who was fired after she arrived three minutes late to work because her son had suffered an asthma attack. A worker at a meatpacking plant was dismissed because she had left work and rushed to the emergency room on learning that her daughter had suffered a head injury. At one factory, whenever the women were ordered to work mandatory overtime, they told their babysitters to drop their children off in the factory lobby, confounding the security guards. The divorced mother of a severely handicapped seventeen-year-old boy failed to report to her janitor's job one Saturday because her son's caregiver could not work because her own child was sick. For missing work that day, the woman, who had been working sixty-hour weeks for several months, was fired after twenty-seven years on the job.[30]

The time bind seems to apply equally to successful white-collar women whose jobs demand more than fifty hours a week and struggling blue-collar women who face problems like mandatory overtime.

"We live in a 'she should work' world," Hochschild wrote. "But we trek to jobs in companies with 'she shouldn't work' cultures."[31]

The time squeeze often applies to men as well. At one factory, a grandfather—in a situation somewhat similar to Jackie Branson's—was fired for insubordination when he refused to remain at work after being ordered to work overtime. He had to rush home to take care of his grandchild.[32]

Lisa Belkin, who has long written about work life issues for the *New York Times*, once wrote that "a modern woman's life journey (and the life journey of any parents who actually wish to spend time with their children) requires [a road with] detours and slow lanes and on-ramps and off-ramps."[33] But many employers refuse to provide slow lanes, and as a result, many women with children feel pushed out. When women do take an off-ramp, it is often at considerable cost. For every two years that a woman is out of the labor force, her earnings drop by about 10 percent. That "mommy penalty" lasts throughout her career.[34] Women who leave the workforce, whether for a year or a decade, also worry about not contributing to their 401(k)s or Social Security accounts. Women who try to balance job and family by working part-time often suffer because part-time female workers generally earn 15 percent less per hour than their full-time counterparts.[35] To reduce the penalty for those who turn to part-time work to balance job and family, the European Union requires that employers pro-rate the pay and benefits to part-time employees so their hourly compensation is comparable to what full-time workers receive.[36]

In addition to the United States' ungenerous approach to vacation days, one study found that of 173 nations surveyed, the United States was one of only four countries—the others are Swaziland, Liberia, and Papua New Guinea— that do not provide paid maternity leave. (Ninety-eight countries provide paid leave for fourteen weeks or more.)[37] As a result—and notwithstanding the Family and Medical Leave Act, which allows American workers to take twelve weeks of *unpaid* leave—many American women feel financially compelled to return to work within two weeks of giving birth.

Working parents are not the only ones who pay a price. According to a study by the Families and Work Institute, companies suffer because employees who are overworked and overstretched make more mistakes on the job and are angrier toward their coworkers and employers.[38] And perhaps toward their customers as well. The nation's overall economy also suffers when women, such as the Princeton graduates in the "Opt-Out" article, drop out of the labor force, because that deprives the nation of the productivity generated by their considerable education, talent, and intelligence.

WHEN PHIL LASKAWY BECAME chairman of Ernst & Young in 1994, about half the accountants the firm hired each year were female. However, most of them left within five years. As a result, less than 5 percent of the firm's partners were women. That troubled him.

"I grew up in the Bronx, right near Yankee Stadium," Laskawy said. "It seemed to me that the smartest kids in the class in grammar school, junior high school, and high school were the girls. This was also becoming more and more true as women were going into the accounting profession. Our top per-formers at the entry level were women, but we weren't keeping them. It seemed like an enormous mistake."

Laskawy was perceptive enough to recognize why this was happening: Ernst & Young's culture was too stressful and not very family-friendly. At the time, it was not unusual for junior accountants to work twenty-four hours straight, shower in the office, and then soldier on the next day. Some partners in the mergers and acquisitions department often worked until midnight five nights a week, plowing through mountains of financial records on takeover targets to discover any hidden problems. "When I started, if you wanted to leave at seven at night to watch your son's basketball game, you had to stay," said one longtime partner. "That's just how it was. It was a work-comes-first mentality."

Many young women at the firm feared that if they had children, the demands of the job would be incompatible with the demands of being a good mother.

"Clearly part of our retention problem was that people were feeling too stressed out and working too many hours," Laskawy said. "From the firm's selfish point of view, we saw we were letting our best people go." So Laskawy began a revolution to make Ernst & Young more family-friendly. In 1996, it created a program of flexible work arrangements, allowing any number of permutations: working four days a week, working three days a week, working sixty hours a week in the months before April 15 and then switching to a three-day week, working full-time during the traditional busy season and then taking the summer off.

Some women were leery of going on a reduced schedule, fearing it would jeopardize their chances of promotion. But Laskawy and his successor as chairman, Jim Turley, backed up their pro-family rhetoric by promoting many women who were on flexible working arrangements. Now 16 percent of the firm's partners are women, and one in three newly named partners is female, a level far higher than that of a decade ago, although the firm's leaders say it's still not as high as they would like. (So as not to discourage workers from adopting flexible working arrangements, Ernst & Young offers full benefits to anyone who works at least twenty hours a week.)

Among those promoted to partner was Carolyn Slaski. For the previous three years, she had been alternating between three-day weeks and four-day weeks, raising her two children, although she occasionally worked six-day weeks during the busy stretch between January 1 and April 15. Slaski, a Rutgers graduate who works in the audit department, made partner thirteen years after joining Ernst & Young—the average length of time to become partner.

"The flexible work arrangements were incredibly important to me," she said. "I'd say there's a real chance I might not be with the firm if I didn't have the opportunity to have that flexibility."

Many of the firm's men eventually admitted that they, too, wanted more flexibility. Now, 2,400 of Ernst & Young's 24,000 U.S. employees are on flexible work arrangements. About 2,000 of them are women and 400 are men. Women are so confident that going on a flexible arrangement won't jeopardize their chances of promotion that 29 percent of the firm's female senior managers—the step before partner—are on flexible arrangements.

When asked whether the firm's flexible policies lead to less productivity, Jim Turley, the current chairman, responded with an emphatic no. He said the firm calculates that the cost of replacing an accountant who leaves is one and a half times that person's annual salary when one adds the cost of hiring and training a new person. The flexible arrangements, he said, help the bottom line by discouraging employees from quitting. "If we have eighty percent of a person's talents and focus, eighty percent of anything is a lot better than zero percent," Turley said.

Ernst & Young made several other sweeping changes in its culture to reduce stress and be more family-friendly. Managers were told to place far less emphasis on face time. The important thing, they were told, was making sure that the work got done and that clients were satisfied. It was fine if a worker went home at three-thirty to attend a child's soccer game and then worked for three hours at home afterward—so long as the employee got the job done.

"We tell managers, 'Don't take attendance to measure results,' " said Maryella Gockel, the Ernst & Young executive who oversees the firm's flexibility programs. "Our people aren't looking for shorter hours; they're looking for more flexible hours, for more ability to control their environment, to be treated more like an adult, to be trusted to get the work done."

Whenever a team is set up to serve a corporate client, whether to conduct an audit or do a due diligence of a client's acquisition target, the team—a mix of partners, senior managers, and junior accountants—holds a preliminary meeting to discuss in detail what personal commitments and conflicts each employee has, be it a child's basketball game, a graduation, knee surgery, or a Pilates class. The team then develops an elaborate schedule that accommodates personal needs and the client's needs. The firm seeks to ensure that there is never just one person handling a particular assignment, so that another person can step in if someone needs suddenly to take off for three days, say, to care for an ailing parent.

Turley says the goal is to help employees balance their lives, "to take away the most insidious stress of all—worrying whether there is something more important that is not being taken care of, your family or something else." "Ten years ago we'd pretend someone didn't have a real life," Turley said. "Sometimes a partner would leave at four p.m. and would make believe he was going to another client when he was going to watch his kid play ball. Now we've authorized having a life."

Bill Stoffel, a partner in the mergers and acquisitions practice, remembers when he was spending several intense weeks in London doing due diligence on a large takeover target. One of his twins was scheduled for a tonsillectomy back home in New Jersey. "My wife was very anxious because our daughter had to go under," Stoffel said. She was eager for him to be home for the operation. "So I flew back for the surgery," Stoffel said. "The senior manager really stepped up, making sure that everything was covered. I went home for one day for the operation, and then flew back. At other companies, you would not have been able to do that."

Women at Ernst & Young now get twelve weeks' paid leave when they give birth, and the firm lets them take another ten weeks of unpaid leave under the Family and Medical Leave Act. Most accountants get four weeks and two days of vacation after five years, with many teams letting their members designate two of those weeks as "red zone" weeks that they can't be forced to change no matter how big the crisis. Many teams work with their members so they can shut off their BlackBerries during vacation.

"The team says, 'Don't turn it on. We'll cover for you. We'll only call you in a dire emergency,' " said Gockel.

Ernst & Young gives all its employees four-day weekends for Memorial Day, July Fourth, and Labor Day. With the firm shut down, workers know there is no need to check their voice mail or e-mail because nobody at the firm is supposed to be working.

Jim Turley said the firm's leaders decided to create these four-day weekends because they saw that the demands on the firm's accountants were greater than ever. Those increased demands resulted from the boom in merger and acquisitions activity, the requirement for more thorough audits after the Enron scandal, and the many new clients who turned to Ernst & Young after Arthur Andersen collapsed.

"When the world began changing and there were dramatically increased expectations from the marketplace, the demand got ahead of the supply of our people, and what was normal hard work became unsustainable," Turley said. "So there was dramatically increased work. We tried to figure out what to do to say thank you to our people. We thought about giving them money, but they would have spent it and they would feel good for ten minutes. We concluded that one of the things that our people value most is time with their loved ones. We decided that this four-day thing would be a big hit."

Ernst & Young has adopted an unusual policy to help make sure that the firm's partners do not push their subordinates too hard. Employees get to write a performance review of their boss. "If partners are setting a tone whereby there's not a work-life balance or you're just expected to work like a dog, they get negative reviews," said Rob Johnson, head of the firm's Cleveland office. "It's all anonymous so the staff can write whatever they want—'This guy's a real hard ass, and he makes us work all the time.' Those reviews are read by the leadership of the firm. They're taken very seriously. If someone is rated pretty low, it hits a partner's annual rating. It hits them in the pocket."

Johnson was the partner who said that when he began in 1989, the firm never would have let him leave early to attend his son's seven p.m. basketball game. Since then, he said, the firm's culture has changed immeasurably.

"We want people to stay," Johnson said. "We want people to make a career at E and Y. I think the firm has come to a realization that we have to do a better job accommodating a person's personal life because this can't be just a meat factory where we grind up people, where people come in and stay two or three years and they work their butts off and leave."

MYRIAD FORCES CONTRIBUTE to the stresses and strains faced by American workers, but one force more than any other is responsible for heightening the pressure in workplaces across the nation—globalization. By opening up borders, expanding imports, and fueling the offshoring boom, globalization is squeezing white-collar and blue-collar workers alike. We will see how.

Chapter Eleven

OUTSOURCED AND OUT OF LUCK

It's hard to imagine a town that embodies Heartland America more than Galesburg, Illinois. Just west of its yellow-brick high school, cornfields stretch mile after mile toward the horizon, with the corn stalks and their golden tassels often melding magically with the golden sunsets. George Washington Gale, a Presbyterian minister from upstate New York, founded the town in 1837 when he established Knox Manual Labor College (now Knox College), where the students paid for their tuition by laboring in the fields. In the 1850s, Galesburg became the main station for the Underground Railroad in Illinois, and in 1858, Abraham Lincoln debated Stephen Douglas before 10,000 people at Knox College, scoring points with the crowd by accusing Douglas of "blowing out the moral lights around us when he maintains that anyone who wants slaves has a right to hold them."

In 1878, Carl Sandburg, the bard of the heartland, was born in a tiny peak-roofed cottage just yards from Galesburg's rail yard, his father a blacksmith's helper for the Chicago, Burlington, and Quincy Railroad. "I was born on the prairie and the milk of its wheat, the red of its clover, the eyes of its women, gave me a song and a slogan," Sandburg wrote in his poem "Prairie."

In 1916, five-year-old Ronald Reagan moved with his family into a rented white wood-framed house at 1260 North Kellogg Street. Up in the attic, to the future president's delight, he found a forgotten collection of birds' eggs and butterflies enclosed in glass cases. "I escaped for hours at a time into the attic, marveling at the rich colors of the eggs and the intricate and fragile wings of the butterflies," he wrote some seven decades later. "The experience left me with a reverence for the handiwork of God that never left me."[1] The Reagans lived in Galesburg during World War I—Ron's father, Jack, sold shoes at O. T. Johnson's department store on Main Street—and like everyone else in town, they rushed down to the depot to cheer whenever troop trains passed through, carrying khaki-clad doughboys on their way to Europe. Coincidentally, Nancy Davis, Ronald's second wife and the future first lady, also had strong ties to Galesburg, spending many vacations at her grandparents' house on Walnut Street.

For much of the twentieth century, Galesburg was a model of progress and prosperity, fueled by three powerful forces: agriculture, manufacturing, and the railroads. So robust was Galesburg's economy that Main Street boasted not just O. T. Johnson's emporium but also a Sears, a JCPenney, and a Carson Pirie Scott—quite an array of department stores, considering that Galesburg was a community of 35,000 out on the prairie between Peoria and Rock Island. On Friday nights, farmers from miles around converged on Galesburg to shop and socialize, at times making it hard not just to park but even to walk on Main Street. While agriculture was big and so were the railroads—the town's rail yard is one of the largest in the Midwest, with seven major lines passing through town—the most important economic engine was the Galesburg Refrigeration Products factory on the south side of town. It was more than a million square feet, the size of twenty football fields, and at peak times it employed more than 3,000 workers. It traces its history to a farm equipment factory built in the early 1900s, which was transformed during World War II into a metal fabrication plant to help the war effort. In 1950, the Admiral Corporation acquired the plant and turned it into a refrigerator factory.

Magic Chef bought Admiral in 1979, and seven years later Maytag, eager to broaden its appliance line, acquired Magic Chef and the Galesburg factory along with it. Under Maytag's ownership, the plant developed a reputation for ingenuity and innovations, introducing the first refrigerators that had internal ice cream makers and the first refrigerator line that dispensed both ice water and crushed ice. *Consumer Reports* awarded its number one rating to the side-by-side refrigerators produced in Galesburg.

Each year, the factory pumped tens of millions of dollars in wages into Galesburg's economy, and in that way, it helped build and sustain the town's— and the country's—middle class. Those dollars flowed to car dealers and supermarkets, bowling alleys and jewelers, even to the Prairie Players' performances at the Orpheum Theater. Drawn by the plant's solid wages and pensions, a steady parade of Galesburg's sons and daughters followed their parents and grandparents into the factory, decade after decade.

One son of Galesburg, Aaron Kemp, began working there on July 1, 1996, starting in its metal-stamping shop, where loud, ferocious machines banged and clanged the refrigerators' sides and cabinets into shape. Having spent several years as a gas station grease monkey, Kemp was hankering for something with better pay, benefits, and job security. When relatives told him that Maytag was hiring, Kemp, twenty-three and already with a young daughter, hurried to apply. He reckoned that a factory that big, the largest employer in

Knox County, one that made an essential appliance, would provide secure employment.

"It was a job where you could raise your family and have decent benefits, good health insurance, and a good pension—all the things that are important to us," Kemp said. A husky five feet ten, he played offensive and defensive line for Galesburg High's football team, but he shunned his parents' advice to go to college. "When I got out of high school, there were girls and parties and all the things that distract a young eighteen-year-old," he said.

Factory work was often monotonous, but Kemp fought the tedium by periodically changing jobs within the plant, moving from metal stamping to making the refrigerators' plastic racks to maneuvering the unfinished three-hundred-pound steel cabinets onto conveyer belts to mounting the doors on Maytag's vaunted side-by-sides. Friendships came easily at the factory—"Our shift was like family," Kemp said—and many evenings after work he and his buddies would down a few beers at the Cactus Corner bar, just across from the local airport. Things fell apart between him and his girlfriend, the mother of his daughter, but another romance bloomed at the factory. It was there he met his bride-to-be, Amanda Williams, who is earnest and hardworking like him, and together they had two boys. "We were starting to really catch our stride," Kemp said. "We could reach out and grab a piece of the American dream. We wouldn't be rich, but we'd be comfortable."

When Kemp reported for work one October morning in 2002, the factory was eerily empty and silent. He walked toward the center of the plant, where finally he heard a voice that grew louder as he approached. The plant manager, Jim Little, was standing on a podium, surrounded by hundreds of workers. Little was saying that Maytag was closing the plant, that the plant was no longer "competitively viable." Sixteen hundred workers would be losing their jobs.

"The news hit us like a ton of bricks," Kemp said. "We weren't prepared for it. No one was. I felt shocked, hurt, and betrayed."

The initial shock turned into anger when Maytag's executives explained why they were closing the plant. They were farming out production of Maytag's lower-cost, top-mount (freezer-on-top) refrigerators to Daewoo of South Korea—the top-mounts represented two-thirds of the plant's production—while they planned to produce Maytag's premier side-by-side refrigerators at a new factory in Reynosa, Mexico, just across the border from McAllen, Texas. There, management said, the workers would earn $2 an hour, compared with the standard pay of $15.14 an hour—$31,500 a year—at the Galesburg factory.

"This is heartbreaking," Kemp said. "This is one of the most unpatriotic, most un-American things I can imagine a company doing. They want Americans to buy their products, but they don't want to put Americans to work making those products."

After the plant manager spoke, several workers burst into tears. Others sat there dazed, while some embraced each other. One worker walked out and made a gesture of slitting his throat. Some angrily questioned why Maytag was closing the plant when by many accounts the factory was plenty profitable. While all this played out, a dozen security guards were standing by, just in case things erupted.

Dave Bevard, the president of the factory's union, Local 2063 of the International Association of Machinists, was quick to take a hard line against Maytag for moving operations to Mexico. "It's all part of a race to the bottom," he said. "It's not that manufacturers can't still make money in these United States. It's that they can't make enough money. It's all about corporate greed."

But to Maytag's executives, the move to Mexico was all about corporate competitiveness. The move made eminent sense to them because competitors like General Electric, Whirlpool, and Frigidaire were already making refrigerators abroad. "Maytag's plans are designed to produce refrigerators more economically and therefore more profitably," said William Beer, the president of Maytag's appliance division. "We don't believe it's possible for the production of side-by-side and top-mount refrigerators in Galesburg to become competitively viable."[2]

"We delayed the inevitable for as long as possible," said Stephen S. Ingham, the senior vice president overseeing Maytag's supply chain. "Many in the investment community have argued that we waited too long."

In the months after Maytag announced the closing, Kemp was sometimes brought to tears by the way his kids reacted. "My daughter, Alixandra, would ask, 'Why is Maytag firing you and your friends? Didn't you guys work hard enough? Didn't you do a good enough job making the refrigerators?' All the kid-type questions that are so hard to answer."

Now and then Kemp and his family drive past the huge plant, which sits lifeless, with foot-tall weeds growing in cracks in the parking lot.

"To this day," Kemp said, "whenever we drive by the Maytag facilities with our boys, they say, 'There's Daddy's work.' "

"It hurts every time."

———

GALESBURG GOT A CRASH COURSE in globalization, and so has much of the nation. Globalization is inarguably painful. It has thrown millions of people out of work and forced millions more to take jobs at lower wages. It should therefore not be surprising that globalization has provoked huge street demonstrations, with protesters shouting that it should be stopped in its tracks. Globalization, however, is unstoppable.

For American workers, globalization—the historical process in which nations and their economies are being bound ever more closely together—has generated huge worries, because more than any other economic force since the Depression, it is creating havoc for blue-collar and white-collar workers alike. In the 1980s, globalization hurt blue-collar America as a wave of imported steel, autos, and machinery hit Rust Belt cities such as Youngstown, Pittsburgh, and Milwaukee. But globalization has extended its reach. It is now hurting many white-collar workers—software developers, database managers, accountants—and it is hitting a very different set of communities: San Jose, Seattle, Austin, and Cambridge. Viewed another way, globalization used to hurt just the Bud crowd, but now it is also hitting the Starbucks crowd.

An explosion of new technologies—including e-mail, digitization, the Internet, broadband technology, scanners, communications satellites, undersea fiber-optic cables, and videoconferencing—has made it convenient for businesses to move white-collar jobs overseas. Before these technological advances, it simply wasn't economical or efficient for companies to send tasks such as designing software or processing insurance claims abroad. Now, radiologists in India are analyzing X-rays for Massachusetts General and other hospitals. Five hundred engineers in Moscow are helping Boeing design and build aircraft, as Boeing lays off engineers in the United States. The Bank of America moved 1,000 technical and back-office jobs to India while cutting 3,700 jobs in the United States.[3] HLW International, an architectural firm based in New York, uses its facilities in Shanghai to design office complexes for upstate New York.[4] American accounting firms had accountants in India prepare 25,000 tax returns in 2003; that number has now increased to several hundred thousand a year.[5]

Of course, the far lower cost of labor in less-developed countries is fueling this trend. American companies that pay a software engineer in Silicon Valley $80,000 a year might pay one in India $15,000, while a call-center worker in Buffalo might earn $22,000 a year, compared with $4,000 for one in Bangalore. In explaining why H&R Block's mortgage division employs 1,000 mortgage processors in India, Mark Ernst, the company's chairman, said, "We have a better-educated workforce in India, and they work for one-fifth the cost."[6]

Several years ago a top executive in Microsoft's Windows division did a PowerPoint presentation that urged managers to "pick something to move off-shore today."[7] H. Ross Perot, chairman of Perot Systems, the man whose main issue when he ran for president in 1992 was "the giant sucking sound" of jobs going to Mexico, plans to double his company's workforce in India to 7,000; India will then account for nearly half the company's worldwide employment. Two professors at Berkeley, J. Bradford DeLong and Stephen S. Cohen, said this move raised a troubling question: "If the economic logic of foreign out-sourcing is so overwhelming that Ross Perot can't resist it, what American CEO will be able to?"[8]

Globalization, according to various studies, threatens the jobs of between 11 million and 42 million white-collar workers in the United States as the range of "tradable" jobs that can be sent offshore continues to expand.[9] Alan Blinder, a Princeton economics professor and the former vice chairman of the Federal Reserve, wrote, "We have so far barely seen the tip of the offshoring iceberg, the eventual dimensions of which may be staggering."[10] One study found that 44 percent of information technology service jobs were vulnerable to off-shoring, as well as 25 percent of retail banking jobs, 19 percent of insurance jobs, and 13 percent of pharmaceutical jobs.[11] Those whose work requires their personal presence in the United States—hair stylists, chefs, elementary school teachers, plumbers, janitors, waiters, surgeons, nurses, dentists, and dental assistants—are secure. But those whose services can be delivered over a wire are in danger.

Forrester Research estimates that 3.4 million white-collar jobs—some 260,000 a year—will be sent overseas between 2003 and 2015.[12] Forrester fore-casts that this exodus will include 1.6 million office-support jobs, 542,000 computer jobs, 259,000 management jobs, 191,000 architecture jobs, 79,000 legal jobs, and 30,000 art and design jobs.[13]

Some economists point out that a loss of 260,000 jobs a year would be just a fraction of the more than two million net jobs created annually during healthy economic times. Indeed, these economists note that 500,000 workers lose their jobs each week (on a gross basis), while somewhat more than 500,000 jobs are created weekly.

Not a few economists warn, however, that the most menacing aspect of off-shoring is not the loss of jobs but its downward pull on wages. Remember Paul Samuelson's admonition, "If you don't believe [offshoring] changes the aver-age wages in America, then you believe in the tooth fairy."[14]

In today's brave new world of offshoring, no one seems sure where to run for safety. Getting a college degree, especially a degree in computer engineering, used to be the ticket to job security. But as Harvard's Richard Freeman has pointed out, the world has changed mightily because hundreds of millions of workers in India and China, not to mention Russia, Hungary, and other former Soviet Bloc countries, have joined the global workforce and are eager to take over work long done by Americans—including highly educated Americans.[15] This has made it hard to advise American college students about what careers to prepare for.

In a candid moment, Craig Barrett, chairman of Intel, a company that does research and manufacturing in many different nations, voiced concern that globalization will portend a dimmer future for young Americans: "Intel will be okay no matter what," Barrett said. "We can adjust to do our R&D and manufacturing wherever it is most economically advantageous to do so. But in addition to being chairman of Intel, I am also a grandfather, and I wonder what my grandchildren are going to do."[16]

Steven Pearlstein, a columnist for the *Washington Post,* took Intel to task for building a $2.5 billion chip fabrication plant on China's northeast coast, encouraged by $500 million in subsidies from China. Pearlstein wrote:

> We can all agree this plant will be a boon to the Chinese economy. And we can be pretty sure it will be in the interests of Intel shareholders. But is it really in the best interests of the U.S. economy?
>
> It would be one thing if the Chinese had developed the capacity to make advanced microchips on the basis of their own investment and ingenuity. But it is quite another when the technology for the chips and chip production has been created by American researchers and American companies, and transferred wholesale to a developing country that makes no secret of its intention to use that knowledge and experience to improve its own industry. By what reasoning is this a net plus for an American economy that is supposed to prosper in this globalized world on the basis of its high-tech know-how? Can you really say that, in such a high-value-added industry, the lower cost of imported computer chips will offset the forgone economic output—jobs and profits—that Intel's move entails?[17]

The other side of the coin is that globalization has improved living standards for hundreds of millions of people in developing nations—consider the "East Asian miracle" that has lifted South Korea, Taiwan, Hong Kong, Malaysia, Singapore, and parts of China, pulling huge numbers of people out of poverty. The blessings of globalization are now transforming pockets of India, including Bangalore and Hyderabad. "One person's economic liberation could be another's unemployment," Thomas L. Friedman wrote in *The World Is Flat,* his insightful book about globalization.[18]

In many countries, however, globalization has continued to leave the great multitudes behind. In much of South America, per capita income has stagnated over the past decade. The North American Free Trade Agreement was supposed to be an elixir for Mexico's economic ills, but ever since NAFTA took effect in 1994, wages for Mexican workers have floundered, illegal immigration has soared, and many Mexican farmers have been devastated by heavily subsidized corn imported from the United States.

Joseph E. Stiglitz, a Nobel Prize winner in economics and a professor at Columbia University, wrote in his book *Globalization and Its Discontents* that even though globalization helped lift total world income by more than 30 percent in the 1990s, the number of people living in poverty worldwide increased by 100 million during that decade.[19] China seems to symbolize the contradictions of globalization. Its economic output is soaring, producing a thriving upper class and raising living standards for tens of millions of workers. Yet millions of Chinese who abandoned their poor rural villages in search of better lives in the cities now find themselves working for a pittance inside factory sweatshops, almost as indentured servants.

For America's multinational corporate giants, globalization has by and large been a blessing, enabling them to increase efficiency, cut costs, and boost profits. Some analysts have even begun to argue that offshoring enables American corporations to preserve jobs in the United States instead of reducing them, by helping them cut costs and solidify their competitiveness.[20]

Globalization is not a zero-sum game. Sending some software programming jobs to India can mean good jobs for Indians and lower software prices for Americans. Globalization can also speed the development and dissemination of new technologies—hybrid car engines, for instance—that might ultimately increase the number of jobs and improve living standards in developed and developing countries alike. And Americans should remember that however much they curse globalization when companies move operations from Galesburg to Mexico or from San Jose to India, South Carolinians and Kentuckians certainly don't see globalization as an evil when BMW and Toyota build assembly plants in their states.

Probably the most beneficial aspect of globalization is that it has been a blessing for consumers. Globalization, in the form of imports, has given us sturdy, fuel-efficient Toyotas and Hondas and has kept down prices on stereos, shirts, and shoes, whether at Wal-Mart or Neiman Marcus. Morgan Stanley estimates that since the mid-1990s, low-cost imports from China have saved American consumers more than $600 billion.[21] As a result of outsourcing, one study found, prices for computer hardware have fallen 10 to 30 percent below what they would have been, and the U.S. economy has grown by an extra $30 billion a year.[22]

But globalization, as a software engineer named Myra knows all too well, has taken its toll on high-tech workers.

THE E-MAIL SEEMED INNOCENT ENOUGH, but something about it worried Myra Bronstein. It instructed her and the seventeen other quality assurance engineers—a fancy term for software testers—to report to the company's boardroom at ten the next morning. *No way can that be good,* she told herself.

At the time, Myra, then forty-seven, was a senior quality assurance engineer at WatchMark, a company that developed sophisticated software for cell phone companies. She and the other quality assurance engineers were a dedicated lot. Sometimes they worked eleven or twelve days straight, sometimes up to eighteen hours a day, as WatchMark rushed to meet deadlines to get new software to customers. WatchMark, based in Bellevue, a Seattle suburb, made software that helped wireless companies determine whether their cell towers were working properly and how many calls were being dropped.

Myra remembers one episode when, after being required to work twenty-four hours in a row testing software, she told her boss that she had to leave for a long-scheduled doctor appointment. Her boss yelled at her, accusing her of lacking dedication.

"If they wanted to wreck our weekends or cancel our vacations," Myra said, "they'd basically say, 'This is a very important release. We need to build this customer's confidence. We have to show them it's good quality, and we need you to work, and basically if we lose this customer then we could fold.' They'd say, 'As long as we're in business, you have a job, so it's in your best interest to work as hard as you can'—weekends, evenings, everything."

Myra is a petite woman, deliberate and not at all showy. She has a reserved smile, a pale, almond-shaped face, deep-set eyes, and thick dark hair that just touches her shoulders. As Myra and the other quality assurance engineers gathered in the boardroom the morning after the e-mail arrived, the director of human resources began giving out large manila envelopes. Once everyone was there, Myra recalled, "The head of HR said, 'Unfortunately, we're having layoffs, and you're in the room because you're being impacted by the layoffs.' "

The eighteen engineers were dumbstruck, but the head of human resources pressed on. "Your replacements," she continued, "are flying in from India, and you're expected to train them if you are going to receive severance."

"People were trying not to cry," Myra said. "We felt sucker-punched. It totally knocked the wind out of me. I had bought into all their motivational tactics. I felt if I helped my company stay afloat, I would ensure my own employment. I believed them."

Uncomfortably, reluctantly, Myra and the others agreed to WatchMark's request to train their replacements beginning the following Monday. They would train their replacements for four weeks and would then receive severance pay. Not to agree would have meant working just a few more days and forgoing any severance.

The following Monday morning, the American engineers gathered inside a conference room, waiting to meet the twenty engineers who had been flown in from India. WatchMark's director of quality assurance began that meeting ever so clumsily by saying, "I'd like my new team to meet my old team."

Once each quality assurance engineer was assigned an Indian to train—Myra was assigned two—WatchMark's vice president of technology began a pep talk, telling the laid-off engineers, "The future welfare of WatchMark depends on how well you train these people."

For the next month, Myra strained to maintain her composure as she trained two Indians at once. "They didn't acknowledge what was going on, that we had to do something upsetting," she said. "It was the most difficult situation in the world."

Soon Myra and the other Americans began calling themselves "The Castaways" and "Dead Man Working." She was told that the Indians would earn $5,000 a year; she had earned $80,000.

After a month of training her replacements, Myra was unemployed. That was the last thing she would have anticipated when, full of lofty expectations, she quit her job as a health inspector in Kansas City to pursue a degree in electrical engineering. She hungered for a job that promised more excitement, more money, and more mobility. "At the time, computer science fit all those criteria," she said.

After obtaining her engineering degree, she landed a job with AT&T in Naperville, Illinois, testing its electronic switching systems. Four years after Myra began, AT&T started downsizing in Naperville, so she transferred to AT&T's operation in Middletown, New Jersey. For her first four years there, she wrote user manuals about telephone systems, and then she transferred into software testing. There, Myra was surprised by how many young engineers from India were being brought in on H-1B visas. After four years, she was the only American left in the twenty-person testing unit. "The writing was on the wall," Myra said.

Worried that she would soon be replaced, Myra quit and moved to Seattle, a city for which she long had a romantic hankering. There she took the testing job with WatchMark, and after three years came the abrupt layoffs. Myra remained unemployed for three months before settling for a job at what she called "a testing sweatshop." It paid twenty dollars an hour, half the rate at WatchMark (which has since changed its name to Vallent and been acquired by IBM). Her new testing company was across the street from a sewage treatment plant, and in summer the workers complained that they were choking from the smell, the heat, and the lack of ventilation. In winter, there was so little heat that many workers wore their coats all day.

"One day it was raining a lot, and I was sitting there at my PC, testing software for bugs, and it started dripping from the ceiling, right into my PC. Before I had time to react, it exploded. Smoke was coming out of it. That was some bug all right."

She soon quit.

Seeing so many jobs being offshored to India, Myra grew convinced that it would be hard to find a high-tech job that paid nearly as much as her Watch-Mark job. She searched in vain for several more months, supporting herself by drawing down her 401(k) and selling off her beloved, painstakingly assembled collection of antique guilloche cosmetic compacts, fine French-made enamel compacts, some of which had silver handles.

Feeling forsaken by the high-tech world, Myra moved back to Kansas City, in large part to take care of her ailing eighty-six-year-old mother.

"I'm giving up on the technology field because it's so difficult to survive now that employers can use so much cheap skilled labor overseas," she said.

Myra is now contemplating a radical career change. She is thinking of becoming a pharmacist, which would entail six years of school. But she has no idea how she would afford the tuition. The Trade Adjustment Assistance Act pays tuition for factory workers who lose their jobs to globalization, but Myra was a software worker, not a factory worker.

"I never would have gone into the technology field in the first place if I had a crystal ball and knew the bottom was going to drop out," Myra said. "People who are staying in this field have to go back to school and continually learn more complicated high-tech things. I thought I could be very competent and learn what I needed to know about my own job and serve the company well. But now they want much more from you for much less."

THERE IS A GLARING DISCONNECT between the way government and business leaders talk about globalization and the way the average American views it. Notwithstanding painful stories like Myra's, political and business leaders almost always talk about globalization as a win-win, as a boon for companies and consumers alike.

But many Americans believe that something has gone badly awry with globalization. In a poll done by the *Financial Times*, nearly half of the Americans surveyed said globalization was having a negative effect on the United States, while just 17 percent said it was having a positive effect.[23] In another poll, 61 percent of Americans surveyed said they feared that they, a family member, or friend would lose their job because an employer would move operations to another country.[24] Even Lawrence Summers, the former Harvard president, former Treasury secretary, and long a leading champion of free trade, remarked on the "growing disillusionment" about globalization. Summers acknowledged that there have largely been two beneficiaries of globalization: an "international elite" whose incomes have climbed strongly, and millions of poor Asians.[25] Summers wrote, "As the great corporate engines of efficiency succeed by using [globalization to combine] cutting-edge technology with low-cost labor, ordinary, middle-class workers . . . are left out." That, he added, is why there is "a degree of anxiety about the market system that is unmatched since the fall of the Berlin Wall and probably well before."[26]

While corporate America continues to clamor for more free trade agreements, many Americans—ranging from the billionaire Warren Buffet to the AFL-CIO—are voicing alarm about another aspect of globalization, the nation's huge trade deficit. In 2006, the deficit climbed to a record $764 billion, by far the largest of any nation in history. With China alone, America's trade deficit was $230 billion. By some estimates, the nation's recurring trade deficits are responsible for destroying two-thirds of the 3.5 million factory jobs the nation has lost since 2000.[27] To finance its trade deficits, the United States has run up $3 trillion in foreign debts. Roughly $1 trillion of that has been borrowed from China's central bank, giving China considerable leverage over the United States. America has also indirectly financed its deficits by selling off assets to foreigners, from Manhattan real estate to large pieces of prestigious investment banks.

Buffett has compared the United States to an extraordinarily rich family that owns an immense farm and consumes considerably more than it produces. To finance its spendthrift ways, this family is constantly selling pieces of its farm and increasing the mortgage on what it still owns. By acting this way, Buffett writes, the United States will grow poorer because it will be "paying ever-increasing dividends and interest to the world."[28]

Various proposals—all of them painful—have been put forward to fix America's huge trade deficit. Some economists say the dollar needs to fall even further to make America's exports more price-competitive and to raise the price of imports. Notwithstanding his reputation for caution, Buffett has proposed a radical solution: importers of goods into the United States would have to pay American exporters a sizable amount to obtain import licenses, which would spur exports by subsidizing them, while forcing up the price of imports.[29] The AFL-CIO has called for emergency temporary tariffs and for "a strategic pause" that would place a moratorium on new free trade agreements while the nation rethinks its trade policies. Such a reevaluation would seek to reduce America's overdependence on imports while reinvigorating the nation's ailing manufacturing base. Organized labor says that Washington has repeatedly pursued trade agreements that helped America's financial and telecommunications companies while hurting its manufacturers. Labor unions say the nation needs to develop a competitiveness policy to strengthen America's industrial base, perhaps by improving worker training and eliminating tax breaks that encourage manufacturers to move operations overseas. With American manufacturers badly trailing their foreign competitors in green industries such as hybrid cars, environmental groups and labor unions are calling on the federal government to invest tens of billions of dollars to help American industry catch up. Such a strategy would help reduce the trade deficit and global warming and would create good manufacturing jobs.

The defenders of free trade decry many critics as alarmist, saying not to worry, that globalization and offshoring increase a nation's wealth and well-being by increasing efficiency. Defenders of offshoring often point to the theory of comparative advantage articulated by David Ricardo in his landmark 1817 treatise, *Principles of Political Economy and Taxation*. In one of the most famous hypotheticals in all of economics, Ricardo assumed that it took 80 Portuguese workers to make a given value of wine and 90 to make a similarly valued amount of cloth, while it took 100 English workers to make the same amount of cloth and 120 for the wine. Ricardo concluded that it would be more efficient, that economic production and economic benefits would be maximized, if Portugal were to make only wine and England only cloth even though

Portugal was more efficient at making both. Economic benefits would be maximized for the two countries if they then traded their wine and cloth.

Applying Ricardo's principles to the twenty-first century, free trade's defenders argue that it makes economic sense for workers in India to process insurance claims and do low-level software programming while American workers concentrate on more sophisticated fields such as designing high-level software or making movies—fields in which workers who lose their jobs to off-shoring can, or so the theory goes, be employed more productively.[30]

But some prominent economists are questioning how well Ricardo's theory works when India and China, with millions of highly educated workers ready to work for a fraction of what Americans earn, are developing high-tech expertise that might someday challenge America's dominance. After examining the dynamics of offshoring, Ralph E. Gomory, the president of the Alfred P. Sloan Foundation and a former IBM senior executive, and William J. Baumol, an economist at New York University, reached some unsettling conclusions. Gomory said in congressional testimony that if the wage difference between two countries is sufficiently large, "the loss of industries to the low-wage, underdeveloped country may well benefit both countries at the national level." But, he added, "as the underdeveloped country develops and starts to look more like the developed one, the balance turns around and further loss of industries becomes harmful to the overall welfare of the more developed nation."[31] In other words, if China's low-wage apparel industry takes some production from the United States, that can benefit both countries. But once China's economy becomes far more sophisticated, once its computer industry becomes so adept that it can challenge America's computer industry, sending high-tech jobs to China can hurt the overall welfare of the United States.[32]

Paul Samuelson voiced some of those concerns in an academic paper that showed that low-wage countries like China and India that are rapidly upgrading their technologies, thanks in part to offshoring, can transform their terms of trade in areas like software design so that per capita income in the United States actually falls (in part by enabling those countries to rely less on trade with the United States for some important, high-value goods and services).[33]

Many economists also note that globalization is a wage-leveling force. Imports and offshoring help to hold down pay for workers in industries in higher-wage countries that are confronted by overseas competition. At the same time, globalization helps to push up wages in export-oriented industries in poorer nations. Three Harvard economists—George J. Borjas, Richard B. Freeman, and Lawrence F. Katz—found that for every 1 percent that employment falls in a manufacturing industry because of imports or operations moving overseas, wages are depressed by five-tenths of 1 percent for the workers who remain. With Forrester Research predicting that 6 percent of America's service-sector jobs will be sent offshore by 2015, Professor Katz estimated that wages for service-sector workers in vulnerable fields could be shaved by 2 to 3 percent as a result. "White-collar workers have a right to be scared," Katz said.[34]

When political candidates campaign, they often hear laid-off factory workers or high-tech workers complain about globalization. The pain is so great that residents of Midwestern communities hobbled by imports often call for unabashedly protectionist measures like banning imports from China or setting an annual dollar cap on the nation's imports.

The vehemence of such sentiments unsettles many supporters of free trade. They worry that a push for protectionism will impede economic progress and free trade agreements. In a column about globalization, George Will noted that the modern welfare state, beginning with unemployment relief, was invented in part by European conservatives, most notably Bismarck, but also Disraeli, to help reconcile people to economic change—to help minimize opposition to the creative destruction that is the way of economics, the turbulence of jobs being created and being lost, that yields innovation, growth, and progress. "It is sound social policy, and simple justice," Will wrote, "that the party who benefits from free trade—the nation as a whole—should be taxed to ameliorate the discomforts of those who pay the short-term price of progress."[35]

Among the measures proposed to reduce the burden on displaced workers are assuring health coverage to the families of workers who lose jobs to globalization and guaranteeing these workers good retraining programs.

Two years before replacing Alan Greenspan as chairman of the Federal Reserve, Benjamin Bernanke warned that the nation needs to do more to help the victims of free trade. "Reducing the burdens borne by displaced workers is the right and fair thing to do," Bernanke said. "If workers are less fearful of change, less pressure will be exerted on politicians to erect trade barriers or to take other actions that would reduce the flexibility and dynamism of the U.S. economy."[36]

THE MAYTAG CLOSING was a body blow not just to hundreds of workers but to Galesburg itself. Housing prices slumped by 15 percent before rebounding slightly, while demand for food and housing assistance jumped at least 25 percent. Eagle Supermarket, a community fixture, closed, while a Family Dollar store opened on Main Street—the chain often opens its downmarket discount outlets in communities that fall into economic distress. At Lindstrom's, a popular appliance store located in the old Carson Pirie Scott building, sales soared at its annual "Scratch and Dent Sale" in which damaged refrigerators, washers, and dryers are sold at hefty markdowns. Western Illinois University issued a study estimating that the Maytag closing would eliminate 4,611 jobs, including the direct layoffs at the factory as well as the 3,000 indirect layoffs involving suppliers, trucking companies, retailers, and even government bodies that relied on Maytag's tax dollars. Senator Barack Obama even highlighted Galesburg's woes when he gave the speech that introduced him to the nation, his keynote address to the 2004 Democratic National Convention, in which he spoke of workers "who are losing their union jobs at the Maytag plant that's moving to Mexico and now are having to compete with their own children for jobs that pay seven bucks an hour."

The man whose job was to stop the economic hemorrhaging was Eric Voyles, the president of the Galesburg Regional Economic Development Association. Voyles is a fireplug of a man, short and stocky with a take-charge manner, ready day or night with an hour-long sales pitch about the countless advantages that Galesburg offers for doing business. His words pour forth in a hyperlogical style, as he breaks every idea into four parts and then three subparts. Voyles dresses with a defiant panache—he has spiky dark hair and a penchant for black leather suspenders.

Voyles sounded far more understanding about Maytag's decision to close than one might expect from Galesburg's leading booster. "Any major company that's not looking to make sure that their capital is allocated in the most effective location will be out of business in the next five to ten years," he said, choosing his words carefully. "The world is changing, and we have to change with it."

Voyles has his hands full. Not only did Maytag close but so did several smaller factories in Galesburg, including the Gates rubber hose factory and the Butler factory that made prefabricated steel-sided sheds and buildings.

"Manufacturing is dead in this part of the world," said John Polillo, chairman of the board of Voyles's agency. "We don't have to like it. But it's a reality."[37]

Voyles is nonetheless trying to attract new factories. He has also set up a "business incubation" center that has helped entrepreneurs create twenty start-ups employing fifty people. He has built a $4 million 350-acre "logistics park" that is focusing on attracting large distribution operations. He hopes to take advantage of the town's central location and its extraordinary rail network—175 trains pass through Galesburg each day. Since 30 percent of the rail freight destined for Chicago passes through Galesburg, Voyles hopes that distribution and logistics can someday be the town's salvation. He points to the recent decision by the Burlington Northern Santa Fe to add 200 yard workers, mechanics, and engineers, bringing its local workforce to 1,000.

"There were Maytag workers who were making thirty thousand dollars a year who were out of work for a year, and then they went to work for the railroad for forty-five thousand a year," Voyles said. "Those people who were picked by the railroad are probably now saying, 'This was probably not too bad a move.' "

Voyles has urged chemical companies in Texas and timber companies in the Northwest to use Galesburg's huge rail yard as a convenient and cheap place—certainly cheaper than Chicago—to transfer their shipments from rail to truck.

"As we continue to move more and more goods from outside the country, more companies will be using the West Coast ports and more and more of their goods will be passing through the Midwest and passing through Galesburg," Voyles said. "Illinois could become the nation's center for distribution."

In its hunt for new business, Galesburg has even sent four delegations to China to encourage Chinese companies to open distribution centers in town, and the Chinese have shown some interest. More than a hundred Chinese from two dozen different groups have visited Galesburg, including a delegation representing 3,000 Chinese companies.

As part of his sales pitch, Voyles emphasizes Galesburg's attractiveness and cost advantages. He is urging Chicagoans to retire in Galesburg, which he says is just a "short" three-hour, 150-mile train ride from Chicago's museums and symphony. He recommends that retirees living in Chicago's affluent suburbs sell their homes for, say, $500,000, and buy a gorgeous Victorian house in Galesburg for $150,000, pocketing the difference to help assure a comfortable retirement.

"We're kind of a blue-collar town with an interesting metropolitan flair," Voyles said. "We have dining. We have our own symphony. We have a multitude of theatrical productions, including the Prairie Players. What you can't find here you can find in Peoria or the Quad Cities." Both places are a forty-five-minute drive.

In his pitch to businesses, Voyles says Galesburg provides "an excellent value." "This is a more cost-effective place for a company to be located," he said, pulling out a chart showing that the average wage of a worker in Chicago is $15.27 an hour compared with $11.98 in Galesburg. "Employing one hundred people here versus one hundred there will mean seven hundred and fifty thousand dollars in annual savings," he said.

Voyles's sales pitch rubs some people the wrong way. Mike Kroll, who runs a shop on Main Street, Dr. Mike, Computer Therapist, said: "To market Galesburg as purely a low-wage town is self-defeating, because you end up creating a town that can't support itself over the long term. If all you have is a town where people are receiving Wal-Mart wages, how are people going to be able to afford to live in the community and raise families?"[38]

SURPRISING AS IT MAY SEEM, some Galesburg residents direct their anger at a former priest 1,100 miles to the south. Their target is Mike Allen, who left the priesthood to devote himself to improving the economic lives, rather than the spiritual lives, of destitute Mexicans. Allen was a maverick priest, moving out of his comfortable rectory in McAllen, Texas, to live in a no-frills trailer alongside his parishioners, many of them migrant farm workers. He is bitter when he describes how miserably those farm workers were treated when they migrated to the Midwest each year to plant and harvest.

After quitting the priesthood, Allen did economic development work in Austin, the state capital. In 1988, he became president of the McAllen Economic Development Corporation. His goal was to woo companies not just to McAllen but to Reynosa, its sister city just south of the border with Mexico— the city that lured away the Maytag plant. In this way, Allen—and McAllen— helped transform Reynosa from a small desert hamlet into an industrial boomtown.

"I don't regret my decision," Allen said about giving up his collar. "I had a parish where most people were unemployed. It's hard to tell people about Jesus when they don't have a job and are hungry."[39]

Allen is a hail-fellow-well-met with a booming voice and a folksy style. Thanks largely to his economic missionary work, Hidalgo County—McAllen is its largest city—has lured 223 new businesses over the past two decades, creating more than 16,000 jobs, while Reynosa, buoyed by NAFTA, has attracted 292 companies, including Maytag, Zenith, Delphi, General Electric, and Black and Decker, creating more than 70,000 jobs. In 2005 alone, Allen helped attract 11,400 new jobs to Reynosa.

"We're living in a global economy," Allen said. "Things are changing. You can't blame McAllen and Reynosa for taking these jobs. The economy took them, I'd say.

"Our struggle here is we have the lowest per capita income in the United States. We've very aggressively gone after companies the last many years. We got a lot of angry calls about Maytag and Galesburg. I can understand the people there. Many have lost their jobs, and that's tough. People have to understand that certain types of manufacturers are going to go to either Mexico or China. We're trying to attract them. We're just attempting to help our community the best we can."

In the 1950s, Galesburg and Reynosa each had about 35,000 people, but Reynosa now has more than 1 million, while Galesburg's population has hardly budged. Reynosa has become a boomtown with dozens of shiny new export-oriented factories, *maquiladoras*, which have lured tens of thousands of Mexican peasants who abandoned subsistence farming to try their luck at factory work. Reynosa has many of the slick emblems of the United States: Burger Kings, Pizza Huts, even an Applebee's and Blockbuster Video. But it also has many neighborhoods filled with shanties made from cinder blocks, corrugated steel, and wood torn from discarded factory pallets.[40] Many of the shanties have dirt floors and crude outhouses, and many of the shantytowns have no sewers, and rutted streets that turn muddy whenever it rains. Reynosa's government seems perpetually starved for funds, partly because Maytag and other foreign companies pay so little in the way of local taxes.

Maytag's new side-by-side refrigerator plant is in the Colonial Industrial Park. Each morning scores of vans drive there to discharge hundreds of workers who earn less in a day than the Galesburg workers earned in an hour. Maytag executives assert that setting up shop in Reynosa has worked out brilliantly. "We have been operating in Reynosa long enough to have validated the fact that our competitive position has improved significantly," said Steve Ingham, the senior vice president overseeing Maytag's supply chain. He says the Mexican factory is producing higher-quality refrigerators than the Galesburg factory did, a statement that Galesburg workers, who received outstanding grades for quality, greet with disbelief.[41]

Mike Allen says the jobs at Maytag and the other *maquiladoras* are definite steps up for the peasants who moved to Reynosa. "In Mexico, there are no food stamps, there is no welfare. If you do not work, you do not eat. We think we have helped thousands. I think the *maquiladoras* have contributed a great deal to people staying in their country instead of coming over here illegally."

This echoes what Mexico's former president, Carlos Salinas de Gortari, once asked to promote NAFTA: "Where do you want Mexicans working, in Mexico or in the U.S.? Because if we cannot export more, then Mexicans will seek employment opportunities in the U.S. We want to export goods, not people."[42]

Chad Broughton, a longtime Knox College political science professor now at the University of Chicago, visited Reynosa and came away convinced that the Maytag refrigerator factory there does not pay its workers enough to support a family. He brought back a copy of a Maytag worker's paycheck, showing wages of one dollar an hour, or eight dollars a day. But Maytag insists that pay comes to nearly two dollars an hour, or sixteen dollars a day, when the value of free lunches and free transportation is included. According to a study by one Mexican workers' group, it costs eighty-three dollars a week to buy food for a family of four in Reynosa, and that does not include money for housing, health care, and education.[43]

One Mexican worker told Broughton that he quit his Maytag job because he was earning too little. "This job doesn't pay nearly enough to raise a family," said the worker, who lives in a shanty with his wife and three children. "My family's economic situation would never allow me to buy one of the refrigerators I make."[44]

For one Maytag worker, Salvador Garza, the company's move to Mexico had special poignancy. Born in rural Mexico, Garza began doing migrant farm work in the Midwest at the age of seven when he accompanied his parents north. He settled in the United States, served in the U.S. Marines, obtained an engineering degree, and married a woman from Galesburg. He rose to become one of the top engineers at the Maytag plant, settling down in Galesburg and buying a house with more middle-class comforts than he ever dreamed of. When Maytag announced the plant closing, it offered Garza one of the top positions in Reynosa, but he turned down the offer, convinced that Maytag's move south of the border would hurt American and Mexican workers alike.

"I have family members who work in Reynosa," said Garza, who has taken a job doing economic development work for the Illinois Department of Commerce. "I understand the conditions there. I understand the wages that the Mexican people receive, and it isn't enough for these folks to thrive. It's just enough to keep them at subsistence, and it doesn't necessarily raise their living standards. Just look at the makeshift housing they're forced to live in. Instead of giving people a job that they can raise their families on, this is merely bankrolling them to finance their trip northward. It does nothing to stem the tide of illegal immigration."

SOON AFTER MAYTAG ANNOUNCED the plant closing, the machinists union asked Aaron Kemp to become a peer counselor, to advise the 1,600 Maytag workers on what to do with the rest of their lives and on how to apply for unemployment insurance, job training funds, and community college courses.

"There's a small handful that says this is the best thing that ever happened to them," Kemp said. "There's a middle group that's still in training, that's in the process of moving on with their new life. There's also a group that's completely lost hope. They really don't know what they're going to do from here. They may not have the type of résumé that's needed to get them hired anywhere else. These people are getting lost in the shuffle."

Kemp, whose counseling job will soon end, is leaning toward getting a commercial truck driver's license. With three children, he hopes that any trucking job he gets will be a local one rather than one that would take him away from his family for days at a time. His wife, Amanda, is earning less in her new job—as an assistant to an insurance agent—than she earned at Maytag. The Kemps have tightened their belts.

"When we were both working at Maytag, on Friday nights we could maybe afford to take the kids to Pizza Hut or to a movie," Aaron said. "Maybe every couple of months we could go to Peoria and see a minor league hockey game and maybe spend the night in a hotel. Those things were within our reach. Now those things are gone."

With so many of the good factory jobs leaving Galesburg and the Midwest, Kemp worries for his children. "I would hope that my kids would have the opportunity to chase the American dream realistically. By that, I don't mean I hope they become millionaires. First of all, I hope they get a better education than I got. When they enter into the workforce, I hope they have a reasonable chance that if they work hard and play by the rules, they can live comfortably."

Having read that many factory workers in Mexico earn a dollar an hour and live in shanties, Kemp says he is not at all angry at the workers in Reynosa who are making the refrigerators that were once made in Galesburg. "The only people who are being exploited and taken advantage of more than us are the people who have our jobs now," Kemp said. "They're family people, just like we are, and they're going to do what they can to support their families, and I don't begrudge them the slightest. I feel sorry for them. I really do."

Postscript: In January 2008, the Whirlpool Corporation, which acquired Maytag in 2006, announced that it would close the refrigerator factory in

Reynosa and consolidate operations in a Whirlpool plant in Ramos Arizpe, Mexico.

THOSE MEXICANS WHO CONTINUE to flee Reynosa are part of a massive flow of immigrants into the United States. Some of those immigrants flourish; for others, life in America has proved far crueler than they ever imagined, in large part because many employers feel little compunction about exploiting them. Immigration has also roiled America's economy, politics, and workforce, generating a political backlash and leaving the nation badly divided over how best to handle the new arrivals.

Chapter Twelve

THE LOWEST RUNG

All across America, industrial bakeries—anonymous, sprawling structures usually built along interstate highways—produce millions of cakes and loaves of bread each day. The Chef Solutions bakery, alongside I-91 just north of New Haven, Connecticut, is one such bakery. It is a cavernous one-story building filled with stainless-steel ovens, freezers, and mixing machines that make bread and rolls for supermarkets and Subway restaurants throughout the Northeast.

The bakery used to be a good place to work, its employees say, so good that soon after Eva Mota took a job there, she urged her three sisters back in Mexico City—Maria Teresa, Maria Elena, and Reyna—to quit their secretarial jobs and join her. Swayed by her talk of good wages and of a place far safer than Mexico's crime-ridden capital, the sisters sneaked across the border and were soon able to land jobs at the bakery. For unskilled immigrant workers, the pay was excellent, nearly ten dollars an hour to start, rising to twelve dollars after two or three years. The work—mixing the dough, putting the bread and rolls into the ovens, and inspecting and packing the baked goods—may have been monotonous, but the pace wasn't frenzied and there was a strong sense of camaraderie among the bakery's 190 workers, a mix of Italians, blacks, Eastern Europeans, and a fast-growing number of Hispanics.

But after several years, the atmosphere at the bakery turned sharply worse when its corporate owner, a large baking and prepared foods company based in Illinois, installed a new top manager. The immigrant women soon became sexual prey.

As a result, three of the Mota sisters eventually filed sexual harassment lawsuits that painted an alarming picture. The harassment began, they said, when the bakery's second-ranking manager, the production manager, started showering Maria Teresa, the oldest sister, with compliments as she worked on the bread-packing line. He started phoning her at home, sometimes in the middle of the night, asking her to go out with him. He often showed up at her apartment and rang the doorbell repeatedly. Maria Teresa told the manager, who had recently married, that she had a steady boyfriend and wasn't interested. But he persisted.

"He told me that he needed me, that he wanted to have sex with me all the time, that he wanted me to be his second wife, that he had to have me," she said. Petite, at most five feet one, Maria Teresa is attractive, with dark brown eyes, bronze skin, full lips, strong, dark eyebrows, and brown hair that she often ties in a bun but occasionally lets fall below her shoulders.

Month after month, the harassment continued, she said. Sometimes the manager phoned Maria Teresa's sisters at their apartments, demanding that they tell him where she was. He often told other workers how attracted he was to her, and some days after work he followed Maria Teresa to her apartment. Still, she managed to keep him at bay.

After two years, the production manager escalated his campaign by making a series of explicit threats, she said. He warned that she would be fired if she did not oblige him. He also said he might retaliate against her sisters, a hint that they, too, might be fired. And the most worrisome threat, albeit unspoken, was that he might tip off immigration authorities to have the sisters deported. Worn down by the threats and psychological pressure, Maria Teresa finally succumbed. Thus began five years of sexual abuse and submission.

After she submitted that first time, the manager often required her to have sex with him in his office and sometimes in his car. At times—Maria Teresa explained at length in interviews and in legal papers—he demanded that she let him into her apartment after she put her daughter to bed. Once when he demanded sex, Maria Teresa told him she was feeling seriously ill. But he insisted. Hours later, she suffered a miscarriage and was hospitalized.

Throughout this ordeal, Maria Teresa feared complaining to the bakery's top manager, convinced that she wouldn't believe her and might even fire her. The top manager had summarily fired other workers who had gone to her with complaints. "I was afraid of her," Maria Teresa said. And her status as an illegal immigrant—she later became legal by marrying a citizen—made her all the more reluctant to complain. And she didn't dare quit to get away from the production manager because she worried that he would carry out his threat of retaliation against her sisters. "I felt trapped," she said.

One of Maria Teresa's sisters said she had a disconcertingly similar experience. Maria Elena, who shares her sister's long dark hair and small stature, but is far shier, also worked as a bread packer. One day, she said, her supervisor took her aside and told her that the bakery's top manager wanted to fire her. But the supervisor quickly reassured Maria Elena that he had saved her job by putting in a good word for her.

Soon, Maria Elena's supervisor began dropping by her workstation, sometimes three or four times a day, to whisper in her ear. "He frequently said that my body made him tremble, that my boyfriend was lucky to have a woman like me," she said. "When I asked him to respect me and to stop making these comments, he would say that he was only telling the truth."

For two months, her supervisor showered her with compliments, and then, just as she feared, he started asking her out. She refused. Her supervisor was unfazed. At the time she told several coworkers who witnessed this awkward courtship that his breath was so foul that it nauseated her.

Shortly afterward, the supervisor told Maria Elena that her job was again in danger. He said he needed to speak with her as soon as possible, but it had to be outside the bakery. She agreed to meet with him.

Later that week, according to a sexual harassment lawsuit that Maria Elena brought, he picked her up at a street corner near her apartment, some two miles west of Yale University. He drove onto the Connecticut Turnpike and after a few minutes he pulled into a McDonald's parking lot. There, he talked to her once again about her tenuous job status and suddenly his lips were moving close to hers. She told him no, but he grabbed her face and kissed her. He then asked Maria Elena to go to a motel with him, but she said no. He persisted, and she managed to put him off by saying she was having her period. But her supervisor insisted that she agree to meet him in two weeks' time, and over the next fortnight, he stopped by her workstation ten, sometimes twelve times a day.

"He told me that I sexually aroused him, that he wanted my body, that he needed me, that he dreamt about me, that he was counting the days until he was with me," Maria Elena said.

Two weeks passed, and the supervisor again told her that he needed to see her urgently. Once more he said her job was in jeopardy, telling her that they had to meet outside of work. When he picked Maria Elena up this time, he drove straight to a motel, and she felt a sense of dread. Inside the motel room, she said in legal papers, her supervisor made it clear that if she did not submit, she could say good-bye to her job. At the same time, he clumsily sweet-talked her, telling her how good a worker she was and how great an injustice it would be if she was fired.

Maria Elena grew panicky. She started to cry. She saw no way out, and she, too, submitted.

For the next six months, she said, the supervisor kept demanding sex and Maria Elena kept submitting, convinced that she would lose her job if she didn't. After six months, the sexual abuse suddenly stopped, mainly because a unionization drive began at the bakery, causing the company's top executives to warn the bakery's supervisors that they needed to treat the workers better.

Like Maria Teresa, Maria Elena concluded that she couldn't complain to the bakery's top manager about the sexual abuse. She was convinced that the top manager would be glad to get rid of her if she did.

Eva, the sister whose upbeat words had persuaded the others to emigrate from Mexico, said she also suffered repeated abuse. Several supervisors squeezed her breasts and buttocks, and one bluntly told her, "I want to fuck you." Once, according to Eva's lawsuit, a manager started ripping off her blouse in his office, while a different manager literally dragged her to a secluded spot in the back of the bakery and tried to force himself on her.

For Eva, too, quitting was out of the question. Not only did her job pay considerably more than most jobs held by unskilled immigrants, but she had family issues to consider. "My mother was dying," she said. "I had children to support. I didn't have any choice."

After months of abuse and sexual taunting, Eva suffered a breakdown. A friend suggested that she contact her local congresswoman, Rosa DeLauro, and DeLauro's aides put her in touch with the Connecticut office of the United Auto Workers. With the help of the union's lawyers, Eva, Maria Teresa, and Maria Elena filed a sexual harassment lawsuit against Chef Solutions.

The sisters eventually reached a settlement with Chef Solutions, but the company insisted that the settlement be sealed. Throughout the litigation, the bakery's managers denied that there had been any sexual abuse, as did corporate headquarters. After reaching the settlement, top executives at Chef Solutions made clear that the accused managers and supervisors were no longer at the bakery.[1]

"They said America is the place to make dreams come true," Maria Teresa said. "But nobody tells you they can also kill those dreams."

THE SISTERS' ORDEAL goes far to show how vulnerable, frightened, and trapped many illegal immigrants feel. Undocumented workers often put up with horrendous conditions for the same reason the sisters did—a fear of being fired or deported. These workers know they won't be the only ones hurt if they lose their jobs. Their children, their spouses, their parents, their brothers and sisters, either in America or back in their native land, often depend on them and their earnings to lift them out of poverty.

Many immigrants are all the more eager to cling to their jobs because they risked their lives and life savings to get to America. Since the beginning of the decade, more than 2,000 immigrants have died in the deserts of the Southwest while seeking to enter illegally. Many Mexican immigrants paid coyotes $2,000, nearly a year's income for many Mexican peasants, to smuggle them in, and they often remain in debt to their coyotes long after arriving. (Chinese immigrants often pay their smugglers more than $30,000.)

Over the past decade the explosion of illegal immigrants has created a huge pool of easy-to-exploit workers. An estimated 7 million immigrants are working illegally in the United States, up from 1.5 million in 1990.[2] Illegal immigrants accounted for about three-fifths of the more than one million immigrants who entered the nation each year from 2000 to 2005.[3]

Illegal immigrants have quietly undermined the nation's workplace standards not only because they are often willing to work for less but because they tolerate conditions Americans wouldn't, including illegal and dangerous ones, such as when they work—and die—in trenches, on scaffolds, or on farms that fail to take the most basic safety protections.[4] In his book *The Short Sweet Dream of Eduardo Gutiérrez*, Jimmy Breslin wrote movingly about a twenty-one-year-old Mexican who died on a construction project in Brooklyn, suffocating in a pool of cement after the scaffolding he was standing on collapsed. "Eduardo represented the most invaluable part of the economy of the world," Breslin wrote. "He was cheap labor."[5]

These workers often necessarily toil in the shadows, making it easier for managers to exploit them. They work in the wee hours washing and waxing floors for giant retailers, sometimes for thirty nights in a row, as we've seen, or they labor in the back of restaurants washing dishes, often not getting paid overtime for the many extra hours they work. Workers who wax the floors late at night at several ethnic supermarkets in New York City say the store managers not only pull down the metal gates at night but, eager to prevent theft, often padlock the emergency exits. One such floor waxer, Gabriel Juarez, a twenty-year-old immigrant from Mexico, has stayed with the job even though he fears being trapped if there is a fire. "I came here to support my family, and that's what I have to do," he said.

At times, employers have deliberately used illegal immigrants to undermine native-born workers. The janitorial industry in Los Angeles is a case in point. In the early 1980s, most office-building janitors in Los Angeles were native-born and unionized, their pay averaging twelve dollars an hour. But building owners were able to break the union by switching to lower-cost, non-union cleaning contractors who relied on illegal immigrants pouring into Los

Angeles. By the early 1990s, janitors' wages in Los Angeles had plunged to seven dollars an hour.

Immigration has been so strong in recent years that foreign-born workers now represent 15 percent of the nation's workforce, the highest percentage since the 1930s. Between 1994 and 2004, the number of immigrant workers, legal and illegal, rose from 13 million to 21 million.[6] So significant are immigrants to the economy that they accounted for more than half the growth in the workforce from 1994 to 2004.[7]

Of the estimated 21 million foreign-born workers, roughly 7 million are undocumented, 5.5 million have green cards, and 8.5 million are naturalized citizens.[8] Even though undocumented immigrants represent just one in twenty workers, they play a huge role in fields that many Americans shun as too menial. Illegal immigrants represent 27 percent of the nation's drywall workers, 24 percent of dishwashers, 22 percent of maids and housekeepers, 22 percent of meat and poultry workers, and 21 percent of roofing workers.[9] By many estimates, 70 percent of the nation's farm workers are unauthorized immigrants, and so are more than 350,000 maids and more than 250,000 janitors.[10] The film *A Day Without a Mexican* made the point that our world of amenities and creature comforts—neatly manicured lawns and hedges, spotless restaurant dishes and tablecloths, spick-and-span hotel rooms—is largely due to these immigrants.[11]

Many immigrants, especially illegal ones, arrive with limited skills and education. Although immigrants represent 15 percent of the workforce, they account for more than 70 percent of the workers in the United States with less than nine years of education and nearly half of those without a high school diploma.[12]

While much of the nation's focus is on unskilled illegal immigrants, many immigrants arrive on America's shores with impressive educations, especially those who enter on visas that require special skills, such as software programmers from India or registered nurses from the Philippines. Immigrants from India average 16.1 years of education and those from China, 14.6 years—higher than American-born workers, who average 13.7 years.[13] Excluding those from Mexico and Central America, the nation's immigrants earn just 3 percent less than native-born workers on average.[14] Immigrants from Mexico and Central America typically earn about half of what native-born workers earn.[15]

Many employers say they have little choice but to hire illegal immigrants. Tom Lippolt, a contractor on Long Island who builds and repairs homes, says, "They're filling in the gaps. It seems like all the [American] kids want to be stockbrokers. We don't have young people coming in to fill these places, all these trade jobs."[16]

Many of the nation's best-known companies have employed illegal immigrants, directly or indirectly. California's three biggest grocery chains—Albertsons, Ralphs, and Vons (part of Safeway)—used a web of contractors that employed more than 2,000 illegal immigrants to clean their floors.[17] Three Tyson managers pleaded guilty to federal charges of smuggling hundreds of Mexican immigrants to poultry plants in seven states.[18] A California cleaning contractor, Global Building Services, hired hundreds of undocumented janitors to clean Target stores in California, Arizona, Nevada, New Mexico, and Texas.[19]

In October 2003, federal agents raided sixty Wal-Marts in twenty-one states, arresting 250 illegal immigrants who were working as floor cleaners. At the time, Wal-Mart said it had "not seen any evidence that its executives knew contractors were using illegal laborers." Wal-Mart was professing ignorance even though federal agents had arrested one hundred undocumented floor cleaners several years earlier at Wal-Marts in Pennsylvania, New York, Ohio, and Missouri.

One of the undocumented janitors was Rolando Ruiz. After leaving his parents' onion farm in Mexico, he boarded a bus to the border, trekked three nights through the desert, and, within weeks, made his way to relatives in New Jersey. There a recruiter persuaded him to take a seven-night-a-week job, from eleven-thirty p.m. to six-thirty a.m., as a floor cleaner at a Wal-Mart in Brick, New Jersey. At the time, Rolando was fourteen. New Jersey, like many states, prohibits minors under age sixteen, whether or not they are in school, from working more than three hours on school days or working past seven p.m. on school days.

Rolando spent hour after hour pushing a giant buffing machine to polish the floors. Many nights he also operated the stripping machine, which used caustic chemicals to remove layers of wax from the floors, chemicals that blister hands, cause nosebleeds, and eat through the soles of sneakers.

"Every time I worked with the stripping machine, I would get a headache from the chemicals," Rolando said.

By the time he turned eighteen, he said, he had worked at four other Wal-Marts in New Jersey—in Howell, Old Bridge, Piscataway, and Toms River—always seven nights a week, always for a cleaning contractor. (His younger brother, Adiel, began working at the Toms River Wal-Mart when he was fifteen.) The best thing about the job, Rolando said, was the pay: $350 a week.

That meant he earned more in a day than many workers in Mexico earned in a week.

"I liked the job," Rolando said. "I slept in the middle of the day. I got used to it."

Rolando said the managers at several of the Wal-Marts knew that a young teenager was working in their stores after midnight. When asked about teenage illegal immigrants working in Wal-Mart stores, a company spokesman said, "No one at the home office was aware of any such practices by contractors. Nor would we ever condone such practices."

AN INSTINCTIVE SENSE of economics would lead one to believe that an influx of immigrants, whether legal or illegal, would push down wages for American workers. But there is a surprisingly fierce debate about that. Some studies have found that immigration caused wages to fall by nearly 10 percent for some groups, while other studies have concluded that immigration had nearly no effect on wages.

"Immigrants provide scarce labor, which lowers prices in much the same way global trade does," Roger Lowenstein wrote in a cover story for the *New York Times Magazine*. "Overall, the newcomers modestly raise Americans' per capita income. But the impact is unevenly distributed; people with means pay less for taxi rides and household help while the less affluent command lower wages and probably pay more for rent."[20]

George Borjas of Harvard University, one of the foremost economists on the effects of immigration, concluded that the influx of immigrants from 1980 to 2000 had pushed down wages for native-born workers by an average of 3.7 percent or $1,600 a year. That influx, he found, reduced the wages of high school dropouts the most, by 7.4 percent.[21] According to Borjas, the wave of immigrants reduced the wages of native-born Hispanics by 5 percent, African Americans by 4.5 percent, whites by 3.5 percent, and Asians by 3.1 percent.[22]

Borjas wrote, "The reduction in earnings occurs regardless of whether the immigrants are legal or illegal, permanent or temporary. It is the presence of additional workers that reduces wages, not their legal status."[23] A restaurant that pays native-born dishwashers $10 an hour may well lower its wages to $7.50 an hour when a new "supply" of immigrant workers shows up, willing to work for the reduced wage.

David Card, an economist at Berkeley, stands in opposition to Borjas. In a study that caused the economics world to rethink the effects of immigration,

Card found that the Mariel boatlift, which brought 125,000 Cuban workers to Miami in 1980, did not pull down wages there even though it increased Miami's workforce by 7 percent. Card found that the wages of Miami's African American workers had even increased slightly after the boatlift, while wages for black workers had declined in several southern cities that did not experience an influx of immigrants.[24] In a subsequent study of three hundred metropolitan areas, Card found that immigration had a negligible effect on wages even though the foreign-born population in those metropolitan areas had risen to 18 percent of the population in 2000, up from 9.5 percent in 1980.[25]

Some economists suggest that Card found no downward effect on wages because immigrants tended to move to cities with robust economies where wages were already rising. Card theorized that one reason wages did not fall was that many immigrants moved to cities where a previous wave of immigrants had founded businesses, such as apparel factories, that could easily absorb a wave of new, low-skilled workers without pulling down the wages of other workers.[26]

Card puts forward another simple yet often overlooked reason that immigrants might not drive down wages—they are not just workers but are also consumers. They create increased demand for everything from housing to groceries, causing investors to build more housing and supermarkets and generating a need for more carpenters, cashiers, and other workers. In other words, immigration increases not just the supply of workers but also the demand for workers.[27] Card points out that immigrants often do not take the jobs of other workers—if low-paid immigrants were not around to mow lawns, homeowners might mow their lawns themselves. Or if low-paid immigrant nannies were not available, many families would conclude that they simply couldn't afford a nanny.[28]

Another respected study found that immigration hurts wages only for workers at the bottom. Its authors, Giovanni Peri of the University of California at Davis and Gianmarco I. P. Ottaviano of the University of Bologna, found that the wave of immigration from 1980 to 2000 pushed down the wages of American-born high school dropouts by 2.4 percent while pushing up the wages of high school graduates, college dropouts, and college graduates by at least 2.5 percent.[29] "I am talking about a negative effect for about nine percent of the population and a positive effect for ninety-one percent of the population," Peri said.[30] Both authors suggested that the influx of immigrants lifted the economy overall, spurring capital investment and creating opportunities for better-educated workers. An influx of foreign-born nurses and nurses' aides might enable a hospital to build another wing, creating jobs for high-paid doctors and radiologists. Or an increase in immigrant construction workers might mean that more native-born workers get promoted to foreman. Or a surge of immigrant child care workers might enable many well-educated American women to reenter the workforce and take high-paying jobs.[31]

Among immigration experts, one of the biggest debates is whether today's new arrivals will be able to catapult themselves into the middle class like previous generations of immigrants. Some economists say the retirement of millions of baby boomers might foster a labor shortage that will create great opportunities for immigrant workers. But others argue that today's immigrants will be held back more than the Italian, Irish, Slovenian, and Slovakian immigrants of years past because manufacturing jobs, which long gave unskilled immigrants a ticket to the middle class, represent an ever smaller percentage of the workforce, while low-paying service-sector jobs represent an ever larger percentage.

Many Hispanic immigrants are held back because the huge size of the Latino population and wide access to Spanish television allow many to get by without learning English, which hampers their assimilation and economic ascent. In an article in the *New York Times,* Anthony DePalma contrasted the prospects of a Greek immigrant who arrived illegally in 1953 with the prospects of an undocumented Mexican who came here in 1990. The Greek is the wealthy owner of a highbrow diner for Manhattan's elite. The Mexican remains stuck in dead-end restaurant jobs, hindered by his lack of English. His father in Huamuxtitlán in Guerrero State has built stairs for a second floor for the family home, confident that his son will make it big in New York and will someday send him money to complete the upstairs. But, the son says, "I've been here fifteen years, and if I die tomorrow, there wouldn't even be enough money to bury me."[32]

WHEN SMITHFIELD FOODS was scouring the South in the early 1990s for a site to build the world's largest hog slaughterhouse, it chose Bladen County, one of the poorest counties in North Carolina, seventy-five miles south of Raleigh. The area had much to offer: there were plenty of hog farms nearby; there was a river, the Cape Fear, where the plant could dump its wastewater; and the area had thousands of residents looking for work—the county's jobless rate was nearly 12 percent—principally because tobacco was in decline and many textile factories had closed. When the pork-processing plant—a gargantuan complex of pipes, conveyers, and steel—opened in 1992, most of its nearly 1,000 employees were African Americans, although there were many whites and Lumbee Indians, too.

Beginning in the mid-1990s, Smithfield's workforce underwent a huge change that surprised many local residents. Its workers were constantly quitting because, as anyone who read *The Jungle* knows, slaughterhouse jobs are bloody, foul-smelling, and grueling. Hour after hour the Smithfield workers slit the hogs' throats, hack at their shoulders, and carve their loins. Even as many workers were quitting, the company was making plans to double the size of the workforce and run two shifts a day instead of one in order to double the plant's killing operation to 32,000 hogs a day. As it sought to expand, Smithfield often found itself desperate for new workers because so many blacks, whites, and Lumbees from the neighboring counties either had worked at the plant and soured on it or hadn't worked there but wouldn't consider it because they had heard how unpleasant it was.

To meet its labor needs, Smithfield, like many American companies that offer arduous, low-wage jobs, began hiring large numbers of Hispanic immigrants. According to many workers, more than half of them were illegal immigrants; some had presented forged green cards or fake Social Security numbers. Smithfield officials insisted that the company had done everything it could to check that the workers were legal; Smithfield didn't want to push too hard, they said, because the company could face lawsuits for discriminating against Hispanics.

The plant's workforce went from being less than 10 percent Hispanic when it first opened to being 60 percent Hispanic by the end of the decade.[33] By the year 2000, the plant had expanded to 5,200 employees; more than 3,000 of them were Hispanic. This increase in Hispanic workers occurred as North Carolina's Hispanic population nearly quintupled from 77,000 in 1990 to 379,000 a decade later as not just Smithfield but poultry plants, furniture factories, hotels, restaurants, and farms increasingly embraced Hispanic workers.[34]

Among the Hispanic workers who found their way to Smithfield was Alfonso Rodriguez, who began harvesting corn and cutting cane at his parents' farm in Mexico at age five. At sixteen he left in search of a better life north of the border. To Alfonso, it was clear why Smithfield was hiring so many Hispanics. "Americans just don't work as hard," he said.

Alfonso is five feet three, trim and athletic—he loves soccer—with lively eyes, an aquiline nose, a thin jaw, and fine short dark hair. After crossing the border, he did construction work in Texas, picked oranges in Florida, and harvested tobacco in North Carolina. He applied to Smithfield at age twenty-one because, unlike those other jobs, it promised year-round work.

Alfonso's wife, who is as soft-spoken as he is assertive, also worked for years at Smithfield, suffering a badly bruised abdomen when a forklift that was carrying a metal crate filled with hog livers crashed into her and pinned her against a wall.

Alfonso said Hispanics work harder than Americans because "in Mexico, we work from the age of five in the cornfields. We're used to working hard." Hispanics also work harder, he said, because managers often seek to squeeze more out of them because they know how desperate immigrant workers are to please their employers and avoid getting fired.

"Americans know that if they don't like their job, they can always leave and find something else," Alfonso said. "The Hispanics know their situation is precarious. The Mexican, no matter how he's treated, he'll work hard. He doesn't have any choice."

Alfonso said many Smithfield managers pushed the workers mercilessly, especially the Hispanics, sometimes ordering a team of three Hispanics to do what is normally done by four workers. Alfonso described the unrelenting pressure of the cutting room floor, where the workers hack and carve with a mindless fury, working just inches from each other with sharp knives, knives that, in the constant rush, sometimes slip and tear into the hand, the shoulder, even the face of a neighboring worker—and sometimes even into one's own arm or hand. On the loin line, Alfonso said, some workers couldn't keep up with the line speed, often causing chunks of meat to back up at their workstations, so much so that meat sometimes tumbled to the floor. At times the loin-line crew, working in forty-three-degree cold, had to rush so much to keep up that they did a bad job cutting the meat and minutes later a supervisor would march over, throw the poorly cut meat at them, and start screaming.

"The line goes so fast that sometimes it feels like we're all going to hell," Alfonso said. "It makes you feel so bad that you don't want to go back after your first break. You feel, 'Oh, fuck.' You're working in this terrible cold, but you're working so hard that you're sweating."

Alfonso said it was well known that many native-born workers couldn't—or wouldn't—take it and would quit after just a week or two at Smithfield.

The pay, he explained, is a major factor why Mexicans are loath to quit or to protest their mistreatment and risk getting fired. "This is a good wage for us," said Alfonso, who earned twelve dollars an hour or nearly one hundred dollars a day. "If a Mexican makes even fifty dollars a day here, that's terrific money for us. In Mexico, I might have made ten dollars a day in farming and a little more than that at a factory."

Smithfield of course profited from the lower wages that Hispanic workers were willing to accept. "They're dragging down the pay," complained Wade Baker, an African American worker at the plant. "It's pure economics. They say Americans don't want to do the job. That ain't exactly true. We don't want to do it for eight dollars. Pay fifteen dollars and we'll do it."[35]

Smithfield also embraced Hispanic workers because it is usually easier to turn them against labor unions. After many blacks voted for a union during an unsuccessful organizing drive at the plant in 1994, Smithfield hired many Hispanics and then worked assiduously to poison their views toward unions. One former Smithfield manager told the National Labor Relations Board that the company kept a list of union sympathizers, firing blacks, many of whom supported the union, and replacing them with Latinos, who were often scared of being seen as union supporters.[36]

Alfonso described one meeting that the immigrant workers were ordered to attend. "A manager said, 'I hear that union people are visiting you,' " he recalled. " 'You shouldn't listen to those people. Those people, they use you. They're manipulators. The union doesn't do anything for you. They drive around in their luxury cars and they stay at the best hotels. If you have a union, you're going to be paying for all that.' "

Alfonso said Hispanics weren't taking jobs from African Americans or other native-born Americans. Rather, he said, Hispanics were merely filling a steady stream of openings at the plant. It's not as if the slaughterhouse, where many workers earn $20,000 to $27,000 a year, is a stable workplace where many Americans stay for a decade and climb into the middle class.

Smithfield executives said the company did not prefer hiring Hispanics over other workers. Nor, they said, did company managers pressure Hispanics to work harder or faster than others. "You got the line running at the same speed for everyone," said Dennis Pittman, a company spokesman. "I don't see how you can work one person harder than another."

Smithfield's enthusiastic embrace of Hispanics came to a sudden end in November 2006. Feeling heat from federal immigration officials, the company started cooperating with the government and sent letters to 640 Hispanic employees, telling them that their identity information did not match government records. The company gave them fourteen days to show that their identification papers were valid, and as soon as that time passed, Smithfield began firing some of those immigrants. In a surprising move, more than 1,000 workers, most of them Hispanic, staged a wildcat strike, angry at the way Smithfield was casting out some loyal, longtime employees. The striking workers—Alfonso was one of the strike's leaders—called on Smithfield to rescind its plan to fire workers who had received no-match letters, but Smithfield, eager not to get on the government's bad side, refused. The company persuaded the strikers to return to work after one day by agreeing to give the immigrants sixty days instead of fourteen to try to show that their papers were legitimate.

Two months later, tensions and fears exploded once again when Smithfield management asked twenty-one Hispanic workers to report to the human resources department, where, to the workers' astonishment, federal agents arrested them. They were soon deported.

Alfonso felt that Smithfield had betrayed those workers. "If workers are having problems with immigration, why does the company collude with ICE [Immigration and Customs Enforcement]?" he said. "Why can't they quietly tell us, 'Leave your job, get out of here'? It would at least show some appreciation for all the work we've done for them."

Those arrests were part of the Bush administration's stepped-up effort in which Immigration and Customs Enforcement arrested 4,393 workers in fiscal year 2007, more than eight times the amount five years earlier. Federal agents sometimes arrested hundreds of immigrants at a time, conducting raids at dozens of facilities, including six Swift meat-processing plants, a Koch Foods poultry plant in Fairfield, Ohio, and Fresh Del Monte Produce in Portland, Oregon.

After the no-match letters were sent out and after the twenty-one arrests in January 2007, hundreds of Hispanics quietly quit their jobs at Smithfield out of fear they would be arrested if they stayed at a plant that was cooperating with immigration authorities. Those fears seemed justified when federal agents, using information provided by Smithfield, raided two dozen homes and trailers in August 2007, banging on doors and windows in the middle of the night. That night they arrested twenty-eight Smithfield workers, with those workers facing not only deportation but more than a year in prison on charges of identity theft for using someone else's ID papers to get hired.

Pittman, the company spokesman, said Smithfield's cooperation with immigration officials improves the company's image and "serves [its] goal of 100 percent compliance 100 percent of the time."

Many North Carolinians applauded the enforcement effort, saying it would open job opportunities for Americans and reduce the burden that illegal immigrants and their children place on schools and other government services. "It is in the long-term interest of the nation to send them back and to send people who break our laws to jail," said William Gheen, a resident of Raleigh who is president of Americans for Legal Immigration.[37]

But Father Carlos Arce, the priest at three Roman Catholic churches in communities near the plant, said the arrests dealt a dispiriting blow to Smith-field's immigrant workers. "They don't know what to do," he said. "They feel unprotected. They feel alone. They are confused because they have been here working a long time at the plant, and they thought the plant would protect them. People are really afraid. Many are afraid to go outside. Many are even afraid to come to church. Some people are thinking about going back to Mex-ico even though their children were born in America and are American citi-zens. It's very sad what's happening."

After nearly seven years at the plant, Alfonso quit. "I saw the writing on the wall," he said. Alfonso, who has taken a construction job that pays $2.50 an hour less than his Smithfield job, is stunned by all the venom being directed against immigrants. "We think people are jealous of us," he said. "They see us advancing. They see us having some success."

As a result of the arrests and turmoil, the percentage of Hispanic workers at the Smithfield plant has dropped to 27 percent, while blacks now represent nearly 60 percent of the workforce, double the percentage in early 2006. After losing longtime employees to immigration raids, some companies in the South rebuilt their workforce by hiring the homeless and newly released pris-oners, while other companies raised wages to attract workers. Smithfield sought to attract workers not by increasing wages, but by running repeated television ads in which workers, most of them black, said Smithfield was a good place to work. Notwithstanding those ads, many local blacks still shun the plant, and as a result, Smithfield has hired a surprising number of blacks from indigent towns in South Carolina, as far as sixty miles away.

Sandy Avila remains shaken by the confrontation in which five armed immigration agents began pounding on her trailer door at four a.m. and arrested her mother, Ana, a Smithfield employee for nearly a decade.

"I was sad and scared," said Avila, who worked at Smithfield alongside her mother. "We're not here to hurt anybody. We're here to make things better for our family. We just want to work."

ILLEGAL IMMIGRANTS CERTAINLY flout our laws by working illegally, but for some observers their poverty and willingness to work hard are mitigating factors. In many ways, their employers deserve more of our disapproval. Many employers violate federal law not just by hiring unauthorized workers but by failing to pay minimum wage, time and a half for overtime, and Social Security and unemployment insurance taxes. Indeed, employers who hire immigrants seem endlessly imaginative in devising ways to skirt the nation's wage, hour, and safety laws.

Isaias Garcia, an immigrant from Mexico, used to work sixteen hours a day, eighty hours a week, cleaning office buildings in the Anaheim area. But in an unusual twist, Garcia said, his managers often insisted on paying him under names other than his own—one name for his first forty hours, a second name for his second forty hours. That way the company never paid overtime.[38]

In Manhattan, Muhammed Kouanda, an immigrant from Burkina Faso in West Africa, said he received $75 in wages for working seventy-two hours a week delivering groceries for Gristede's, a supermarket chain. With tips included, Kouanda said, his earnings averaged $175 a week ($2.43 an hour). Gristede's said that Kouanda and hundreds of other workers who made deliveries from its stores were not its employees but employees of a contractor. That contractor, Great American Delivery, asserted that its deliverymen were independent contractors, who, unlike regular employees, are not covered by minimum wage and overtime laws. Eliot Spitzer, then New York State's attorney general, disagreed. He got Gristede's to agree to pay $3.2 million in back wages to more than three hundred deliverymen to cover minimum wage and overtime violations.

Mei Ying Liu said she never received any wages whatsoever while working eighty-hour weeks as a waitress at King Chef, a Chinese restaurant in Wayne, New Jersey. During her seventeen months there, she said, all she received was tips, with the managers often letting her keep just eighteen dollars in tips for a twelve-hour day. New Jersey law requires that wages be paid to tipped employees. Liu said the balance of her tips was withheld ostensibly to pay for a squalid apartment that the restaurant's managers told her to live in. Five unknown men slept in the living room, she said, while eight women squeezed into a bedroom without dressers and with bunk beds crammed so closely together that the women often had to climb over one another to get to their beds.[39]

Soon after leaving Mexico, Moises and Rigoberto Xaca landed jobs in Blythewood, South Carolina, digging trenches for electrical and telecommunications lines for a new high school. On their first day on the job, the two brothers were crushed to death when the trench's sandy walls collapsed. Moises was seventeen, and Rigoberto, fifteen. OSHA fined the contractor $42,075 for six violations, including failure to analyze the soil and failure to instruct the workers on how to prevent a trench collapse. Maria Smoak, director of the Hispanic ministry at St. Peter's Catholic Church in Columbia, South Carolina, asked whether the contractor would "be as careless or as negligent if they had been non-Hispanic workers."[40]

In Georgia and Mississippi, Mexican and Guatemalan guest workers toil fifty to sixty hours a week planting seedlings, but their employers— contractors hired by corporate giants such as International Paper—often pay them for fewer hours, often not paying them for the ninety-minute round-trip drive between the warehouse where they pick up seedlings and the planting areas.[41] The tree planters, who receive visas to work under the H-2B program, dare not complain for fear of getting fired, partly because many had already paid more than $1,500 in visa and transportation fees to get to their jobs. To make sure that tree planters do not quit, some contractors require the planters to give them the deeds to their homes while they work in the United States.[42]

In addition to the savings achieved through such familiar practices as making immigrants work endless hours or not giving them breaks, many employers recognize that there are huge advantages in working them off the books. "When you don't pay taxes, don't pay Social Security, and don't pay workers' comp, you have a forty percent cost advantage, and that makes it hard for companies that follow the rules," said Lilia Garcia, executive director of the Maintenance Cooperation Trust Fund, a Los Angeles group backed by business and labor that monitors cleaning contractors for wage violations.

Patricia Smith, the State of New York's labor commissioner, said many businesses that employ immigrants seem to slide toward a lowest common denominator. "When we ask owners why they're paying so little," she said, "they say, 'That's what everybody else pays.' "

AMERICANS HAVE A LOVE-HATE relationship with illegal immigrants. Many Americans are seething about the wholesale lawbreaking that illegal immigration represents, yet many Americans gladly hire illegal immigrants to mow their lawns or work as nannies, and many economists say the flood of these immigrants benefits the economy. Some economists say that howling against illegal immigration makes as little sense as howling against air that is rushing to fill a vacuum. Daniel T. Griswold, an economist at the Cato Institute, wrote: "Demand for low-skilled labor continues to grow in the United States, while the domestic supply of suitable workers inexorably declines—yet U.S. immigration law contains virtually no legal channel through which low-skilled immigrant workers can enter the country to fill that gap . . . American immigration laws are colliding with reality, and reality is winning."[43]

The friends and foes of illegal immigrants agree that something must be done. To many hard-line critics of illegal immigration, the solution is to crack down at the borders, to build a 700-mile-long fence, and to expel the seven million foreigners who are working here illegally. But to the illegal immigrants and their advocates, the solution is to somehow regularize these immigrants so that they can remain in the United States and gain a path to citizenship, which would mean they would no longer have to live and work outside the law and suffer exploitation.

There is widespread consensus that any sensible immigration policy would contain three elements: getting control of the border, restoring legality to the labor market, and meeting the economy's needs for labor. Some believe that the best way to control the border is to spend billions more on border guards, but past spending increases on stepped-up patrols did little to stanch the flow. Some say a smarter way to reduce the flow would be to make it harder for employers to hire illegals. That would probably entail, first, setting up a system that requires all workers to have counterfeit-proof IDs, and second, creating a national database that would be used to check the Social Security numbers of all job applicants to help prevent the hiring of immigrants who use fake or stolen numbers. Such a system would be far more foolproof than the nation's longtime system in which immigrants often trick employers—who can seem easily tricked—with counterfeit green cards or Social Security cards. Under a 1986 law, employers were largely free to hire any worker as long as they made a good-faith effort—read fumbling and halfhearted effort—to determine whether IDs were legitimate.

To stop employers from hiring illegal workers will require something that has, until very recently, been sorely lacking: political will. In 1998, just hours after forty-five federal agents raided the Vidalia onion fields of Georgia with plans to arrest more than 1,000 illegal immigrants, the government faced a fierce backlash from growers and politicians. Senator Paul Coverdell, a Republican, led the fight, denouncing the enforcement effort as "a moonshine raid" against "honest farmers who are simply trying to get their products from the field to the marketplace."[44] Days later, the government backed off, granting temporary amnesty to the illegal onion pickers. "There was hypocrisy," said Doris Meissner, who was director of the Immigration and Naturalization Service at the time. "On one hand, you say you want enforcement, and then you see it's not so easy to live with the consequences."[45]

For the next eight years, federal immigration officials, fearing similar backlashes, did hardly any workplace enforcement. But in 2006, the Bush administration, after being derided for doing next to nothing to crack down on illegal immigration, began its series of high-publicity raids. The administration arrested thousands of undocumented workers, but it still went easy on employers, arresting fewer than one hundred business owners and officials in 2007 for employing illegal immigrants. But even a vigorous crackdown on employers will not be nearly enough to solve the nation's immigration problems. There will have to be a sensible way to meet the nation's labor market needs as well, because as long as there is a shortage of workers, immigrants will find a way to fill the void.

To satisfy labor needs in sectors such as vegetable picking, meatpacking, and hotel housekeeping, many lawmakers and businesses have called for admitting at least three times as many foreign guest workers each year. Under existing law, some 200,000 foreigners receive H-1B, H-2A, or H-2B work visas each year that last from two months to two years. Guest worker programs, however, often encourage employers to hire low-paid foreign workers instead of American workers who might be happy to take the jobs if they paid somewhat more. Moreover, many employers cheat guest workers by paying them less than legally required and putting them in substandard housing. If Congress approves a larger guest worker program, it is imperative that American workers are given priority for those jobs the guest workers would take; it is also important to significantly strengthen federal laws and enforcement to protect guest workers from exploitation.

The fiercest debate about illegal immigration is how to treat the seven million undocumented workers who are already here. Hard-liners like Representative Tom Tancredo, a Colorado Republican, say these workers should be expelled forthwith. Others have called for granting illegal immigrants a path to legalization and citizenship, but only if they first return to their native lands for a year or so and apply for visas from there. That means these workers must quit their jobs, but that is not realistic because many of them fear they will never be allowed to return to the United States, let alone get their jobs back.

Senators John McCain and Edward Kennedy have long argued that the best way to restore law and order to the job market would be to let undocumented workers pay a fine and then apply for work authorization that might ultimately lead to citizenship.[46] That proposal, combined with counterfeit-proof

ID cards and a national database to screen job applicants, would go far to end today's chaos. In June 2007, the Senate killed a bill backed by President Bush, McCain, and Kennedy that would have increased border security and granted legal status to most of the nation's illegal immigrants while also requiring them to pay fines and return to their homelands at least once.

Many critics derided that proposal as rewarding those who break the law. A strong response to that argument came from the *Wall Street Journal* editorial page: "This amnesty charge may be potent as a political slogan, but it becomes far less persuasive when you examine its real-world implications . . . Those who wave the 'no amnesty' flag are actually encouraging a larger underground illegal population . . . The only reform that has a chance to succeed is one that recognizes the reality that 10 or so million illegal aliens already work in the U.S. and are vital to the economy and their communities. More enforcement is a slogan, not a solution."[47]

WHEN IT COMES TO IMPROVING their lives, many of today's immigrants are looking to the same solution that immigrants looked to a century ago—a union. Successful unions could do a great deal to induce employers to ease the squeeze on American workers. But as we are about to see, America's unions are in deep trouble.

Chapter Thirteen

THE STATE OF THE UNIONS

In 1997, Ercilia Sandoval took a part-time job as a janitor at Ben Taub Hospital in Houston. The pay was $5.25 an hour, $104 a week. For the next nine years, she hopped between janitorial jobs, spending the last few years cleaning floors eighteen through twenty at the Aon Building, an exclusive office tower near the opulent Galleria Mall. Throughout those nine years her pay remained the same.

"Everything has gone up except our wages," she said. "If we ask for a raise, they say, 'Anyone who doesn't like it here, there's the door. There are lots of people waiting to take your job.'"

To Ercilia, an immigrant from El Salvador, not having health insurance was as big a problem as her puny paycheck. When her seven-year-old daughter, Genesis, had an allergy attack that caused vomiting, fever, and a rash, the doctor's visit cost $165, far more than Ercilia's weekly pay. And then a dentist at the school health fair found that Genesis had six cavities, which would cost a total of $750 to fill.

"To pay for the allergist, we had to take from our food money," Ercilia said. "How we're going to pay for the dentist, I have no idea."

It was not until two organizers from the Service Employees International Union appeared at her church one Sunday morning, seeking to persuade the janitors in the congregation to unionize, that it dawned on Ercilia that unionization might be the best vehicle to pull her out of her rut. She was moved by what they told her about a campaign to unionize 4,500 janitors in New Jersey. Before that effort began, those janitors earned $5.85 an hour, worked part-time, and didn't have health benefits. As a result of the unionization effort and the contract that followed, their hourly wage doubled within five years, they obtained health coverage, and many of their jobs were converted to forty hours a week from twenty. Janitors who were earning $6,000 a year in 2001 were earning nearly $25,000 five years later.

Ercilia wanted the same thing, so she threw herself wholeheartedly into a campaign to unionize more than 5,000 office-building janitors in Houston.

"We don't have anything," she said. "That's why we're in this struggle. We need the union."

More than any other institution in America, labor unions work to improve the lives of low-wage workers and to reduce inequality. More than any other institution, unions seek to ensure a fair distribution of productivity and profits. If America's political leaders are serious about helping low-income workers and putting an end to wage stagnation and widening inequality, they would push for ways to make it easier for workers to join unions. Today's leaders could look to the example of Franklin Delano Roosevelt, who viewed unions as an important tool for lifting workers out of poverty and building a prosperous economy.

To be sure, many unions have been afflicted by corruption, overpaid bosses, suffocating bureaucracy, and a lack of energy and vision. But ever since the American Federation of Labor was founded in 1886, unions have pushed, albeit with occasional stumbles, to better the lives of the nation's workers. The forty-hour week, the minimum wage, health coverage, pensions, Social Security, unemployment insurance, workers' compensation, occupational safety rules, and prohibitions on child labor were all made possible by labor's moral vision, political muscle, and bargaining clout. A popular bumper sticker puts labor's role in perspective: "The Labor Movement—The Folks Who Brought You the Weekend."

Economic studies have found an unquestionable financial advantage for workers who join unions. Unions raise workers' wages by 20 percent on average, and when health coverage and other benefits are added, they increase total compensation by 28 percent.[1] Unionized workers are 28 percent more likely to have employer-provided health insurance than nonunion workers and 54 percent more likely to have employer-provided pensions, and the benefits union members receive are usually more generous than those received by nonunion workers. Union members usually pay lower health insurance premiums and receive higher pension payouts. They receive 26 percent more vacation days on average.[2] One Bureau of Labor Statistics survey found that unionized women earn 33 percent more than nonunion women on average, African American union members earn 35 percent more, and unionized Hispanic workers earn 51 percent more.[3]

Unionized plants have greater productivity per worker, several studies have found, because employee turnover is generally lower, workers are often trained better, and managers, knowing they have higher labor costs, often push harder to increase productivity. One survey of the economic literature found "a positive association" between unions and productivity,[4] while another study found that unionized factories were 22 percent more productive than nonunion ones.[5] That can often offset higher pay and benefits.

Labor's detractors say, accurately, that unionization has contributed to factory closings, corporate bankruptcies, and outsourcing. In the years after the Congress of Industrial Organizations began unionizing millions of auto, steel, and rubber workers in the 1930s, manufacturing became the heart of organized labor. Unionization in those industries did wonders to build America's middle class, but it made those industries vulnerable when imports from lower-wage countries began to soar in the 1980s. As foreign competition intensified, a unionized auto parts factory that paid eighteen dollars an hour was more likely to close than a nonunion one paying ten dollars an hour.

IT IS HARD TO OVERSTATE how much America's labor unions have declined in power, in prestige, and in the public's consciousness. There was a time when, to borrow Michael Lewis's phrase, unions were the "new, new thing." That was in the 1930s after Franklin Roosevelt and Congress enacted the National Labor Relations Act (the Wagner Act), which not only gave workers a federally protected right to form unions but also gave the government's blessing to unions. It was an era when millions of workers flooded into unions and unions inspired. They were beacons for progress and prosperity. Leading songwriters wrote songs about them. John L. Lewis and Walter Reuther became household names. Sidney Hillman, the president of the Amalgamated Clothing Workers, was one of Roosevelt's top advisers. Unions were so much at the center of things that some mornings six labor-related stories ran on the front page of the *New York Times*. By the mid-1950s, 35 percent of American workers belonged to unions.

But today, Big Labor is no longer so big. Just 12.1 percent of American workers are in unions, and in the private sector, just 7.5 percent are, the lowest level since 1901.[6] Reuther's mighty UAW has shrunk from 1.5 million workers to 500,000. Just six states—California, New York, Illinois, Michigan, Ohio, and Pennsylvania—account for half of all union members. In candid moments, some labor leaders confess that American unions seem to be sliding toward irrelevance and oblivion.

Beginning in the 1950s, many labor leaders largely abandoned the ambitious, inspiring organizing efforts that had not long before turned unions into powerhouses. Several unions, most notably the Teamsters and the East Coast longshoremen, became notorious for mob corruption, and many union locals became little more than moneymaking enterprises for union officials. Far too many union leaders forgot that they had an image to worry about, and soon the image of labor became not a scrappy organizer or a gutsy striker bloodied by Pinkertons but instead a paunchy, cigar-chomping union leader stretched out at a hotel swimming pool in Florida.

Some people say unions should be written off as hopelessly corrupt because of the many labor scandals over the years. But it makes no more sense to dismiss unions on these grounds than it would be to dismiss all American corporations because of the Enron, Tyco, and WorldCom scandals. Unions need what American corporations need—tougher penalties for corrupt officials and tougher scrutiny by government and auditors.

At many unions, the notion of union democracy became an oxymoron. Many union presidents saw themselves as presidents-for-life. Too often they surrounded themselves with yes-men who were scared to challenge them or raise fresh ideas. And too often union leaders deliberately kept the rank and file uninvolved and in the dark, usually because they knew that an informed, invigorated rank and file could someday rise up against them on anything from bloated leader salaries to terrible contracts. A movement that was once inspiring became a champion of the status quo. It had lost its vigor, its vision, and its way.

Many union leaders took far too long to realize that the economy was moving away from them. Factory jobs were under assault from automation and imports, and the service sector was growing dominant. Many union officials tried to stop some of the most powerful economic trends—imports, deregulation, and globalization—but of course they could not. Many unions failed to see that they had two choices, adapt or die, and they did very little to adapt. Too often union leaders dug in to defend mindless featherbedding rules instead of working to make companies more efficient, to help them compete and survive and save union members' jobs. Too often union leaders viewed their role as clinging to a status quo for white male craft workers and defending those workers' privileged positions. Too often they saw their role as helping only union members and not all workers. Too often they showed little concern about women, African Americans, Hispanics, and low-wage workers—the workers who needed unions most.

In a field where the motto had once been "Don't Mourn, Organize," organizing, and growth, became an afterthought. At times labor's motto seemed to have become "Don't Organize, Mourn."[7]

At the same time that labor was stumbling, powerful economic forces were at work to weaken it further. The surge in imports dealt a body blow to manufacturing, labor's longtime base, while the deregulation championed by presidents Carter and Reagan destroyed unionized companies and union members' jobs in airlines, trucking, and telecommunications. New technologies, such as robots in auto plants, also took a heavy toll on union jobs. Facing ever-fiercer competitive pressures, corporate America moved jobs to the lower-cost, anti-union South and then overseas. Pummeled by recession, imports, and deregulation, unions lost one-fifth of their private-sector membership during the 1980s. Most new jobs were in the service sector, for instance, in banks, law firms, specialty stores, and hair salons, fields where unions faced an especially hard time organizing. And as we've seen, corporate America hired more and more contingent workers—temps, freelancers, and independent contractors—workers who were usually beyond the grasp of union organizers.

Entrepreneurialism and individuality became America's animating notions as the concept of solidarity was largely forgotten. As a result, many workers, especially young workers, saw unions as irrelevant, even antithetical, to the brilliant careers they sought for themselves. They would pull themselves up on their own, or so they thought, and they didn't think unions could help. This was especially true during the high-tech boom when career opportunities seemed limitless and companies showered benefits on their workers.

"It is a culture of the individual," said Julie Bick, who worked developing CD-ROMs at Microsoft. "It's entrepreneurial. Everyone writes their own six-month objective, and you have stock options, a great health club, great health benefits, maternity leave. The purpose of a union is to get better benefits, but it's pretty hard to beat the benefits we were already getting. What would a union be bargaining for?"

FROM SEVEN A.M. TO THREE P.M., Marie Sylvain had to take care of fourteen nursing home patients, not the recommended maximum of ten. She had to feed each of them breakfast, ferry their trays to and from the kitchen, brush their teeth, change their linens, give many of them a bath or shower, dress many of them, and take them to the dining room for lunch.

"They give you too many patients," said Marie, an immigrant from Haiti who is in her early forties. "You can't relax. You can't talk to them. Sometimes three o'clock comes, and you have two patients left to do. Your lunchtime comes, and you don't have time to take it."

One day Marie's sister, Esther, told her that a union organizer wanted to talk with her, and Marie couldn't wait to pour out her heart about conditions at the nursing home, Palm Gardens in North Miami. Marie was seething about the pace of work and the pay—she earned so little that she and her two teenage daughters were on food stamps and Medicaid. ("You can't take the health insurance, honey, it costs too much," Marie said.) She was also upset about unsafe conditions because her sister had severely injured her back at Palm Gardens when she slipped on a wet floor while lifting a patient.

"I know if I got a union, maybe they'd help us to find a better wage, maybe they don't give you too many patients," Marie said. "When you have the union at your job, when they think of doing something to you, they think about the union and they don't do it. They know you have the union to fight for you."

Marie is short and surprisingly muscular, with intense dark eyes, a thick head of hair, a loud contralto voice, and an unabashed fervor about her evangelical beliefs. She left Haiti for South Florida in 1980 and received her green card six years later.

Soon after meeting with the union organizer, Marie began urging her coworkers to sign cards calling for a union election. As soon as the managers got wind of Marie's efforts, they ordered the workers to attend meeting after meeting where the workers were warned that the union only wanted their dues money. At one meeting, managers staged mock contract negotiations in which the union officials were dunces who agreed to cut the workers' pay to the minimum wage. The managers warned that unions meant strikes and weeks without pay. They gave out buttons saying "Vote No."

"They do so many things to make you scared," Marie said. "They always say the union can do nothing for us. I tell them, 'If the union's so bad for the workers, why do you even fight it?' "

After a month of threats and propaganda, the nursing home aides finally voted on whether to join a union called Unite for Dignity, an unusual joint venture formed by the service employees and Unite Here, the union representing apparel, hotel, and restaurant workers. Before the votes were counted, Marie left for a vacation in Haiti.

When she returned, she was stunned to learn that the nursing home's employees had voted against unionizing, thirty-five to thirty-two. She was also surprised that her name had been removed from the work schedule, indicating that she might have been terminated.

Marie went to talk to her supervisor. "I say, 'You have to give me my job. I have my family to feed.' " But the supervisor told Marie that she was being fired because she had gone on vacation without submitting the required vacation request form and without getting a manager to sign it. Marie swears that she filed the form and had a supervisor sign it. Many years, according to NLRB statistics, thousands of workers are illegally fired, demoted, or otherwise retaliated against because they supported a union.[8]

The union now sought to rally the workers, vowing to seek a new election on the grounds that the nursing home's managers had illegally poisoned the atmosphere through intimidation and lies. But on learning of Marie's dismissal, the other workers grew too scared to speak out in favor of a union. The termination took a heavy personal toll, making it hard for Marie to feed her daughters. The termination also sucked all the wind out of the unionization drive.

Marie's story is part of a trend in which much of corporate America has taken a far more hostile attitude toward unions. Until the early 1980s, American companies generally saw unions as a sometime partner, sometime antagonist that they had to deal with, however reluctantly. But then came a sharp change in attitude as many corporate executives concluded that they should undertake all-out battles to keep unions out or render them insignificant. Part of this new attitude stemmed from heightened competitive pressures from imports and deregulation, and part stemmed from Wall Street's stepped-up demands to maximize profits. Martin Jay Levitt, a former anti-union consultant who wrote a book about union busting, said that President Reagan's aggressive anti-union behavior in firing 11,500 air traffic controllers who had engaged in an illegal strike also had a powerful effect on corporate attitudes. "In ninety days Ronald Reagan recast the crimes of union busting as acts of patriotism," Levitt wrote.[9]

In some corporate milieus, any manager who failed to keep out a union was viewed as not being tough enough. Such a failure often led to demotion or even dismissal.

With great sophistication and lots of money, many companies turned up the heat against unions. Kate Bronfenbrenner of Cornell University found that 75 percent of companies facing organizing drives hired anti-union consultants. Ninety-two percent forced employees to attend meetings to hear anti-union propaganda, while 78 percent required workers to attend one-on-one meetings in which managers force-fed them the company's anti-union message. The study found that 51 percent of companies threatened to close plants if unions won, while just 1 percent actually closed operations after a union victory.[10]

Many companies keep unions at bay through a kinder, gentler strategy—

they offer union-level wages and benefits, and they treat their workers well. For instance, union leaders have asked why they should bother to devote their energy and money to seek to organize all Costco stores—only about 15 percent of them are unionized—when Costco already treats its workers so well and so many other retailers do not.

A federal commission headed by John Dunlop, the Harvard University labor relations professor who served eleven presidents, found that union supporters were retaliated against in one in four union elections.[11] Another study found that during organizing drives one in eighteen union supporters were somehow victimized—for example, fired, demoted, or moved to a worse shift.[12] American workers have certainly gotten the message about the perils they face if they seek to unionize. A poll conducted for the Dunlop Commission found that 79 percent of Americans believe that it is "very" or "somewhat likely" that "nonunion workers will get fired if they try to organize a union."[13]

When two hundred U-Haul mechanics in Nevada sought to unionize, the company—according to charges filed by the National Labor Relations Board—illegally discharged forty-one of them for backing a union.[14] After unions sought to organize 4,100 workers at the giant Avondale shipyard outside New Orleans, a federal administrative law judge found that the company had illegally fired twenty-two workers for supporting a union. The judge ordered them reinstated with full back pay four years after they were fired.[15]

It took four and a half years for Marie Sylvain to get her job back. That was only after the union had spent tens of thousands of dollars on litigation that included administrative law hearings, an appeal to the full five-person NLRB in Washington, and an appeal to a United States Court of Appeals. At each level, the judges agreed that Marie's nursing home was so eager to fire her for supporting the union that it fabricated the story that she had failed to file a vacation form. By the time the appeals court ordered Marie's reinstatement, the unionization drive at Palm Gardens had fizzled out.

It took even longer, six years, for Marie's friend, Ernest Duval, to be reinstated. A judge found that his employer, the King David Nursing Home in Palm Beach, had concocted a story to fire him by claiming that he had sought to choke a nurse. The judge ordered the nursing home to pay Duval just $1,757 in back wages even though he had been terminated six years earlier. That amount was so small because federal law allows companies that illegally dismiss union supporters to subtract, from the back pay owed, whatever money the workers earned in other jobs after they were fired. (Duval, an immigrant from Haiti, had become a translator for Catholic Charities.) For the nursing home, $1,757 was a modest investment to get rid of the head of the unionization drive and effectively kill the unionization effort.

"They were supposed to punish them for that wrongdoing," Duval said, "but there was really no punishment."[16]

FOR THOSE WHO HOPE the labor movement will regain its strength, there is one especially tantalizing statistic: 53 percent of nonmanagerial, nonunion workers—nearly 50 millon workers—say they would definitely or probably vote to join a union today if they could.[17] So why does union membership remain stuck somewhere below 16 million?

The answer can be found in part in labor's failure to inspire, but even more so in the behind-the-scenes work of one of America's stealthiest, least-known industries. It euphemistically calls itself "the union-avoidance industry." Others call it union busting.

In the 1960s, there were perhaps one hundred "union-avoidance" consultants; today there are some 2,000, ranging from shady outfits that routinely break the law to some of the nation's most respectable law firms.[18]

"Union busting is a field populated by bullies and built on deceit," wrote Martin Jay Levitt, the former anti-union consultant. "A campaign against a union is an assault on individuals and a war on the truth. As such, it is a war without honor. The only way to bust a union is to lie, distort, manipulate, threaten, and always, always attack. The law does not hamper the process."[19]

Levitt admitted that during his union-busting days he planted contraband in the lockers of pro-union workers who had drug records. He made anonymous telephone calls to the wife of a union activist, telling her a concocted story that her husband was with another woman. Through such tactics, he succeeded in keeping out unions more than 98 percent of the time.[20]

Over the years, union-avoidance consultants have advised companies to adopt no-solicitation policies, announcing that they won't even allow the Salvation Army on their property. They then threaten to arrest union organizers for trespass if they even set foot in the employee parking lot.[21] The consultants tell companies to warn employees that bullying union organizers will make unwarranted intrusions on their privacy by calling them at home or knocking on their doors. Union organizers often must resort to contacting workers that way because they can't set foot on company property. Meanwhile, inside the workplace, management often shows anti-union videos and forces workers to hear anti-union propaganda in large meetings and in one-on-one sessions with their supervisors. Richard Bensinger, the AFL-CIO's former organizing director, once likened the situation to a presidential campaign in which Bill Clinton had access to voters in all fifty states twenty-four hours a day, while Bob Dole had to stand on the Canadian border with a bullhorn, desperately shouting to voters.

Frequently, the anti-union consultants fill a prominent bulletin board inside the workplace with disparaging newspaper stories that tell of union corruption, high-living union bosses, months-long strikes, and plants that closed soon after workers voted to unionize. Some managers facing unionization drives have parked flatbed trucks outside their plant and loaded machinery in back with a sign saying MEXICO.[22]

If the union still has the upper hand as a unionization election approaches, consultants frequently tell companies to delay, delay, delay. They tell them to file lengthy legal challenges about which workers should be in the bargaining unit and which ones should be considered supervisors and thus not be included in the bargaining unit. Sometimes companies seek to illegally skew the vote by transferring out pro-union workers and transferring in known union opponents.

The consultants often advise managers to ease out or force out pro-union workers by giving them unfavorable evaluations or transferring them to the most onerous jobs so they quit, or writing them up two or three times for being two minutes late when they return from lunch, creating a pretext to fire them. Consultants tell some managers to lean on their loyal anti-union friends to file reports, perhaps even fictitious ones, saying they saw pro-union workers curse, fight, or bad-mouth a coworker, giving managers the excuse needed to fire the union supporters.

Jon Lehman, who worked for seventeen years as a Wal-Mart store manager in Kentucky, said that just hours after he called the company's anti-union hotline to report a flyer in his store's bathroom that read THIS STORE NEEDS A UNION, Wal-Mart dispatched a corporate jet to his store, carrying an anti-union SWAT team from Bentonville. He said the SWAT team asked for incriminating information about likely union supporters that might help get them fired.

"As soon as they determine you're pro-union, they go after you," he said. "They go after you any way they can to discredit you, to fire you. It's almost like a neurosurgeon going after a brain tumor: We got to get that thing out before it infects the rest of the store, the rest of the body."[23]

"Union-avoidance" consultants don't just help keep out unions; they also help companies get rid of unions they already have. And their methods can often be innovative.

In late 1994, more than two hundred workers at the EnerSys battery factory in Sumter, South Carolina, petitioned for a unionization election because they were unhappy about stingy pensions, production speedups, and bullying supervisors. The workers also complained about safety hazards, especially the high temperatures in the factory and the lead used in making the giant batteries, which power forklifts and provide backup power to cell phone towers. Supporters of unionization acted quietly to round up support, catching EnerSys largely unaware. Management ultimately mounted a fierce battle to keep out the union—it even put pictures of tombstones in the cafeteria—but its efforts failed.

On February 23, 1995, the workers voted, 191 to 185, to join the International Union of Electrical Workers. Management was livid, and so was Sumter's chamber of commerce. With most of the area's textile factories closing in what seemed like an epidemic of deindustrialization, the chamber's leaders were eager to attract new industry, and they feared that the union's success at EnerSys, one of labor's rare successes in the Carolinas, would sabotage their sales pitch that Sumter was passionately pro-business.

Even though federal law requires employers to bargain with a union once a majority of workers vote to unionize, EnerSys largely refused to do so as it began an unrelenting six-year campaign to drive out the union. A former director of human resources disclosed some embarrassing company secrets when he testified in litigation that John Craig, the president of EnerSys, had said, "We need to do whatever we've got to do to get rid of the union, regardless of what it may cost us."[24]

Adopting highly aggressive tactics, EnerSys fired or pushed out the union local's top seven leaders. One union president, Sharon Brown, said she quit after managers harassed her by following her everywhere she went in the factory and by ordering her to do demeaning, dangerous work, such as cleaning obscure, hard-to-reach vents and spouts on the factory roof.

Management challenged the validity of the unionization election. The company finally agreed to begin bargaining only after an expensive two-year legal battle in which a federal appeals court ruled that the union's victory was legitimate and that the company would be breaking the law if it refused to bargain. The factory granted no raises during that two-year legal fight.

When the bargaining finally began, the nation's economy was booming, but EnerSys nonetheless warned the union that it would begin laying off workers unless the union accepted a 10 percent pay cut. Management promised, however, that it would offset those cuts through a new "gain-sharing" plan that would provide bonuses for increased productivity. The union leaders and workers in Sumter reluctantly approved the contract mainly because of pressures from top union officials in Washington who were eager to have a signed contract. They feared that support for the union would soon melt away without one.[25]

Soon after the contract was signed, EnerSys cut most workers' pay by 16 percent, not the 10 percent that had been agreed to. Workers grew even more enraged when the company gave out minuscule gain-sharing bonuses even though productivity had risen strongly.

"They gave us a bum deal on that gain-sharing," said David Bunker, a machine operator whose pay fell to $11.07 an hour from $13.26. "The union was trusting the company to do what is right. That didn't work."

The union demanded arbitration, insisting that EnerSys had violated the contract's provisions on gain-sharing. After two more years of legal wrangling, an arbitrator ruled that EnerSys had improperly manipulated its productivity calculations as a way to give paltry bonuses. (The company prolonged that arbitration by taking a highly unorthodox step: it challenged the impartiality of the arbitrator it had helped select.)

A former human resources director at the factory, Choice Phillips, testified during the arbitration that the factory's budget had provided no money whatsoever for gain-sharing bonuses, indicating that management had never intended to offset the pay cuts. His testimony also helped clarify the behind-the-scenes role of some union-avoidance consultants.[26]

He said the factory's top manager used to leave cash on a table in his office for a longtime maintenance man named Tom Brown to help finance a campaign to get rid of the union. The plant manager, Phillips testified, pretended that the cash was "trash" that Brown was to pick up as part of his daily maintenance chores. Brown, a short, wiry man, acknowledged during later litigation that a mysterious consultant—a man known as Mr. X—had advised him in his anti-union efforts. Mr. X had guided Brown on writing flyers that repeatedly insulted the union's leaders, calling them "trailer trash," "Uncle Tom," "wimpy pig," and "dog woman."

Brown said that in addition to the money the manager left for him, envelopes stuffed with cash had often been sent to his home to further his anti-union campaign. He said he had no idea where the money came from. "I don't look a gift horse in the mouth," he said. Federal law prohibits companies or managers from contributing money to employee efforts, known as decertification campaigns, that seek to get rid of unions. (In such campaigns, workers can oust their unions if a majority vote to do so.)

Slowly, but inevitably, the EnerSys workers were growing angry with the union, not just because of the pay cuts but because the company hadn't given any raises for six years—from 1995 to 2001. "They did everything they could to make the union look bad," said Larry Brown, a union vice president.

All the frustration fueled Tom Brown's anti-union efforts. He distributed thousands of flyers, organized meetings with refreshments, and sent several mailings to the plant's five hundred workers. Brown later admitted that managers had given him more than 1,000 stamps for the mailings—another illegal donation. All the while, Brown was urging the factory's workers to sign cards saying they wanted the union out. Later, during the litigation, EnerSys officials admitted that they had illegally paid Mr. X $39,000 to help guide Brown during the anti-union campaign.

In June 2001, EnerSys surprised the workers by firing the union's newest president, Vincent Gailliard, supposedly because he had lied about something. The NLRB brushed aside those claims and accused EnerSys of illegally dismissing Gailliard in retaliation for being a union leader.

"They figured that if they got rid of the leaders, the rest of us would buckle under," said Cathy Moody, another fired union leader.

The same day Gailliard was fired, EnerSys announced it was withdrawing recognition from the union. The company said a majority of workers had signed Tom Brown's cards saying they no longer wanted a union.

As the battle raged between EnerSys and its union, the company suffered an economic downturn. It began several rounds of layoffs, fueled in part by its decision to move much of its battery production to its nonunion plants in other states. (The NLRB later asserted that the company's decision to move production to nonunion plants was illegal because it was designed to punish the Sumter workers for unionizing.)

On September 10, 2001, the company announced it was closing the Sumter factory altogether. "These guys hated the union so bad, they would do anything to get rid of it, and that included closing the plant," said Gailliard.

After the plant closed, the litigation multiplied. In addition to the NLRB charging EnerSys with 120 separate labor law violations, the electrical workers union sued the company for failing to give it sixty days' advance notice of the plant closing, as federal law generally requires. Thrown on the defensive by all the lawsuits, EnerSys agreed to a $7.75 million settlement.

Then came a big surprise. EnerSys filed a malpractice lawsuit against Jackson Lewis, the anti-union law firm it had hired. EnerSys alleged that Jackson Lewis, one of the nation's most prominent anti-union firms, had repeatedly advised it to break the law to eliminate the union—allegations that the law firm vigorously denied. EnerSys also accused the law firm of misleading federal investigators, giving illegal assistance to Tom Brown, and engineering "a relentless and unlawful campaign to oust the union."

"The company gave carte blanche to the law firm—the law firm was pretty much running the plant," Gailliard said. "It came back and slapped them [EnerSys] in the face, and now they want someone to blame."

Like a battlefield long after the violence has ended, the EnerSys factory lies eerily quiet. Many of its workers remain unemployed. Jackie Clemmons, a machine operator who was one of the earliest union supporters, said the firings, the lack of raises, and the plant closing all sent a powerful message.

"After all this, I don't think you could pay the people here to join a union, to mess with a union," he said. "And I don't believe the union would want to deal with us anymore down here."

IF ORGANIZED LABOR has a future in the United States, what the Service Employees International Union has done in Houston could serve as a model. When so much seems to be going wrong for organized labor, the union did everything right in its campaign to unionize Ercilia Sandoval and 5,300 other Houston janitors. But for American labor to enjoy a true resurgence, it will require far more than one successful organizing drive—it will require hundreds and perhaps thousands of them.

In an impressive showing, the SEIU, in one fell swoop, unionized the lion's share of office-building janitors in one of America's largest cities. And it did so in a state that is especially hostile to unions and among a population that would seem extraordinarily hard to unionize. The janitors worked part-time, they didn't speak English, they worked for outside contractors, and many were illegal immigrants, a group that is normally reluctant to back a union, terrified as they are of getting fired and perhaps deported. Remarkably, the SEIU organized the cleaning workers in a city where it had no permanent staff and no union local to build on.

Stephen Lerner, the architect of the service employees' Justice for Janitors campaign, long had his eye on Houston. Beginning in the mid-1980s, Justice for Janitors adopted a smart and at the time novel approach for labor. Unionizing janitors was trumpeted as a social justice movement to lift one of society's most invisible groups out of poverty. Often using headline-grabbing tactics, such as staging sit-ins on bridges and harassing cleaning company executives at their country clubs, the Justice for Janitors campaign unionized office-building cleaners in Denver, Pittsburgh, Washington, and Los Angeles during the 1980s and 1990s. In the late eighties, the SEIU undertook an initial foray into Houston. It followed labor's traditional pattern of seeking to organize one workplace at a time by getting a few dozen janitors in one office tower after another to unionize. But in the handful of buildings where the janitors . voted in favor of unionizing, the building owners contracted out the cleaning work to a new, nonunion company.

Lerner, widely considered one of the labor movement's most farsighted strategists, decided that the SEIU would do it right the second time around. "We decided that Houston would be the place to bring to bear everything we've built in the last fifteen years," he said. "That would allow us to organize a whole city at once."

The service employees began slowly, sending in a full-time bilingual strategist and liaison in 2002, three years before the janitors' organizing drive was officially announced. That liaison developed ties with community groups, politicians, immigrant organizations, and religious congregations. Meanwhile, the SEIU's research staff investigated who owned Houston's buildings, which cleaning contractors served which buildings, and which public-employee pension plans held sizable stakes in the companies that owned the buildings. The union also distributed questionnaires to ask the janitors what issues concerned them most.

By the time the union officially kicked off the janitors' drive in April 2005—in the George H. W. Bush Ballroom at the city's convention center—the service employees had lined up the backing of Houston's mayor, half the city council, several members of Congress, and eighty members of the clergy, including one especially prized ally, the city's Roman Catholic archbishop. At the kickoff rally, Archbishop Joseph Fiorenza delighted the janitors by proclaiming that God was unhappy that they had such meager wages and no health coverage. In a city where street protests are as rare as blizzards, the service employees generated plenty of media coverage on kickoff day by having nearly 1,000 supporters march through downtown Houston to decry the janitors' meager pay and benefits. That their church was behind them emboldened many normally frightened immigrant janitors to openly embrace the unionization drive.

That summer Archbishop Fiorenza celebrated a special mass for the janitors. "The right to live is the basis of all other human rights," the archbishop told hundreds of janitors at Immaculate Heart of Mary Catholic Church. Then, citing Pope John Paul II, he said the right to live included "the right to obtain a job that provides the means to sustain you and your family . . . Today a job paying five-fifty an hour without pensions or with no medical benefits is not a fair-paying job. Janitors in Houston should get a salary like the rest of the janitors in Los Angeles, Chicago, Boston, and New York."

The union put the building owners and cleaning companies on the defensive by running a full-page ad in the *Houston Chronicle* that was signed by several dozen political leaders and members of the clergy. Their statement noted that many janitors earned just $450 a month and had to work two, even three jobs to support their families. "We believe that Houston can do better," they wrote. The SEIU sent the city's political and business leaders a well-researched, slickly printed report about the huge number of uninsured residents of Texas and Houston and about the burden that the uninsured put on the state's taxpayers and hospitals. The union even commissioned a Los Angeles artist, Irene Carranza, to do a theme painting for the campaign—a wistful, swirling, Munch-like picture of janitors that was emblazoned on posters and T-shirts across Houston.

To meet one-on-one with thousands of Spanish-speaking janitors, the SEIU needed foot soldiers. So it had its huge janitors' local in Chicago "adopt" the Houston drive, and that local not only lent a top official to run the Houston campaign but sent more than thirty janitors for weeks at a time to spread the union message to Houston janitors at their homes and outside their workplaces. While the Chicago union local provided the bodies, the parent union put up more than $1 million to finance the campaign.

"One of the key questions in labor is, how do we use our existing strength to help workers who don't have a union?" Lerner said. "In Chicago, more than ninety percent of the janitors are unionized, and we've figured out how to use the strength of those unionized workers to help nonunion workers in Houston."

This burst of activity sought, as a first step, to persuade Houston's cleaning contractors to agree to grant union recognition not through the traditional method, that is, a unionization campaign and election that can drag on for months, with management often intimidating and firing union supporters. Instead, the SEIU wanted the janitorial companies to agree to a faster, simpler unionization technique known as card check neutrality. Under that procedure, companies agree not to mount an anti-union campaign and promise to grant union recognition as soon as a majority of workers sign cards expressing support for a particular union. Labor unions are increasingly seeking to use card check neutrality because they win a far higher percentage of organizing drives through that method than through expensive adversarial election battles. (In the two years after the Communications Workers of America persuaded Cingular Wireless to agree to card check neutrality, the union got 23,000 workers in Cingular facilities nationwide to join by signing pro-union cards.)

To pressure Houston's cleaning companies into accepting card check neutrality, the SEIU asked several allies—including several state treasurers and comptrollers who oversee pension funds with large real estate holdings—to urge Houston's building owners to press their cleaning contractors to agree to card checks. A huge concern for many cleaning contractors was that they would be put at a major cost disadvantage if they were unionized and their competitors were not. To allay that concern and the fierce anti-union resistance that often stems from it, the union made an innovative proposal not to begin bargaining with any cleaning contractor until contractors representing at least 55 percent of Houston's janitors had been unionized.

To add some bite to its message, the SEIU staged a twelve-day strike at one Houston building, asserting that the cleaning contractor, ABM, had improperly retaliated against a union supporter by transferring her to clean bathrooms. The SEIU raised the ante by flying several Houston janitors to California, Illinois, New York, and Connecticut, where they picketed seventy-five buildings that were cleaned by ABM. Janitors at those seventy-five buildings joined a sympathy strike, causing cleaning operations to be suspended and sowing alarm among tenants and building owners alike. Mirna Blanco, one of the Houston janitors who were flown to other cities, relished the experience, saying, "I was happy because we were invisible, and now we're not." With the service employees threatening to spread the sympathy strikes to additional cities, building owners soon pressured Houston's five largest cleaning companies to accept card check neutrality and to pledge not to punish any janitors for backing a union.

As soon as the fear of retaliation was removed, Houston's immigrant janitors rushed to sign pro-union cards.

THE ORGANIZING VICTORY in Houston grew directly out of what the service employees have become: a well-oiled organizing machine. While the labor movement has been shrinking, the SEIU has grown to 1.9 million members from 1.1 million in 1996. It became the first major union to devote 50 percent of its budget to organizing nonunion workers at a time when many unions were spending just 1 or 2 percent. The SEIU now spends nearly $200 million a year on organizing, probably three times the amount of any other union. It has pioneered efforts to transform labor into a social justice movement that seeks to help workers who need unions most—those on the bottom, such as janitors and nursing home aides. Through such strategies, the SEIU, much like the civil rights movement of old, has become a magnet for idealistic young college graduates intent on addressing the nation's economic inequities.

While the service employees union is spearheading labor's hoped-for revival, it has been widely attacked for engineering the schism within organized labor. Andy Stern, the SEIU's president, led the exodus of several unions from the AFL-CIO in 2005 after he grew impatient with the federation's lumbering bureaucracy and its failure to reverse labor's decline. Stern's detractors voiced fears that the schism would undercut labor's effectiveness in politics and spark destructive rivalries in which unions spend millions of dollars trying to steal each other's members instead of organizing nonunion workers.

At the moment, the schism appears to have sparked a healthy rivalry in which the two sides—the AFL-CIO unions and the breakaway unions, which include the Teamsters, the laborers, the carpenters, Unite Here, the farm workers, and the UFCW—have begun a competition to show who can unionize more workers, a rivalry that just might spur a long-desired burst of organizing. The schism might also help labor by taking two major unions that have long been largely ineffective in organizing, the Teamsters and the UFCW, and transforming them into more aggressive and effective organizing outfits. But that has not happened yet. If the Teamsters and UFCW begin to realize their ambitions, that could lead to organizing large numbers of workers who have been ripe for unionization for years—supermarket cashiers and stockers, school bus drivers, poultry workers, warehouse workers, department store workers, pharmacy workers, and maybe even Home Depot and Wal-Mart workers. If those two unions are transformed, that would be a substantial boost for organized labor.

The breakaway unions' plan is to focus largely on low-wage workers, recognizing that for organized labor to regain momentum, it makes sense to go after the workers who need unions most. Sweeping those workers into unions could significantly help labor increase its numbers, improve its image, and transform it into a social justice movement, perhaps giving labor some of the same fire and ire that it had when it was organizing immigrant sweatshop workers a century ago.

If labor is to thrive again, it also needs to reconnect with middle-class workers. Unions already represent many middle-class groups: auto workers, teachers, steelworkers, government employees, construction workers, telephone workers, nurses, and airline mechanics. Indeed, once upon a time some of those jobs were low-wage, but unions helped transform them into middle-class jobs. Nonetheless, millions of workers in these groups remain nonunion and might be ripe for being organized by a rejuvenated labor movement.

It will be far harder for unions to connect with white-collar workers such as insurance agents, software developers, and commercial bank employees, because many of them are too independent and entrepreneurial-minded to consider joining a union. Nonetheless, unions might still find a way to win the hearts and support of these white-collar workers. With benefits under siege, millions of Americans recognize that unions are doing more than any other group to protect health coverage and pensions from further erosion. Software developers and mortgage processors might never want to become full union members with unions negotiating contracts for them. But these workers just might be interested in becoming associate union members (paying partial dues), with unions fighting, perhaps, to get them better pharmaceutical benefits or to better protect their pensions and 401(k)s. Unions might also win the interest and support of white-collar workers if they become smart—and entrepreneurial—about delivering services that these workers want, such as pension plans and health coverage that workers can take from job to job, or affordable training, such as sophisticated computer courses, to help prepare workers for future, higher-paying jobs.

The economy has changed, workers have changed, and to survive, unions need to change along with them. But so many forces are arrayed against the labor movement that any revival is bound to be a long, tough slog.

FOR ERCILIA SANDOVAL, the union couldn't arrive soon enough. A big problem, she said, was that her boss kept foisting more work on her each four-hour shift. Someone else used to mop the kitchens on the three office floors that she cleaned, but now she had to mop them in addition to her regular dusting, sweeping, vacuuming, and trash-emptying.

"They increase my workload, but they don't increase my pay," Ercilia said. "Is that fair?"

She was also angry about an injury she suffered while pushing her cleaning cart onto an elevator. It got wedged in the elevator door, and when she pulled with all her might to dislodge the cart, it crashed into her foot, badly injuring a bone.

"I took three days off because I could hardly walk, but they wouldn't pay for those days off," Ercilia said. "My supervisor told me it was my fault, that it wasn't an accident, that it was stupidity on my part. The company sent me to a doctor, and he said, 'There's nothing wrong. You need to go back to work.' All he did was give me some pills for the pain."

A year later, Ercilia's foot still ached. It had never been X-rayed because the doctor said X-rays weren't necessary, and, without insurance, she couldn't afford them on her own.

Ercilia is no whiner; she exudes energy, talking in bursts. Forty-two years old, she is five feet three and compact, with dyed red hair, a glowing copper complexion, and prominent Indian cheekbones. She loves vibrantly colored clothes, especially fiery orange dresses.

Her dresses resemble the tiger-stripe theme in her modest ground-floor apartment—the curtains, the upholstery, even the shower curtain, are filled with tiger stripes. In her tiny garden, she has planted luxuriant ferns and flowers, and in her living room, every shelf is covered with plastic petunias and daffodils. The bathroom has a large framed poster of Van Gogh's *Sunflowers*.

"They don't give us what we deserve," Ercilia said. "I have seen how they humiliated my coworkers. One coworker from Honduras, she was cleaning floors, and the supervisor grabbed the bag with the worker's cleaning chemicals and threw them on the floor. She said, 'Pick them up.'

"The woman started to cry, and I got involved. I asked, 'Why are you bothering her? If you're a supervisor, why don't they give you a talk on how to treat workers?' She said, 'Don't get involved. I'm not talking to you.'

"I said, 'I know you're not talking to me, but just because you're a supervisor doesn't mean you should abuse people.' "

Ercilia feels emboldened, knowing that the union will back her if a supervisor punishes her for standing up for herself or for a coworker.

In El Salvador, Ercilia took in laundry and sold empanadas in the village market, but she and her husband weren't earning enough to support their four daughters. So they moved to the United States in 1997, leaving their four daughters with Ercilia's mother. She hasn't seen those daughters since.

"My dream is to bring my daughters here," she said.

After arriving in Houston, she and her husband had two more daughters.

(She has legitimate working papers. The federal government gave her a work permit when she obtained Temporary Protected Status after applying to be admitted as a refugee.)

In the fall of 2005, Ercilia started feeling nauseous and weak, and soon she was feeling pain in her shoulder. She held off on seeing a doctor because she was uninsured. Month by month the pain spread, to her back and then to her arm and her heart—she started to feel an irregular heartbeat. Finally, a full seven months after she first felt sick, she saw a doctor.

"I didn't have money to go to the doctor," said Ercilia, whose husband has a job doing asbestos removal. "I finally went because the pain wouldn't go away."

The doctors found that she had breast cancer. (Her first mammogram and ultrasound cost four hundred dollars—equal to four weeks of her take-home pay.) The doctors told her that if they moved quickly she could likely avoid chemotherapy. But the doctors didn't move quickly because Ercilia didn't have health insurance. It took nearly two months to be approved for health coverage under the state's Medicaid program. During that time, the cancer spread—the doctors now found a lump in her right lung.

Ercilia continued working after being diagnosed with cancer, even during her two months of chemotherapy. "I would vomit sometimes during work," she said. "I would have fever, I would get tired, I would have to sit down every few minutes. But I needed to work."

In October 2006, while Ercilia was being treated for cancer, Houston's janitors went out on strike after management rejected the union's demands for health insurance and a raise to $8.50 an hour, up from $5.25. The union staged sit-ins on Houston's main boulevards, organized sympathy strikes in other cities, and picketed the offices of Chevron and Shell—all to press Houston's building owners and major tenants to pressure the city's five largest cleaning contractors to be more generous toward the union.

Ercilia became a prominent spokeswoman for the strike, not least because health insurance was at the center of the dispute. She marched at the head of protests, gave television interviews, even appeared in a YouTube video.

After a month of escalating actions and tensions, the cleaning companies agreed to raise wages to $7.75 an hour over two years (a 48 percent increase) and to lengthen the janitors' workday to six hours from four. As a result, the janitors' weekly pay will more than double.

To Ercilia, the most important breakthrough was the companies' promise to begin offering health coverage in 2009.

"This was a big victory," she said. "People said this wouldn't be possible, but with the union, it was possible."

IN THE UNITED STATES, it was always assumed that your children would earn more and live better than you do. For the first time, however, many Americans are worried that their children's generation will actually live worse than they do. Those fears, as we are about to see, are fully justified.

Chapter Fourteen

STARTING OUT MEANS A STEEPER CLIMB

From seven a.m. to three p.m. each day, John Arnold darts around Caterpillar's "materials handling facility" in his forklift truck, maneuvering it with the deftness of a NASCAR driver. His job is to unload tractor parts from flatbed trucks and then deposit those parts—from engine gaskets to one-ton tractor buckets—in the enormous store yard at the plant, which is located just east of Peoria, Illinois. An earnest, deep-voiced giant of a man, Arnold likes his job, but with one major reservation—twenty-somethings like him can earn only three-fourths as much as the fifty-somethings who work alongside him.

Under the two-tier contract at Caterpillar, the most that Arnold can ever earn is $14.90 an hour or $31,000 a year—so little, he says, that some of his coworkers are living at home with their parents. "Some," he said, "are even on food stamps."

A fifty-two-year-old who works alongside Arnold, doing the exact same work, earns $19.03 an hour, or just under $40,000 a year, because employees who started before Arnold began in 1999 are on a higher wage scale.

"I don't like it," Arnold said. "I wish I was at least able to get to the pay scale that the guys who are right next to me are making."

Scott Wilcoxon, a twenty-six-year-old navy veteran who not long ago served as an electrician on a nuclear submarine, operates five computer-controlled metal-cutting machines at Caterpillar. The maximum he can ever earn is $19.84 an hour, 21 percent below the maximum for the fifty-year-olds working next to him. Wilcoxon says it's a struggle to support his wife and three children. "We can buy our food and our gas," he says. "But we can't go out to eat at a nice restaurant. We can't go to a movie. We can afford very few extras. The only way I can afford Christmas presents is by working seven days a week to make extra money."

Caterpillar, based in Peoria, is an enduring symbol of America's industrial prowess, thanks to the success of its earthmoving machinery. At the end of World War II, the U.S. Army left behind thousands of Caterpillar tractors to help a devastated Europe and Asia rebuild, a generous gesture that ultimately established Caterpillar worldwide. For decades after the war, Caterpillar reigned as the king of tractor production, and it was the company's factories in and around Peoria that built that dominance, factories that paid some of the best wages in the American heartland. In the late 1980s, Caterpillar's factory workers earned sixteen dollars an hour on average, equivalent to twenty-eight dollars an hour in 2007 dollars.

"My dad's worked at Caterpillar for thirty-seven years, and when I was a kid, he was making some good money," Arnold said. "I was hoping that I could eventually get to where my dad's at." His father, a millwright who repairs conveyor belts and other machinery, works in the same giant materials handling facility and earns twenty-five dollars an hour, nearly twice as much as his son. (Arnold's pay is lower than his father's not just because he is on the bottom tier of a two-tier pay scale but also because he works in a less-skilled pay grade.)

Arnold acknowledged that his modest paycheck was dampening his interest in getting married. "Let's say I got married and my wife and I have a kid—I don't know how you can do it on what I'm making," he said.

John Arnold and Scott Wilcoxon are the type of workers on whom America's industrial success was built: diligent, dedicated, and determined. But because their wages are lower than those of the previous generation, young workers like them are part of a reverse economic evolution. Young Americans are confronting the same reversal at many workplaces across the country: at General Motors, Ford, and Chrysler; the Dana Corporation's twenty-five auto parts plants; American Axle's three plants in upstate New York; ACF's railcar plant in Pennsylvania; longshoremen's hiring halls along the East Coast; and, as we have seen, the Tyson pepperoni plant in Wisconsin. Manufacturing companies have pushed hardest for a lower wage tier for their young workers, and as a result this phenomenon is most prevalent among the nation's 13.7 million factory workers.

Caterpillar began insisting on a lower wage tier in the early 1990s. After losing more than $1 billion in the 1980s, in part because of lower prices offered by Komatsu and other foreign competitors, Caterpillar decided to take a hard line in bargaining with the United Auto Workers. Convinced that it needed to cut costs, the company demanded a dual wage scale that would pay new workers 60 percent less than what experienced workers earned. The UAW resisted those demands and called a strike by 12,000 Caterpillar workers in late 1991. After five months, Caterpillar emerged victorious and instituted a system that paid new workers 20 to 40 percent less than the other workers received.[1]

In Caterpillar's parlance, the lower pay scale is called "a competitive wage"—not so high that Caterpillar becomes uncompetitive against foreign tractor makers, yet high enough to attract the workers it needs. The company seems confident that its pay strategy will assure its future as a thriving company.

But Wilcoxon's wife, Anessa, views the competitive wage from a different perspective. "My parents' house was bigger," said Anessa, whose father worked for Caterpillar for three decades. "We always had two cars when I was growing up. When we went out to eat—we had a family of five—we'd always go to a sit-down place. When we go out to eat now, it's McDonald's or Hardee's." The Wilcoxons rent a run-down three-bedroom house and have a second car only because Anessa's parents gave them their old GMC Sierra truck.

Caterpillar's CEO, Jim Owens, says the company's competitive wage strategy isn't destroying middle-class jobs so much as it's preserving jobs in America, a common refrain, as we've seen. If Caterpillar did not maintain its competitive wage rates, Owens says, his company would be closing plants in the United States or moving operations overseas, or perhaps both. But thanks to its competitive wages, Owens says, Caterpillar has been able to increase its Midwest workforce, expanding it by 5,000 in 2005.

"What we've done is reposition ourselves to actually grow employment in our Midwestern plants," Owens said. "We finally have a labor cost that is viable."[2]

Caterpillar's posture points to a rough future for millions of young Americans who may someday want factory jobs, jobs that workers without college degrees embraced in decades past to lift themselves into the middle class. Not long ago, the typical compensation package for unionized factory workers in the Midwest was forty dollars an hour including benefits, but that package, according to Daniel Luria, an economist at the Michigan Manufacturing Technology Center, is now around twenty-five dollars an hour—thirteen dollars to eighteen dollars an hour in wages plus nine dollars or so in benefits.[3]

Among young workers at Caterpillar, the company's two-tier wage scale has engendered huge resentment. "Caterpillar," Wilcoxon said, "has monthly business meetings in the factory where managers talk about how the company is doing. They talk about their record sales and record profits, and we sit there, and they wonder why we're still bitter about the contract. I sometimes call those monthly meetings our monthly slap in the face. And each year the top executives' salaries are printed on the front page of the newspaper. They may not mean to, but it feels like they're rubbing it in our faces."

Recently, Caterpillar has piled up record earnings year after year. Its net profits soared to $3.5 billion in 2006, up 74 percent from two years earlier. Those profits amount to $37,000 per employee, almost as much as Wilcoxon earns each year, convincing him and many other young workers that Caterpillar can easily raise wages without jeopardizing its competitiveness.

Shane Hillard, a twenty-nine-year-old who works at the same factory as Wilcoxon, said, "I don't understand how you're supposed to be able to buy a house and live the American dream when you work for one of the biggest companies in the United States and it's paying you just twelve dollars an hour."

AMERICA HAS ALWAYS STOOD for progress, for economic advancement and upward mobility. But for many of today's young Americans, progress seems uncertain because entry-level wages and benefits have languished while housing costs and college tuition have risen. As one expert put it, "The next generation is starting their economic race fifty yards behind the starting line."[4]

Entry-level wages for college graduates and high school graduates fell from 2001 to 2006, after factoring in inflation, and median income slipped in families with at least one parent aged twenty-five to thirty-four.[5]

Today's young workers face these wage problems because they are the first generation to come of age after the high-tech bubble burst, after offshoring jobs to India and elsewhere became popular, and after millions of factory jobs disappeared in a new wave of de-industrialization. "Young workers are on the cutting edge of experiencing all the changes in the economy," said Lawrence Mishel, president of the Economic Policy Institute.[6]

Longer-term wage trends have been just as troubling. From 1979 to 2005, entry-level wages for male high school graduates without college degrees slid 19 percent (after inflation); for their female counterparts, they fell 9 percent. For young Americans with college degrees, entry-level wages did rise, although modestly and still far slower than wages for most older workers with college degrees.[7]

One study found that men who were in their thirties in 2004 had a median income 12 percent less, after factoring in inflation, than their fathers' generation did when they were in their thirties. The study, sponsored by the Pew Charitable Trusts, said, "There has been no progress at all for the younger generation . . . The up-escalator that has historically ensured that each generation would do better than the last may not be working very well."[8]

The changing job market is undercutting entry-level wages for those who do not go to college. "In the 1960s and 1970s, you saw high school graduates getting good jobs at Ford and AT&T, jobs that in inflation-adjusted terms were paying twenty or twenty-five dollars in today's wages," said Sheldon Danziger, a professor of public policy at the University of Michigan. "Nowadays most kids with just high school degrees will work in service-sector jobs for ten dollars or less. That's where you see a big drop."

All told, more than one-fourth of the 45 million workers under age thirty-five do not have health insurance from any source, by far the highest rate of any age group.[9] As for young workers with just high school degrees, two-thirds do not receive health coverage in their entry-level jobs, up from just over one-third in 1979.[10] In her book *Generation Debt*, Anya Kamenetz tells the story of Katy, an uninsured young violinist who gave music lessons and played in bluegrass and punk bands. Katy had an abnormal Pap smear, and to raise $3,500 to help her pay for lab tests and outpatient procedures, her musician friends organized, sold tickets to, and played at a fund-raiser billed as "Katy's cervix benefit and thirtieth birthday party."[11]

Corporate America's increasing tightfistedness over pensions is also hitting young workers hard. The share of workers twenty-five to thirty-four participating in an employer-sponsored pension plan or 401(k) slid to 42 percent in 2005, down from 50 percent five years earlier. As for workers aged thirty-five to sixty-four, 55 percent participate in employer-sponsored retirement plans.[12] The picture is worst for young high school graduates; less than one in five participate in a retirement plan in their entry-level jobs.[13]

The Internet generation will, as *Generation Debt* points out, enter the prime of life in a nation as gray as Florida is today, and as a result that generation will face an unprecedented burden in sustaining the Social Security system.[14] In 1960, sixteen Americans were working for each retiree. Today there are four active workers contributing taxes to Social Security for each retiree. In 2030, there are expected to be just two and a half workers per retiree.[15] Today's young workers may well face a double squeeze—to keep Social Security solvent, Congress might increase the younger generation's payroll taxes as well as trim their Social Security benefits.

Young Americans also face a tough time because of the explosion in housing prices over the past fifteen years, notwithstanding the recent weakening of the real estate market. The median price of homes soared from $23,000 in 1970 to $212,000 in 2007, rising almost twice as fast as inflation.[16] The price pressures have been worst in many of the metropolitan areas that most attract college graduates—New York, Boston, Los Angeles, Silicon Valley, and Seattle.[17] It was very different for young people starting out after World War II. They could buy a brand-new home in Levittown, that quintessential New York suburb, for $6,700, helped by mortgage subsidies from the GI Bill. Now that home would cost more than $300,000, and now there's no GI Bill to help.[18]

As a result of these trends, many young people are being forced to wait longer to purchase housing, especially on the coasts. Indeed, many college graduates—so-called boomerang kids—have reluctantly moved back in with their parents, especially in high-rent metropolitan areas such as New York and Los Angeles, until they land a job that pays enough that they can live on their own.

These trends have fostered considerable pessimism. Fifty percent of adults surveyed in a Pew Research Center poll in 2006 said life would be worse for the next generation, while just 34 percent said it would be better.[19] Still, it is important to remember that many things are better for the younger generation—longer life spans, lower crime rates, and wondrous developments such as the Internet and breakthrough pharmaceuticals.

But today's young adults are entering a harsher, less forgiving workplace where job security is often treated as an anachronism. The unspoken message is that you have to work hard and perform well to make sure your employer keeps you. You also have to earn your pay increases, because automatic raises are increasingly a thing of the past. As Steve Lohr wrote in the *New York Times*, "The new mantra is to have employees who are 'productive' and 'engaged,' human resources experts say. Pay and bonuses are based on performance measures instead of seniority."

"It's an 'If you give, you'll get' model," said David Ulrich, a professor at the University of Michigan business school. "Corporate loyalty is seen as a market transaction—a bond that will last as long as it clearly benefits both the employee and the company. It's very much at-will employment."[20]

Some young workers are of course doing very well. That's especially true for those who get the most advanced or prestigious diplomas, especially MBAs, law degrees, and medical degrees. At some corporate law firms, starting pay for twenty-five-year-olds out of top-notch law schools is $160,000 a year. "Young adults perceive that having just a BA isn't going to get you a really good job as it did three or four decades ago," said Frank Furstenberg, a sociology professor at the University of Pennsylvania. "There's a signal from the market and the current winner-take-all approach that you should get more than a college degree."

In an era when good jobs increasingly require specialized skills, it appears that young workers without college degrees will generally end up worse than those without college degrees did in the past, while those with superior credentials will do better. "You're much better off as a young worker today if you're the child of the well-to-do and you get a good education, and you're much worse off if you're a child of a blue-collar worker and you don't go to college," said Professor Danziger. "There's increasing inequality among young people just as there is increasing inequality among their parents."[21]

AT THE SAME TIME THAT millions of young Americans are convinced they need more than a bachelor's degree to succeed, many students feel too daunted to even consider a four-year college. The reason: they are scared off by soaring college costs.

Each year more than 400,000 high school graduates who are fully qualified to attend a four-year college fail to do so for financial reasons. More than 200,000 of them attend a two-year college, while 170,000 do not attend any college at all.[22] As a result, over a full decade more than 4 million qualified high school graduates will not attend four-year colleges, and this, says Juliet Garcia, chairwoman of the Advisory Committee on Student Financial Assistance, "will exact a serious economic and social toll for much of this century."[23]

Her committee, which Congress created to advise its members as well as the executive branch, found that 43 percent of qualified students from moderate-income families (with annual incomes of $25,000 to $50,000) are unable to attend a four-year college.[24]

A big part of the problem is that Pell Grants—the main federal grant for low-income students—have not nearly kept up with tuition. For the 1975–76 school year, the maximum Pell Grant covered 84 percent of the average annual costs for a four-year public college. By 2007–8, it had fallen to 32 percent.[25] Tuition and fees at four-year public universities climbed 40 percent from 2002–3 to 2007–8, the largest increase ever over a five-year period after factoring in inflation.[26]

"There is no question that the bulk of the impact of that is falling on lower- and lower-middle-income students," said Donald Heller, a professor of education at Penn State and one of the nation's foremost experts on college finance and student access. "They are getting killed on the aid side, and they are getting killed on the tuition side."[27]

At private colleges nationwide, tuition, room, and board averaged $32,307 in academic year 2007–8 (up from $4,240 in 1977–78, a 124 percent jump after inflation). At four-year public universities, costs per year totaled $13,589 (up from $2,038 in 1977–78, a 96 percent increase after inflation).[28] One dismaying result of these aid and tuition trends is that after decades of steady increases, the percentage of twenty-five- to twenty-nine-year-olds with bachelor's degrees has declined since the beginning of this decade.[29]

Meanwhile, many private universities and states—states of course finance public universities—have increasingly awarded financial aid on the basis of merit rather than need. These merit-based awards favor wealthier students over poorer ones, and white students disproportionately over minority students. At the nation's private universities, merit-based aid was 50 percent of all aid in 2003–4, up from 33 percent in 1995–96, while public universities increased merit aid to 62 percent of all aid, up from 45 percent in 1995–96.[30]

"In the last decade or so there's been more focus in terms of policy on making college affordable for middle- and upper-middle-class students," said Professor Heller. "And if you go back to the creation of the Higher Education Act in 1965, the focus was on making college accessible for kids who wouldn't otherwise have been able to go. The primary focus has really shifted. And from my perspective, it makes little sense to be spending public money to subsidize the cost of college for kids who are going there anyway."[31]

Trends like these make the climb steeper for young people like Melissa Diviney, who was an honors student at Peoria High School. Both of her parents—her father has a slight mental handicap—worked for three decades as dishwashers at Peoria's largest hospital, St. Francis Medical Center. Her mother, who still earned less than ten dollars an hour after thirty years there, had drilled into Melissa's head that she should go to college. "If you don't go to school, this is what it will be like," her mother warned.

Melissa took her studies seriously, graduating in the top tenth of her class even though she held a full-time job her last two years of high school. As a junior, she went to work as a counter girl at Hardee's, and the following year she worked as the night manager, responsible for closing the restaurant at eleven p.m. and overseeing the cleanup of the floors, tables, and grills until midnight.

"One of my big dreams was to go away to a four-year university," said Melissa, warm, winning, and energetic, with a big smile, plump cheeks, and a pale complexion. "I wanted to go to Illinois State. And my parents were saying I should go to a four-year school."

But at decision time, her parents told her they simply couldn't afford Illinois State. It cost $15,000 a year, more than a third of their annual income. "My parents always worked extremely hard, but they were never able to save for college," Melissa said.

Recognizing financial realities, Melissa's high school guidance counselor recommended a well-regarded community college in Peoria, Illinois Central College. Melissa applied, and because of her academic achievements and financial needs, she was awarded a full scholarship, covering the $2,000 in annual tuition costs. On a bluff overlooking the Illinois River, Illinois Central doesn't have the elaborate science facilities, football stadium, or arts complex that many four-year colleges have, but as community colleges go, it is respected for the individualized attention it gives its students and for sending many to four-year colleges such as Illinois State.

During her first year there, Melissa juggled her courses with her full-time position at Hardee's, which she was reluctant to give up. Notwithstanding the scholarship, she left Illinois Central after one year because of financial pressures from having to pay for her food, rent, car, and gas. She spent the following year at Hardee's as the morning manager.

Having saved up $5,000 that year, she decided to quit Hardee's and return to Illinois Central, with the goal of becoming an accountant. Once again she was awarded a full scholarship, but to pay for her living expenses she took a thirty-hour-a-week job as a restaurant hostess at Baker's Square in the Grand Prairie Mall. It paid $7.25 an hour.

Like Melissa, about half of the nation's 6.6 million community college students work more than thirty hours a week, usually in low-wage jobs.[32] And even when these students move to four-year colleges, they often continue holding outside jobs. This helps explain why 23 percent of students take more than six years to graduate from college, up from 15 percent in 1970.[33]

With grades somewhat lower than she would like—her jobs took a toll on her studies, she acknowledges—Melissa hopes to be accepted by the University of Illinois at Springfield. But she has a recurring worry: how will she afford the $12,000 in costs for tuition, room, and board? Once again her parents have made clear that they don't have money to help, and Melissa worries that she will not be able to swing it through grants and loans.

As Melissa continues to juggle school and job, it remains unclear whether she will achieve her dream of graduating from a four-year college. "Unfortunately," Professor Heller said, "the majority of students who go to community colleges never graduate from a four-year institution."[34]

FAR MORE THAN PREVIOUS GENERATIONS, today's young Americans have piled on debt—college loans, housing loans, auto loans, and credit card debt. Many young people have borrowed heavily for what they view as a necessity for moving up in the world: getting a college degree. But many have taken on debt for another reason, as a handy way to improve their living standards in an age of stagnating wages and low entry-level salaries.

In households headed by someone aged twenty-five to thirty-four, average debt has climbed to over $55,000, up 70 percent from the 1980s, after accounting for inflation.[35] Indeed, the average debt load for young Americans actually exceeds their annual household income, a sharp change from two decades ago.[36]

Debt has become a worrisome burden for many young Americans, with one study finding that one in two twenty-somethings has defaulted on at least one loan.[37] In her book *Strapped: Why America's 20- and 30-Somethings Can't Get Ahead*, Tamara Draut wrote, "Compared to previous generations, today's young adults have been forced to borrow to get a life."[38]

College debt has been marching upward, the result of soaring tuition, stagnating family incomes, and shrinking Pell Grants, after factoring in inflation. (Congress voted in 2007 to increase the maximum Pell Grant to $5,400 in 2012, from $4,050.) Students who borrow to go to college borrow 50 percent more on average than students did a decade ago, after adjusting for inflation. Three out of four students attending private colleges take out educational loans during their undergraduate years, with those who graduated in 2004 borrowing a total of $19,500 on average, compared with $15,500 for students at public universities.[39] Nationwide, nearly one in five students borrows more than $30,000 to obtain a bachelor's degree.[40]

With tuitions climbing and family incomes stagnating, "the costs of education are moving from the government to families, and in families, from parents to kids," said a top official at the American Council on Education, an association of colleges.[41]

Nellie Mae, a student lending company, found that among those who borrowed to obtain bachelor's degrees, 13 percent devote 20 percent or more of their income toward repaying education debts—a dangerously high ratio.[42] As evidence of how stretched students are, some experts point out that 27 percent of undergraduates charge part of their college expenses on a credit card, with 40 percent of that group graduating with credit card balances exceeding $5,000.[43]

"This debt-for-diploma system is strangling our young people right when they're starting out in life," says Draut.[44] But some experts are hardly alarmed by the increase in education debt, saying that borrowing to obtain a bachelor's degree is the smartest loan a young person can make. One study found that students will earn $402,959 more on average over their lifetime as a result of obtaining a bachelor's degree.[45]

But even those, like Michelle Young, who take out college loans with the best of intentions can later find those loans a daunting burden. Michelle was the first in her family to attend college, all but defying her parents by pursuing a bachelor's degree. Intent on becoming a teacher—"it's what I always knew I wanted to be"—she began at a community college outside Oklahoma City before transferring to the University of Oklahoma. Pell Grants financed one-third of her college costs, and to finance the rest she took out loans and worked thirty hours a week, first as a cashier at Target for the $5.15-an-hour minimum wage and then at a golf course (where her father worked as a maintenance man), operating the beer and soda cart for the minimum wage plus tips. Because it was hard to juggle her studies with her job, it took Michelle three years to complete community college and then four years to finish at the University of Oklahoma, where it was supposed to take three years (in theory, two years of classes and a year of student teaching).

Michelle took out $53,000 in educational loans during her seven years in college. She said she lived modestly, driving a 1984 Oldsmobile Cutlass that she had bought for $1,000. For a doctor or lawyer, educational debt of $53,000 might not be onerous, but for Michelle it was terrifying, especially because she was earning just $34,000 after five years as a ninth-grade geography teacher.

She was supposed to repay $295 each month to Sallie Mae, the nation's largest student lender, but she applied to postpone her payments. She said she couldn't afford to repay that amount because it represented nearly one-sixth of her $1,850 monthly take-home pay. (She was also obligated to pay $300 a month to a hospital for back surgery she once had.) Sallie Mae granted her a postponement, but that did not stop interest from pushing her debt to $64,000.

Michelle would like to pursue a master's degree in education to increase her expertise and salary, but she said she has ruled that out because it would mean at least $15,000 more in debt.

"Nothing would make me happier than to be able to repay them the money I owe, but I just don't have it," Michelle said. "It's like blood from a stone."

For many young Americans, college debt has influenced important life decisions. In one survey, 29 percent of respondents, much like Michelle, said they delayed getting more education or dropped the idea altogether because they already had so much college debt, while 17 percent said pressures from student loans forced them to change career plans.[46] Thirty-eight percent said student debt made them delay buying a house, 13 percent said it delayed them from moving out of their parents' home, and 21 percent said it caused them to delay having children.[47]

As serious as the college debt burden is, mortgage loans are the main factor behind the rising debt load for young Americans. Mortgage debt has climbed to $41,000 on average for households headed by someone age twenty-five to thirty-four, nearly double the amount in 1983, after factoring in inflation.[48] This increase stems directly from the rise in housing prices, including starter houses, as well as the lenient lending standards that led to the subprime mortgage crisis, which has hurt many young homeowners.

"There's the common misconception that [young Americans] have these debts because they're buying iPods or cable TV," said William Strauss, coauthor of *Millennials Rising: The Next Great Generation*. "It's not that. It's student loans and housing."[49]

FRUSTRATED BY HIS ECONOMIC SITUATION at Caterpillar, Scott Wilcoxon has enrolled in an online college program with Colorado Technical University. He was a star student in high school, studying two foreign languages and planning to major in physics in college. But he fell in love with Anessa, married at eighteen, and suddenly had a child to support. He joined the navy instead of going to college because that enabled him to serve his country while his military pay supported his family. With the navy now providing tuition assistance, he has decided to pursue a bachelor's degree in business, specializing in human resources. He used to dream of becoming a teacher, but he has since decided against it because "teachers don't exactly make enough to support a family of five." Now he hopes to work for a large corporation, training employees on mechanical operations. That way he can still teach, while earning more than a public school teacher.

Many nights after he returns home from Caterpillar at eleven-thirty p.m., Wilcoxon studies until one-thirty a.m. Sometimes he even hits the books during his half-hour lunch break at Caterpillar.

"I've reached the top of the unskilled job market," Wilcoxon said. "This is the only thing that's going to allow us to get out of this upper-lower-class way we live. It's a way up."

———

NOT ONLY DO YOUNG AMERICANS entering the workforce face tough times, but so do older Americans about to leave the workforce. Some economists foresee a severe retirement squeeze because many companies have jettisoned traditional pension plans and because many workers are saving too little for retirement. We will now see why retirement security is growing less and less secure.

Chapter Fifteen

THE NOT-SO-GOLDEN YEARS

Harold Danley worked for more than three decades as an auditor and trainer for a leading insurance company. Then, shortly after turning sixty-seven, he had quadruple bypass surgery, fully intending to retire afterward. But eighteen months after his surgery, Danley discovered that his Social Security benefits and his retirement savings weren't enough for him and his wife to make ends meet. Their out-of-pocket health care costs alone—she suffers from arthritis and sleep apnea—topped $14,000 a year.

"We saw we would really have to cut back unless I started to work again," Danley said. "So I started looking around for something part-time. Wal-Mart and Target were paying six-fifty and seven dollars an hour, and most grocery stores were in the area of eight or nine dollars an hour. But security companies were willing to hire me at ten-fifty, so I took that."

At age seventy-three, Danley now holds two part-time jobs as a security guard, at Ecolab's corporate headquarters in St. Paul, Minnesota, and at Metropolitan State University, a four-year college in the Twin Cities. It won't be easy to retire, he admits, partly because the insurance company where he worked terminated his pension plan in the 1990s and replaced it with a far less generous 401(k).

When Danley was planning for his golden years, retirement planners told him what they invariably tell other Americans: they should view their retirement security as a three-legged stool, with one leg of personal savings, one of Social Security, and one as a pension. But for millions of American workers, that stool looks awfully shaky—all three of its legs are having problems. For the first time since the Depression, the nation's personal savings rate fell below zero in 2005—and it has remained there since—meaning that Americans are spending more than they earn and saving nothing on a net basis. Social Security benefits, some economists predict, will fall from 42 percent of the average worker's pre-retirement earnings to 32 percent over the next two decades.[1] And companies are moving aggressively away from pensions. In 1982, 84 percent of full-time workers in companies with more than one hundred workers had traditional pensions, which promise a monthly income stream for life after retirement. Today less than 33 percent do.[2]

As a result of these trends, says Teresa Ghilarducci, a pension expert at Notre Dame, "the baby boom generation may be the last generation to enjoy a more comfortable retirement than their parents."[3]

Among retirement planners, the rule of thumb is that for people to maintain their lifestyle, their income after they stop working should be 70 to 80 percent of their pre-retirement earnings. Baby boomers who are retiring now, often in their late fifties or early sixties, average 77 percent. But many leading experts say that Americans who reach retirement age in ten or twenty years will fall to 65 percent.[4] A study by the nation's leading research center on retirement, the Center for Retirement Research at Boston College, estimates that 40 percent of baby boomers, born between 1946 and 1964, will not be able to maintain their standard of living when they retire.[5] That rises to half for those workers in Generation X who were born between 1965 and 1972.

"This is a crisis in the making," said Alicia Munnell, a former White House economist and now director of the Boston College Center. "I think ten or fifteen years from now, people who approach their early sixties are simply not going to have enough money to retire on."[6]

Experts point out that things will grow worse from a retirement situation that is already far from ideal. For recent retirees, age sixty-five to sixty-nine, median total income was just $17,934 in 2005.[7]

Corporate America's flight from traditional pensions is contributing greatly to the crisis. CEOs have grown uncomfortable with the idea of making a commitment to pay decade after decade of benefits to retirees, especially when pension burdens have pushed several major corporations toward bankruptcy. Robert Miller, the chief executive of Delphi, the beleaguered auto parts giant, probably spoke for many business executives when he complained about a pension system in which some employees begin work at twenty, retire at fifty and live into their eighties. "These pensions were created when we all us to work until age seventy and then poop out at seventy-two," he said. "N you live past eighty, a not uncommon demographic, you're going to b benefits for longer than you are working. That social contract is un pressure."[8]

The corporate flight from pensions has taken numerous for lines, US Airways, Bethlehem Steel, and LTV all dumped th pension plans onto the federal government earlier this d bankruptcy. United had fallen $10 billion behind in plans, while Bethlehem was $3.5 billion behind. As a result, many workers will receive smaller benefits than those companies had promised.

IBM angered its workers in 1999 when it announced that it would jettison its traditional pension plan and replace it with a newfangled plan known as "a cash balance plan." Traditional pensions favor long-term workers because retirement benefits accrue much faster in a worker's final years of employment. Cash balance plans use a far different formula that, in IBM's case, cut the anticipated monthly pension benefits of many of the company's long-term workers so severely that their furious reaction led to a congressional hearing and a class action lawsuit accusing IBM of discriminating against older workers.[9]

Earl Mongeon had worked for IBM for two decades when the company switched to a cash balance plan. He said his expected pension fell from $2,200 a month to $1,243.

"They've broken their promises," said Mongeon, a quality control worker at IBM's chip fabrication plant in Burlington, Vermont. "They told us throughout our career, 'Your salary might not be that high, but you'll have a good pension.' And when they change all that, it feels criminal. . . . I'm definitely going to have to work longer to make ends meet."

The pension-cutting trend has spread to many of the nation's most prosperous blue chips, including Verizon, Hewlett-Packard, Lockheed Martin, and Motorola. Corporations are largely free to revamp their pension plans as they see fit because the system is by and large a voluntary arrangement. The main exception is when a company's hands are tied by a union contract.

The most popular pension-cutting strategies are for companies to freeze their pension plans for current employees and close them to new employees, while offering 401(k) plans to their workers. When companies freeze their plans, it means that the anticipated pensions of workers in the plan will never increase, even if they stay with the company another decade or two.

For companies, the math is simple. Large companies typically pay 7 to 8 percent of a worker's wages into traditional pension plans, but just 3 percent of a worker's wages into 401(k)s.[10] As a result, a company with 50,000 workers can easily save $100 million or more a year by switching from pensions to 401(k)s. For workers, 401(k) plans are essentially an individual investment account, with companies often providing a match for employee contributions (often in the form of company stock); sometimes dollar for dollar, sometimes just ten cents to the dollar.

When Verizon announced its freeze, it promised to contribute more to its employees' 401(k) plans. Even so, the company estimated its savings would be $300 million a year. A month after Verizon acted, IBM announced that it, too, would freeze its main pension plan, which covered 117,000 employees, vowing to contribute more to its workers' 401(k) plans. IBM told its shareholders that these changes would increase its profits by more than $2.5 billion over five years.[11]

"We're seeing a brand-new phenomenon: healthy companies are closing their pension plans to existing employees and new employees," said Professor Munnell. "Employers want out of the benefits game. They just do not want to be responsible for providing pensions."[12]

As a result of corporate America's shift toward 401(k)s, the number of workers in such employer-sponsored plans has climbed from 14 million in the early 1980s to more than 50 million today.[13] This trend has accelerated partly because older companies such as IBM and Sears feel they should shun traditional pensions when competitors such as Microsoft and Wal-Mart do not offer them. Moreover, companies argue that traditional pensions, which employees cannot take with them from job to job, might have made sense in decades past when workers typically stayed at a company for twenty or thirty years, but make little sense in today's economy in which workers frequently move from job to job.

Advocates of 401(k)s say they are preferable to pensions because they place a smaller cost burden on corporations and because they foster self-reliance. But 401(k)s are usually far less effective and reliable than pensions in assuring retirement security. With 401(k)s, retirees essentially receive a lump sum, which they must manage. Not all retirees do that effectively, however; many workers, in fact, have scant expertise in investing. And nearly half of workers cash out their 401(k) accounts when they change jobs, often leaving them with a small nest egg when they retire.[14] The median amount that Americans have in their 401(k)s is surprisingly small, just $28,000 in 2004,[15] with the bottom half of workers by income having a balance averaging less than $6,000. For workers on the cusp of retirement, between fifty-four and sixty-five, median 401(k) holdings were $61,000 in 2004.[16] That is not a reassuring amount if you retire at age sixty-five and live another twenty years.[17]

The *Washington Post*'s longtime pension reporter, Albert B. Crenshaw, wrote that the move away from pensions is "part of a fundamental shift in our sense of what American society owes individuals in the form of financial protection." Crenshaw added, "Employers, unwilling and increasingly unable to promise their workers a secure retirement, are handing that problem off to the workers themselves . . . But if things don't work out a few decades from now—well, tough."[18]

BOTH LARRY CUTRONE AND DON JENSEN began working at AT&T around 1970. Cutrone was a get-your-hands-dirty blue-collar guy who repaired phone lines. Jensen was a polished college graduate who began in facilities planning and later moved into human resources. Both men spent three decades at the company, and both became managers—Cutrone oversaw the installation of computers and telecommunications equipment at AT&T's vast office complex in Bridgewater, New Jersey; Jensen became a top human resources executive at Lucent, a telecommunications equipment company that AT&T spun off in 1996. Jensen oversaw the hiring of thousands of workers over the years, heading a staff of twenty-five and supervising recruitment at fifty leading universities, including Cornell, Stanford, MIT, and Purdue.

"I made a choice back in 1970," Cutrone said, "to go to work at a company that offered a good job and good pension benefits and stable employment."

In 1997, AT&T offered a buyout to its management employees, and Cutrone, after twenty-seven years at the company, applied, confident that the $44,000 annual pension he anticipated would be sufficient for his retirement. His application was rejected because AT&T management still deemed his services valuable. The next year, AT&T replaced its traditional pension plan with a cash balance plan, and Cutrone was shocked to learn that his retirement benefit would now be $23,000 a year.

"Some smarter heads than I did some calculations and discovered that for people with my type of seniority, we'd lose almost half," Cutrone said. "I was of course upset and angry. We weren't given a choice. All they did was shove it down your throat."

In traditional pension plans, benefits are typically calculated by multiplying years of service times a percentage of final salary. Cash balance plans use a different formula that hurts longtime workers the most: companies typically credit a worker's account each year with a percentage of that worker's annual pay. Like many other companies that replaced traditional pension plans with cash balance plans, AT&T argued that its cash balance plan was better because workers can essentially take their accrued cash balances with them when they leave and roll them over into an IRA.

Three years after AT&T introduced its cash balance plan, Cutrone faced another shock. He was laid off—at fifty-three.

To stretch his $23,000 pension, he and his wife, a paralegal, headed to Montana, moving in with his mother-in-law in Big Fork. Notwithstanding Montana's lower cost of living, Cutrone soon realized they couldn't make ends meet on his pension. So he began doing part-time work as a landscaper and computer consultant. Soon, feeling a pressing need for a bigger, steadier income, he and his wife opened a full-time business in his mother-in-law's home, doing process serving for lawsuits.

"We're not living out of garbage cans," Cutrone said, "but a $23,000 pension doesn't go nearly as far as I would like."

When Don Jensen retired in 1998, he began receiving the pension that had been promised him, $32,000 a year. Eager to escape the Northeast's winters, he and his wife, a retired schoolteacher, moved to Tucson, where he planned to concentrate on golf. Jensen left Lucent with the understanding that it would shoulder the cost of his post-retirement health insurance. The year after he retired, he had to pay only $180 annually in health insurance premiums. But by 2006, when Jensen was fifty-nine, six years from qualifying for Medicare, Lucent was asking him to pay premiums of $8,280 a year.

"It came to about twenty-five percent of my pension," Jensen said. "That's pretty onerous."

His wife's pension would not begin for several years, and it would be small when it did. So Jensen now took a job as a bank teller. It paid ten dollars an hour.

"That felt pretty bad," he said. "But I took it for the health benefits." By obtaining health coverage through his bank job, he could let his Lucent insurance lapse.

Lucent was among the one-third of companies with more than two hundred employees that offer health benefits to their retirees. That was down from two-thirds in 1988. Indeed, many other retirees are facing Jensen's predicament—in 2004, eight out of ten companies that provide retiree health coverage increased their retirees' monthly premiums.[19]

The nation's accounting rules give companies a strong incentive to transfer more of their health costs to retirees by, for example, increasing retirees' premiums. A company can count as increased profits whatever money it expects to save when it transfers health costs to retirees. In this way, Caterpillar increased its profits by $75 million one year.[20]

Many Americans are delaying retirement because of worsening retiree health coverage. One survey found that the absence of employer-financed retiree health benefits increases the average retirement age by one and a half years for men and two years for women.[21] Indeed, partly as a result of the pension and health insurance squeeze, the percentage of men fifty-five to sixty-four who are working is rising again after having fallen steadily from 1950 to 1994. And the percentage of American men over sixty-five who are working has jumped to 21 percent, from 15 percent in 1993.[22]

"I'm coming up on sixty, and I'm back in the full-time workforce," said Jensen, who left his bank teller's job to take a human resources position with a mail-order company. "I commute one hour each way to work. I leave the house at six-thirty in the morning, and I don't come home until six-thirty. My wife isn't happy with it, and I can't say I'm happy about working these hours at my age."

In 2003, Lucent dealt the Jensens another blow. It informed its retired managers that it would no longer pay the death benefits it had long promised to widows and widowers. Those benefits usually equaled a year's salary. That maneuver enabled Lucent to save $464 million.[23]

"I don't think it's fair to change the rules after people leave," Jensen said. "People in the gap like me [people who retire before age sixty-five when Medicare coverage kicks in] are being forced back into the workforce based on broken promises. It pretty much stinks."

IN 1875, AMERICAN EXPRESS, then a stagecoach delivery company, became the first American corporation to offer pensions. The goal was to help the company retain its workforce and to ease older workers into retirement. Not long after, many railroads began offering pensions, usually requiring employees to stay for thirty years to qualify. In 1901, Andrew Carnegie went far to popularize pensions in the manufacturing sector by becoming the first major industrialist to provide them to his workers. Ten years later Massachusetts became the first state to promise pensions to its employees, and in 1926, Congress gave its blessing to employer-provided pensions by granting tax exemptions to the money that companies put into pension plans for their workers.

When the Great Depression hit in 1929, pensions were far from widespread, and many elderly Americans found themselves in serious financial peril. Franklin Roosevelt in response pushed through the Social Security Act in 1935, landmark legislation that provided modest monthly payments to older Americans.

Pensions mushroomed in popularity during World War II largely as an unintended consequence of the wage controls that Roosevelt had adopted.

Many companies, restricted in raising wages to help recruit and retain workers, began offering pensions, with organized labor's enthusiastic support. Moreover, the era's high income tax rates made pensions an attractive tool for sheltering income.

After the war, labor unions made a huge push to expand pension coverage. John L. Lewis, the renowned mine workers leader, spearheaded a strike that won pensions for coal miners, and in 1949, Walter Reuther pressured the Ford Motor Company into offering pensions. General Motors followed in Ford's footsteps in 1950 despite the warnings of its chairman, Alfred P. Sloan, Jr., who had cautioned that pensions could prove "extravagant beyond reason."[24] The UAW proclaimed that these hard-won pensions "laid the foundation" for "a full measure of dignity and security" for retirees.[25]

Ford and GM's embrace of pensions helped generate what was widely called "the pension stampede." From 1940 to 1960, the number of private-sector workers with pension coverage soared from 4 million to 23 million, representing half of the nation's private-sector workers.[26]

Then, in 1963, America's smooth ride toward retirement security hit a bump. Studebaker, the automaker, went bankrupt, leaving 4,100 workers, some employed there for three decades, with just 15 percent of their promised pensions.[27] Suddenly the pension system was seen to have a gaping hole; pensions could evaporate when companies failed to set aside enough money to finance them. After a decade-long tug-of-war between business and labor, Congress enacted the Employee Retirement Income Security Act of 1974 (ERISA), which required companies to set aside adequate funding for the pensions they promised. (That legislation had numerous loopholes and flaws that did not become fully apparent until years later.) ERISA created a federal agency, the Pension Benefit Guaranty Corporation (PBGC), charged with protecting the pensions of workers whose companies might, like Studebaker, declare bankruptcy, leaving underfunded pension plans.

In 1978, four years after ERISA was enacted, Congress passed a provision, little noticed at the time, that authorized the creation of 401(k) plans. These plans were originally intended to help high-paid corporate executives reduce their income taxes by enabling them to defer part of their salaries. In the early 1980s, many large companies began offering 401(k)s to regular workers to promote employee savings, often while maintaining their pension plans. At the same time, many small businesses, including some that later became large, such as Starbucks, Dell, and Home Depot, opted to offer 401(k)s rather than traditional pensions.

Corporate America's shift away from pensions was hastened early this decade by what some actuaries called a "perfect storm" of unfavorable circumstances. When the stock market soared in the 1990s, many corporations hardly gave a thought to their pension obligations. The assets in their pension plans soared in value, and their plans became overfunded, meaning that plan assets were more than enough to meet long-term obligations. This in turn enabled hundreds of companies to skip pension contributions for years in so-called contribution holidays.

But when the stock market began a three-year slide in 2000, many companies saw how costly pension plans could be. According to Bear Stearns, corporate pension plans went from being 23 percent overfunded in late 2000 to being 19 percent underfunded two years later.[28] (Lucent's plan, for example, was $5.5 billion overfunded on September 30, 2001; a year later it was underfunded by $1.7 billion.)[29] The era's low interest rates aggravated the underfunding because companies had to assume a lower rate of return on pension assets in calculating their long-term obligations. And the 2001 recession hurt company profits, further straining corporate America's ability to keep up with its pension burdens.

While United Airlines and Bethlehem Steel abandoned their pension plans, concluding that they could no longer fund them, many other companies were chilled by the specter of paying indefinitely large pension obligations thirty and forty years into the future. Since then, Verizon and IBM have frozen their plans, and many companies have closed their plans to newly hired workers. Because of such moves, the number of traditional pension plans at large companies and small businesses plunged from 114,396 in 1985 to 30,336 in 2005.[30]

When United Airlines and Bethlehem unloaded their pensions on the Pension Benefit Guaranty Corporation, labor unions, politicians, and others woke up to the problem of underfunded plans. (The PBGC can pay a maximum of $45,000 a year in benefits to a retiree, well below what many pension plans would have provided.) As a result of the moves by United, Bethlehem, and other companies, the PBGC's deficit swelled to $23 billion. In 2005, with corporate America's pension plans underfunded by an estimated $450 billion, up from $39 billion five years earlier, many experts warned that so many companies might dump their plans that the PBGC could face a $100 billion deficit and require a huge taxpayer bailout, just like the savings and loan industry once did.[31]

With fears of a bailout growing, the PBGC and federal lawmakers faced stinging criticism for lax oversight. Bethlehem Steel's plan, for instance, had only 45 percent of its theoretically required funding. Congress and President Bush enacted the Pension Protection Act of 2006, which tightened requirements to make sure that far more corporate pension plans were adequately funded. Companies were given seven years to assure full funding, far stricter than the thirty years allowed previously. The law also increased most companies' premiums from nineteen dollars a year per worker to thirty dollars to help finance the pensions of workers whose companies dump their underfunded plans on the PBGC.

Some critics warned that the 2006 law, by setting stricter funding requirements for companies, would ultimately undermine the pension system by persuading more companies to stop providing traditional pensions. Seeming to justify such fears, DuPont announced just two weeks after the law was enacted that it was slashing its pension contributions by two-thirds for current employees and closing its pension plan to new hires. At the same time, DuPont substantially increased its 401(k) match.[32]

CEOs who failed to jump on the pension-cutting bandwagon feared that Wall Street would criticize them for missing an opportunity to reduce costs.[33] All this, at least from the worker's perspective, is spurring an unhealthy race to the bottom on retirement benefits.

WHEN CONGRESS ENACTED ERISA in 1974 with the aim of requiring companies to fund their pension plans adequately, it sought to discourage corporations from lavishing oversize pensions on their top executives. Under ERISA's original provisions, a company's pension plan would not qualify for federal tax deductions if the pension for any executive in the plan was more than seven times the wage of the average full-time worker. (A 1982 law reduced that ratio to four times the average worker's pay.)[34] But many companies showed their contempt for this rule by creating a separate "supplemental" pension plan for their top executives, often giving them pensions that were forty times the pay of the average worker.

On many corporate boards, the CEO's friends sit on the compensation committee and often look to pensions as another way to increase the chief executive's pay. They often hide such pension-boosting moves in the footnotes of regulatory filings. Pfizer, the pharmaceutical company, promised its chief executive, Harry McKinnell, an annual pension of $6.6 million, representing 100 percent of his annual salary and bonus, even though Pfizer's stock had plunged $137 billion in value—43 percent—during his tenure as CEO.[35] Pfizer's

board forced McKinnell into early retirement in 2006 because of his poor performance, but the board left his $200 million retirement package intact.

Lee Raymond, Exxon's chairman, did even better. He retired with a package
worth nearly $400 million, including $199 million in restricted shares, $70 mil-
lion in stock options, and the $98 million lump-sum value of his pension plan.

What is more, as Ellen Schultz and Theo Francis explained in the *Wall Street
Journal*, many companies are lavishing extraordinary post-retirement health
benefits on their top executives even as they trim health benefits to other
retirees. Citigroup has pledged to pay all the health insurance premiums as
well as all out-of-pocket health expenses for its longtime chairman, Sanford I.
Weill, and his wife, for the rest of their lives.

Most employees at Northwest Airlines must work there twenty-three years
to qualify for retiree health coverage, but Northwest's senior executives qualify
for lifetime health coverage for themselves and their families after three
years.[36]

To fatten executive pensions, some companies have engaged in some creative counting. When John Snow left his job as CSX's chief executive to become
Treasury secretary, CSX, the biggest railroad network on the East Coast, gave
him a $33.2 million lump-sum pension. The board based this pension on com-
putations that Snow had worked at CSX for forty-four years even though Snow
had worked there only twenty-six. At Delta Airlines, the chairman, Leo Mullin,
left with a $16 million retirement package based on calculations that he
had worked there twenty-eight and a half years even though he had worked
there just seven years.[37] Many Delta workers resented this generosity because
Mullin had forced a far worse pension plan on the airline's nonunion workers.[38]

AS COMPANIES INCREASINGLY SHUN traditional pensions, 401(k)s have
become the dominant work-based savings plan for retirement. But 401(k)
plans, as I said earlier, are far from an ideal solution.

"In practice, 401(k)s have turned out to be much worse [than traditional
pension plans]," says Professor Munnell. "Workers have to decide whether to
join the plan, how much to contribute, how much to allocate to what plan,
when to change contribution formulas, how to handle things when they move
from one job to the other. The data show very clearly that many people make
mistakes every step of the way."[39]

Moreover, when invested heavily in stocks, as they often are, 401(k)s can be
dangerously volatile. One study, conducted by the Watson Wyatt consulting

firm, examined what would happen to a hypothetical worker who put 6 percent of his or her pay into a 401(k) account for forty years and then retired at age sixty-five. The worker would then use the 401(k) to buy an annuity, a financial product that, like a pension, pays a monthly benefit for as long as one lives. If that worker retired in 2000, when the stock market was booming, that 401(k) account would buy an annuity paying 134 percent of pre-retirement income. But if that worker retired in 2003, when the stock market was far lower, that worker's 401(k) would buy an annuity paying only 57 percent of pre-retirement income.[40]

There are many other shortcomings to 401(k)s. At large corporations, 34 percent of employees' 401(k) plans are invested in their own companies' stock, while 9 percent of workers invest at least 80 percent of their accounts in their company's stock.[41] Such investment strategies can spell disaster. During his more than twenty years at Enron, Charles Prestwood loyally heeded management's advice and invested all of his 401(k) in Enron stock. When the company collapsed, his 401(k) holdings tumbled in value from $1.3 million to just $3,600. Jack VanDerhei, a research fellow at the Employee Benefit Research Institute, says it is foolish for workers to invest their 401(k)s heavily in their own companies. "The problem," he said, "is you not only have your entire job future invested in that company, but now you have your entire retirement security also."[42]

More than 20 percent of workers whose companies offer 401(k) plans don't even sign up, either because they are inattentive or because they are struggling to make ends meet, without money to set aside for retirement.[43] Moreover, nearly 50 percent of workers don't contribute enough to obtain the full company match, essentially giving away money that is within reach. About half of 401(k) participants cash out rather than roll over their investments when they change jobs, turning 401(k)s into a self-generated severance package.[44] This can badly deplete the money they should be setting aside for retirement.

According to the Employee Benefit Research Institute, more than one-third of workers aged fifty-five to sixty-four do not have retirement savings accounts, while six in ten workers have no idea how much they need to save for retirement.[45] All too many workers just a year or two from retirement are still investing more than 80 percent of their 401(k)s in stocks, when any retirement adviser would warn them to move their investments into less volatile bonds or money market accounts.[46]

The median amount that workers age fifty-five to sixty-four have in their

401(k) plans, you'll remember, is $61,000. A retiree who establishes an annuity with $61,000 would typically receive a monthly annuity of $400, or $4,800 a year. That annuity, plus Social Security benefits (which typically come to $12,500 a year), would add up to $17,300 a year in annual retirement income. That is not much to live on.

In the view of many pension experts, someone who earns $50,000 a year should aim to have at least $300,000 in a 401(k) to assure adequate retirement income. That could produce annuity payments of $24,000 a year, which with $12,500 in Social Security benefits puts the worker near the goal of three-fourths of pre-retirement income. According to Vanguard, only one-third of Americans are on track to achieve this goal.[47]

Karen Ferguson, director of the Pension Rights Center, a retirees' advocacy group, said, "The 401(k) system is built on great optimism; educate everyone to save for themselves and they'll live happily ever after. But it's not happening."[48]

Aggravating matters, the age for receiving full Social Security benefits will increase to sixty-seven for people born after 1960. And many economists predict that monthly Social Security benefits will fall as a percentage of pre-retirement income.[49]

As a result of all these factors, many Americans are going to have to continue working well past today's average retirement age of sixty-two. Professor Munnell says that if Americans work an additional four years, pushing back the average retirement age to sixty-six, that will solve the problem of inadequate retirement income for most workers. Those who work the extra years will be in better financial shape for retirement, she said, because their retirement will be four years shorter and they will have squirreled away additional savings during their four extra years of work. But this solution of working several more years to assure sufficient retirement income will be especially troublesome for older Americans who are too infirm or ill to work. Like Harold Danley, many Americans will be toiling into their sixties and seventies in what are often viewed as low-skill, entry-level jobs. "Instead of sixty being the new thirty," Professor Ghilarducci of Notre Dame wrote, "it has become the new seventeen, as older people fill the job segment with the predicted largest growth in new jobs—retail clerks."[50]

"What is the meaning of retirement if the only way you can live is to work?" Professor Ghilarducci said on the PBS *Frontline* documentary "Can You Afford to Retire?" "The answer is there is no meaning to retirement anymore. We are now shifting from lifetime pensions to lifetime work. It's the end of retirement."[51]

Chapter Sixteen

LIFTING ALL BOATS

President John F. Kennedy used a memorable phrase to describe the economy of his day: "A rising tide lifts all boats." During the Kennedy era, not only did low-income, middle-class, and wealthy Americans all enjoy growing incomes, but their incomes more or less increased at the same rate. The dinghies and the yachts rose in tandem.

That is no longer the case.

Even though the economic tide has risen in recent years, even though economic growth, corporate profits, and worker productivity have all climbed strongly, many middle-income and low-income families have been left behind. What can be done about that?

First of all, the public conversation needs to be changed. Too often workers are not even part of the discussion, or part of the equation. Whether the subject is corporate takeovers, trade deals, or cuts in capital gains taxes, the discussion often glosses over what it means for the nation's 145 million workers. To insert the American worker back into the national conversation won't be easy. But imagine if a presidential candidate vowed that his or her top legislative priority would be universal health coverage for every worker, three weeks' paid vacation a year for every worker, five paid sick days a year for every worker, and six weeks' paid maternity leave for women.

Many business executives would no doubt complain that they couldn't possibly afford such measures, but it would be healthy to have a vigorous debate about these proposals because that would go far to put workers' concerns back into the conversation.

FIGHTING WAGE STAGNATION

To address the worst effects of the squeeze on the American worker, it is of course vital to tackle the problem of languishing incomes. Fortunately, there are many strategies to address this problem, among them a higher minimum wage, greater unionization, and keeping unemployment low to increase workers' bargaining power. Continued productivity growth is, of course, important, too.

There are two prevailing schools of thought regarding the minimum wage. One argues that only the market should set wages and that whatever a worker's wages are, no matter how low, is fair because that's where the market set them. The other school of thought holds that every full-time worker should earn enough to assure a life of dignity.

That second school of thought holds that something is badly awry because 13.5 million Americans, including 7.7 million children, live below the poverty line even though at least one adult in their household holds a full-time job. To help reduce that disturbing number, the nation should embrace the official goal of assuring that every household in which the parents are working has enough income to meet its basic needs. As a first step, the president and Congress should appoint a bipartisan commission that would have six months to determine how much income is needed to meet a household's basic needs in each of the fifty states.[1] Since living costs are far higher in some states than in others, the basic needs budget would vary significantly. The federal government has set the nationwide poverty line at $20,614 for a family of four, but one study estimated that a basic budget for four in 2005 was $31,284 in Caspar, Wyoming, $42,732 in Charlotte, North Carolina, $47,520 in Denver, $54,948 in the Twin Cities, and $64,656 in Boston.[2]

After the bipartisan commission makes its recommendations, Congress should make vigorous use of the minimum wage and the earned income tax credit (EITC) to assure that all full-time workers have sufficient income to support their families. In May 2007, Congress raised the minimum wage from $5.15, the first increase in nearly a decade, following the longest stretch without an increase since the minimum wage was first enacted in 1938. Under the new legislation, the minimum wage will increase in three steps, with it reaching $7.25 in July 2009.[3] At that point, a full-time minimum-wage worker will earn $15,080 a year. Many economists, citing a landmark economic study by David Card and Alan Krueger, have said that this increase will do little to cause business to reduce hiring.

The increase to $7.25 is expected to raise wages for nearly six million workers who earn less than $7.25 an hour, and through a ripple effect, it is expected to push up wages for another seven million who earn slightly more than $7.25.[4] Because the minimum was not raised for nearly ten years, inflation had badly eroded its value, with the minimum falling to less than one-third of the average wage—the lowest level since World War II and down from half the average wage during John F. Kennedy's presidency. To prevent another long stretch without a minimum wage increase, many advocates say Congress should enact legislation that pegs the minimum wage to half the average wage (currently $17.71 an hour, which would yield a minimum wage of $8.85).

At $7.25 an hour, the minimum wage will leave many workers with incomes well below the poverty line and well below what it takes to meet a family's basic needs. That is why the federal government should substantially increase the EITC, a tax credit received by many low-wage workers, perhaps by several thousand dollars above the current ceiling of $4,520. States with the highest basic-needs budgets should pitch in with their own state-financed earned income tax credit. Conservatives and liberals alike should embrace the EITC; President Ronald Reagan once called it "the best anti-poverty, the best pro-family, the best job creation measure to come out of Congress."[5]

Macroeconomic policy is another important tool, too often forgotten, for lifting all boats. When the labor market was tight from 1995 to 2000, real wages rose at their fastest pace in three decades, helped by the unemployment rate's falling to 3.9 percent, its lowest level in decades. Between 1995 and 2000, incomes for the bottom fifth of families rose as fast as incomes for the highest fifth (more than 13 percent after inflation).[6] During those five years, family income for blacks rose by 16 percent and for Hispanics by 25 percent.[7] Without that five-year burst of earnings growth, the wage stagnation of the past three decades would have been far worse. The lesson of the late 1990s is that a strong economy and low unemployment are vital to higher wages.

CRACKING DOWN ON WAGE THEFT

As we have seen, far too many workers have had their wages cut because of lawbreaking by their bosses. The government must assume some of the blame. Far too many states have mimicked the federal government and cut the number of workplace investigators when more are needed. The ratio of federal wage-and-hour investigators per million workers has dwindled to one-third of what it was a half century ago. Hiring new workplace investigators should easily earn back the cost given the drastic increase in lawbreaking in the workplace.

If the nation is serious about increasing wage and hour compliance, then federal and state lawmakers should increase the puny penalties now imposed. The federal penalty for falsifying wage documents, for example, is just $1,000. In some states, the penalty for minimum wage and overtime violations is just 25 percent more than the amount workers are cheated. With penalties so small and the likelihood of getting caught so minuscule, many managers see a bright green light to take illegal actions.[8] To deter lawbreaking, fines should be four or five times the amount that workers are cheated. To show their seriousness about stopping theft of wages, prosecutors should seek to send some executives to prison for cheating workers. Executives are serving time for bilking investors; is cheating workers any less serious a crime?

Congress and state legislatures should prohibit companies from pressuring plaintiffs to seal settlements in workers' lawsuits. Such wrongdoing should be made public. Being able to hide their malfeasance through sealed settlements emboldens companies to cheat workers again.[9]

Congress and the states should also enact laws making companies jointly liable for any wage violations committed by the contractors they hire. This should go far to stop corporations from contracting out janitorial and other low-wage work to firms that brazenly violate wage laws.

When Eliot Spitzer was New York State's attorney general, his office did an impressive job uncovering violations among Manhattan's greengrocers, many of whom paid their workers less than $3.50 an hour. To help ensure future compliance, Spitzer pressured two hundred greengrocers to sign a code of conduct in which they pledged to follow the law and to let a private outside monitor inspect their stores and interview their workers. (The monitoring company brought any violations it found to Spitzer's attention.) Spitzer threatened to bring enforcement actions against lawbreaking greengrocers who refused to sign the code. Ultimately the code greatly increased compliance, and for that reason it is a model that workplace regulators in other states should use for industries with widespread violations, including restaurants, construction companies, laundries, landscapers, car washes, and janitorial services.

To help increase enforcement, worker advocates, community groups, and labor unions should join with law-abiding companies to pressure government regulators not to ignore employers who show contempt toward workplace laws. (Law-abiding companies that pay on the books and pay overtime are obviously at a competitive disadvantage to lawbreaking companies, so they should be involved, too.) Beyond pressing government regulators to act, advocates should establish independent enforcement efforts modeled on the Maintenance Cooperation Trust Fund, based in Los Angeles. That group has seven investigators who crisscross California in search of violations in the janitorial industry. The trust fund is financed by unionized janitorial companies that worry about being undercut by low-priced lawbreaking contractors. Its investigators uncovered minimum wage and overtime violations involving 2,000 late-night janitors at California's three largest supermarket chains, helping to produce a $22.4 million settlement. The group also helped unearth over-time violations involving 775 janitors at Target stores in five states, leading to a $1.9 million settlement between Target and the federal government.

SAFEGUARDING THE SAFETY NET

Given how rapidly corporations are cutting back on health and pension bene-fits, the nation should move quickly to build new structures that will lead to more security for the ill and the elderly. Moreover, with workers moving from job to job as never before, the nation needs to build a system of health and retirement security that is not so closely tied to one's job.

CURING AN UNHEALTHY HEALTH CARE SYSTEM

The United States is the only major industrial nation that does not guarantee universal health coverage. It spends far more on health per person than any other nation, yet the number of uninsured keeps climbing; it's now 47 million people, nearly one in six Americans. Health outlays have soared to more than 16 percent of gross domestic product, up from 5 percent in 1960. America spent $6,102 on health per person in 2004, far more than France ($3,159), Germany ($3,043), and Japan ($2,249), yet those countries boast a higher life expectancy and a much lower infant mortality rate.[10] America's health system ranks thirty-seventh in the world, according to the World Health Organization, while France's ranks first.[11]

America's employer-based health care system was essentially created by happenstance. Because of wage controls during World War II, many compa-nies, as we've seen, could not raise wages to attract or retain workers, so they instead began offering generous health benefits. This employer-based system more or less worked for decades, but with health costs rising rapidly, many companies have either stopped offering coverage or made their insurance premiums so expensive that many workers have dropped their coverage.[12]

The solution would seem to be clear: the United States must make univer-sal coverage one of its highest priorities, the sooner the better. Every American is given the right to a public school education. Is the right to health coverage any less important?

Our system should guarantee that every American can obtain coverage without financial hardship, it should bring health care inflation under control, it should ensure that people don't go without coverage because they changed jobs or lost their job or had a preexisting condition, and it should prevent health costs from undermining the nation's industrial competitiveness. A Pew poll found that 67 percent of Americans want the government to guarantee health insurance, even if it means raising taxes.[13]

One way to achieve these goals would be to extend Medicare to all Americans, emulating Canada's system in which the government pays nearly all medical bills. The government would finance coverage for everyone, with Americans able to choose their doctors exactly as elderly Americans now do under Medicare. (Americans who want treatment above what Medicare covers would be free to pay for it out of their own pocket or through supplemental insurance.) Some economists estimate that moving to such a program would save $200 billion a year, more than enough to provide coverage to the nation's 47 million uninsured. That $200 billion would be saved mainly because administrative costs represent just 3 percent of Medicare's overall costs, while in today's system, administrative costs for insurers, HMOs, doctors, and employers account for nearly 25 percent of costs.[14]

Or every state could copy the innovative programs proposed in Massachusetts and California by Mitt Romney and Arnold Schwarzenegger, respectively, requiring every resident to buy health insurance the way states require every driver to buy automobile insurance. Those states would provide subsidies to help low- and moderate-income residents obtain health insurance. Romney and Schwarzenegger, hoping to create a more level playing field, believe that companies that don't provide health coverage should pay a special assessment for each of their uninsured workers. The huge obstacles that Schwarzenegger's plan has faced in the state legislature argue in favor of having Washington develop a nationwide solution.

Hillary Clinton, John Edwards, and Barack Obama have all outlined plans to create universal or near universal coverage, with all three proposing that Americans of all ages have the choice of buying coverage through a government-run plan modeled on Medicare. Americans could turn to that plan if they believed that private insurers were rejecting them unfairly, charging too much, or providing poor service or coverage.[15]

These proposals would eliminate billions of dollars in insurance industry profits, so we must be prepared for as intensive an industry lobbying effort against them as we've ever seen.

INCREASING RETIREMENT SECURITY

There are options for solving the looming retirement crisis, and they all involve taking some big steps to increase workers' savings.[16] One solution would be to borrow an idea that Italy and Sweden have embraced and Germany is considering. Under one version of such a plan—here I borrow greatly from Professor Teresa Ghilarducci of Notre Dame—all workers would have a retirement account that would piggyback on top of their Social Security balances. Workers would be required to contribute several percent of their wages into that account—Ghilarducci recommends 2.5 percent—with employers required to match that amount. As with Social Security, the federal government would administer these accounts, which Ghilarducci calls "guaranteed retirement accounts."[17] As the federal government does with its main retirement plan for federal employees, these retirement accounts would promise a specific rate of interest each year, perhaps 3 percent after inflation.* A full-time worker who contributes 2.5 percent of pay for forty-four years, working from age twenty-three to age sixty-seven, aided by an employer match, could expect a monthly benefit of around 30 percent of pre-retirement income. Higher earners would contribute more and would accordingly receive higher monthly benefits. Together with Social Security, these monthly benefits would give workers a healthy replacement rate of around 70 percent of pre-retirement income.[18]

This proposal builds on the founding concept of Social Security but goes beyond it by seeking to assure that every worker has adequate income in retirement. Unlike Social Security, these retirement accounts would never face a funding shortfall because they would be pre-funded. Employees and their employers would have already paid into the fund the full amount that employees draw on when they retire.[19]

At retirement, workers would be allowed to withdraw up to 10 percent of their account balance in a lump sum. The rest would be paid in lifelong monthly annuities. (Workers would be barred from taking full lump-sum payouts at retirement because far too many retirees spend all of their lump sums by the time they turn seventy-five, leaving them with little but Social Security benefits if they live another ten or fifteen years.)[20]

This proposal would be an improvement over today's system because every worker would have a retirement account; workers, who are often ignorant about investing, would no longer be managing their retirement accounts; and investment firms would no longer be siphoning off large annual fees for handling those accounts.

---

*This proposal also mirrors important aspects of the pension offerings of TIAA-CREF, the giant financial services company that serves college professors and many medical and nonprofit employees.

Meanwhile, some stopgap fixes are needed. Because the workforce is increasingly mobile, Congress should reduce vesting for pension plans to one year from the current five. Too often workers leave a job after three or four years and lose whatever had been accrued toward their pension.[21] Also, Congress should require companies that have 401(k) plans to enroll all their employees automatically, although employees could opt out if they want. Moreover, as a default, 401(k) plans should be structured so that a worker's savings are automatically invested in a prudent manner and are automatically rebalanced as a worker ages. Workers, however, would retain the option of managing and allocating their 401(k)s themselves.[22]

PUTTING SOME MOVEMENT BACK INTO THE LABOR MOVEMENT

Labor unions once were, and could be again, the most effective tool to improve the lot of the American worker. As Gene Carroll of the Cornell University School of Industrial and Labor Relations said: "Can anyone expect companies to suddenly give workers better wages and benefits and treat them better unless they face some outside pressure, and where can that pressure come from except from unions?"

Unions have certainly brought some problems on themselves. But, as discussed earlier, intense employer opposition is by far the leading factor behind labor's decline. Employers flout the law far too often in opposing unions, and unfortunately the nation's system of labor law enforcement has grown so ineffective, with its long delays and insignificant penalties, that it has often served as an enabler for such corporate lawbreaking.

As we've seen, it took six years of litigation before a federal court finally ordered a Florida nursing home to reinstate Ernest Duval, an aide it had illegally fired for leading a unionization effort. The nursing home was ordered to pay just $1,757 in back wages to cover the six years between Duval's firing and reinstatement—a negligible price to pay to cripple the unionization drive he had led.

A long series of judicial and NLRB decisions has further tilted the playing field in favor of employers. In one such example, the Supreme Court ruled that companies have the right to bar union organizers from setting foot on their property, even their parking lot, during organizing drives. The court concluded that a company's property rights trump the union organizers' need for access to help assure a fair election. Using similar reasoning, the NLRB ruled in December 2007 that employers have the right to prohibit individual workers from using their employer's e-mail system to send out union-related messages. Today, with companies deluging employees with anti-union propaganda and threatening, and even firing, many pro-union workers, elections to determine whether employees want a union are often as fair as elections in Cuba or China.

Convinced that this election process is skewed in favor of management, union advocates favor legislation that would give workers the right to use card checks—that is, signing pro-union cards—to determine whether a majority wants a union. Many labor leaders believe that if Congress enacts such a law, it would be the single biggest step to enable unions to grow again. Under current law, companies have a right to demand elections, but as good as elections sound in theory, they often involve widespread intimidation and lawbreaking by management. Because current law contains no monetary penalties to deter such lawbreaking, labor leaders have called for fines of up to $20,000 per violation. With cases like Ernest Duval's in mind, union leaders say that to prevent illegal firings, penalties should be increased to triple or quadruple back pay from the time of firing to the time of reinstatement, period. But even those measures are questionable deterrents given all the money that companies can save if they remain nonunion.[23]

As happened with EnerSys, companies often seek to get rid of unions by dragging their feet for years on negotiating a first contract after workers decide to unionize. To prevent such tactics, many union advocates have called for requiring binding arbitration if no contract is reached within six months of a union's winning recognition.

To help reverse labor's decline, every union should be required to spend at least 25 percent of its budget on organizing. That would be an investment in the betterment of American workers. Any union that falls short of this requirement should face sanctions up to and including expulsion from its respective federation, the AFL-CIO or Change to Win. Union leaders should recognize that they have a responsibility to organize nonunion workers, not just to help those workers but because failing to organize nonunion workers in their industries often undercuts the wages and benefits of members of their own unions.

In light of the embarrassing pay excesses of the past, the two labor federations and Congress should take strong action to impose salary limitations on labor leaders. To prevent unions from turning into a family business, union leaders should also be prohibited from having any family members on the payroll of their union or union benefit fund.[24]

To survive and grow, unions desperately need to stir more member interest. Every union should be required to spend at least 5 percent of its budget on educating and mobilizing rank-and-file members, because an informed, involved membership means a stronger, smarter, and more democratic labor movement. Moreover, every union should have a Web site with a members' blog and chat room that allows workers to air their views and grievances—and if need be lambaste their union leaders—free of censorship by union officials. To help the rank and file kick out incompetent, inattentive, or corrupt leaders, Congress should enact a law mandating recall votes once 20 percent of a union's members sign a petition.

Unions need to do more to appeal to a more mobile, better-educated work-force, one with an increasing number of white-collar workers, temps, and freelancers. To help these workers, unions have to offer something different from the traditional bargaining for an overall contract. To attract these work-ers, unions should help provide services these workers desperately want, such as affordable training courses, health insurance, and advice on investing for retirement. The Freelancers Union could serve as a model; that Brooklyn-based group has helped thousands of temps, independent contractors, and freelancers obtain good, affordable health insurance and disability insurance. Finally, unions need to adapt to the fiercely competitive global marketplace of the twenty-first century. Unions need to relinquish the view that the employer is always wrong whenever it wants to cut costs or expand a worker's responsi-bilities. Unions also need to cooperate (wisely) with management to help ensure the survival of corporate operations and union members' jobs.

GRAPPLING WITH GLOBALIZATION

In a world in which corporations can move operations wherever they wish, there are no easy answers to stop the sting of globalization. Some Americans have called for crude measures such as import quotas or tariffs to protect workers in particular industries. But even economists who have highlighted the downside of offshoring, such as Paul Samuelson, warn that protectionist measures would hurt more than help. Such measures are hard to administer, could spark a trade war, and could undermine economic efficiency by enabling domestic industries to keep prices artificially high.

In *The World Is Flat*, Tom Friedman wrote, "The Indians and Chinese are not racing us to the bottom. They are racing us to the top—and that is a good thing."[25] To be sure, many Chinese workers are producing toys, shirts, and furniture (often in deplorable sweatshops) that American workers once made. Americans have to accept that such labor-intensive, low-value-added jobs will inevitably be lost to low-paid workers in China and other countries. But the loss of high-tech, high-value-added jobs to China, India, and elsewhere is not something Americans should readily accept. Not only are hundreds of thousands of high-paying high-tech jobs in play, but so is the future of many high-tech industries and perhaps our global economic leadership as well.

While the Bush administration has focused on fighting terrorism, it seems to have engaged in unilateral disarmament in the struggle for global competitiveness. The administration has repeatedly cut the federal budget for science research, after factoring in inflation, when such research is pivotal to staying ahead of the pack. President Bush has largely taken a "What, me worry?" attitude about the nation's colossal trade deficit, which is undermining our manufacturing base and, as Warren Buffett warned, our long-term living standards as well.

Americans can boast of world-leading universities such as MIT and Caltech, but we allow far too many of our schools and children to wallow in mediocrity and worse. Not only that, we seem to be surrendering our lead in science and engineering. United States eighth-graders rank fifteenth out of forty-five countries in international math rankings, behind Singapore, South Korea, and Russia.[26] Three decades ago, the United States ranked third in awarding science degrees; it has sunk to seventeenth.[27] Each year in the United States, 60,000 students receive bachelor's degrees in engineering; in China, 700,000 do.[28] In 2010, the American share of the science and engineering PhDs awarded worldwide is expected to be 15 percent, down from 50 percent in 1975.[29]

The nation needs a scientific and economic call to arms, like the one that President Kennedy made after the Soviet Union launched the first human into space. America needs to boost basic R&D spending and to steer more students into science and engineering. We as a nation need to give some of the same acclaim to academic and scientific achievement that we give to athletic achievement.

Although this might be wishful thinking, corporate attitudes do need to change. Far too many business executives seem predisposed to laying off workers at home and moving operations abroad. The corporate mentality should instead be "How can we make it work in the USA?" Political leaders rarely criticize companies that move operations overseas, in effect, giving them a green light. Just as President Kennedy intervened with U.S. Steel to help hold down steel prices, some high-level jawboning might persuade some companies to keep jobs in the United States. This is not a call for protection, just a call for a change in attitudes.

Congress should require companies that plan to lay off five hundred or more employees because they are moving production overseas or offshoring white-collar jobs to issue a report sixty days they take such a move. The report should explain the reasons for such a move and analyze the costs that such a move would have on the affected workers and community. Those companies should also be required to hold a meeting with their employees and the local community to discuss the layoffs.[30]

With most Americans gaining from globalization, the nation should take some steps to help those who lose out. Retraining needs to be expanded and upgraded to make sure it produces results. Moreover, federal retraining funds should go not just to factory workers who lose jobs to foreign competition but also service-sector workers and white-collar workers, such as software developers and customer service representatives. Just as important, the nation—if it hasn't already enacted universal health insurance—should provide at least two years of health insurance to workers (and their families) who lose jobs to globalization. And to pay for such measures, the government might look to increase taxes on those who Lawrence Summers said were the biggest winners from globalization, those at the top of the income pyramid.

With the country losing hundreds of thousands of good-paying jobs to globalization, government should use its economic might and foresight to plant the seeds for the industries of the future. The Apollo Alliance, a coalition of environmentalists, unions, and political leaders, has proposed making America a leader, rather than a laggard, in energy efficiency, all while creating at least one million good-paying jobs. That alliance has called on the federal government to use billions in subsidies, grants, and tax credits to spur companies to build hybrid cars as well as energy-efficient appliances, factories, and office towers. The idea is simple: a good environment and good jobs.

As the world's richest nation, the United States should use its consumer buying power to improve the lot of factory workers in developing countries such as China and Bangladesh, just as the National Consumers League used consumer power in the early 1900s to fight sweatshop wages and conditions in American factories. A first step would be to boycott products made in overseas sweatshops.[31] Second, the United States should make sure that in all its trade agreements, signatory countries pledge to enforce their own workplace laws (such as their minimum wage laws) and the international labor conventions they've already pledged to follow, like barring child labor and guaranteeing workers the right to form unions. This is a modest step that even free traders should not balk at—asking other countries to do what they're already supposed to be doing.

EASING THE CLIMB UPWARD

If the United States is serious about being the land of equal opportunity that it says it is, it needs to take some vigorous steps to increase economic mobility. A childhood of poverty creates unfertile terrain for youngsters to grow and flourish, and the nation therefore needs to take meaningful steps, as we discussed earlier, to increase incomes for low-wage workers and their families.

In light of the studies showing that child readiness programs lead to better results in school and lower dropout and incarceration rates, the nation should guarantee Head Start places to all three- and four-year-olds in families earning less than $50,000 a year. At present, just 40 percent of the three- and four-year-olds in households earning $20,000 to $30,000 are in preschool programs, half the rate for families earning $100,000 or more.[32]

With so many poor children held back by dismal schools and a lack of positive role models, the Center for American Progress has made the interesting proposal to create two million "opportunity" housing vouchers that would enable families locked in poor inner-city neighborhoods to move to "opportunity-rich" neighborhoods where children would enjoy better schools, greater safety, and better job opportunities.[33]

In every state in which inner-city schools perform far worse than schools in affluent areas, the courts should rule, as courts have already done in several states, that the inferior education in the worst school districts violates students' rights by denying them an adequate education or the equal protection of the law or both. Such rulings should require states to increase spending on the lowest-performing schools. This should lead to smaller class sizes, stepped-up remedial efforts, more honors classes, and higher teacher salaries—all important ways to improve schools and better prepare students.[34]

Because many high school dropouts are relegated to poverty or near poverty, the nation should create more second-chance schools, such as those assisted by the Bill and Melinda Gates Foundation, that work with dropouts and potential dropouts to ensure that they obtain diplomas and skills for today's economy.[35]

Far too many qualified students just can't afford to go to college. Congress should make sure that Pell Grants keep pace with soaring college tuitions.

States should experiment with making the first year of community college free, both to encourage students to continue their education and to make clear that it is government policy that having a high school diploma is no longer enough. Other states should seek to copy an innovative program in Greene County, North Carolina, in which low-income students in four-year state colleges have their tuition paid their first year if they agree to work part-time that year. To further mobility, colleges should adopt an affirmative action policy that favors poorer applicants. If an applicant from a $30,000-a-year household has done as well as, or perhaps slightly worse than, one from a $200,000-a-year household, admissions officers should look more favorably on that poorer applicant.

For many low-wage workers, a well-designed career ladder is the answer. More cities should emulate New York and Los Angeles programs that help $18,000-a-year teachers' aides go to school and become full-fledged teachers with bachelor's degrees, enabling them to more than double their salaries. In another program worth taking nationwide, labor unions working with hospitals in New York enable $17,000-a-year nurses aides and home-care workers to study tuition-free to become $35,000-a-year medical technicians and, for those with the head and heart, to become nurses, who can earn $50,000 and often far more.

It does not make sense for the nation to bring in tens of thousands of foreign nurses and software engineers on special visas when the nation's schools should be training more Americans for those high-paying jobs. The United States had 120,000 job vacancies for nurses in 2007, with industry officials predicting a shortage of nearly 400,000 nurses over the next dozen years. Yet the nation's nursing schools turned away 43,000 qualified applicants in 2006 because of insufficient budgets, faculty and classroom space. Government and educational institutions should work together to guarantee that there are enough places to train all Americans interested in such good jobs.

RESPECT AS A REMEDY

As another important step to end the big squeeze, there needs to be a "revalorization" of the worker. Plain and simple, revalorization means treating workers with a newfound respect, to start treating them as if they and their concerns matter. The nation's politicians, news media, and public discourse have largely ignored the struggling worker, except every four years when presidential candidates descend on factories in Iowa, Ohio, and Pennsylvania, with TV cameras in tow, and lend an ear to the concerns of the poor workingman.

This is the era of the investor, the entrepreneur, the consumer, the CEO, the media mogul, the billionaire, the Internet whiz. It is certainly not the era of the worker. America's workers are viewed as voters, as NASCAR fans, as *Oprah* watchers, as Bud drinkers, as potential members of the ownership society, but they are rarely viewed as workers qua workers. All this has made it easier for corporations to continue squeezing the nation's workers and for political leaders to largely ignore their problems (while cozying up to corporate donors).

To be sure, workers will never be as sexy a story as Paris Hilton or Bill Gates, but society needs to begin paying more attention to workers and their concerns. Invisibility begets neglect, while attention begets respect. If society—and the news media—were to start treating workers with more respect, corporations would feel pressure to do likewise, and managers just might feel some pressure to stop squeezing so hard.

Imagine the effect of a White House conference on job safety, with television cameras and heartrending stories of workers maimed and killed. Or imagine the president and secretary of labor holding a conference with workers who suffered minimum-wage violations to highlight that problem. They could also hold a conference on the dark side of offshoring to which they could invite software developers whose jobs were moved to India and accountants and call center workers whose jobs were shipped to various countries. That might cause Congress and the public to focus more on the phenomenon of sending good jobs overseas.

Make no mistake: America is paying a considerable price for outsourcing jobs. Only those directly affected and their immediate families are feeling it now, but soon its impact will grow in the form of fewer high-tech opportunities for American college graduates and greater pressures to hold down American wages.

Workers' concerns have retreated from the nation's consciousness. But if we don't address those concerns, we do so at the workers' peril—and our own.

Acknowledgments

I first want to thank my editor at Knopf, Jonathan Segal, who played an invaluable role in shaping and editing this book. His wisdom and guiding hand have made this a far better book. I also want to thank his assistant, Kyle McCarthy, for her kind help.

I am very grateful to my agent, Vicky Bijur, for her enthusiastic backing of this project. She has been a valuable sounding board and invariably gave me wise advice.

This book would not have been possible were it not for my wife, Miriam. Without her patience, support, and love, in myriad ways large and small, I don't know how I would have written this book. I also want to thank my wonderful children, Emily and Jeremy, both for encouraging me to write a book and for enduring a project in which they lost their father for long stretches.

I want to thank my mother and father, Cyril and Mortimer Greenhouse, my brother, Andrew, and my nephew, Jared, for their enthusiasm and support throughout this project. I also want to thank Lee Reinharth and Françoise Rothman for their keen interest and backing.

As I wrote this book, I often found myself inspired by—and indebted to—other books about American workers, most notably *The Other America* by Michael Harrington, *Working* by Studs Terkel, *The New Deal at Work* by Peter Cappelli, and *Nickel and Dimed* by Barbara Ehrenreich.

It is hard for me to give enough thanks to the workers who appear in this book. They opened their lives and homes to me, and they were often highly courageous in speaking out about the conditions where they worked. Without their cooperation and courage, this would have been a far less compelling work. I want to voice my regrets to Gale Stubbs, Theodore Faulders, and the other workers whom I interviewed at length for this book but was not able to include because of space limitations.

I am very grateful to the *New York Times* for letting me roam the country to write about the nation's workers and working conditions. I am greatly indebted to many friends at the *New York Times*. I thank Bill Keller, Jill Abramson, and John Geddes (and Max Frankel and Joe Lelyveld before them) for recognizing the importance of having a labor and workplace beat. Many editors, notably Susan Edgerley, Jim Roberts, Joe Sexton, Suzanne Daley, Bill Schmidt, and Kevin Flynn, showed patience and understanding in giving me the time and freedom to write this book. I also owe thanks to Mike Oreskes and Dean Baquet for originally putting me on the labor beat for the Metro and National desks.

I thank Daryl Alexander, Rusha Haljuci, and Alex Pelletier for all their kind, behind-the-scenes assistance.

Many colleagues at the *Times* gave me encouragement, kicked around ideas with me, and gave me pointers on writing a book. Among those I want to thank especially are Michael Barbaro, Joe Berger, Nina Bernstein, Ray Bonner, Ethan Bronner, Lawrence Downes, Jim Dwyer, Peter Edidin, David Firestone, Soma Golden, David Cay Johnston, Leslie Kaufman, Peter Kilborn, N. R. Kleinfield, David Leonhardt, Steve Lohr, Floyd Norris, Tom Redburn, Alan Riding, Sara Rimer, Somini Sengupta, Robin Toner, Lou Uchitelle, Mary Williams Walsh, and Ben Weiser.

I want to thank the many people who helped arrange my interviews with the workers who appear in this book: Tarik Ajami, Deborah Axt, Dave Bevard, Gina Bowers, Alan Collinge, Mairead Connor, Amanda Cooper, Marcus Courtney, Rick Doty, Julie Eisenberg, Fred Feinstein, Andrea Fleischer, Andrew Friedman, Lilia Garcia, Artemio Guerra, Ron Hira, Robert C. Huntley, Nancy Hwa, Russell Lloyd, Tom Meiklejohn, Denise Mitchell, Lars Negstad, Eduardo Pena, Mike Rice, Shannon Liss Riordan, Monica Russo, Brad Seligman, Justin Swartz, D. Taylor, Michele Vana, Lane Windham, and Shane Youtz. I am also grateful to those who kindly translated for me, including Lisa Hoyos, Linda Morales, Betzabeth Sanchez, and Elizabeth Wagoner. Susan Grebner and other officials at Illinois Central College were extremely generous in arranging interviews for me with several talented students.

I owe a deep debt of gratitude to Bill Moyers and the Schumann Center for Media and Democracy for awarding me a grant to do the considerable travel required to research this book. I also thank Lynn Welhorsky for her kind assistance in administering that grant.

I want to thank Bob Dilenschneider and Wayne Kabak for giving me valuable insights about book writing and the book business.

I am indebted to numerous experts who helped me on various parts of this book: Nelson Lichtenstein on Walter Reuther and General Motors, Beth Shulman on low-wage workers, Rosemary Batt on call centers, Teresa Ghilarducci, Karen Friedman, Karen Ferguson, and Alicia Munnell on pensions, and Jared Bernstein and Lawrence Mishel on economic statistics and economic trends. I am also grateful to Annette Bernhardt, Janice Fine, Richard Hurd, Mark Levinson, and Kathy Ruckelshaus for sharing their expertise with me.

I owe thanks to numerous officials at Cooperative Home Care, Costco, Ernst & Young, Patagonia, and Wal-Mart, who answered my many questions.

I have also gotten strong support from the small (and dwindling) group of colleagues who write (or until recently wrote) about labor and workplace matters. Here I single out Steve Franklin of the *Chicago Tribune*, Nancy Cleeland, who recently left the *Los Angeles Times*, and Aaron Bernstein, who recently left *BusinessWeek*.

Lastly, I would like to thank many other friends, too many to name, who provided me with invaluable support and encouragement.

Notes

Introduction

1. In 2007, the Service Employees International Union succeeded in unionizing 4,000 Los Angeles security guards, including Michael Johnson. In January 2008, the SEIU negotiated the first labor contract for those guards, a five-year agreement that the union says will raise overall compensation—pay and benefits taken together—by 40 percent. The contract will give Johnson raises of fifty cents a year for five years, and those wage increases, together with a raise tied to his recent promotion to supervisor, will lift his pay to $13.55 an hour in 2012. The contract sets a wage floor of $10.50 an hour in downtown Los Angeles, so guards earning $9 an hour will climb immediately to $10.50.

Chapter One: WORKED OVER AND OVERWORKED

1. Michell and more than a dozen other Wal-Mart workers said in interviews that they were terminated or pushed out after being injured on the job. Wal-Mart denies having a policy to eliminate injured workers.

2. U.S. Bureau of the Census, *Income, Poverty, and Health Insurance Coverage in the United States 2006* (Washington, D.C.: GPO, 2007), p. 6. Median household income for nonelderly households slid to $54,001 in 2005, down $3,100 or 5.4 percent from five years earlier, after accounting for inflation (in 2006 dollars). For all households, including elderly households, median income rose by 1.1 percent in 2005, after having slid the previous five years. The figure for all households, including elderly households, was down 2.7 percent from 2000.

3. U.S. Bureau of the Census, *Income, Poverty, and Health Insurance 2006*, p. 5. In 2006, median income for nonelderly households was $54,726, up $725 or 1.3 percent from the previous year. For all households, median income was $48,201, up $360 or .7 percent.

The economist Stephen Rose argues that median household income has been held down by numerous factors, including more single-parent households, more elderly widows, and more young adults living on their own. Stephen Rose, "Does Productivity Growth Still Benefit Working Americans?: Unraveling the Income Growth Mystery to Determine How Much Median Incomes Trail Productivity Growth," Washington, D.C., Information Technology and Innovation Foundation, June 2007.

4. Lawrence Mishel, Jared Bernstein, and Sylvia Allegretto, *The State of Working America 2006/2007* (Ithaca: Cornell University Press, 2007), p. 119.

5. Ibid., p. 115.

6. Within the economics profession there is a debate over just how much wages have stagnated, with some economists arguing that the consumer price index overstates inflation and that as a result wages have risen somewhat faster than official Bureau of Labor Statistics (BLS) figures indicate.

7. Perhaps the most compelling statistic showing the economy's increased tilt against workers is the decline in the share of national income going to wages and salaries. The wage share fell to its lowest level on record in 2006, with data going back to 1929, while the share going to overall employee compensation, including health and pension benefits, slid to its lowest point in four decades, except for 1997. But the share of national income going to corporate profits has climbed to its highest level since 1942. Steven Greenhouse and David Leonhardt, "Real Wages Fail to Match a Rise in Productivity," *New York Times*, Aug. 28, 2006, p. A1; Aviva Aron-Dine and Isaac Shapiro, "Share of National Income Going to Wages and Salaries at Record Low in 2006," Center on Budget and Policy Priorities, Washington, D.C., March 29, 2007.

8. U.S. Bureau of the Census, *Income, Poverty, and Health Insurance 2006*, pp. 12, 21.

9. Elizabeth Warren and Amelia W. Tyagi, *The Two-Income Trap* (New York: Perseus Books, 2003), p. 20. Warren and Tyagi show that foreclosures were increasing even before the subprime mortgage crisis. Many bankers asserted that one reason for the increase in bankruptcies was that many Americans were taking advantage of lenient provisions in the bankruptcy laws.

10. Richard B. Freeman, *America Works: The Exceptional U.S. Labor Market* (New York: Russell Sage Foundation, 2007), pp. 41–45.

11. Mishel, Bernstein, and Allegretto, *State of Working America 2006/2007*, p. 91.

12. Ellen Galinsky, James T. Bond, and E. Jeffrey Hill, "When Work Works," New York, Families and Work Institute, April 2004, p. 1.

13. *OECD Employment Outlook 2007* (Paris: Organization for Economic Co-operation and Development, 2007), table F, p. 263.

14. Michael Mandel, "Which Way to the Future?" *BusinessWeek*, Aug. 20, 2007, p. 45, quoting Lynn Franco, director of consumer research for the Conference Board; "In Pursuit of Satisfaction: U.S. Job Satisfaction Declines," News Release, Conference Board, Feb. 23, 2007.

15. Bob Davis, "Extra Credit: Lagging Behind the Wealthy, Many Use Debt to Catch Up," *Wall Street Journal*, May 17, 2005, p. A1.

16. At the same time, household debt soared to a record 132 percent of disposable income, an all-time record, up from 74 percent a quarter century earlier. Mishel, Bernstein, and Allegretto, *State of Working America*, p. 271.

17. Brian K. Bucks, Arthur B. Kennickell, and Kevin B. Moore, "Recent Changes in U.S. Family Finances: Evidence from the 2001 and 2004 Survey of Consumer Finances," *Federal Reserve Bulletin*, 2006, p. A35.

18. Vikas Bajaj and Edmund L. Andrews, "Broader Losses from Mortgages," *New York Times*, Oct. 25, 2007, p. A1. The Joint Economic Committee of Congress estimated up to two million foreclosures. The Bush administration predicted up to 500,000, which, in itself, would be a tidal wave compared with recent years.

19. Congressional Budget Office, *Historical Effective Federal Tax Rates* (Washington, D.C.: GPO, 2007), table 1C. As a result of such trends, the share of the nation's overall income going to the top 1 percent of earners has leaped from 9 percent in 1980 to 22 percent in 2005, reaching heights not seen since the Roaring Twenties. Thomas Piketty and Emmanuel Saez,

"Income Inequality in the United States: 1913–1998," *Quarterly Journal of Economics* 68, no. 1 (Feb. 2003): 1–39 (elsa.berkeley.edu/~saez/pikettyqje.pdf). An updated series can be found at elsa.berkeley.edu/~saez/TabFig2005prel.xls. Also see David Cay Johnston, "Income Gap Is Widening, Data Shows," *New York Times,* March 29, 2007, p. C1.

20. Congressional Budget Office, *Tax Rates,* table 1C. President Bush has been able to boast that average income is up—the upper crust's income boom has pulled up everyone else's mean income. But there's a catch: *median* income, with half of Americans above and half below, has remained depressingly flat. According to a 2007 study based on IRS data, income for the bottom 90 percent of Americans fell in 2005, before government payments are included, while income for the top 1 percent—they average $1.1 million a year—climbed by $139,000 on average. Piketty and Saez, "Income Inequality."

21. Paul Krugman, "Left Behind Economics," *New York Times,* July 14, 2006, p. 19.

22. Mishel, Bernstein, and Allegretto, *State of Working America 2006/2007,* p. 121.

23. U.S. Bureau of the Census, *Income, Poverty, and Health Insurance 2006,* p. 12. The earned income tax credit has certainly been a salve to many low-income families, giving them a few thousand extra dollars, but even with this boost, far too many Americans—12.3 percent—remain in poverty.

There is considerable debate about how to define the poverty threshold. Based on recommendations of the National Academy of Sciences, the Census Bureau calculated that the poverty rate in 2003 would have been 16 percent if one added housing subsidies, food stamps, subsidized school lunches, and the income tax credit to family income and then subtracted federal and state taxes, child care, and commuting costs. Another Census Bureau calculation would figure in the imputed return of home equity for homeowners, and that would have reduced the 2003 rate to 9 percent. See David Wessel, "Counting the Poor: Methods and Controversy," *Wall Street Journal,* June 15, 2006, p. A10.

24. Mishel, Bernstein, and Allegretto, *State of Working America 2006/2007,* pp. 135, 138; Alicia H. Munnell and Pamela Perun, "An Update on Private Pensions," Center for Retirement Research at Boston College, Aug. 2006, p. 2.

25. Beth Shulman, *The Betrayal of Work* (New York: New Press, 2005), p. 31.

26. Tom Waldron, Brandon Roberts, and Andrew Reamer, "Working Hard, Falling Short: America's Working Families and the Pursuit of Economic Security," Working Poor Families Project, Oct. 2004, p. 3.

27. Barbara Ehrenreich, *Nickel and Dimed* (New York: Henry Holt, 2001), p. 221.

28. U.S. Bureau of Labor Statistics, "2004–14 Employment Projections," USDL News Release 05-2276, Dec. 7, 2005 (www.bls.gov/news.release/ecopro.nr0.htm).

29. U.S. Bureau of the Census, *Income, Poverty, and Health Insurance 2006,* p 21.

30. Sara R. Collins, Karen Davis, Michelle M. Doty, Jennifer L. Kriss, and Alyssa L. Holmgren, "Gaps in Health Insurance: An All-American Problem," Commonwealth Fund, April 2006, p. vii. The study defined moderate-income as having household income of $20,000 to $40,000 a year.

31. Kaiser Family Foundation and Health Research and Educational Trust, "Survey of Employer Health Benefits 2007," Sept. 11, 2007, charts 4 and 5.

32. "Can You Afford to Retire?" *Frontline,* Public Broadcasting System, May 16, 2006. In an interview with correspondent Hedrick Smith, the lawyer for United Airlines was James H. M. Sprayregen, who said, "Chapter Eleven has become somewhat of a more accepted strategic tool than just companies filing who are about to go out of business, or something like that."

33. Donald L. Bartlett and James B. Steele, "The Broken Promise: It Was Part of the American Dream," *Time*, Oct. 31, 2005, p. 32.

34. Brian Bergstein, "HP Struggling with Pension Costs," Associated Press, July 19, 2005.

35. Peter G. Gosselin, "If America Is Richer, Why Are Its Families So Much Less Secure?" *Los Angeles Times*, Oct. 10, 2004, p. A1. Gosselin has done extraordinary work on the growing risks that American workers face.

36. Jacob S. Hacker, "The Privatization of Risk and the Growing Economic Insecurity of Americans," Social Science Research Council, posted Feb. 14, 2006. (privatizationofrisk .ssrc.org/Hacker/). See also Jacob S. Hacker, *The Great Risk Shift: The Assault on American Jobs, Families, Health Care and Retirement—and How You Can Fight Back* (New York: Oxford University Press, 2006).

37. At the same time, the share of national income going to employee compensation overall—wages and benefits taken together—has, except for 1997, sunk to its lowest level since 1968. The wage share fell to 51.6 percent of national income in 2006, from 55 percent in 2001, while the share of employee compensation fell to 64 percent, from 66.2 percent in 2001. Aron-Dine and Shapiro, "Share of National Income Going to Wages and Salaries at Record Low in 2006."

38. Telephone interview with Lawrence Katz, April 6, 2005.

39. For a haunting account of this problem, see David Barstow, "A Trench Caves In; a Young Worker Is Dead. Is It a Crime?" *New York Times*, Dec. 21, 2003, p. 1.

40. This means that if each investigator visited one establishment per workday, it would take forty-two years to inspect every single one. Annette Bernhardt and Siobhan McGrath, "Trends in Wage and Hour Enforcement by the U.S. Department of Labor, 1975–2004," Brennan Center for Justice, Sept. 3, 2005 (www.brennancenter.org/programs/downloads/ trendswageshours.pdf). Although many critics say the Labor Department's wage and hour division should be far more aggressive, it did collect a record $221 million in back wages in fiscal 2007, including $181 million for minimum wage and overtime violations.

41. "Remarks by Labor Secretary Elaine Chao on the National Day of Prayer," Federal News Service, May 4, 2006.

42. Ian Urbina and Andrew W. Lehren, "U.S. Is Reducing Safety Penalties for Mine Flaws," *New York Times*, March 2, 2006, p. A1.

43. Steven Greenhouse, "Among Janitors, Violations Go with the Job," *New York Times*, July 13, 2005, p. A1.

44. Steven Greenhouse, "Forced to Work off the Clock, Some Fight Back," *New York Times*, Nov. 19, 2004, p. A1.

45. Steven Greenhouse, "Altering of Worker Time Cards Spurs Growing Number of Suits," *New York Times*, April 4, 2004, p. A1.

46. Steven Greenhouse, "Suits Say Wal-Mart Forces Workers to Toil off the Clock," *New York Times*, June 25, 2002, p. A1.

47. Steven Greenhouse, "Neighbors Take Up Cause of Higher Pay at Some Stores," *New York Times*, Oct. 18, 2004, p. B1.

48. Steven Greenhouse, "In-House Audit Says Wal-Mart Violated Labor Laws," *New York Times*, Jan. 13, 2004, p. A16; Rachel Osterman, "Lunch and the Law; Workers Split on Timing of Breaks," *Sacramento Bee*, Dec. 29, 2004, p. D1.

49. Greenhouse, "In-House Audit."

50. Steven Greenhouse, "Abercrombie & Fitch Bias Case Is Settled," *New York Times,* Nov. 17, 2004, p. A16; Steven Greenhouse, "Clothing Chain Accused of Discrimination," *New York Times,* June 17, 2003, p. A21.

51. Carlos Tejada and Gary McWilliams, "New Recipe for Cost Savings: Replace Expensive Workers—In a Tight Market, Employers Are Finding Job Seekers Willing to Accept Less," *Wall Street Journal,* June 11, 2003, p. A1.

52. Sherri C. Goodman, "Fired Worker Feels Betrayed by Circuit City; 17 Employees in Area Laid Off," *Birmingham News,* April 12, 2007, p. 1D.

53. Greenhouse, "Forced to Work off the Clock."

54. Rachel Williams, "400 Workers 'Eliminated' by Email," Press Association, Aug. 31, 2006.

55. Joel J. Smith, "NWA Layoff Tips Offend Workers," *Detroit News,* Aug. 17, 2006, p. 1C.

56. Jared Bernstein and Isaac Shapiro, "Buying Power of Minimum Wage at 51-Year Low," Washington, D.C., Economic Policy Institute and Center on Budget and Policy Priorities, June 20, 2006 (www.epinet.org/issuebriefs/224/ib224.pdf#search=%22economic%20policy %20institute%20minimum%20wage%20cbpp%22).

57. Tax Policy Center, "Combined Effect of the 2001–2006 Tax Cuts," Washington, D.C., table T06-0279, Nov. 13, 2006.

Chapter Two: WORKPLACE HELL

1. Steven Greenhouse, "Factory Finds Itself Up Against a Woman with a Mission," *New York Times,* April 7, 1997, p. B1. Workers who were desperate to reduce their points had one unappealing option—Landis would subtract one point whenever an employee agreed to work a half dozen six-day weeks in a row.

2. Steven Greenhouse, "Labor Strife and Amputations Roil a Plastics Factory," *New York Times,* Oct. 2, 1996, p. B1.

3. Greenhouse, "Woman with a Mission." Also see Landis Plastics Decision by NLRB Administrative Law Judge Steven Davis, May 22, 1998 (1998 NLRB Lexis 308), p. 99.

4. John O'Brien, "Landis Worker Claims Harassment," *Syracuse Post-Standard,* Oct. 16, 1996, p. C2.

5. Greenhouse, "Woman with a Mission."

6. Interview with Kathy Saumier, Syracuse, March 10, 2003. Also see Landis Plastics Decision by NLRB Administrative Law Judge Steven Davis, pp. 31–32. Judge Davis found that Russell had illegally intimidated and interrogated Saumier when she asked her about the aid the steelworkers union had given her in how to deal with the harassment by the technician.

7. "Syracuse Bishop Decries Worker Injuries," *National Catholic Reporter,* Sept. 20, 1996, p. 3.

8. Greenhouse, "Woman with a Mission."

9. After protracted negotiations, Landis and OSHA ultimately reached a settlement in which the company agreed to pay $425,520. John O'Brien, "Landis Agrees to Pay Record $425,520 Fine," *Syracuse Post-Standard,* June 6, 1998, p. B1.

10. Steven Greenhouse, "Plastics Factory Is Fined for Failure to Register Work Injuries," *New York Times,* Jan. 15, 1997, p. B2.

11. John O'Brien, "Judge Fines Landis for Breaking Law, Company Failed to Report Injuries," *Syracuse Post-Standard,* Nov. 12, 1996, p. A10.

12. Greenhouse, "Labor Strife and Amputations."

13. Ibid. Later, Gregory Landis said, "That was the dumbest statement that ever came out of our company." Quoted in John O'Brien, "Union Advocate Always Stood Up for Others," *Syracuse Post-Standard*, March 23, 1998, p. B1.

14. Greenhouse, "Strife and Amputations."

15. John O'Brien, "In the Past Year, Four Workers Have Lost Fingers While Working at the Solvay Plastics Plant," *Syracuse Post-Standard*, Aug. 29, 1996, p. B1.

16. Ibid.

17. Craig Urey, "NLRB May Push Landis Plastics to Rehire Fired Union Organizer," *Plastics News*, April 7, 1997, p.3.

18. Telephone interview with Gregory Landis, March 1997.

19. John O'Brien, "Fired Landis Worker Sues Accuser for $1 Million," *Syracuse Post-Standard*, Feb. 27, 1997, p. B1.

20. Personal interviews with Kathy Saumier and Mairead Connor, Syracuse, Dec. 16, 2005.

21. Editorial, "Whistle Blower Fired, Another Vindication for Landis?" *Syracuse Post-Standard*, Feb. 12, 1997, p. A8.

22. John O'Brien, "Landis Slapped by Labor Board," *Syracuse Post-Standard*, April 3, 1997, p. A1.

23. John O'Brien, "NLRB Cites Landis Again," *Syracuse Post-Standard*, June 25, 1997, p. B1.

24. *Dunbar v. Landis Plastics*, 996 F Supp. 174 (N.D.N.Y. 1998).

25. Ibid. Judge Pooler also ordered the reinstatement of Clara Sullivan, a recently hired African American union supporter who was fired on charges of alleged sexual harassment.

26. Landis Plastics Decision by NLRB Administrative Law Judge Steven Davis, p. 98.

27. John O'Brien, "Union Lawyer Trips Up Landis' Witness," *Syracuse Post-Standard*, Sept. 27, 1997, p. B4.

28. *NLRB vs. Landis Plastics*. Transcript of hearing before NLRB Administrative Law Judge Steven Davis, pp. 3788–3801.

29. Ibid, p. 3801.

30. Landis Plastics Decision by NLRB Administrative Law Judge Steven Davis, p. 99.

31. Judge Davis also found that Landis had broken the law by putting pro-union workers in isolation to punish them, by installing video cameras to spy on union supporters, by interrogating employees about which of their coworkers supported the union, and by urging managers to take smoking breaks with their pro-union subordinates to eavesdrop on them. Ibid., pp. 112–14.

32. John O'Brien, "Union Organizers Back at Landis," *Syracuse Post-Standard*, April 7, 1998, p. B7.

33. Steven Greenhouse, "Plastics Company to Pay $782,000 in Sex Discrimination Case," *New York Times*, Dec. 7, 2000, p. B14. In announcing the settlement, EEOC officials said they expected that more than five hundred current and former female Landis workers would apply for part of the $782,000. Landis said it had pushed for the settlement, and as usual, it refused to admit any mistakes or wrongdoing. Landis officials said the company had agreed to the settlement to avoid costly litigation and to get the issue behind it.

Chapter Three: **THE VISE TIGHTENS**

1. Steven Greenhouse, "Unions Finding That Employers Want More Concessions," *New York Times,* July 11, 2003, p. A12.

2. U.S. Bureau of the Census, *Income, Poverty, and Health Insurance Coverage in the United States: 2005* (Washington, D.C.: GPO, 2006), p. 6. For all households, including elderly households, median income rose slightly in 2005, edging up by 1.1 percent after falling the previous five years in a row. Nonetheless, the 2005 median for all households remained 2.7 percent below 1999 levels.

3. U.S. Bureau of the Census, *Income, Poverty, and Health Insurance Coverage in the United States: 2006* (Washington, D.C.: GPO, 2007), p. 5; Jared Bernstein, Elise Gould, and Lawrence Mishel, "Poverty, Income and Health Insurance Trends in 2006," Washington, D.C., Economic Policy Institute, Aug. 28, 2007.

4. Productivity growth was robust from 2001 to 2004 but slowed to a moderate pace from 2004 to 2007.

5. In sharp contrast, during the first five years of the seven other postwar expansions, compensation climbed *half* as fast as profits on average. There are other troubling measures showing that corporations are grabbing more and more of the economic pie. Corporate profits took 47 percent of the increase in national income in the four and a half years after the recession ended, compared with an average of just 17.5 percent after other postwar recessions. Aviva Aron-Dine and Isaac Shapiro, "Share of National Income Going to Wages and Salaries at Record Low in 2006," Washington, D.C., Center on Budget and Policy Priorities, March 29, 2007.

6. Steven Greenhouse and David Leonhardt, "Real Wages Fail to Match a Rise in Productivity," *New York Times,* Aug. 28, 2006, p. A1.

7. That represents a sharp break from what happened during the previous seven postwar recoveries, when compensation rose roughly *three-fourths* as fast as productivity on average.

8. Lawrence Mishel, Jared Bernstein, and Sylvia Allegretto, *The State of Working America 2006/2007* (Ithaca: Cornell University Press, 2007), pp. 48, 121. Jared Bernstein and Lawrence Mishel, "The Growing Gap Between Productivity and Earnings," Washington, D.C., Economic Policy Institute, Oct. 5, 2006.

9. Mishel, Bernstein, and Allegretto, *State of Working America 2006/2007,* p. 122. For men in the eightieth percentile, pay climbed by 9 percent from 1979 and 2005, after factoring in inflation, reaching $26.71 an hour or about $55,000 a year, while for men at the ninety-fifth percentile, pay rose by 30 percent to $46.40 an hour or $96,000 a year.

10. Stephen J. Rose, "The Myth of Middle-Class Job Loss," *Wall Street Journal,* October 24, 2007, p. A21. Rose found that the share of male workers earning less than $25,000 a year jumped to 36 percent in 2005, from 23 percent in 1979, after adjusting for inflation.

11. Ibid., p. 124; U.S. Bureau of the Census, *Income, Poverty and Health Insurance 2006,* p. 8.

12. Mishel, Bernstein, and Allegretto, *State of Working America 2006/2007,* p. 150. For workers with a high school degree but no college diploma, wages were $14.14 an hour in 2005 (about $29,400 a year for a full-time worker), while for those without a high school diploma, the median wage was $10.53 an hour (or nearly $22,000 a year). For those with a college

degree, the median wage was $24.67 an hour in 2005, or around $51,300 a year. And for those with advanced degrees, real wages averaged $31.49 an hour (or $65,500 a year).

In the early years of this decade, it should be noted, wages for the college-educated dipped slightly (although they remained considerably higher than in 1979), because of the bursting of the high-tech bubble, pressures from offshoring, and new rounds of white-collar downsizing during the 2001 recession.

13. Richard B. Freeman, *America Works: The Exceptional U.S. Labor Market* (New York, Russell Sage Foundation, 2007), p. 48.

14. Elizabeth Warren and Amelia W. Tyagi, *The Two-Income Trap* (New York: Perseus Books, 2003), pp. 51–52.

15. Ibid.

16. Elizabeth Warren, "Rewriting the Rules: Families, Money and Risk," Social Science Research Council, privatizationofrisk.ssrc.org/Warren/, posted Oct. 20, 2005. In households in which both parents work, the average income, Warren found, was $73,770 in 2005, 75 percent higher than the average for single-earner households in the early 1970s, after factoring in inflation. Despite that increase, Warren concluded, discretionary income was $1,500 less than for the single-earner households of the 1970s. She found that in middle-class families, discretionary income was squeezed by mortgage payments averaging $10,500 a year, day care payments averaging $5,700 per child, and $8,000 in annual spending on cars and auto insurance. Health coverage eats up another $2,000, and taxes take a $22,000 bite.

17. Congressional Budget Office, *Historical Effective Federal Tax Rates, 1979 to 2005,* Dec. 2007, table 1C.

18. Ibid.

19. Thomas Piketty and Emmanuel Saez, "Income Inequality in the United States: 1913–1998," *Quarterly Journal of Economics* 68, no. 1 (Feb. 2003): 1–39, (elsa.berkeley.edu/~saez/pikettyqje.pdf). An updated series can be found at elsa.berkeley.edu/~saez/TabFig2005prel.xls.

One can see the economic divide widen in another way. In 1979, average income for the top 1 percent of households was ten times that for the middle fifth, but by 2004 those in the top 1 percent earned twenty-two times as much on average as those in the middle. Average income for the top 10 percent of households was eleven times that of the bottom fifth in 1979, but a quarter century later, it was nineteen times greater. Mishel, Bernstein, and Allegretto, *State of Working America 2006/2007*, p. 65.

20. David Wessel, "One Pay Gap Shrinks, Another Grows," *Wall Street Journal*, Nov. 1, 2007, p. A2.

21. Tax Policy Center, "Combined Effect of the 2001–2006 Tax Cuts," tables T06-0273 and T06-0279, Nov. 13, 2006. The top 1 percent already controlled 34 percent of the nation's wealth, while the next 9 percent of households had 37 percent and the bottom 90 percent, just 29 percent. Mishel, Bernstein, and Allegretto, *State of Working America 2006/2007*, p. 251.

22. Joann S. Lublin and Scott Thurm, "Behind Soaring Executive Pay, Decades of Failed Restraints," *Wall Street Journal*, Oct. 12, 2006, p. A1, citing Kevin Murphy of Marshall School of Business at the University of Southern California.

23. Ben Stein, "In Class Warfare, Guess Which Class Is Winning," *New York Times*, Nov. 26, 2006, sec. 3, p. 3.

24. Bloomberg News, "Buffett Says No Estate Tax Would Be a Gift to the Rich," *New York Times*, Nov. 15, 2007, p. C8.

25. Mishel, Bernstein, and Allegretto, *State of Working America 2006/2007*, pp. 101–2.

26. Ibid., pp. 94–95, citing Chul-In Lee and Gary Solon, "Trends in Intergenerational Mobility," NBER Working Paper No. 12007, Feb. 2006.

27. That study also found that someone born into the top fifth was five times as likely to end up in the top fifth as a person born into the bottom fifth. "Ever Higher Society, Ever Harder to Ascend," *Economist*, Jan. 1, 2005, p. 22, citing paper by Thomas Hertz of American University, "Rags, Riches and Race: The Intergenerational Economic Mobility of Black and White Families in the United States," Washington, D.C., April 9, 2003.

28. Mishel, Bernstein, and Allegretto, *State of Working America 2006/2007*, p. 95, citing Gary Solon. According to another study, slightly more than half of Americans who started the 1990s in poverty remained in poverty at the end of the decade. See Aaron Bernstein, "Waking Up from the American Dream," *BusinessWeek*, Dec. 1, 2003, p. 54. Another study found that among sons born to fathers in the bottom quarter of income earners, 68 percent remained in the bottom half when they were in their twenties and thirties while just 32 percent rose into the top half. Only 14 percent of the men whose fathers were in the bottom 10 percent of the wage ladder climbed to the top 30 percent. David Wessel, "Moving Up: Challenges to the American Dream Escalator Ride: As Rich-Poor Gap Widens in the U.S., Class Mobility Stalls," *Wall Street Journal*, May 13, 2005, p. A1; Bhashkar Mazumder, "Earnings Mobility in the U.S.: A New Look at Intergenerational Inequality," Federal Reserve Bank of Chicago, Dec. 2001.

29. A white born into the bottom fifth has a 45 percent chance of rising into the top three-fifths, but an African American born into the bottom fifth has just a 25 percent chance. Not only are blacks hampered by much less mobility, but they start out in a far worse position. The median wage for black men was $12.48 an hour in 2005, some 28 percent below the median for white men, while the median for black women, $11.22, was 19 percent below that for white women. Mishel, Bernstein, and Allegretto, *State of Working America 2006/2007*, p. 163. Even more disconcerting, the median wealth for black households was a paltry $11,800 in 2004, just one-tenth the $118,000 median for white households. What is more, 29 percent of African American households have zero or negative net worth, more than twice the rate for whites. Ibid., p. 258. The average wealth for blacks was $101,000 in 2004, less than one-fifth the $534,000 for whites. The poverty rate for African Americans is 24.3 percent, versus 10.3 percent for whites (and 10.3 percent for Asians and 20.6 percent for Hispanics). U.S. Bureau of the Census, *Income, Poverty, and Health Insurance Coverage: 2006*, p. 12.

30. A low-income high school student with low test scores has just a 3 percent chance of completing college, while a high-income student with low test scores has ten times as great a chance, a 30 percent chance. Taken together, these statistics reveal that a low-income student with high test scores has a smaller chance of finishing college (29 percent) than a high-income student with low test scores (30 percent). Mishel, Bernstein, and Allegretto, *State of Working America 2006/2007*, pp. 99–100, citing Mary Ann Fox, Brooke A. Connolly, and Thomas D. Snyder, "Youth Indicators 2005: Trends in the Well-Being of American Youth," Washington, D.C., National Center for Education Statistics, July 2005, table 21.

31. "Ever Higher," *Economist*, p. 22.

32. Samuel Dillon, "Commencement Speeches; Threats to Rights and Financial Barriers to Poor Are Cited at Graduations," *New York Times*, June 6, 2004, sec. 1, p. 31. Princeton, Harvard, and several other schools have recently eased the way for low- and moderate-income

students by providing financial aid to them only in the form of grants and no longer in the form of loans.

33. Radio Address on the Third Anniversary of the Social Security Act, Aug. 15, 1938. See American Presidency Project Archive at the University of California at Santa Barbara, www.presidency.ucsb.edu/ws/index.php?pid=15523&st=&st1=.

34. Ibid.

35. Peter G. Gosselin, "If America Is Richer, Why Are Its Families So Much Less Secure?" *Los Angeles Times*, Oct. 10, 2004, p. A1.

36. *EBRI Data Book on Employee Benefits*, Employee Benefit Research Institute, Dec. 2005, table 10.1a (www.ebri.org/pdf/publications/books/databook/DB.Chapter%2010.pdf).

37. Gosselin, "If America Is Richer."

38. General Accounting Office, *Unemployment Insurance: Role as Safety Net for Low-Wage Workers Is Limited*, Dec. 2000, p. 15.

39. Mishel, Bernstein, and Allegretto, *State of Working America 2006/2007*, p. 135.

40. Ibid.

41. Gosselin, "If America Is Richer."

42. Ibid.

43. Advisory Committee on Student Financial Assistance, *Access Denied: Restoring the Nation's Commitment to Equal Educational Opportunity* (Washington, D.C.: GPO, 2001), p. 8; College Board, *Trends in Student Aid, 2007* (New York: College Board, 2007), p. 18.

44. Louis Uchitelle, *The Disposable American: Layoffs and Their Consequences* (New York: Knopf, 2006), p. 68. Another result of today's greater economic volatility is that the average American family can expect its income to swing by 26 percent in any given year, twice the level in the 1970s. The fact that many households have two parents working increases income volatility because it means that in any given year there is a greater chance that one of the wage earners will lose a job. Peter Gosselin, "How Just a Handful of Setbacks Sent the Ryans Tumbling out of Prosperity," *Los Angeles Times*, Dec. 30, 2004, p. A1.

45. Warren and Tyagi, *The Two-Income Trap*, p. 20. Increased foreclosures also resulted from the riskier mortgages that finance companies were offering to less credit-worthy households. Many bankers said that the increased bankruptcies stemmed in part from people taking improper advantage of the bankruptcy law.

46. Vikas Bajaj and Edmund L. Andrews, "Broader Losses for Mortgages," *New York Times*, Oct. 25, 2007, p. A1.

47. Elizabeth Warren, "The Middle Class on the Precipice," *Harvard Magazine*, Jan.–Feb. 2006, p. 27.

48. Kimbro was interviewed on "Downward Mobility," *Now with Bill Moyers*, Public Broadcasting System, Oct. 24, 2003.

49. Interview with Mike Rice in Jefferson, Wisconsin, July 7, 2003.

Chapter Four: DOWNRIGHT DICKENSIAN

1. Steven Greenhouse, "Workers Assail Night Lock-ins by Wal-Mart," *New York Times*, Jan. 18, 2004, p. A1; Bob Ortega, *In Sam We Trust* (New York: Times Business, 1998), p. 363.

2. Greenhouse, "Workers Assail Night Lock-ins."

3. Under New York State law, Julia was supposed to be paid for eleven and a half hours of work each day even though she worked from eight-thirty a.m. to seven-thirty p.m. Her half-

hour lunch break was not paid time, but under the state's spread-of-hours provision, hourly employees who work a shift of ten hours or more are to be paid for an extra hour of work.

4. Rentway, Toys "R" Us, and Family Dollar all said they have strict policies requiring managers to pay employees for every single hour worked.

Chapter Five: THE RISE AND FALL OF THE SOCIAL CONTRACT

1. Telephone interview with Greg Wallace, general manager of the GM Heritage Center, April 30, 2007.

2. Nelson Lichtenstein, *The Most Dangerous Man in Detroit* (New York: Basic Books, 1995), pp. 220–41. This history relies heavily on Lichtenstein's excellent biography of Reuther.

3. Ibid., p. 231.

4. Lizabeth Cohen, *A Consumers' Republic: The Politics of Mass Consumption in Postwar America* (New York: Vintage Books, 2003), p. 155.

5. *Fortune* hailed the agreement as "the Treaty of Detroit," while the *Washington Post* called it "a great event in industrial history." Lichtenstein, *Most Dangerous Man*, p. 280.

6. Cohen, *Consumers' Republic*, p. 154.

7. Lawrence Mishel, Jared Bernstein, and Sylvia Allegretto, *The State of Working America 2006/2007* (Ithaca: Cornell University Press, 2007), p. 48.

8. "*Fortune* Magazine Applauds the U.S. Labor Movement, 1951," in *Major Problems in the History of American Workers*, ed. Eileen Boris and Nelson Lichtenstein (Lexington, Mass.: D.C. Heath, 1991), p. 507.

9. Keith Bradsher, "Ford's 70-Year Itch Could Be Relieved: As G.M. Stumbles, Its Perch at the Top Is Within Reach," *New York Times*, May 3, 2001.

10. Cohen, *Consumers' Republic*, p. 125.

11. Ibid., p. 126.

12. Mishel, Bernstein, and Allegretto, *State of Working America 2006/2007*, pp. 58–63.

13. Peter Cappelli, *The New Deal at Work: Managing the Market-Driven Workforce* (Boston: Harvard Business School Press, 1999), p. 66.

14. William H. Whyte, *The Organization Man* (New York: Doubleday, 1956), p. 1.

15. Paul Osterman, *Securing Prosperity: The American Labor Market: How It Has Changed and What to Do About It* (Princeton: Princeton University Press, 1999), p. 29.

16. Peter Gosselin, "If America Is Richer, Why Are Its Families So Much Less Secure?" *Los Angeles Times*, Oct. 10, 2004, p. A1.

17. Peter Gosselin, "The Poor Have More Things Today—Including Wild Income Swings," *Los Angeles Times*, Dec. 12, 2004, p. A1.

18. Jill Andresky Fraser, *White-Collar Sweatshop: The Deterioration of Work and Its Rewards in Corporate America* (New York: W. W. Norton & Co., 2001), p. 100.

19. Thomas J. Peters and Robert H. Waterman, Jr., *In Search of Excellence: Lessons from America's Best-Run Companies* (New York: Warner Books, 1982), pp. 238–39.

20. Thomas F. O'Boyle, *At Any Cost: Jack Welch, General Electric, and the Pursuit of Profit* (New York: Vintage Books, 1998), pp. 85–86.

21. Osterman, *Securing Prosperity*, p. 158.

22. Richard Witkin, "Threat of a Strike by Air Traffic Controllers Rises as Talks Fail," *New York Times*, Aug. 2, 1981, p. 1.

23. Richard Witkin, "U.S. Says Goal Now Is to Reconstruct Air Control Force," *New York*

Times, Aug. 7, 2001, p. A1; Ed Magnuson, "The Skies Grow Friendlier: Reagan Holds Firm, and the Air-Control System Regroups," *Time*, Aug. 24, 1981, p. 14.

24. Herbert E. Meyer, "The Decline," *Fortune*, Nov. 2, 1981, p. 66.

25. "Louisiana-Pacific: Says Workers at 17th Struck Mill Vote to Oust Union," Business Wire, Sept. 25, 1984; Paul Davenport, "Copper Workers Vote to Oust Unions; Sides Debate Whether Strike Over," Associated Press, Jan. 25, 1985.

26. Bill Keller, "Unionists See Labor Day '84 as a Time to Weigh Setbacks," *New York Times*, Sept. 3, 1984, p. 1.

27. Peter T. Kilborn, "Replacement Workers: Management's Big Gun," *New York Times*, March 13, 1990, p. A24.

28. Michael H. Belzer, *Sweatshops on Wheels: Winners and Losers in Trucking Deregulation* (New York: Oxford University Press, 2000), pp. 44, 121.

29. Paul Osterman, Thomas A. Kochan, Richard M. Locke, and Michael J. Piore, *Working in America: A Blueprint for the New Labor Market* (Cambridge: MIT Press, 2001), p. 66.

30. John Judis, "Why Your Wages Keep Falling," *New Republic*, Feb. 14, 1994, pp. 26–29.

31. Glenn Collins, "Tough Leader Wields the Ax at Scott," *New York Times*, Aug. 15, 1994, p. D1.

32. Ibid.

33. Ibid.

34. Tony Jackson, "Scott's Clean Sheet," *Financial Times*, Oct. 27, 1994, p. 18. While staying at the Four Seasons hotel in Philadelphia during his first seven weeks at Scott, Dunlap took advantage of the company's generosity by giving his two German shepherds, Cadet III and Brit, their own suite at another hotel. Paul Davies, "Downsized: The Rise and Fall of Chainsaw Al," *Philadelphia Daily News*, Dec. 20, 1999, p. 52.

35. John A. Byrne, "The Shredder," *BusinessWeek*, Jan. 15, 1996, p. 56.

36. Ibid.

37. Ibid. With regard to Dunlap's problems after leaving Scott, see Floyd Norris, "Former Sunbeam Chief Agrees to Ban and a Fine of $500,000," *New York Times*, Sept. 5, 2002, p. C1; Floyd Norris, "Justice Dept. Starts Inquiry at Sunbeam," *New York Times*, Sept. 9, 2002, p. D1.

38. O'Boyle, *At Any Cost*, p. 32.

39. Ibid, p. 71.

40. Steven Flax, "The Toughest Bosses in America," *Fortune*, Aug. 6, 1984, p. 18.

41. "Jack Welch: 'I Got a Raw Deal,'" *Fortune*, July 7, 1986, p. 45.

42. Jon Ashworth, "Welch: 'I Gave It My Best Shot,'" *Times* (London), Sept. 8, 2001, Business.

43. Thomas Stewart, "GE Keeps Those Ideas Coming," *Fortune*, Aug. 12, 1991, p. 40.

44. Janet Guyon, "Combative Chief, GE Chairman Welch, Though Much Praised, Starts to Draw Critics," *Wall Street Journal*, Aug. 4, 1988, p. A1.

45. O'Boyle, *At Any Cost*, pp. 73–74.

46. Cappelli, *New Deal*, p. 25.

47. Jack Welch with John A. Byrne, *Jack: Straight from the Gut* (New York: Warner Business, 2001), p. 161.

48. Ibid., p. 158.

49. Tim Smart, "Jack Welch's Encore," *BusinessWeek*, Oct. 28, 1996, p. 154.

50. Geoffrey Colvin, "The Ultimate Manager," *Fortune*, Nov. 22, 1989, p. 185.

51. William Glaberson, "An Uneasy Alliance in Smokestack U.S.A.," *New York Times*, March 13, 1988, sec. 3, p. 1.

52. Cappelli, *New Deal*, p. 22.

53. See Michael Useem, *Investor Capitalism: How Money Managers Are Changing the Face of Corporate America* (New York: Basic Books, 1996).

54. Osterman, *Securing Prosperity*, p. 151.

55. Stephanie Strom, "Sears Eliminating Its Catalogue and 50,000 Jobs," *New York Times*, Jan. 26, 1993, p. A1.

56. Laurie Hays and Gautam Naik, "Xerox to Cut 10,000 Jobs, Shut Facilities," *Wall Street Journal*, Dec. 9, 1993, p. A3.

57. Claudia H. Deutsch, "Kodak Raises Its Job-Cut Total Sharply," *New York Times*, Dec. 19, 1997, p. D1.

58. N. R. Kleinfield, "In the Workplace Musical Chairs: The Company as Family, No More," *New York Times*, March 4, 1996, p. A1.

59. Matt Murray, "Thanks, Goodbye: Amid Record Profits, Companies Continue to Lay Off Employees," *Wall Street Journal*, May 4, 1995, p. A1.

60. Procter & Gamble Announcement, PR Newswire, July 15, 1993.

61. Murray, "Thanks, Goodbye."

62. Bloomberg Business News, "G.M.'s New Development Plan Would Cut 5,000 Engineer Jobs," *New York Times*, Aug. 11, 1995, p. D3.

63. Michael Hammer and James Champy, *Reengineering the Corporation* (New York: Harper Business, 1993), pp. 36–39, 67–71.

64. Simon Head, *The New Ruthless Economy: Work and Power in the Digital Age* (New York: Oxford University Press, 2003), p. 5.

65. Louis Uchitelle and N. R. Kleinfield, "On the Battlefields of Business, Millions of Casualties," *New York Times*, March 3, 1996, p. A1.

66. Steve Lohr, "Though Upbeat on the Economy, People Still Fear for Their Jobs," *New York Times*, Dec. 29, 1996, p. A1.

67. Osterman, *Securing Prosperity*, p. 20.

68. Murray, "Thanks, Goodbye."

69. Louis Uchitelle, "Job Insecurity Is a Big Factor in Fed Policy," *New York Times*, Feb. 27, 1997, p. D6.

70. Cappelli, *New Deal*, p. 126.

71. Ibid., p. 131.

72. John Markoff and Matt Richtel, "Profits, Not Jobs, on the Rebound in Silicon Valley," *New York Times*, July 3, 2005, p. A1.

73. Steve Lohr, "Cutting Here, but Hiring over There," *New York Times*, June 24, 2005, p. C1.

74. Ibid.

75. John C. McCarthy, "Near-Term Growth of Offshoring Accelerating," Forrester Research, May 14, 2004; Pete Engardio, Aaron Bernstein, and Manjeet Kripalani, "The New Global Job Shift," *BusinessWeek*, Feb. 3, 2003, p. 50. The wages associated with all the U.S. jobs moving offshore will total $151 billion per year by 2015, Forrester estimates.

76. Lohr, "Cutting Here."

77. Steven Greenhouse, "Falling Fortunes of the Wage Earner: Average Pay Dipped Last Year for First Time in Nearly a Decade," *New York Times*, April 12, 2005, p. C1.

78. Steve Lohr, "An Elder Challenges Outsourcing's Orthodoxy," *New York Times,* Sept. 9, 2004, p. C1.

79. Bill Vlasic and Brett Clanton, "Delphi Defends Big Pay Cuts," *Detroit News,* Oct. 13, 2005, p. 1A.

80. Tom Walsh and Jason Roberson, "Unions Irate over Delphi's New Offer," *Detroit Free Press,* Oct. 22, 2005, p. 1A.

81. George Will, "A Right Turn Back to Making Cars," *Washington Post,* Oct. 20, 2005, p. 1A.

82. Joy Guy Collier, "UAW Workers Rejoice, Worry," *Detroit Free Press,* Sept. 27, 2007, p. 2.

Chapter Six: LEANER AND MEANER

1. Andrew S. Grove, *Only the Paranoid Survive: How to Exploit the Crisis Points That Challenge Every Company* (New York: Currency/Doubleday, 1996), p. 6.

2. Jill Andresky Fraser, *White-Collar Sweatshop: The Deterioration of Work and Its Rewards in Corporate America* (New York: W. W. Norton & Co., 2001), p. 15.

3. ea-spouse.livejournal.com/274.html.

4. Ibid.

5. Daniel Nelson, *Managers and Workers: Origins of the New Factory System in the United States, 1880–1920* (Madison: University of Wisconsin Press, 1975), p. 35, cited in Peter Cappelli, *The New Deal at Work: Managing the Market-Driven Workforce* (Boston: Harvard Business School Press, 1999), pp. 56–57. I am indebted to Professor Cappelli for this history of the drive system.

6. Sumner H. Slichter, *The Turnover of Factory Labor* (New York: D. Appleton, 1919), p. 375, cited in Cappelli, *New Deal,* p. 57.

7. Sanford M. Jacoby, *Employing Bureaucracy: Managers, Unions, and the Transformation of Work in American Industry, 1900–1945* (New York: Columbia University Press, 1985), p. 21, quoted in Cappelli, *New Deal,* p. 57.

8. Telephone interview with Carl M. Van Horn, Feb. 6, 2006.

9. Louis Uchitelle, "Pink Slip? Now, It's All in a Day's Work," *New York Times,* Aug. 5, 2001, sec. 3, p. 1.

10. Cappelli, *New Deal,* p. 128.

11. Ibid., p. 121.

12. Martin Feldstein, "Why Is Productivity Growing Faster?" NBER Working Paper 9530, March 2003.

13. Telephone interview with Richard S. Wellins, May 12, 2006.

14. See Jerry Newman, *My Secret Life on the McJob* (New York: McGraw-Hill, 2006).

15. Telephone interview with Jerry Newman, March 9, 2006.

16. Brian Meyer, "TeleTech Marks Grand Opening with Forecast for 250 More Jobs," *Buffalo News,* Dec. 2, 1997, p. 3D.

17. Rosemary Batt, Virginia Doellgast, and Hyunji Kwon, "Service Management and Employment Systems in U.S. and Indian Call Centers," in *Brookings Trade Forum 2005: Offshoring White-Collar Work—The Issues and Implications,* ed. S. Collins and L. Brainard, (Washington, D.C.: Brookings Institution, 2006).

18. Rosemary Batt, Larry W. Hunter, and Steffanie Wilk, "How and When Does Management Matter? Job Quality and Career Opportunities for Call Center Workers," in *Low-Wage*

America, ed. Eileen Appelbaum, Annette Bernhardt, and Richard J. Murnane (New York: Russell Sage Foundation, 2003), p. 270.

19. www.TeleTech.com/careers.opp.html, accessed on Sept. 24, 2006.

20. Batt, Hunter, and Wilk, "How and When Does Management Matter?" pp. 272–73.

21. Louis Uchitelle, "Answering '800' Calls, Extra Income but No Security," *New York Times,* March 27, 2002, p. A5.

22. Steve Hillmer, Barbara Hillmer, and Gale McRoberts, "The Real Costs of Turnover: Lessons from a Call Center," *Human Resource Planning* 27, no. 3 (Sept. 1, 2004): p. 34.

23. David Holman, "Employee Well-Being in Call Centers," *Human Resource Management Journal* 12, no. 4 (2002): p. 35.

24. At TeleTech, the computer was programmed to subtract thirty minutes for each worker's lunch. If workers took a thirty-seven-minute lunch, they were docked seven minutes, one top call center executive explained, but if managers pressured a customer service representative to return to work after twenty-three minutes because the phone queue had mushroomed, the worker was not credited for those extra seven minutes of work.

25. David Streitfeld, "No Gain, Know Pain: Incentive-Driven Countrywide Financial Is a Model on How to Boost Output," *Los Angeles Times,* March 2, 2004, p. A1.

26. Ibid.

27. Richard L. Worsnop, "Privacy in the Workplace: Does Electronic Monitoring Violate Workers' Privacy?" *CQ Researcher* 3, no. 43 (Nov. 19, 1993): 1019.

28. Robert H. Moorman and Deborah L. Wells, "Can Electronic Performance Monitoring Be Fair?" *Journal of Leadership & Organizational Studies* 10, no. 2 (Sept. 22, 2003): 2.

29. Simon Head, *The New Ruthless Economy: Work and Power in the Digital Age* (New York: Oxford University Press, 2003), p. 109.

30. Telephone interview with Julian Barling, March 9, 2006.

Chapter Seven: HERE TODAY, GONE TOMORROW

1. The federal government estimates that there are 18 million just-in-time workers, although a far more expansive measure that includes part-time workers and self-employed workers puts the total of contingent workers at 43 million, nearly one-third of the workforce. Government Accountability Office, *Employment Arrangements: Improved Outreach Could Help Ensure Proper Worker Classification,* July 2006, p. 11.

2. Paul Osterman, *Securing Prosperity: The American Labor Market: How It Has Changed and What to Do About It* (Princeton: Princeton University Press, 1999), p. 54.

3. Dallas Salisbury, president of the Employee Benefit Research Institute, quoted in Michael Jonas, "Lone Rangers," *Commonwealth Magazine,* Summer 2005, p. 62.

4. Quoted in Jonas, "Lone Rangers."

5. Louis Uchitelle, "More Downsized Workers Are Returning as Rentals," *New York Times,* Dec. 8, 1996, p. 1.

6. Michele Matassa Flores, "Microsoft Toughens Pay Policy for Temps," *Seattle Times,* June 24, 1997, p. A1.

7. Jonathan Weisman, "Permanent Job Proves an Elusive Dream," *Washington Post,* Oct. 11, 2004, p. A1.

8. Steven P. Berchem, "American Staffing 2007: Annual Economic Analysis," Alexandria, Va., American Staffing Association 2007, p. 2.

9. Leslie Helm, "Microsoft Testing Limits on Temp Worker Use," *Los Angeles Times*, Dec. 7, 1997, p. D1.

10. *American Staffing 2007*, p. 4.

11. Ibid., p. 5.

12. GAO, *Employment Arrangements*, p. 11.

13. Ibid.

14. Laurence Mishel, Jared Bernstein, and Sylvia Allegretto, *State of Working America 2004/2005* (Ithaca: Cornell University Press, 2005), p. 260.

15. Daniel H. Pink, *Free Agent Nation: How America's New Independent Workers Are Transforming the Way We Live* (New York: Warner Books, 2001), p. 216; Katharine Mieszkowski, "Don't Wanna Be Your (Temp) Slave," *Fast Company*, Aug. 1998, p. 40.

16. Pink, *Free Agent Nation*, p. 214.

17. Sharon R. Cohany, "Workers in Alternative Employment Arrangements: A Second Look," *Monthly Labor Review* 121, no. 11 (Nov. 1998): 12.

18. Mishel, Bernstein, and Allegretto, *State of Working America 2004/2005*, p. 260.

19. Yukako Ono and Alexei Zelenev, "Temporary Help Services and the Volatility of Industry Output," *Economic Perspectives* (Federal Reserve Bank of Chicago), Second Quarter 2003, vol. 27, p. 16.

20. Susan N. Houseman, "The Benefits Implications of Recent Trends in Flexible Staffing Arrangements," W. E. Upjohn Institute Staff Working Paper 02-88, Aug. 2001, p. 9.

21. Ibid., p. 33.

22. Massachusetts and several other states have enacted laws that bar discrimination against independent contractors.

23. GAO, *Employment Arrangements*, p. 2.

24. Various regional offices of the National Labor Relations Board have rejected FedEx's assertions, concluding that the delivery drivers are regular employees who have a right to unionize. After those rulings FedEx Ground drivers in Wilmington, Massachusetts, and Windsor, Connecticut, voted to join the International Brotherhood of Teamsters. The company said it would refuse to bargain with the union, evidently hoping that the five-person NLRB in Washington will reverse the decisions of its regional offices.

25. While FedEx's overnight air-freight division—unlike its ground division—treats its drivers as employees, FedEx has taken extraordinary steps to prevent its air-freight drivers from unionizing. In 1996, in a dazzling display of lobbying prowess, FedEx persuaded Congress to enact a special provision that applied to FedEx alone. Under the special provision, the drivers in FedEx's air-freight division would henceforth be covered by the Railway Labor Act rather than the National Labor Relations Act. This means that any organizing drive would have to seek to unionize the company's 40,000 express air-freight drivers in one national unit rather than in smaller, terminal-by-terminal units. To accomplish this lobbying tour de force, FedEx relied on not just its sizable political contributions but on the many IOU's it collected by giving scores of senators and representatives rides on its jet fleet to get to political events. See Neil A. Lewis, "A Lobby Effort That Delivers the Big Votes; Federal Express Knows Its Way Around Capital," *New York Times*, Oct. 12, 1996, p. 37.

26. *Estrada v. FedEx Ground*, Statement of Decision, L.A. Superior Court, BC 210130, July 26, 2004.

27. *Estrada v. FedEx Ground,* 154 Cal. App. 4th 1 (2007).

28. Sara Horowitz, Stephanie Buchanan, Monica Alexandris, Michel Anteby, Naomi Rothman, Stefanie Syman, and Leyla Vural, *The Rise of the Freelance Class: A New Constituency of Workers Building a Social Safety Net* (New York: Freelancers Union, 2005), p. 4.

29. Cohany, "Workers in Alternative Employment Arrangements," p. 12.

30. Pink, *Free Agent Nation,* p. 19.

31. Ibid., p. 21. The free agents of today can draw encouragement from the man credited with inspiring the term *freelancer:* Sir Walter Scott. In *Ivanhoe,* Sir Walter wrote of a knight "who offered Richard the service of [his] Free Lances." Sir Walter added, "Thanks to the bustling times, a man of action will always find employment."

32. Horowitz et al., *The Rise of the Freelance Class,* p. 4.

33. Ibid, pp. 5–7.

34. Brian Stelter, "Freelancers Walk Out at MTV Networks," *New York Times,* Dec. 11, 2007, p. C7.

35. Mishel, Bernstein, and Allegretto, *State of Working America 2004/2005,* p. 260. When part-time jobs are controlled not just for personal characteristics but also for job characteristics, the hourly wage for female part-time workers is 1.2 percent below that of regular full-time workers, and for male part-time workers it is 11 percent below.

36. Mishel, Bernstein, and Allegretto, *State of Working America 2006/2007* (Ithaca: Cornell University Press, 2007), pp. 242–45.

37. Steven Greenhouse and Michael Barbaro, "Wal-Mart to Add More Part-Timers and Wage Caps," *New York Times,* Oct. 2, 2006, p. A1.

38. GAO, *Employment Arrangements,* p. 11. These numbers exclude self-employed workers, who represented another 6.1 million workers in 2005.

39. Osterman, *Securing Prosperity,* p. 60.

40. Mishel, Bernstein, and Allegretto, *State of Working America 2006/2007,* p. 241.

41. Ron Lieber, "The Permatemps Contretemps," *Fast Company,* Aug. 2000, p. 198.

42. Helm, "Microsoft Testing Limits on Temp Worker Use." Ballmer was executive vice president at the time.

43. Steven Greenhouse, "Equal Work, Less-Equal Perks; Microsoft Leads the Way in Filling Jobs with 'Permatemps,' " *New York Times,* March 30, 1998, p. D1.

44. Dan Richman, "Former 'Permatemps' at Microsoft Get Checks," *Seattle Post-Intelligencer,* Oct. 25, 2005, p. A1. The federal appeals court also ruled that not just permatemps but independent contractors whom Microsoft had treated like regular employees should also qualify for the stock purchase plan.

Chapter Eight: WAL-MART, THE LOW-WAGE COLOSSUS

1. Jerry Useem, "One Nation Under Wal-Mart," *Fortune,* March 3, 2003, p. 64.

2. Wal-Mart's stock performance seems even worse when compared with the Morgan Stanley retail index, which covers most large American retailers. That index more than doubled during Scott's first eight years as CEO. Floyd Norris, "Paranoia and Bugging at Wal-Mart," *New York Times,* April 13, 2007, p. C1.

3. Dexter Roberts and Aaron Bernstein, "A Life of Fines and Beating," *BusinessWeek,* Oct. 2, 2000, p. 122.

4. E-mail interview with Sandy Skrovan, senior vice president of TNS Retail Forward, Nov. 7, 2007.

5. After interviewing Scott, one Arkansas newspaper reported, "Scott said the seeds of Wal-Mart's troubles lie in the financial stress suffered by the poorest shoppers in the United States, Wal-Mart's core customer. In the past five years, federal overhauls to the tax system have largely benefited the wealthiest Americans, Scott said." Christopher Leonard, "Wal-Mart Chief Sees a Sunnier Day Ahead," *Arkansas Democrat-Gazette,* June 3, 2005.

6. Parija Bhatnagar, "Wal-Mart Lumbers Toward $500B in Sales," CNN Money, Jan. 10, 2005; Pete Hisey, "Can Wal-Mart Become the First Trillion Dollar Company?" *Retail Merchandiser,* May 1, 2003, p. 20.

7. "Wal-Mart's Growth Opportunities in Food and Fashion Explored in New Retail Forward Reports," Market Wire, Sept. 17, 2003.

8. E-mail interview with Sandy Skrovan, Nov. 7, 2007; Anthony Bianco and Wendy Zellner, "Is Wal-Mart Too Powerful?" *BusinessWeek,* Oct. 6, 2003, p. 100.

9. Bianco and Zellner, "Is Wal-Mart Too Powerful?"

10. Katherine Bowers, "Annual Meeting: Wal-Mart CEO Vows to 'Stay the Course,' " *Supermarket News,* June 13, 2005, p. 26.

11. "Lee Scott Discusses His Ideas," Tavis Smiley Show, National Public Radio, March 31, 2004.

12. An economics consulting firm that Wal-Mart hired, Global Insight, found that Wal-Mart, by keeping its prices down and pressuring other retailers to do likewise, saved American consumers $263 billion annually. But Global Insight added—in an aside that it underplayed—that because Wal-Mart played a role in reducing inflation and that in turn helped hold down wage increases, the net increase in consumer purchasing power thanks to Wal-Mart was $118 billion annually. See Steven Greenhouse, "Mixed Grade for Wal-Mart on Report Card," *New York Times,* Nov. 5, 2005, p. C4. Some economists have suggested that Global Insight's conclusions are greatly exaggerated. Jared Bernstein, L. Josh Bivens, and Arindrajit Dube, "Wrestling with Wal-Mart: Tradeoffs Between Profits, Prices, and Wages," Working Paper 276, Economic Policy Institute, 2006.

13. "Wal-Mart CEO Credits Consumers' 'Negotiating Power' in Creating Savings That Are Improving Lives," PR Newswire, Feb. 23, 2005.

14. Brent Schlender, "Wal-Mart's $288 Billion Meeting," *Fortune,* April 18, 2005, p. 90.

15. Arindrajit Dube and Steve Wertheim, "Wal-Mart and Job Quality—What Do We Know and Should We Care?" Paper prepared for Center for American Progress, Oct. 16, 2005, p. 3. (These numbers take into account that Wal-Mart's wages are somewhat lower because its stores are concentrated in lower-wage states.)

16. Ibid.; Reed Abelson, "States Are Battling Against Wal-Mart over Health Care," *New York Times,* Nov. 1, 2004, p. A1.

17. Susan Chambers, "Reviewing and Revising Wal-Mart's Benefits Strategy," internal Wal-Mart memorandum, p. 24 (www.nupge.ca/publications/wal-mart_nytimes_memo_28oc05 .pdf). In January 2008, Wal-Mart announced very different numbers, saying that the percentage of its workers who were uninsured had fallen to 7.3 percent, down from 9.6 percent in 2007.

18. The internal study noted that Wal-Mart's annual health spending was $1.5 billion in 2005, meaning the company spent a meager $1,100 on average for each of its 1.33 million U.S.

workers. Steven Greenhouse and Michael Barbaro, "Wal-Mart Memo Suggests Ways to Cut Employee Benefit Costs," *New York Times*, Oct. 26, 2005, p. C1; Panjak Ghemawat, Ken Mark, and Stephen Bradley, "Wal-Mart Stores in 2003" (case study, Harvard Business School, revised Jan. 30, 2004), p. 13.

19. Michele Chandler, "Grocery Strife: Wal-Mart Opening Scores of Stores That Sell at Rock-Bottom Prices," *San Jose Mercury News*, Jan. 25, 2004, p. 1F; Jerry Hausman and Ephraim Leibtag, "Consumer Benefits from Increased Competition in Shopping Outlets: Measuring the Effects of Wal-Mart," NBER Working Paper 11809, Dec. 2005.

20. John Stark, "Contract Dispute Looms over Union Workers' Health Benefits," *Bellingham (Washington) Herald*, April 4, 2004, p. 8A.

21. Abelson, "States Are Battling Against Wal-Mart."

22. David Neumark, Junfu Zhang, and Stephen Ciccarella, "The Effects of Wal-Mart on Local Labor Markets," NBER Working Paper 11782, Nov. 2005.

23. Elliot Zwiebach, "Strike Settlement May Set Standard for Others," *Supermarket News*, March 8, 2004, p. 1. In a 2007 contract with the three California supermarket chains, the UFCW recouped some of what it conceded in the earlier contract. As part of the 2007 settlement, all workers, regardless of when they started, will be eligible to reach the same top pay in their job classification.

24. Steven Greenhouse, "Wal-Mart, Driving Workers and Supermarkets Crazy," *New York Times*, Oct. 19, 2003, sec. 4, p. 3.

25. "Is Wal-Mart Good for America?" *Frontline*, Public Broadcasting System, Nov. 2004 (www.pbs.org/wgbh/pages/frontline/shows/walmart/etc/script.html).

26. Abigail Goldman and Nancy Cleeland, "The Wal-Mart Effect: An Empire Built on Bargains Remakes the Working World," *Los Angeles Times*, Nov. 23, 2003, p. 1.

27. Bob Ortega, *In Sam We Trust* (New York: Times Business, 1998), p. xiv.

28. Ibid., pp. 86–87.

29. Sam Walton with John Huey, *Sam Walton, Made in America: My Story* (New York: Doubleday, 1992), p. 127.

30. Mike Michell and another loss-prevention worker later filed a lawsuit accusing Wal-Mart of refusing to pay them for the hours they worked installing the cameras and for other off-the-clock work. The two sides reached a settlement for an undisclosed amount. Wal-Mart declined to comment on Mike Michell's case.

31. "Wal-Mart Stores Inc. Shareholders Meeting," Fair Disclosure Wire, June 3, 2005.

32. Joshua L. Weinstein, "Wal-Mart Fined $205,650 in Child Labor Case," *Portland (Maine) Press Herald*, March 2, 2000, p. 1A.

33. Steven Greenhouse, "Wal-Mart Agrees to Pay Fine in Child Labor Cases," *New York Times*, Feb. 12, 2005, p. A9.

34. When Sam Walton's brother, Bud, was making the introductory remarks at one shareholders meeting, he stunned David Glass, then the CEO, by complaining that the widespread practice of slashing employees' work schedules was particularly callous. "I think that's wrong," Bud Walton said, as thousands of employee shareholders applauded. "I know we got to cut expenses, but we can find another way." For the rest of the meeting, Glass simply ignored the issue, notwithstanding his statement that employees should be treated as partners. Ortega, *In Sam We Trust*, pp. 346–47.

35. Steven Greenhouse, "Wal-Mart Workers Are Finding a Voice Without a Union," *New York Times*, Sept. 3, 2005, p. A11.

36. Steven Greenhouse, "Workers Assail Night Lock-ins at Wal-Mart," *New York Times*, Jan. 18, 2004, p. 1.

37. Molly Selvin and Abigail Goldman, "Wal-Mart Workers Win Suit," *Los Angeles Times*, Dec. 23, 2005, p. A1.

38. Steven Greenhouse, "Wal-Mart Faces Lawsuit over Sex Discrimination," *New York Times*, Feb. 16, 2003, p. 22.

39. Ibid. Odle and Durfey are plaintiffs in the sex discrimination lawsuit against Wal-Mart. For a detailed account of that lawsuit, see Liza Featherstone, *Selling Women Short: The Landmark Battle for Workers' Rights at Wal-Mart* (New York: Basic Books, 2004).

40. Ortega, *In Sam We Trust*, pp. 223–28.

41. Roberts and Bernstein, "A Life of Fines and Beating."

42. Steven Greenhouse and Michael Barbaro, "Wal-Mart to Add More Part-Timers and Wage Caps," *New York Times*, Oct. 2, 2006, p. A1.

43. Chambers, "Reviewing and Revising Wal-Mart's Benefits Strategy," p. 14.

44. "The Age of Wal-Mart: Inside America's Most Powerful Company," CNBC, Nov. 24, 2004. David Faber, the CNBC correspondent, asked: "Wal-Mart gets blamed, fairly or not, for being part of this cycle. You pressure your suppliers, they have to find the lowest-cost producer. That generally means not the United States. You're the biggest importer from China, jobs get lost here. True or not true?"

Lee Scott responded: "Do I think Wal-Mart's responsible for it? Clearly the answer is no. Moving offshore started a long time before we got to be the largest sales company in the world. I think it's only reasonable to assume we're going to be the largest importer from China simply because we are the largest company in America. I think Wal-Mart reflects the globalization."

Faber: "Do you accelerate that process?"

Scott: "Do you accelerate it? No, I don't think so."

See Kris Hudson and Ellen Byron, "Textile Deal Could Spur China to Improve Quality," *Wall Street Journal*, Nov. 25, 2005, p. A8. Wal-Mart "imported $18 billion in goods from China last year."

45. "Wal-Mart Stores Inc. Shareholders Meeting," Fair Disclosure Wire, June 3, 2005.

46. Steven Greenhouse and Michael Barbaro, "On Private Web Site, Wal-Mart Chief Talks Tough," *New York Times*, Feb. 17, 2006, p. C1.

47. Wal-Mart's efforts to portray itself as a scrupulously law-abiding company were undermined when its vice chairman, Tom Coughlin, a man who was Sam Walton's hunting buddy, a man who was second only to Mr. Sam in personifying Wal-Mart and its culture, pleaded guilty to federal fraud charges in February 2006. He had been accused of embezzling more than $400,000 from the company.

48. In addition to whatever employee mistreatment the company may have been guilty of, an overzealous Wal-Mart employee eavesdropped on calls made to Wal-Mart by Michael Barbaro of the *New York Times*. Wal-Mart fired the employee in 2007, and Scott apologized about the eavesdropping.

49. Steven Greenhouse, "Lawsuits and Change at Wal-Mart," *New York Times*, Nov. 19, 2004, p. A25.

50. Telephone interview with Abi Morales, Aug. 27, 2005.

51. Telephone interview with Catherine Kandis, Aug. 31, 2005.

52. Sydney P. Freedberg and Connie Humburg, "Lured Employers Now Tax Medicaid," *St. Petersburg Times,* March 25, 2005, p. 1A.

53. Michael Barbaro, "Wal-Mart Chief Makes Plea to States on Health Care Costs," *New York Times,* Feb. 27, 2006, p. C2.

54. Michael Barbaro, "A New Weapon for Wal-Mart: A War Room," *New York Times,* Nov. 1, 2005, p. A1. McKinsey & Company conducted a study of 1,800 shoppers and found that 2 to 8 percent said they had ceased shopping at the chain because of "negative press they ha[d] heard."

55. Dube and Wertheim, "Wal-Mart and Job Quality," table 3, p. 6.

56. Michael Barbaro, "Wal-Mart Crosses a Health Insurance Threshold," *New York Times,* Jan. 23, 2008, p. C2. Target provides health insurance to an estimated 40 percent of its workforce.

57. Referring to the 11,000 job applicants in Oakland, one Wal-Mart Web site boasted that getting a job at Wal-Mart can be "statistically more competitive than gaining admission to Harvard."

58. "Wal-Mart's Impact on Society: A Key Moment in Time for American Capitalism," *New York Review of Books,* April 7, 2005, pp. 6–7.

59. Dube and Wertheim, "Wal-Mart and Job Quality," table 1, p. 4.

60. In 2005, Wal-Mart's health care spending came to only seventy-five cents per hour per worker, with the company anticipating only modest increases in subsequent years. This figure is based on the Chambers memo, which says Wal-Mart spent $1.5 billion on health care for its U.S. employees in 2005. This figure is also based on the computation, taken from Dube and Wertheim, that Wal-Mart employees average 30.5 hours per week.

Chapter Nine: **TAKING THE HIGH ROAD**

1. If anything, these numbers are skewed in Wal-Mart's and Sam's favor because their figures include only full-time workers while Costco's cover full-time and part-time workers.

2. Stanley Holmes and Wendy Zellner, "The Costco Way," *BusinessWeek,* April 12, 2004, p. 76.

3. Steven Greenhouse, "Woman Sues Costco, Claiming Sex Bias in Promotions," *New York Times,* Aug. 18, 2004, p. C3.

4. Steven Greenhouse, "How Costco Became the Anti-Wal-Mart," *New York Times,* July 17, 2005, section BU, p. 1.

5. In 2007, Sinegal's compensation included an $804,000 restricted stock award, putting his pay that year at $1.23 million, twenty-seven times what the typical Costco worker earns. The typical American CEO earns 369 times as much as the average worker.

6. Jeff Swartz, "Doing Well and Doing Good," *Brookings Review,* Sept. 22, 2002, p. 20.

7. Cara Mia DiMassa, "Being a CEO 'in the Tradition of Abraham,' " *Los Angeles Times,* Nov. 10, 2002, part 2, p. 2.

8. Richard Florida and Jim Goodnight, "Managing for Creativity," *Harvard Business Review,* July 2005, p. 124.

9. Geoff Colvin, "The 100 Best Companies to Work for 2006," *Fortune,* Jan. 23, 2006, p. 74.

10. Cooperative's employees belong to New York's giant health care union, 1199 SEIU

United Healthcare Workers East. They joined because they wanted to help the union spread better wages and treatment throughout New York's home-care industry.

11. Yvon Chouinard, *Let My People Go Surfing: The Education of a Reluctant Businessman* (New York: Penguin Press, 2005), p. 165.

12. Ibid., p. 44.

13. Under California law, the state pays working mothers—but not fathers—eight weeks of disability leave after their baby is born, and Patagonia tacks eight weeks onto that.

14. Telephone interview with Hal Rothman in May 2004. Professor Rothman, one of the foremost experts on the history and culture of Las Vegas, died in March 2007.

Some critics of labor argue that Las Vegas's hospitality workers obtained their impressive wages and benefits not because of the Culinary but only because of Las Vegas's booming economy and low unemployment rate. But that argument fails to explain why unionized hotel housekeepers in Las Vegas earn 40 percent more than those in nearby nonunion Reno, which also has a thriving casino-based economy and an even lower jobless rate. Harold Meyerson, "Las Vegas as a Workers' Paradise," *The American Prospect*, Jan. 2004, p. 38.

15. The average number of hours that housekeepers work nationwide has fallen from forty a week in 1960 to thirty-one today. Annette Bernhardt, Laura Dresser, and Erin Hatton, "The Coffee Pot Wars: Unions and Firm Restructuring in the Hotel Industry," in *Low-Wage America: How Employers Are Reshaping Opportunity in the Workplace*, ed. Eileen Appelbaum, Annette Bernhardt, and Richard J. Murnane (New York: Russell Sage Foundation, 2003), p. 44.

Chapter Ten: OVERSTRESSED AND OVERSTRETCHED

1. For this scene, I owe credit to a book review by Nicholas Lemann: "Honey, I'm Not Home," *New York Times*, May 11, 1997, sec. 7, p. 8.

2. Telephone interview with Carl M. Van Horn, Feb. 6, 2006.

3. Linda Tischler, "Extreme Jobs (and the People Who Love Them)," *Fast Company*, April 2005, p. 54.

4. Ellen Galinsky, James T. Bond, and E. Jeffrey Hill, "When Work Works," Families and Work Institute, April 2004, p. 1.

5. Katharine Mieszkowski, "Santa's Sweatshop," *Salon*, Dec. 2, 2004.

6. Jody Miller and Matt Miller, "Get A Life!" *Fortune*, Nov. 28, 2005, p. 108.

7. Steven Mufson, "Video of Sleeping Guards Shakes Nuclear Industry," *Washington Post*, Jan. 4, 2008, p. A1.

8. National Institute for Occupational Safety and Health, "Stress . . . at Work," NIOSH Publication 99–101, 1999.

9. Ellen Galinsky et al., "Overwork in America: When the Way We Work Becomes Too Much," Families and Work Institute, March 2005, p. 14.

10. Lisa Girion, "Office Pressure Cookers Stewing Up 'Desk Rage,' " *Los Angeles Times*, Dec. 10, 2000, part W, p. 1; "Stress Producing 'Desk Rage,' " *USA Today*, Dec. 29, 2000, p. 1A, citing telephone survey of 1,305 workers done for Integra Realty Resources.

11. *OECD Employment Outlook 2007* (Paris: Organization for Economic Co-operation and Development, 2007), table F, p. 263.

12. Reuters, "U.S. Leads Productivity Ranking, China Gains," *New York Times*, Sept. 4, 2007, p. C3. "When productivity was measured by the hour . . . Norway, an oil nation, was the

most productive." Also see Lawrence Mishel, Jared Bernstein, and Sylvia Allegretto, *The State of Working America 2006/2007* (Ithaca: Cornell University Press, 2007), p. 330.

13. Rebecca Ray and John Schmitt, "No-Vacation Nation," Center for Economic Policy Research, May 2007, p. 2.

14. Galinsky et al., "Overwork in America," p. 7.

15. Lisa Belkin, "Putting in the Hours and Paying a Price," *New York Times*, Dec. 3, 2006, sec. 10, p. 1.

16. Phil Leggiere, "What Happened to the Leisure Society?" *Across the Board*, July/Aug. 2002, p. 42.

17. Carolyn Jones, "Battle of the Beds," *San Francisco Chronicle*, Dec. 19, 2005, p. A1.

18. Telephone interview with Phyllis King, April 13, 2006.

19. According to Jackie Branson, soon after I wrote a story for the *New York Times* in April 2006 about stress and injuries faced by housekeepers at the Chicago Hilton and other hotels, officials at the Hilton began recommending that housekeepers participate in a modest stretching and exercise program to reduce ergonomic injuries. Jackie said that the program has helped somewhat, but that she still suffers serious pain in her shoulders and back. See Steven Greenhouse, "Hotel Rooms Get Plusher, Adding to Maids' Injuries," *New York Times*, April 21, 2006, p. A20.

20. Lisa Belkin, "The Opt-Out Revolution," *New York Times*, Oct. 26, 2003, sec. 6, p. 42.

21. Joan C. Williams, Jessica Manvell, and Stephanie Bornstein, " 'Opt Out' or Pushed Out?: How the Press Covers Work/Family Conflict," Center for WorkLife Law, 2006.

22. Marilyn Gardner, "The Truth Behind Women 'Opting Out,' " *Christian Science Monitor*, Oct. 30, 2006, p. 13.

23. Arlie Russell Hochschild, *The Time Bind* (New York: Henry Holt, 1997), p. 6.

24. Heather Boushey, "Values Begin at Home, but Who's Home?" *American Prospect*, March 2007, p. A2.

25. Hochschild, *The Time Bind*, p. xix.

26. Mishel, Bernstein, and Allegretto, *State of Working America 2006/2007*, p. 91.

27. Joan Williams and Ariane Hegewisch, "All Work and No Play Is the U.S. Way," *Los Angeles Times*, Aug. 30, 2004, p. B9.

28. Galinsky, Bond, and Hill, "When Work Works," p. 1,

29. Seventy-seven percent of workers in the lowest quarter by wages do not have paid sick days, and 43 percent of middle-class workers do not. Vicky Lovell, "No Time to Be Sick: Why Everyone Suffers When Workers Don't Have Paid Sick Leave," Institute for Women's Policy Research, May 2004, p. 12.

30. Joan C. Williams, "One Sick Child Away from Being Fired: When 'Opting Out' Is Not an Option," Center for WorkLife Law, 2006.

31. Arlie Russell Hochschild, "A Work Issue That Won't Go Away," *New York Times*, Sept. 7, 1998, p. A17.

32. Williams, "One Sick Child Away from Being Fired."

33. Lisa Belkin, "Envisioning a Career Path with Pit Stops," *New York Times*, Jan. 30, 2005, sec. 10, p. 1.

34. Boushey, "Values Begin at Home."

35. Mishel, Bernstein, and Allegretto, *The State of Working America 2004/2005* (Ithaca: Cornell University Press, 2005), p. 260.

36. Janet C. Gornick, "Atlantic Passages," *American Prospect*, March 2007, p. A19.

37. Jody Heymann, Alison Earle, and Jeffrey Hayes, "The Work, Family, and Equity Index: How Does the United States Measure Up?" Institute for Health and Social Policy, 2007; Jody Heymann, *Forgotten Families: Ending the Growing Crisis Confronting Children and Working Parents in the Global Economy* (New York: Oxford University Press, 2006).

38. Galinsky et al., "Overwork in America."

Chapter Eleven: OUTSOURCED AND OUT OF LUCK

1. Ronald Reagan, *An American Life: The Autobiography* (New York: Simon and Schuster, 1990), p. 24.

2. Steven Greenhouse, "City Feels Early Effects of Plant Closing in 2004," *New York Times*, Dec. 26, 2002, p. A26. The Whirlpool Corporation acquired Maytag in 2006. After the acquisition, more plants were closed, including Maytag's washing machine factory in Newton, Iowa, where the company's founder, Fred L. Maytag, produced his first washing machine in 1907.

3. Pete Engardio, Aaron Bernstein, and Manjeet Kripalani, "The New Global Job Shift," *BusinessWeek*, Feb. 3, 2003, p. 50.

4. Peter S. Goodman, "White-Collar Work: A Booming U.S. Export," *Washington Post*, April 2, 2003, p. E1.

5. Thomas L. Friedman, *The World Is Flat* (New York: Farrar, Straus and Giroux, 2005), p. 13.

6. Chris Lester, "U.S. Jobs: Road Ahead a Rocky One," *Kansas City Star*, Nov. 22, 2005, p. D10.

7. Engardio, Bernstein, and Kripalani, "New Global Job Shift."

8. Stephen S. Cohen and J. Bradford DeLong, "Shaken and Stirred," *Atlantic Monthly*, Jan./Feb. 2005, p. 112.

9. Ashtok D. Bardhan and Cynthia A. Kroll, "The New Wave of Outsourcing," Fisher Center for Real Estate and Urban Economics, University of California at Berkeley, Fall 2003. Bardhan and Kroll estimate 11 million jobs. Alan S. Blinder, "Offshoring: The Next Industrial Revolution?" *Foreign Affairs*, March/April 2006, p. 113. Blinder estimates 28 to 42 million jobs. "The total number of current U.S. service-sector jobs that will be susceptible to offshoring in the electronic future is two to three times the total number of current manufacturing jobs (which is about 14 million)."

10. Blinder, "Offshoring."

11. Diana Farrell and Jaeson Rosenfeld, "U.S. Offshoring: Rethinking the Response," McKinsey & Company, Dec. 2005, p. 5. Farrell and Rosenfeld write, "Our research shows that, even theoretically, only 11 percent of all U.S. services jobs could possibly be performed offshore."

12. Forrester's estimates are based on intelligent speculation and are lower than some (Economy.com estimates that the nation will lose 600,000 jobs a year to offshoring) and higher than some others. But Forrester's estimates are fully consistent with McKinsey's: "We expect that U.S. companies will create 200,000 to 300,000 offshore jobs per year over the next 30 years." Farrell and Rosenfeld, "U.S. Offshoring," p. 8.

13. John C. McCarthy, "Near-Term Growth of Offshoring Accelerating," Forrester Research, May 14, 2004, p. 5.

14. Steve Lohr, "An Elder Challenges Outsourcing's Orthodoxy," *New York Times*, Sept. 9, 2004, p. C1.

15. Richard B. Freeman, *America Works: Critical Thoughts on the Exceptional U.S. Labor Market* (New York: Russell Sage Foundation, 2007), pp. 128–29.

16. Quoted in Clyde Prestowitz, *Three Billion New Capitalists: The Great Shift of Wealth and Power to the East* (New York: Basic Books, 2005), p. 149. Prestowitz also quotes a surprisingly candid venture capitalist who acknowledged that he urges all the biotech start-ups he finances to move as much R&D as possible to China and India. "When I asked how he felt about the long-term implications of that to the U.S. economy, he acknowledged some concern, but then said, 'Look, I'm a loyal citizen but what happens to the United States is not my job. I have a fiduciary responsibility to my investors. The guys in Washington are supposed to be worrying about the United States." Ibid., p. 148.

17. Steven Pearlstein, "From Old World to Real World," *Washington Post*, April 25, 2007, p. D1.

18. Friedman, *The World Is Flat*, p. 205.

19. Joseph E. Stiglitz, *Globalization and Its Discontents* (New York: W. W. Norton, 2002), p. 5.

20. Pete Engardio, "The Future of Outsourcing: How It's Transforming Whole Industries and Changing the Way We Work," *BusinessWeek*, Jan. 30, 2006, p. 50.

21. Friedman, *The World Is Flat*, p. 120.

22. Catherine L. Mann, "Globalization of IT Services and White Collar Jobs: The Next Wave of Productivity Growth," Institute for International Economics, Dec. 2003, pp. 1–2.

23. Chris Giles, "Globalisation Backlash in Rich Nations," *Financial Times*, July 22, 2007, p. 2.

24. Ron French, "Desperate People Line Up for Jobs," *Detroit News*, Nov. 21, 2004, p. 5B.

25. David Leonhardt, "Larry Summers's Evolution," *New York Times*, June 10, 2007, sec. 6, p. 22.

26. Lawrence Summers, "The Global Middle Cries Out for Reassurance," *Financial Times*, Oct. 29, 2006, p. 17.

27. Lawrence Mishel, Jared Bernstein, and Sylvia Allegretto, *The State of Working America 2006/2007* (Ithaca: Cornell University Press, 2007), p. 175.

28. Warren E. Buffett and Carol J. Loomis, "America's Growing Trade Deficit Is Selling the Nation Out from Under Us," *Fortune*, Nov. 10, 2003, p. 106.

29. Ibid.

30. John Cassidy, "Winners and Losers: The Truth About Free Trade," *New Yorker*, Aug. 2, 2004, p. 24.

31. Ibid.

32. In an incisive article in the *New Yorker*, John Cassidy wrote, "This conclusion directly challenges [the claim of Gregory Mankiw, the former chief White House economist] that free trade must, as a matter of economic logic, benefit the United States. It supports the common-sense notion that what helps one nation can hurt another, and that countries adversely affected by foreign competition can lose out permanently." Ibid.

33. Paul A. Samuelson, "Where Ricardo and Mill Rebut and Confirm Arguments of Mainstream Economists Supporting Globalization," *Journal of Economic Perspectives* 18, no. 3 (summer 2004): 135.

34. Aaron Bernstein, "Shaking Up Trade Theory," *BusinessWeek*, Dec. 6, 2004, p. 116.

35. George Will, "Old Lesson Applies to New Situation," *Seattle Post-Intelligencer,* Feb. 19, 2004, p. B6.

36. David Leonhardt, "How Bernanke Could Outshine Greenspan," *New York Times,* Feb. 1, 2006, p. C1.

37. David Moberg, "Industrial Evolution: A Prairie Fire of Factory Closings Has Hit Galesburg," *Chicago Tribune Magazine,* July 10, 2005, p. 12.

38. In 2006, Voyles left Galesburg to become the head of economic development for the City of Rockford.

39. Enrique Rangel, "Following NAFTA's Calling," *Dallas Morning News,* Dec. 11, 1994, p. 2H.

40. I am greatly indebted to Chad Broughton for his help, guidance, and expertise on Reynosa.

41. Chad Broughton, "Maytag Refrigerators Roll Out of Reynosa," *(Galesburg, Ill.) Register-Mail,* Feb. 6, 2005, p. 1.

42. "Bush, Mexico's President Say Free-Trade Pact in the Works," *Chicago Tribune,* June 12, 1990, business section, p. 1.

43. Chad Broughton, "Working and Living in Reynosa," *(Galesburg, Ill.) Register-Mail,* Sept. 28, 2003, p. 1.

44. Broughton, "Maytag Refrigerators."

Chapter Twelve: THE LOWEST RUNG

1. Chef Solutions has since changed the name of its bakery division to Pennant Foods.

2. Congressional Budget Office, *The Role of Immigrants in the Labor Market* (Washington, D.C.: GPO, 2005), p. 4; Jeffrey S. Passel, "Unauthorized Migrants: Numbers and Characteristics," Pew Hispanic Center, June 14, 2005, p. 26; Eduardo Porter, "Here Illegally, Working Hard and Paying Taxes," *New York Times,* June 19, 2006, p. A1.

3. Passel, "Unauthorized Migrants," p. 6.

4. In an extraordinary investigative piece, David Barstow of the *New York Times* describes how two illegal immigrants drowned in a farm's waste sump, their lungs filled with bovine excrement. David Barstow, "California Leads Prosecution of Employers in Job Deaths," *New York Times,* Dec. 23, 2003, p. A1.

5. Jimmy Breslin, *The Short Sweet Dream of Eduardo Gutiérrez* (New York: Crown, 2002), p. 196.

6. CBO, *Role of Immigrants,* pp. 1–2.

7. Ibid., p. 2.

8. Ibid.

9. Passel, "Unauthorized Migrants," p. 27.

10. Porter, "Here Illegally."

11. These immigrants are not the huge drain on the public fisc that many people suggest. Government officials estimate that illegal immigrants, often using false ID numbers, have paid billions in Social Security taxes that they, because they are illegal, will never collect. Some estimate that this subsidy totals $7 billion a year. See Eduardo Porter, "Illegal Immigrants Are Bolstering Social Security with Billions," *New York Times,* April 5, 2005, p. A1. Undocumented immigrants rarely seek welfare or food stamps, although because so many have no health insurance, they often use emergency rooms in public hospitals, meaning

that taxpayers often pay their medical bills. The presence of their children in American schools does push up school budgets, although illegal immigrants help finance school districts because they often pay property taxes, either directly as homeowners or indirectly as renters.

12. CBO, *Role of Immigrants*, pp. 4, 8.

13. Ibid., p. 6.

14. Ibid, p. 16.

15. Ibid.

16. Michelle Garcia, "Contractors Divided over Day Laborers," *Washington Post*, July 4, 2006, p. A4.

17. Bloomberg News, "Janitors Get Class-Action Status on Market Suit," *Los Angeles Times*, April 10, 2001, p. 2; Nancy Cleeland, "Heartache on Aisle 3: Sweatshop for Janitors," *Los Angeles Times*, July 2, 2000, p. A1.

18. Sherri Day, "Prosecutors in Smuggling Case Against Tyson Contend Trial Is About 'Corporate Greed,' " *New York Times*, Feb. 6, 2003, p. A26.

19. Steven Greenhouse, "U.S. Wins Back Pay for Janitors," *New York Times*, Aug. 26, 2004, p. A16.

20. Roger Lowenstein, "The Immigration Equation," *New York Times*, July 9, 2006, sec. 6, p. 36.

21. CBO, *Role of Immigrants*, p. 7.

22. Borjas also found a 2.1 percent drop for high school graduates and a 3.6 percent decline for college graduates. One reason that wages fell the most for the 6 percent of Americans who are high school dropouts is that so many immigrant workers do not have high school degrees. George J. Borjas, "Increasing the Supply of Labor Through Immigration: Measuring the Impact on Native-Born Workers," Center for Immigration Studies, May 2004, pp. 5–6.

23. Ibid., p. 1.

24. David Card, "The Impact of the Mariel Boatlift on the Miami Labor Market," *Industrial and Labor Relations Review* 43, no. 2 (Jan. 1990): 245–57.

25. David Card, "Is the New Immigration Really So Bad?" NBER Working Paper 11547, Aug. 2005.

26. Card, "Impact of the Mariel Boatlift." Another possible explanation is that an influx of immigrants into certain cities might have dissuaded others from moving to those cities, helping to keep wages from falling.

27. Lowenstein, "Immigration Equation."

28. Carolyn Said, "The Immigration Debate," *San Francisco Chronicle*, May 21, 2006, p. A13. David Card said, "Twenty years ago when I first moved to the U.S., only very rich people had their lawns cut by someone else. The cost of hiring someone to do that got so low because of the supply of landscapers and firms that specialized in hiring immigrants, it created a sector of the economy that . . . wasn't counted as part of GDP before."

29. Gianmarco I. P. Ottaviano and Giovanni Peri, "Rethinking the Gains from Immigration: Theory and Evidence from the U.S," NBER Working Paper 11672, Sept. 2005.

30. Virginia Postrel, "Yes, Immigration May Lift Wages," *New York Times*, Nov. 3, 2005, p. C2.

31. CBO, *Role of Immigrants*, p. 20; Lowenstein, "Immigration Equation."

32. Anthony DePalma, "Fifteen Years on the Bottom Rung," *New York Times*, May 26, 2005, p. A1.

33. Smithfield officials maintained that Hispanics represented at most 50 percent of the plant's workers, but union organizers, many workers, and Charlie LeDuff, a *New York Times* reporter who worked for several weeks at the plant, said its workforce was at least 60 percent Hispanic.

34. Rakesh Kochhar, Roberto Suro, and Sonya Tafoya, "The New Latino South: The Context and Consequences of Rapid Population Growth," Pew Hispanic Center, July 26, 2005, p. 3.

35. Charlie LeDuff, "At a Slaughterhouse, Some Things Never Die; Who Kills, Who Cuts, Who Bosses Can Depend on Race," *New York Times*, June 16, 2000, p. A1.

36. Ibid. The National Labor Relations Board found that Smithfield had repeatedly broken the law during the 1994 unionization election as well as in a 1997 election in which the workers again voted against joining the United Food and Commercial Workers Union.

37. Kristin Collins, "Crackdown Separates Mobs, Kids; Raids Targeting Illegal Workers Pull in More Women," *Raleigh News & Observer*, Sept. 2, 2007, p. A1.

38. Steven Greenhouse, "Among Janitors, Labor Violations Go with the Job," *New York Times*, July 13, 2005, p. A1.

39. Robert Ratish, "Waitress Hopes Suit Ends 'Injustice,' " *(Bergen County, N.J.) Record*, Sept. 30, 2003, p. L1; Hugh R. Morley, "Workers Protest Conditions, Chinese Buffet Is Target in Wayne" *(Bergen County, N.J.) Record*, Aug. 30, 2001, p. B1.

40. Noelle Phillips, "Immigrant Brothers' Dreams End in Trench," *The State (Columbia, S.C.)*, March 20, 2005, p. A1.

41. Steven Greenhouse, "Migrants Plant Pine Trees but Often Pocket Peanuts," *New York Times*, Feb. 14, 2001, p. A16.

42. Tom Knudson and Hector Amezcua, "Forest Workers Caught in Web of Exploitation," *Sacramento Bee*, Nov. 13, 2005, p. A1.

43. Daniel T. Griswold, "Willing Workers: Fixing the Problem of Illegal Mexican Migration to the United States," Center for Trade Policy Studies, Oct. 15, 2002, pp. 1–2.

44. Editorial, "No More Amnesty Deals," *Augusta (Georgia) Chronicle*, May 22, 1998, p. A4.

45. Steven Greenhouse, "Going After Migrants, but Not Employers," *New York Times*, April 16, 2006, sec. 4, p. 3.

46. During the 2008 presidential campaign, Senator McCain backed away from taking a lead role on this issue. He was evidently concerned that many conservative Republicans deplore anything that can be construed as amnesty.

47. Editorial, "Fortress America," *Wall Street Journal*, July 20, 2005, p. A12.

Chapter Thirteen: THE STATE OF THE UNIONS

1. Lawrence Mishel and Matthew Walters, "How Unions Help All Workers," Economic Policy Institute, Aug. 2003.

2. Ibid.

3. U.S. Bureau of Labor Statistics, *Union Members in 2003*, Jan. 21, 2004.

4. Chris (Hristos) Doucouliagos and Patrice Laroche, "What Do Unions Do to Productivity? A Meta-Analysis," *Industrial Relations* 42, no. 4 (Oct. 2003): 650–91, cited in Harley Shaiken, "The High Road to a Competitive Economy: A Labor Law Strategy," Center for American Progress, June 25, 2004.

5. Charles Brown and James L. Medoff, "Trade Unions in the Production Process," *Journal of Political Economy* 86, no. 3 (June 1978): 355–78.

6. Richard Hurd, "The Failure of Organizing, the New Unity Partnership and the Failure of the Labor Movement," *WorkingUSA: The Journal of Labor and Society* 8, no. 1 (Sept. 2004): 13. According to the Bureau of Labor Statistics, union membership climbed by 311,000 in 2007, the largest annual increase since 1979. Labor leaders hailed this as the harbinger of a turnaround, but some labor experts said this increase might be a mere statistical fluctuation resulting from inexact surveying techniques. The BLS said the percentage of workers in unions was 12.1 percent in 2007, up from 12 percent in 2006, the first such increase since 1983. The percentage of private-sector workers in unions was 7.5 percent in 2007, up from 7.4 percent in 2006. The BLS said these percentage changes were statistically insignificant.

7. When George Meany, the AFL-CIO's president, was asked in 1972 if he should worry about organizing and about the decline in labor's numbers, he had a startling response: "Frankly, I used to worry about the members, about the size of membership. But quite a few years ago, I just stopped worrying about it because to me, it doesn't make any difference." When labor's membership shrinks, its power of course shrinks as well. Charles Craver, *Can Unions Survive?* (New York: New York University Press, 1993), p. 3.

8. In fiscal year 2003, 23,144 workers received back pay from their employers after the NLRB charged their employers with illegally retaliating against them for demonstrating support for a union. *Sixty-Eighth Annual Report of the National Labor Relations Board, for the Fiscal Year Ended Sept. 30, 2003*, table 4.

9. Martin Jay Levitt and Terry Conrow, *Confessions of a Union Buster* (New York: Crown Publishers, 1993), p. 217.

10. Kate Bronfenbrenner, "Uneasy Terrain: The Impact of Capital Mobility on Workers, Wages, and Union Organizing" (paper for the United States Trade Deficit Review Commission, Sept. 2000), pp. 18, 52, 64, 73.

11. "The Dunlop Commission on the Future of Worker-Management Relations: Final Report" (Cornell University, Dec. 1994), p. 40.

12. Human Rights Watch, "Unfair Advantage: Workers' Freedom of Association in the United States Under International Human Rights Standards," Aug. 2000, p. 94.

13. "Dunlop Commission," p. 40.

14. *NLRB v. U-Haul Company of Nevada*, Decision by Administrative Law Judge John J. McCarrick, Sept. 30, 2005

15. "Avondale Ordered to Reinstate Workers," *Baton Rouge Advocate*, July 12, 2001, p. 1-D.

16. Labor leaders are urging Congress to increase the penalties for firing union supporters. Some human rights experts have also decried the modest penalties and huge delays. Kenneth Roth, executive director of Human Rights Watch, wrote, "Loophole-ridden laws, paralyzing delays, and feeble enforcement have led to a culture of impunity in many areas of U.S. labor law and practice. Legal obstacles tilt the playing field so steeply against workers' freedom of association that the United States is in violation of international human rights standards for workers." Kenneth Roth, "Workers' Rights in the United States," Industrial Relations Research Association, *Perspectives on Work*, vol. 5, no. 1 (2001): 19–20.

17. Peter D. Hart Research Associates, "Labor Day 2005: The State of Working America," Aug. 2005.

18. Kris Maher, "Unions' New Foe: Consultants," *Wall Street Journal*, Aug. 15, 2005, p. B1.

19. Levitt and Conrow, *Confessions of a Union Buster*, p. 1.

20. Union busters do not come cheap. ConAgra, for example, paid a firm $194,000, coming to nearly $1,000 per worker, to help it fight a unionization effort at a two-hundred-employee meatpacking plant in Omaha. Maher, "Unions' New Foe."

21. The U.S. Supreme Court has ruled that the company's property rights trump the union organizers' need for access to help assure a fair election. See two Supreme Court decisions, *NLRB v. Babcock & Wilcox Co.*, 351 U.S. 105 (1956) and *Lechmere, Inc. v. NLRB*, 502 U.S. 527 (1992).

22. Jeff Faux, *The Global Class War* (Hoboken, N.J.: John Wiley & Sons, 2006), p. 131.

23. Lehman quit Wal-Mart out of frustration with how it treated its workers and took a job as an organizer with the United Food and Commercial Workers.

24. Steven Greenhouse, "How Do You Drive Out a Union? South Carolina Factory Provides a Textbook Case," *New York Times*, Dec. 14, 2004, p. A30.

25. One reason that the union's top leaders were eager for ratification was that one-third of the time that workers vote to join a union, no contract is signed within a year, often because of management intransigence. Such delays often cause many workers to sour on their new union, and ultimately to vote to get rid of it.

26. EnerSys said Phillips had been fired for sexual harassment, an allegation he denied, saying it was no more credible than management's other assertions.

Chapter Fourteen: STARTING OUT MEANS A STEEPER CLIMB

1. For an impressive retelling of this showdown, see Stephen Franklin, *Three Strikes: Labor's Heartland Losses and What They Mean for Working Americans* (New York: Guilford, 2001).

2. Louis Uchitelle, "Two Tiers, Slipping into One," *New York Times*, Feb. 26, 2006, sec. 3, p. 1.

3. Ibid.

4. Quoted in Brendan I. Koerner, "Generation Debt—The New Economics of Being Young," *Village Voice*, March 23, 2004, p. 28.

5. Steven Greenhouse, "Many Entry-Level Workers Feel Pinch of Rough Market," *New York Times*, Sept. 4, 2006, p. A10. From 2000 to 2005, median income for those families fell by $3,009, sliding to $48,405 a year, in 2005 dollars, according to the Census Bureau. That's a 5.9 percent drop—a sharp contrast to the late 1990s, when median income for young households climbed by 12 percent, lifted of course by the high-tech boom.

From 2001 to 2005, entry-level wages for male college graduates fell 7.3 percent, to $19.72 an hour, according to the Economic Policy Institute, while entry-level wages for female college graduates slipped 3.5 percent, to $17.08. For men with high school diplomas, entry-level pay fell 3.3 percent, to $10.93, over that period, while for female high school graduates, pay slid 4.9 percent, to $9.08 an hour. Lawrence Mishel, Jared Bernstein, and Sylvia Allegretto, *The State of Working America 2006/2007* (Ithaca: Cornell University Press, 2007), p. 155.

6. Greenhouse, "Many Entry-Level Workers Feel Pinch."

7. Ibid. For young college graduates, the news was better but by no means great. Entry-level pay for female college graduates, age twenty-three to twenty-nine, climbed a healthy 21 percent from 1979 to 2005, but that was less than half the 47 percent wage increase for

female college grads age thirty-four to forty. For male college graduates, entry-level pay rose 11 percent over that quarter century, but that was lower than the 14 percent pay increase for thirty-four- to forty-year-olds.

8. The report found that men who were in their thirties in 2004 had median incomes of $35,010, while men in their fathers' cohort, those now in their sixties, had a median income of $40,210 in 1974, adjusted to current dollars. The report found that the families of men who were in their thirties in 2004 had incomes that were 9 percent higher than their fathers' families had in 1974, but the report added that this increase was due to the greater participation of women in the workforce. Isabel Sawhill and John E. Morton, "Economic Mobility: Is the American Dream Alive and Well?" Economic Mobility Project, May 2007, p. 5.

9. U.S. Bureau of the Census, *Income, Poverty, and Health Insurance Coverage in the United States 2006* (Washington, D.C.: GPO, 2006), p. 21.

10. Mishel, Bernstein, and Allegretto, *State of Working America 2006/2007*, pp. 154–56. In a surprisingly rapid fall, the portion of college graduates receiving health coverage in entry-level jobs dropped to 64 percent in 2004 from 71 percent just five years earlier. (That's down from 78 percent in 1979.)

11. Anya Kamenetz, *Generation Debt: Why Now Is a Terrible Time to Be Young* (New York: Riverhead, 2006), p. 130.

12. Patrick Purcell, "Pension Sponsorship and Participation: Summary of Recent Trends," Congressional Research Service, Aug. 31, 2006, p. 10. The share of workers age twenty-five to thirty-four whose employers sponsor a retirement plan fell from 63 percent in 2000 to 54 percent just five years later. Mishel, Bernstein, and Allegretto, *State of Working America 2006/2007*, p. 156.

13. Mishel, Bernstein, and Allegretto, *State of Working America 2006/2007*, p. 157.

14. Kamenetz, *Generation Debt*, p. 13.

15. Sylvester J. Schieber, "Paying for It," *Wilson Quarterly* 30, no. 2 (spring 2006): 62.

16. Mindy Fetterman and Barbara Hansen, "Young People Struggle to Deal with Kiss of Debt," *USA Today*, Nov. 20, 2006, p. 1A.

17. As a result of these trends, young adults devoted 22 percent of their incomes to rent in 2002, up from 17 percent in 1970, with 30 percent spending at least 30 percent of their income on rent, up from 20 percent paying that percentage in 1970. Tamara Draut, *Strapped: Why America's 20- and 30-Somethings Can't Get Ahead* (New York: Doubleday, 2005), p. 128.

18. Ibid., p. 132.

19. "Once Again, the Future Ain't What It Used to Be," Pew Research Center, May 2, 2006.

20. Steve Lohr, "Outlook on the Workplace: How Is the Game Played Now?" *New York Times*, Dec. 5, 2005, p. C1.

21. Greenhouse, "Many Entry-Level Workers Feel Pinch."

22. Advisory Committee on Student Financial Assistance, *Empty Promises: The Myth of College Access in America*, June 2002, p. v.

23. Statement of Dr. Juliet V. Garcia, president, University of Texas at Brownsville, Committee on House Education and the Workforce, July 16, 2002.

24. Advisory Committee on Student Financial Assistance, *Empty Promises*, p. v.

25. Advisory Committee on Student Financial Assistance, *Access Denied: Restoring the Nation's Commitment to Equal Educational Opportunity* (Washington, D.C.: GPO, 2001), p. 8; College Board, *Trends in Student Aid, 2007* (New York: College Board, 2007), p. 18.

26. College Board, *Trends in College Pricing 2007*, p. 11.

27. Quoted in Robert Tomsho, "As Tuition Soars, Federal Aid to College Students Soars," *Wall Street Journal*, Oct. 25, 2006, p. B1.

28. College Board, *Trends in College Pricing 2007*, p. 11.

29. Michael Mandel, "Which Way to the Future?" *BusinessWeek*, Aug. 20, 2007, p. 46.

30. Donald Heller, "Need and Merit in Financial Aid," presentation at National Scholarship Providers Association Annual Conference, Oct. 20, 2005, p. 17 (www.personal.psu.edu/faculty/d/e/deh29/papers/NSPA_2005.pdf).

31. Quoted in Kamenetz, *Generation Debt*, p. 42.

32. Ibid., pp. 84–86.

33. Maria D. Fitzpatrick and Sarah E. Turner, "The Changing College Experience for Young Adults," policy brief, Network on Transitions to Adulthood, iss. 34, Sept. 2006.

34. Telephone interview with Donald Heller, Nov. 6, 2006.

35. Ngina S. Chiteji, "To Have and to Hold: An Analysis of Young Adult Debt," Network on Transitions to Adulthood, May 2006, p. 10.

36. Ibid., p. 16. Debt for the typical young adult's household was 111 percent of annual income in 2001, up from 66 percent two decades earlier. A recent Federal Reserve study shed some light on this debt overload—14 percent of families with a head of household under age thirty-five have at least one payment more than sixty days past due (compared with 9 percent for all families). Brian K. Bucks, Arthur B. Kennickell, and Kevin B. Moore, "Recent Changes in U.S. Family Finances: Evidence from the 2001 and 2004 Survey of Consumer Finances," *Federal Reserve Bulletin*, 2006. p. A35.

37. Fetterman and Hansen, "Young People Struggle."

38. Draut, *Strapped*, p. 12.

39. The biggest borrowers are part of an often overlooked group—those who attend for-profit schools such as culinary schools or the University of Phoenix. They borrowed $24,600 on average. "Trends in Student Aid," p. 12. For an excellent analysis of this problem, see Kim Severson, " 'Top Chef' Dreams Crushed by Student Loan Debt," *New York Times*, May 8, 2007, p. A1.

40. Sandy Baum and Marie O'Malley, "College on Credit: How Borrowers Perceive Their Education Debt; Results of the 2002 National Student Loan Survey," Nellie Mae Corporation, Feb. 6, 2003, p. 6.

41. Susan Berfield, "Thirty & Broke: The Real Price of a College Education Today," *BusinessWeek*, Nov. 14, 2005, p. 76, quoting Melanie E. Corrigan, associate director of national initiatives and analysis at the American Council on Education.

42. Baum and O'Malley, "College on Credit," p. 11.

43. Ibid., p. 8.

44. Fetterman and Hansen, "Young People Struggle."

45. For students who began college in 2003, the gain will be $295,682 on a net basis after subtracting the $107,277 in total college costs. The study said, "A student entering college today can expect to recoup her investment within ten years of graduation." Lisa Barrow and Cecilia Elena Rouse, "Does College Still Pay?" *Economists' Voice* 2, no. 4 (2005).

46. Fetterman and Hansen, "Young People Struggle"; Baum and O'Malley, "College on Credit," p. 27.

47. On the positive side of the ledger, 70 percent said college loans were very important in enabling them to continue their education after high school, while 59 percent said the ben-

efits of student debt outweighed the disadvantages. Baum and O'Malley, "College on Credit," p. 27.

48. Chiteji, "To Have and to Hold," p. 10.

49. Fetterman and Hansen, "Young People Struggle."

Chapter Fifteen: THE NOT-SO-GOLDEN YEARS

1. Alicia H. Munnell, Marric Buessing, Mauricio Soto, and Steven Sass, "Will We Have to Work Forever?" Center for Retirement Research at Boston College, July 2006, p. 2.

2. *EBRI Databook on Employee Benefits,* Employee Benefit Research Institute, Dec. 2005, table 10.1a (www.ebri.org/pdf/publications/books/databook/DB.Chapter%2010.pdf).

3. Telephone interview with Teresa Ghilarducci on Oct. 30, 2006.

4. Telephone interview with Alicia Munnell on March 23, 2006.

5. Alicia H. Munnell, Anthony Webb, and Francesca Golub-Sass, "Is There Really a Retirement Savings Crisis? An NRRI Analysis," Center for Retirement Research at Boston College, Aug. 2007, p. 2.

6. Online interview with Alicia Munnell, "Can You Afford to Retire?" *Frontline,* Public Broadcasting System, posted May 16, 2006 (www.pbs.org/wgbh/pages/frontline/retirement/interviews/munnell.html).

7. Debra Whitman and Patrick Purcell, "Topics in Aging: Income and Poverty Among Older Americans in 2005," Congressional Research Service, updated Sept. 21, 2006, p. 2.

8. Roger Lowenstein, "The End of Pensions?" *New York Times,* Oct. 30, 2005, sec. 6, p. 56.

9. A federal appeals court in Chicago ruled in 2006 that IBM's cash balance plan did not discriminate against older workers. Judge Frank H. Easterbrook wrote, "Removing a feature that gave extra benefits to the old differs from discriminating against them." See Mary Williams Walsh, "Court Rules for IBM on Pension," *New York Times,* Aug. 8, 2006, p. C1.

10. Alicia H. Munnell, Francesca Golub-Sass, Mauricio Soto, and Francis Vitagliano, "Why Are Healthy Employers Freezing Their Pensions?" Center for Retirement Research at Boston College, March 2006, p. 4.

11. As part of a decade of maneuvering to push down pension costs, IBM moved to a cash balance plan in the late 1990s. In 2004, it announced that future employees could not even join that pension plan but could instead participate in the company's riskier, less generous 401(k) program.

12. Telephone interview with Alicia Munnell on March 23, 2006.

13. Beth Shulman, "Sweating the Golden Years," *Wilson Quarterly* 30, no. 2 (spring 2006): 57.

14. Alicia H. Munnell and Annika Sundén, "401(k) Plans Are Still Coming Up Short," Center for Retirement Research at Boston College, March 2006, p. 5.

15. Patrick Purcell, "Retirement Savings and Household Wealth: Trends from 2001 to 2004," Congressional Research Service, updated May 22, 2006, p. 10. The mean value of 401(k) accounts was $98,395. Including IRAs and Keoghs, $34,000 was the median amount that Americans had in all their retirement accounts in 2004.

16. Ibid., p. 15. For workers in this age group, the mean value of 401(k) accounts was $202,425. When IRAs and Keoghs are included, the median amount that fifty-five- to sixty-four-year-olds had in their retirement accounts was $88,000.

17. As bad as the pension squeeze is, like so many trends, it squeezes those on the bottom the most. Just 13 percent of male workers and 10 percent of female workers in the bottom quintile participate in pension plans or 401(k)s. That compares with 67 percent of men and women in the top quintile. Alicia H. Munnell and Pamela Perun, "An Update on Private Pensions," Center for Retirement Research at Boston College, Aug. 2006, p. 2. Someday those not participating in pension plans are likely to be among the nearly one in four retirees for whom Social Security provides their only retirement income. Shulman, "Sweating the Golden Years."

18. Albert B. Crenshaw, "A Retirement Crapshoot," *Washington Post,* Dec. 12, 2004, p. F1.

19. Eduardo Porter and Mary Williams Walsh, "Retirement Becomes a Rest Stop as Pensions and Benefits Shrink," *New York Times,* Feb. 9, 2005, p. A1.

20. Ellen E. Schultz and Theo Francis, "Financial Surgery: How Cuts in Retiree Benefits Fatten Companies' Bottom Lines," *Wall Street Journal,* March 16, 2004, p. A1.

21. Porter and Walsh, "Retirement Becomes a Rest Stop."

22. Ibid. The percentage of men fifty-five to sixty-four years old in the workforce fell steadily from 87 percent in 1950 to less than 65 percent in 1994. Then it began inching back up, reaching 70 percent in 2007, according to the Bureau of Labor Statistics. Other factors—among them improved health, increased longevity, and the federal law barring age discrimination—are also helping push up the labor force participation rate for these workers as well as for workers over age sixty-five.

23. Ellen E. Schultz, "Widows' Lament—As Companies Cut Spousal, Death Benefits for Retirees, Survivors Suffer More Loss," *Wall Street Journal,* June 29, 2005, p. B1. Here I should voice my admiration and debt to Schultz and her colleagues at the *Journal* for their excellent coverage of retirement benefits.

24. Lowenstein, "End of Pensions." I am indebted to Lowenstein's excellent article for help on the history of pensions.

25. James A. Wooten, "The Most Glorious Story of Failure in Business: The Studebaker-Packard Corporation and the Origins of ERISA," *Buffalo Law Review,* vol. 49, 2001, p. 731.

26. Donald L. Barlett and James B. Steele, "The Broken Promise," *Time,* Oct. 31, 2005, p. 34.

27. David Wessel, Ellen E. Schultz, and Laurie McGinley, "Pressured GM Slashes Pay, Benefits," *Wall Street Journal,* Feb. 8, 2006, p. A1.

28. Theo Francis and Ellen E. Schultz, "Is Pension Crisis a Scapegoat?" *Wall Street Journal,* Nov. 18, 2003, p. C1.

29. Ellen E. Schultz, "Coming Up Short: Firms Had a Hand in Pension Plight They Now Bemoan," *Wall Street Journal,* July 10, 2003, p. A1.

30. Patrick Purcell, "Pension Sponsorship and Participation: Summary of Recent Trends," Congressional Research Service, Aug. 31, 2006, p.4. The number of pension plans at companies with more than one hundred employees has fallen by more than half since 1985, from 22,147 that year to 10,772 in 2005.

31. Marilyn Adams, " 'Fundamentally Broken' Pension System in 'Crying Need' of a Fix," *USA Today,* Nov. 15, 2005, p. 1B. After United Airlines and Bethlehem dumped their plans, politicians, economists, business executives, and labor leaders were all pointing to the many chinks in the system. One problem was that companies and their labor unions, knowing that the federal government was there to guarantee pension plans, sometimes agreed to oversize pension increases, often at the expense of pay increases, even though it was a big stretch for those companies to finance the more generous pensions.

ERISA left companies lots of wiggle room on accounting, so much so that by some measures GM's pension plans were adequately funded, while by other measures its plans were underfunded by $31 billion.

32. Gary Haber, "DuPont Cutting Pension Plan," *Wilmington (Delaware) News Journal*, Aug. 29, 2006, p. 1A. DuPont's announcement angered many workers, but the company said the move would help it attract new workers who were "looking for more control and portability of benefits."

33. There are many other forces fueling the shift away from pensions. Life expectancy is rising, meaning that pension plans will require even more funding because plans will, over time, have to pay out more years of benefits per retiree. In 2005, men age sixty-five were expected to live 17 more years, but men who turn sixty-five in 2055 are projected to live 19.9 more years. In 2005, women age sixty-five were expected to live 19.7 more years, while women who turn sixty-five in 2055 are projected to live 22.5 more years. See Munnell, Golub-Sass, Soto, and Vitagliano, "Why Are Healthy Employers Freezing Their Pensions?" p. 6.

Adding to corporate America's distaste for pensions, the panel that sets rules for the accounting profession, the Financial Accounting Standards Board, has begun requiring companies to list all unfunded pension liabilities on their balance sheets. The rule aims to help investors by increasing financial transparency, but many CEOs loathe this transparency because it can push down their stock prices.

34. Munnell, Golub-Sass, Soto, and Vitagliano, "Why Are Healthy Employers Freezing Their Pensions?" pp. 7–8.

35. Gretchen Morgenson, "Fair Game; A Lump of Coal Might Suffice," *New York Times*, Dec. 24, 2006, sec. 3, p. 1.

36. Ellen Schultz and Theo Francis, "The CEO Health Plan—In Era of Givebacks, Some Executives Get Free Coverage After They Retire," *Wall Street Journal*, April 13, 2006, p. B1.

37. Janice Revell, "CEO Pensions: The Latest Way to Hide Millions," *Fortune,* April 28, 2003, p. 68.

38. Barlett and Steele, "Broken Promise."

39. Telephone interview with Alicia Munnell, March 23, 2006.

40. Mary Williams Walsh, "More Companies Ending Promises for Retirement," *New York Times,* Jan. 9, 2006, p. 1.

41. Jack VanDerhei, Sarah Holden, Craig Copeland, and Luis Alonso, "401(k) Plan Asset Allocation, Account Balances, and Loan Activity in 2006," Employee Benefit Research Institute, Aug. 2007, p. 16.

42. Online interview with Jack VanDerhei, "Can You Afford to Retire?" *Frontline,* Public Broadcasting System, posted May 16, 2006 (www.pbs.org/wgbh/pages/frontline/retirement/interviews/vanderhei.html).

43. Munnell and Sunden, "401(k) Plans Are Still Coming Up Short," p. 3.

44. Alicia H. Munnell and Annika Sunden, *Coming Up Short: The Challenge of 401(k) Plans* (Washington, D.C.: Brookings Institution, 2004).

45. Ruth Helman, Matthew Greenwald, Jack Van Derhei, and Craig Copeland, "The Retirement System in Transition: The 2007 Retirement Confidence Survey," Employee Benefit Research Institute, April 2007, figure 8.

46. Another problem with 401(k)s is that workers generally get a lower rate of return from those plans than they obtain from traditional pension plans, partly because many investment companies take sizable undisclosed fees each year from the 401(k)s they manage. One

study found that the rate of return for 401(k)s is 1 percentage point lower per year than for traditional pension plans, although another study found that the returns on 401(k)s were 2 to 4 percentage points lower. A return that is 1 percent lower may sound modest, but consider that a 401(k) account with a balance of $30,000 will grow to about $106,000 over twenty years, with a net return of 6.5 percent a year. But with a return that is 1 percentage point lower (5.5 percent), the account will end up with about $88,000 after twenty years, meaning a difference of 17 percent, or $18,000. See Government Accountability Office, *Private Pensions: Changes Need to Provide 401(k) Plan Participants and the Department of Labor Better Information on Fees*, Nov. 2006, p. 7.

47. Teresa Ghilarducci, "The Changing Role of Employer Pensions: Tax Expenditures, Costs, and Implications for Middle Class Elderly," Working Paper 469, Annandale-on-Hudson, N.Y., Levy Economics Institute of Bard College, Aug. 2006, p. 25.

48. Interview with Karen Ferguson in Washington, D.C., March 25, 2006.

49. Munnell, Buessing, Soto, and Sass, "Will We Have to Work Forever?"

50. Ghilarducci, "The Changing Role of Employer Pensions," p. 27.

51. "Can You Afford to Retire?" *Frontline*, Public Broadcasting System, May 16, 2006.

Chapter Sixteen: LIFTING ALL BOATS

1. Some advocates will no doubt call for an official benchmark not just for every state but for every metropolitan area because living costs can vary so greatly in different parts of a single state. The benchmark typically used is the poverty line set by the Census Bureau—$16,079 for a family of three and $20,614 for a family of four in 2006. But many economists, sociologists, and poor people say those numbers are unrealistically low in that they do not provide for an adequate standard of living. In 1959, the federal poverty line represented about 50 percent of the median income for a family of four, but today it has slid to about 30 percent of median income. Center for American Progress Task Force on Poverty, "From Poverty to Prosperity: A National Strategy to Cut Poverty in Half," April 2007, p. 17.

2. Sylvia Allegretto, "Basic Family Budgets: Working Families' Incomes Often Fail to Meet Living Expenses Around the U.S," Briefing Paper 165, Economic Policy Institute, Sept. 1, 2005.

3. Under the law, the minimum rose to $5.85 an hour on July 24, 2007, and rises to $6.55 a year later and to $7.25 a year after that.

4. Center for American Progress Task Force on Poverty, "From Poverty to Prosperity: A National Strategy to Cut Poverty in Half," April 2007, p. 2.

5. Jack Nelson, "Administration to Fight Plans to Curb Poor's Tax Break," *Los Angeles Times*, Aug. 17, 1995, p. A11. Many free marketers warn against raising the minimum wage, saying the earned income tax credit should be increased instead as a way to help low-income Americans. But there are strong reasons to raise the minimum wage and not rely on just the EITC. First, many policy makers are averse to any substantial increase in the earned income tax credit because that could cost the government billions of dollars. Second, it would be unwise to rely on only an increase in the EITC because many companies that pay the minimum wage or just above it arguably receive an indirect subsidy from the government (in the form of the EITC, Medicaid, and food stamps for their employees). The more generous the EITC and other government programs are, the easier it is for companies to keep their pay levels to a minimum. Those companies that pay the minimum wage to their

workers arguably have an unfair advantage over competitors that want to do the right thing and pay their workers a living wage. Accordingly, it would be wise to look to both a higher minimum wage and EITC to combat poverty wages.

6. Lawrence Mishel, Jared Bernstein, and Sylvia Allegretto, *The State of Working America 2006/2007* (Ithaca: Cornell University Press, 2007), p. 43.

7. Ibid., p. 20.

8. David Weil, an economics professor at Boston University who has studied the apparel industry, found that the financial benefits of breaking wage laws far outweigh the chances of getting caught. Weil found that given the industry's average annual illegal underpayment per worker ($338), the median civil penalty ($1,086), and the very small likelihood of being inspected and caught, the potential cost of not complying was $121 a year versus a benefit of $12,205 a year for not complying. That, Weil wrote, implies "that an apparel employer should choose not to comply." David Weil, "Improving Labor Standards in the Apparel Industry: Can Government Make a Difference?" Boston University and Harvard Center for Textile and Apparel Research, Jan. 2004, pp. 6–7.

9. A big problem with sealed settlements is that they fail to alert other employees and other judges about a company's or a manager's pattern and practice of wrongdoing. Similarly, sealed settlements often prevent the news media from reporting on such malfeasance. To paraphrase Justice Louis Brandeis, sunlight can be the best disinfectant—and best disincentive.

The federal Fair Labor Standards Act has numerous provisions that make it harder for workers to file complaints about wage violations. Workers can't have a union or immigrant rights group bring the complaint on their behalf, and the law's class action language is quite restrictive, discouraging lawyers from bringing lawsuits. These provisions discourage workers from seeking redress, because the amount a worker is cheated, perhaps $1,000 or $2,000, is often less than it costs to hire a lawyer. With regard to violations of minimum wage and overtime laws, class actions are often the most effective deterrent and arguably a more efficient use of judicial resources than individual cases. Some companies, most notably Wal-Mart, argue that class action lawyers have ganged up on them, especially in state courts, and there might be some truth to that, but it is doubtful that Wal-Mart would be facing so many class actions unless its wage violations were fairly prevalent in the first place. Take another huge employer: McDonald's. It has faced very few class actions over off-the-clock work, and there is a simple reason: from its early days, it has aggressively pressured its managers to comply with wage-and-hour laws.

10. Organization of Economic Cooperation and Development, *Health Data 2006* (www.oecd.org/dataoecd/20/51/37622205.xls). In 2004 dollars in purchasing power parity (which compares living standards in different countries by seeking to equalize the purchasing power of those countries' currencies for a given market basket of goods).

11. Ray Moseley, "Health Care in France Gets Top Marks," *Chicago Tribune,* July 8, 2001, p. 4.

12. Paul Krugman and Robin Wells, "The Health Crisis and What to Do About It," *New York Review of Books,* March 23, 2006, p. 38.

13. "Bush Approval Slips—Fix Economy, Say Voters," Pew Research Center for the People and the Press, Aug. 7, 2003.

14. Krugman and Wells, "The Health Crisis." One reason for the astronomical administrative expenses is that insurance companies and HMOs spend huge amounts of money and

employee hours trying to reject high-risk individuals and trying to figure out ways to deny coverage for any number of doctor visits and medical procedures, generating a never-ending series of disputes with doctors' offices and patients.

15. As part of their proposals, Clinton, Edwards, and Obama would require employers to provide coverage or pay a certain percentage of wages to the government. All three would prohibit health insurers from rejecting anyone because of a preexisting condition, medical history, job, or age. All three would subsidize low-income and moderate-income Americans to help them afford insurance. They would also encourage the creation of regional insurance pools that would give individual Americans more bargaining power to push private insurers to cut costs and improve coverage. Clinton would require all individuals to have coverage; Obama would require that all children have coverage.

16. Many union leaders say the answer to this gathering crisis is simple: restore the old pension system in which corporations invested billions of dollars to guarantee their workers a lifetime stream of monthly payments after retirement. But that idea is a pipe dream—many corporations have moved decisively away from conventional pensions and their open-ended liabilities (which often soared when the stock market stumbled). Besides, in an era when workers average fewer years with a particular employer, traditional pension plans—which favor those who spend two or three decades at a company—do not make nearly as much sense as they once did. Corporations much prefer 401(k)s because in those plans companies' contributions are limited and predictable.

17. Teresa Ghilarducci, "Guaranteed Retirement Accounts: Toward Retirement Income Security," Notre Dame University, Feb. 2007. Under her proposal, mandatory contributions would be deducted only on earnings up to the Social Security earnings cap of $98,000, but workers could contribute above that cap if they desired.

18. Under Ghilarducci's plan, someone who worked, say, twenty-five years and thus contributed to a retirement account for twenty-five years would receive lower benefits than someone who worked forty-four years. To prevent undue penalties against women who leave the workforce to give birth and raise children, some economists have proposed that the government credit women's accounts for the period they are out of the workforce to raise their children. Unemployed workers with the wherewithal would be allowed to contribute to their accounts to give themselves larger retirement incomes.

19. These accounts might call for some minor government subsidies when the financial markets' rate of return falls below the promised rate of return of 3 percent after inflation. At the same time, these accounts could provide the same sweetener that TIAA-CREF does: when financial markets are booming, the rate of return can be temporarily increased above the promised return—a sort of bonus.

20. Workers who worry that their annuities will leave nothing for their spouse when they die should be given an option to have survivor benefits. This would give a retiree a lower monthly annuity check but would assure an annuity for survivors.

21. Companies will argue that letting workers vest after just one year will cause companies to run up high administrative costs for workers who have very little in their pension accounts. The companies should be given the right to give workers who leave after one year but before they finish their fifth year their accrued pension savings in a lump sum to roll over into an IRA.

22. See William G. Gale, Jonathan Gruber, and Peter R. Orszag, "Improving Opportunities

and Incentives for Saving by Middle- and Low-Income Households," Hamilton Project, April 2006. As a default option, a plan might automatically channel most of a thirty-year-old's 401(k) investments into stocks and, as the worker ages, switch more of the investments into bonds. These "prudent" default options would improve on the status quo because many workers act unwisely about their 401(k) investments and because about half of workers touch their allocation formula just once in all their years on the job—the day they sign up for their 401(k).

23. There are strong economic incentives for anti-union companies to flout the law. Hypothetically, if a company fires the four workers who spearhead a unionization drive, it might have to pay them a total of $80,000 in back wages ($20,000 each, after subtracting what they earn elsewhere) if NLRB officials rule two years later that they were dismissed illegally. If those firings cripple a unionization drive of five hundred hourly employees, the savings for the company could be many times the $80,000 in back pay. If a union contract were to add two dollars an hour to the five hundred workers' wages and benefits, that could cost the company $4 million over two years. So firing the four employees becomes a shrewd business move, saving $4 million minus the $80,000 in back pay.

24. Union nepotism can often be laughably crude. The benefits fund of a laborers local in New Jersey paid $3 million over nine years to the relatives of an executive board member. The official's son-in-law was paid $119,000 a year to administer a scholarship fund that awarded just $28,000 a year in scholarships, while the official's daughter was hired as a confidential secretary to check phone messages. One year she was paid $117,799 when all she had to do was answer 109 phone messages, coming to $1,025 a message.

25. Thomas L. Friedman, *The World Is Flat* (New York: Farrar, Straus and Giroux, 2005), p. 233.

26. Michael Dobbs, " 'Good News, Bad News' About U.S. Students Released," *Washington Post*, Dec. 15, 2004, p. A2.

27. Friedman, *The World Is Flat*, p. 257.

28. Richard B. Freeman, "Doubling the Global Workforce: The Challenge of Integrating China, India, and the Former Soviet Bloc into the World Economy," Presentation at Center for Economic Performance, London School of Economics, Nov. 8, 2004, p. 11.

29. Ibid.

30. All this could be an amendment to the WARN Act, which requires sixty days' advance notice before a company lays off five hundred or more workers.

31. To preserve the jobs of workers in overseas sweatshops, a boycott should not be carried out if a factory improves its awful conditions soon after they have been uncovered. As a condition for avoiding a boycott, the factory should agree to periodic monitoring by an independent group that interviews workers at a location other than the factory so that the workers can speak freely. Ideally, the government of a country where a sweatshop faces a boycott would, perhaps with the assistance of the United States government or nongovernmental organizations, help find new jobs for the sweatshop's workers.

32. Deborah Solomon, "As States Tackle Poverty, Preschool Gets High Marks," *Wall Street Journal*, Aug. 9, 2007, p. A1. The government should also make the Child Tax Credit fully refundable so that low-income families with children can benefit fully from the credit. The credit gives families up to $1,000 per child for up to three children. The credit is available to families with incomes as high as $110,000, but it provides no benefit to the poorest families

because it is nonrefundable. If a family doesn't owe income taxes, then it does not receive the credit. As a result, the poorest 10 million children receive no help from this credit. Making the credit fully refundable would lift two million children and one million parents out of poverty. Center for American Progress Task Force, "From Poverty to Prosperity," p. 29.

33. Center for American Progress Task Force, "From Poverty to Prosperity," p. 3.

34. Some commentators argue that increased spending in no way guarantees improved educational results, and to be sure, little in life is guaranteed. But if those who argue that increased spending does not guarantee improvement were given the choice of sending their child to school in Sausalito, which spends $16,000 a year per student, or in Los Angeles, which spends $9,000, it is easy to guess which district they would pick.

35. There are many other options to improve schools. For instance, set statewide limits on class size or legislate that class size in a city's schools can be no higher than those in the affluent suburbs that surround it. Or enact a law requiring that teacher pay in urban districts be equal to that of teacher pay in the surrounding suburbs. Or to make sure that public schools receive the attention they deserve, enact a law prohibiting all elected or appointed federal, state, and local officials from sending their children to private schools. These officials are the guardians of the public schools, so why exactly shouldn't they be sending their own children to public schools? Are their kids too good for public school?

Index